FSC
www.fsc.org
MIX
Papier aus ver-
antwortungsvollen
Quellen
Paper from
responsible sources
FSC® C105338

NO-POINT PERSPECTIVE

ANDREAS MÜLLER
JUSTIN ALLEN

Imprint

Impressum

Bibliografische Information der Deutschen Nationalbibliothek: Die Deutsche Nationalbibliothek verzeichnet diese Publikation in der Deutschen Nationalbibliografie; detaillierte bibliografische Daten sind im internet über www.dnd.de abrufbar.

Bibliographic information from the German National Library: The German National Library lists this publication in the German National Bibliography; detailed bibliographic data are available on the Internet at www.dnb.de.

Herstellung und Verlag: BoD - Books on Demand, Norderstedt

ISBN: 9783751979504

Acknowledgements from Andreas Müller:

Thanks to Nadine and Soham, Tony and Claire Parsons and Dorothea

Acknowledgements from Justin Allen:

Thanks to my family, close and far friends, Andreas and Dorothea

CONTENTS

CONTENTS

June 21, 2020 JUSTIN ALLEN

PREFACE

This is at most a collection of talks between a self-confirmed apparent person and an unconfirmed non-person, which ultimately offers nothing of value to any persons. It is not a book which you will read and then be able to do something afterwards with some newly acquired knowledge, like understand the equation E = mc2 or bake a cake or know what is right or wrong, and it won't provide any helpful or useful information on how to live life better or worse.

Yet there are illustrations, and it is possible that the reader relates to and identifies with myself as an apparent person trying to figure something out unsuccessfully. Maybe reading these talks triggers an apparent clarity regarding the absurdity of seeking in which ever form it comes, through teachers, gurus, jobs, family, relationships, location, rebellion, diet, meditation, therapy, drugs, partying, sport, a combination of things or giving up or "letting go." At least, this book captures the absurdity of my seeking.

I consider myself to be average. I am of an average age (40), an average upbringing, an average social status and a sort of well-rounded every-person of sorts. I have dabbled in several paths to fulfillment as mentioned above, and I am unconvinced of every path I have tried. I was even unconvinced while trying them and unconvinced of my "unconvincement." By "fulfillment" I mean that search for the thing or things, in whichever form or forms they may come, that you think will end the search for fulfillment and leave you contented. For example, when I finally find the right place to live, with the right partner and a good job, I will have it all (and be done searching). And even though I am confessing that I am unconvinced of the search for fulfillment in whatever form it comes, I still can't stop searching.

This project that I have undertaken with Andreas Müller was a setup to share this dilemma of seeking, which you can't seem to stop and doesn't seem possible for you to end, even when you know it's basically futile. I use the word "basically" because it softens the seeming fact that there is no point. In our talks, in this sense, I am the experimental lab rat or the average Joe, and I wanted to share my dilemma in the form of a chronologically ordered series of talks between myself as a self-confirmed person or a "me" and Andreas Müller as a non-person or a "no me," to see what happens. In a sense we have put the dilemma on display with me as the mannequin.

Originally, before we started our talks, I thought of this project as a modern-day, normal-people, non-stigmatized *Bhagavad Gita* in that it follows a similar framework of the *Gita*, which is that of a dialogue between the prince Arjuna (Justin Allen) and his guide Krishna (Andreas Müller). But I am not a prince and Andreas is not a guide, and this is just a collection of talks between two apparent people with no spiritual, religious or scientific intentions, which took place from October 23, 2019 to March 23, 2020.

June 21, 2020 ANDREAS MÜLLER

INTRODUCTION

This book is a collection of talks between Justin Allen and myself. To suggest that we had a goal or purpose was not my intention, although there might have been one originally for Justin. In the end, we talked about the nature of apparent separation in an undefined outline beginning broadly with teachers and gurus to "getting down to the point," even though there is not really a point.

When Justin contacted me with his proposal, which was to start a dialogue and possibly turn it into a book to share, I was surprised and curious. We had never met before, so I only heard his voice on the telephone. On the one hand, there was this instantaneous "yes," but on the other hand, there was a bit of skepticism. To me, Justin seemed to have had some kind of picture and idea of what he wanted to achieve or what he was hoping may or may not happen. Usually, I am open for having a conversation on this "topic," especially when it comes from a genuine and sincere interest, but there seemed to be a potentially disingenuous aspect as well – a personal goal maybe or the "making a of book."

However, as the conversations started, I liked them right away. And as they continued, so did my own interest and enjoyment. In the early talks, we addressed deceased and current spiritual teachers as a place of reference and in order to compare apparent differences to the "no-point perspective." Looking back, there seemed to have been an apparent movement from rather superficial aspects (like comparing teachings and gurus) to a rather distinct examination of this apparent topic. Now, having the text in my hands, I am very happy with it.

October 23, 2019 Talk 01

TEACHERS AND GURUS

Justin Allen: So, one thing is that I've started reading this Ramana Maharshi book called *Be As You Are*.

Andreas Müller: All right.

Justin Allen: I haven't read that much of it yet, but what I notice is that it's almost verbatim what Rupert Spira is talking about.

Andreas Müller: All right.

Justin Allen: So, last time we talked, kind of an interesting thing that we came upon was that if there is only "oneness," then it seems logical that there would only be one message.

Andreas Müller: So to speak, yes.

Justin Allen: Yeah, and one of the things that Ramana Maharshi has already talked about and also Rupert Spira talks about a lot and probably they all do in some sense is this analogy of the "screen." Have you heard this?

Andreas Müller: Yes.

Justin Allen: So, it's more or less like you watch a movie, and there's the screen and there's really nothing on the screen. It's just light.

Andreas Müller: Yes.

Justin Allen: But it creates the image as if something's happening, but nothing can happen without the screen.

Andreas Müller: Yes.

Justin Allen: And there, the message is that we are consciousness – "me" as myself and "you" as yourself, you're just a screen, and I'm a screen –, and as consciousness we somehow create our physical body and this idea of being separate and there being objects and that there's things happening.

Andreas Müller: Yes.

Justin Allen: And that's what I've always understood. That the illusion is not realizing that "you" are the "screen," even though that's all that you are and that's all that you can be. Somehow you're not aware that "you're" the "screen," you're only aware of the objects and things appearing on the screen.

Andreas Müller: Yes.

Justin Allen: And so, when I hear that, it all seems logical ...

Andreas Müller: Yes.

Justin Allen: And then I think, "Okay, how do I realize that 'I'm' the screen?" And then that's where it all gets ... I don't know if it gets illogical, but that's where the kind of practice comes in, in a sense of ...

Andreas Müller: Yes.

Justin Allen: Somehow trying to abide as that, like abide as the awareness and somehow deny the ...

Andreas Müller: Whatever the technique is, "to bring the awareness back," "to abide as awareness," "to bring awareness to awareness," "to just be," or "to learn how to consciously be awareness."

Justin Allen: Right.

Andreas Müller: All that stuff, yes.

Justin Allen: Right, and then that's where I see that even that seems so convincing in a way, but at the same time you realize that you're still ... There's still somebody that's doing all that.

Andreas Müller: Oh, of course, and as far as I would see it it's a complete personal teaching. Because in a way, they state, or the statement in that picture is that there is something which you are and something which you are not. So, they give a solution and a promise and say, "If you learn to be how you are or if you recognize who you actually are, then you are free." What I'm actually saying is that there is no screen either. I would say exactly that's the illusion: that there is something which you are, namely awareness, and that there is something which you are not, the options in awareness or the appearance in awareness, all that stuff. And I would say, that's the reason why it's logical and understandable because it perfectly reflects and describes the personal experience.

Justin Allen: Yeah, that's true.

Andreas Müller: All that comes out of that again is another teaching (laughing). There is no other possibility, because it's a personal teaching right from the start. The whole picture is personal.

Justin Allen: Well, but at the same time it still seems kind of ... It still does seem possible. Of course, it's possible because there's no formula and there's no real way to recognize when it's equally ... In a sense, it's possible that you might follow these teachings and somehow come to a recognition, and you might attribute it to the teachings then and say, "Ah, I can't say for sure that it's because of this teaching ," but you would think that there was a correlation, possibly.

Andreas Müller: I wouldn't really say so, to be honest. Not if the apparent recognition happened that it's an illusion. For me, it's rather impossible to come to the conclusion that it happened because of the teaching.

Justin Allen: Right, but if you were following Ramana Maharshi for ten years, and then all of a sudden you had this enlightenment experience or this recognition or whatever, some part of you would have to think it had something to do with your meditating or with your inquiring, no?

Andreas Müller: Not really, it's a story, but when the "me" dies, it's ... No, it's not possible to entertain that idea in the end.

Justin Allen: So, would you want to say, not that you can make these conclusive statements, but would you say that if someone like Ramana Maharshi is giving this kind of personal teaching, and his and Rupert Spira's message is that they haven't really recognized the absence of the "me"? Or is it possible that they've understood or recognized the absence of the "me," but they're just somehow flawed in their teaching?

Andreas Müller: Well, it's really in a way hard to talk about it because there are no "persons" doing that either. But yes, my impression is that whenever that statement was made, it wasn't really coming from a "no me" position, so to speak.

Justin Allen: And then I've heard of the necklace analogy where there's a woman that can't find her necklace, and she goes all around her house looking for it. Then she starts to ask her friends, and then at some point somebody comes along and says, "Hey, have you tried feeling for the necklace around your neck?" And then she reaches for her neck and finds it and goes, "Oh, I found it," and then she's happy. And then if somebody later on says, "Hey, did you ever find your necklace?" she again replies, "Yeah, I found it." And then they use this analogy to explain how she didn't actually find it, right? Because it was always there. It wasn't lost in the first place. It was around her neck all the time.

Andreas Müller: Yes. I mean the dilemma with all those stories is that they're fine, but in the end you're just left with "someone" seeing something.

Justin Allen: Yeah.

Andreas Müller: And that's just what remains for the seeker: That there is something to be seen and something to be found, and that there is "someone" who can see or find something.

Justin Allen: Okay.

Andreas Müller: In a way, that's the dream. I mean, one could say, "Yes, it's already there." Me too, I sometimes say, "What you are looking for is already what happens."

Justin Allen: Right.

Andreas Müller: So, maybe this part would fit the analogy, but this can't be found and it's not to be seen for "someone," and that's where the analogy doesn't fit anymore.

Justin Allen: Okay, and that's why I wanted to bring up that analogy.

Andreas Müller: The dilemma for the seeker is that the only thing he or she can do is process that analogy. That's totally fine, but of course, the seeker will always be left with the assumption that there is another circumstance to be seen. Namely, "Oh, I have the necklace already around my throat."

Justin Allen: Or to realize that I am already the thing that I'm seeking.

Andreas Müller: Exactly. Seen by the seeker, this would just be another circumstance that "I" have to realize, probably beating up himself because it sounds so easy (laughing).

Justin Allen: Right, yeah, it's making it worse.

Andreas Müller: Yeah, exactly (laughing).

Justin Allen: But that's the thing they point out in this book ... That's what's so confusing to me, because they also point out the exact same thing, always. There's even this, "Hence I say no; you are really the infinite peer being the self," and by self he means consciousness. "You are always that self and nothing but that self. Therefore, you can never be really ignorant of the self. Your ignorance is merely an imaginary ignorance, like the ignorance of the ten fools about the lost tenth man. It's this ignorance that caused them grief." Do you know that analogy about the ten men?

Andreas Müller: No, I don't know that.

Justin Allen: That's where ten men cross a river, and when they get to the other side, one of them counts off how many there are to make sure nobody was lost in the river, but he forgets to count himself, so he only counts nine men.

Andreas Müller: Alright.

Justin Allen: And so, he says, "We're only nine," and then somebody else does the counting and makes the same mistake. It's only until they meet a passerby that lines them all up and says ...

Andreas Müller: "You are ten."

Justin Allen: "State your name and then count 'one', and then the next 'two' and so on," and then they realize. Then they go, "Oh, we didn't lose somebody."Throughout this book, so far it's saying that the whole point of trying to find yourself or realize that this is the ignorance is already the misstep. And that's what causes all the suffering and all the pain because you're just kind of inflating the problem the whole time by trying to figure it out, but there's essentially nothing to figure out. You're already that which you're seeking.

Andreas Müller: Yes.

Justin Allen: And that's where there's a correlation. That's why I think people can read this and then also find similarities with your message or Tony Parsons's message.

Andreas Müller: Yes, yes.

Justin Allen: And that's why sometimes I'm not sure if maybe this teaching is the same as yours in a way, but it's ... Or not that yours is a teaching, but that the message is the same as your message, just maybe that the strategy there is to try to ...

Andreas Müller: I think it's hard to say, and this is only referring to Ramana Maharshi. It's really hard to say because all we have from him are those few books. And he was sitting there for, I don't know, thirty, forty years?

Justin Allen: Yeah.

Andreas Müller: Speaking, talking to people every day?

Justin Allen: Yeah.

Andreas Müller: Talking to people about all kinds of stuff and all kinds of concepts during these forty years. And it's possible that at the beginning he said something completely ... Not completely, but he said something different than twenty years later. Maybe there was a subtle movement away from an awareness teaching to what I would call non-duality, and that's what I mean. You have those few books extracted from those forty years, from someone who chose exactly those dialogues, maybe from someone who felt much more attracted to this awareness thing. But maybe Ramana was just pointing out the concept.

I do that too in my talks. Not the concept, but I describe the personal experience. That's why I think it's very hard to talk about Ramana and every statement of his because it's the same for me. I see statements which would exactly fit that, and then there is this awareness stuff mixed in, to which, if I just got the statement, I would definitely say, "No, that's not what I would say."

Justin Allen: Yeah, and another topic that's running like a thread throughout this whole thing is the continuity through the waking state, the dream state and the sleep state, yes?

Andreas Müller: Yes.

Justin Allen: So, this is being talked about a lot, and the point is that you ... Or at least the point is that in the wake state you feel like you are yourself. And in the sleep state you could be sleeping in your bed in your home or wherever, but you're dreaming that you're in London, right?

Andreas Müller: Yes.

Justin Allen: And in the dream, you think that you're in London, and it's all real to you until you wake up in your bed and then you think, "Oh, it was just a dream." So that's one of the analogies they use to try to explain this. And then when you're in deep sleep, supposedly there's no objects that exist. There's no ...

Andreas Müller: Subject?

Justin Allen: Yeah, but you still know that while you're sleeping that's you.

Andreas Müller: Well, I think no.

Justin Allen: I mean like you do in the sense that somebody from the outside still says, "That's you sleeping," even though you can't relate to them while you're sleeping. And then when you wake up, you don't feel like you're a new person. You feel like, "Oh, I was sleeping," or like, "I had a good night's sleep." To be able to say that, their argument is that it's because somehow there was an awareness while you were sleeping ...

Andreas Müller: Yeah, which is utterly (laughing) ... I think that's just made up. That's assumptions. It's logic. It's thinking how it could be. It's philosophy, in the end. It's thinking about, "Hmm, which story would fit my experience? Which story would explain that? Which story would explain that I was there in the night, too?" (laughing) It's inventing a story to prove that I am.

Justin Allen: But I don't think that they're saying that "you" as a physical body are there in the sleep, but that "you" as an individual are there in the sleep.

Andreas Müller: Yeah, just as something.

Justin Allen: As "being". That's like Ramana saying, "There is continuity of being in all three states, but no continuity of the individual and the objects in all three states."

Andreas Müller: Yes.

Justin Allen: So, the individual and the objects are continuous in the waking state, so I feel like I can touch things and see objects. But in deep sleep, all objects have disappeared, or apparently there's nothing there, and there's no way I can even know what happened in deep sleep because there's no memory. There's no time, because time and memory only exist in the waking state.

Andreas Müller: I would say there is no experience.

Justin Allen: Yeah, they also say there's no experience, but they still might say that there's the awareness of no experience or something like that.

Andreas Müller: Mm-hmm (affirmative), yes. But yeah, I wouldn't say so.

Justin Allen: But still, wouldn't you say that there's a continuity of being or the continuity of ...?

Andreas Müller: No, I wouldn't even buy into that idea of continuity, because in order to know continuity you would already need someone to experience continuity. For me, change and continuity are two sides of the same coin. Something is constantly changing and moving, and something is going on continuously. Both would, for me, imply time. That's why I sometimes say it's timeless, but there isn't really something going on. Again, that's another thing. Maybe continuity was meant to be timeless. Maybe ... You know, that's what I mean. Again, it's hard with Ramana. It's seventy years ago. It's translated. I don't know how he actually used the words. But for me, continuity is definitely an experience. And again, it's an experience that the seeker is looking for to find something that's always there as a conscious experience.

Justin Allen: But even "oneness," if you take it as a message, is also ...

Andreas Müller: Yes.

Justin Allen: It can be seen as continuity of "oneness"?

Andreas Müller: That's how the "person" would understand it, yes. That there is something called "oneness." Meanwhile, I actually say "noneness."

Justin Allen: "Noneness" ...

Andreas Müller: But yes, the "person" will always turn it into something which is in time and space. Always.

Justin Allen: And even if the "person" isn't there, we say that without the "person" there's nothing, or without the "person" there's just "oneness" or "noneness."

Andreas Müller: Oh, but in the end, nothing can be said when there is no "person."

Justin Allen: Right, but then even in that case there's no waking state, dream state or sleep state. There's just ...

Andreas Müller: Yes, exactly. The waking state is the illusion. And when something wakes up in the morning, when the illusion wakes up in the morning, that's the only thing which makes a break. That's the only thing which has the experience that, "Oh, now something else is happening," or, "Now something is happening." And then all the ideas start, of continuity, of what really is, et cetera ...

Justin Allen: But they have to because that's the ... But even that's a change. So, it's saying that before that, let's say, there's no experience.

Andreas Müller: Yes.

Justin Allen: And then the illusion is the experience?

Andreas Müller: Yes.

Justin Allen: So, there's a change from no experience to experience.

Andreas Müller: But I would say that's the illusion; that waking up in the morning or having the experience of waking up in the morning makes for a real change. No, it doesn't.

Justin Allen: But the illusion is a change?

Andreas Müller: Yeah, but it's not a real change. It's not real. "Me" isn't real, so the illusion isn't real either (laughing).

Justin Allen: But it's apparently different. It's an apparent change, or it's an apparent experience even though it's also not an experience.

Andreas Müller: Exactly, and it's not a change. And it's a bit conceptual now, but it's not a change for wholeness. But to experience oneself as "I'm here now" is the apparent experience of the change. Nothing else experiences that change. Nothing else does experience a change in "me" waking up. It's only the "me" that believes itself to have woken up which makes the difference. "Oh, I'm here." But there's nothing else that experiences a "me" waking up.

Justin Allen: Right, unless you're in the illusion; then there is (laughing).

Andreas Müller: One could say it's only the illusion itself that experiences itself as "I'm here." Nothing does that. Nothing knows about the existence of "me," except the "me."

Justin Allen: Yeah, except that's also … It's so absurd.

Andreas Müller: Yes, it's wonderful (laughing).

Justin Allen: Because it doesn't make any sense either, right? Because it doesn't make sense that an illusion which isn't real could even have ...

Andreas Müller: Yes.

Justin Allen: I mean, it makes sense, and it doesn't make sense.

Andreas Müller: Yes.

Justin Allen: Because an illusion can do whatever it wants because it's an illusion. But logically you'd think that something that's not real could never be real or never think that it's real.

Andreas Müller: Yes, that's the thing. It can't even do that. It's what apparently happens. It can't do. It can't think it's real. That's just what happens. And it's interesting what you just said because that's when we come to that message: It's not logical. Seen from the separate perspective, it's totally without sense. It can't be comprehended. It has nothing to do with these logical awareness teachings where everybody who can follow it a bit can say, "Yeah, true, true. That's right, mm-hmm (affirmative). I understand. I get it. Yes, mm-hmm (affirmative), right." All that stuff, that's all within the person. But what this is pointing to, apparently, is really beyond. It's almost difficult to say, but it's not within that setup. Because exactly that question is the impossible thing for the person: How can I experience myself to be here and hearing this message that I'm not here? Eh? How is that?

Justin Allen: I mean, even that ... But I think there's even something more subtle that ... It's like when you watch a movie on a screen: From the audience's perspective you know that nothing is real. You know totally that this is all an illusion.

Andreas Müller: Yes, but there is someone who really knows that.

Justin Allen: Yeah, right. But I'm just saying, you know that it's an illusion, so you know that when you're looking at a mountain in a movie. Even though sometimes you might forget for a second and really think that the mountain is real. Or with this new 3D technology: Sometimes I've been in those 3D movies where you see people trying to grab something (laughing).

Andreas Müller: Yes, yes.

Justin Allen: And so when they're trying to grab something, they're at least momentarily convinced that there's something floating one meter in front of them.

Andreas Müller: Yeah, yeah.

Justin Allen: So, when you look at them, you think, "That's crazy that they're reaching out for something. Don't they know?" And it's the same thing here. Even though you know that it's an illusion or a fake – something that doesn't really exist, so it doesn't make any sense to try to grab it or touch it –, it still seems to be there. And it's the same with this: How can an illusion create anything, in a sense, because it's just ... It's not real.

Andreas Müller: Exactly. That's why I would say, in that sense, there isn't an autonomous illusion. That would again be the dream; that there is something autonomous at all.

Justin Allen: But then in the same way, would you say that there's only illusion?

Andreas Müller: No, not at all.

Justin Allen: So, you'd say there's only not ... I mean, you can't say that there's only not illusion.

Andreas Müller: Well, the word "illusion" in a way only applies to the illusion. I would say that everything just is what apparently happens. There is no real illusion anywhere, so if people think they're someone, that's not an illusion in the end. That's just what apparently happens. And it would be the apparent illusion to think that there is someone who is in an illusion and could or should wake up from that.

Justin Allen: Right.

Andreas Müller: In that sense, there is no illusion at all. Or if you go into the story, you have to say the only illusion is that there are separate people; that there is something autonomous. Call it people, call it an autonomous illusion, call it "I" – whatever. That would be the only illusion. This conversation is not an illusion. It's "wholeness" or "noneness" or "oneness" or whatever you want to call it.

Justin Allen: But the illusion is also "wholeness" or "oneness," yeah?

Andreas Müller: Yes, and one of us would believe, "Yeah, but I'm a separate person."

Justin Allen: Which would also be an illusion.

Andreas Müller: Yeah, but as you said, it would be an apparent illusion.

In the end, it would just be what apparently happens.

Justin Allen: Right.

Andreas Müller: It would be "noneness" or "wholeness" or "oneness." It would be what is.

Justin Allen: Yeah, but that ... I mean, that applies to everything.

Andreas Müller: Oh, yes, exactly.

Justin Allen: I mean, you can say whatever's happening, that's what's happening. You can apply that to everything.

Andreas Müller: Yes.

Justin Allen: And you can apply the "whatever."

Andreas Müller: Oh, yes. This is what this message does. It addresses everything, but seen from the "person," it's just a dead concept.

Justin Allen: Right.

Andreas Müller: Because the "person" says, "Yeah, but ..." Like you did. Sorry, I'm not mocking, but the "person" said, "Yeah, but you can say that to everything."

Justin Allen: Right. That's what I was trying to point out: For the "person" hearing that it's just the same as how I hear about God, or when you hear a Christian talk about something. They say, "Everything's God," or, "Why do children die of starvation if God's real?" And then they answer, "Because that's part of God's plan." "But why is there a God's plan?" And they can just keep on, and so it's not satisfying. That's why I never was interested in religion because I was like, "Well, I don't see God. None of this makes sense."

Andreas Müller: Yes, it's the same here, but the thing is that this doesn't try to answer your seeking with this concept.

Justin Allen: Right.

Andreas Müller: The "person" can only understand that as a concept, and religions, for example, do that. They try to answer the "person's" needs. They see a "person" and try to provide an answer. I mean, in Christianity they say, "You have to believe it." That's their method.

Justin Allen: Yeah, you have to have faith.

Andreas Müller: Yeah, "Just have faith. Believe that it's like that," which is very elegant, I think, to be honest.

Justin Allen: But that's also the same as Adyashanti's and Rupert Spira's message. This notion of grace or faith, like you said, is their elegant escape maybe, or a concession in a sense ...

Andreas Müller: Yes.

Justin Allen: Because they also kind of say that you can't do it; you're not going to figure it out, because they also say that there's "no one" there to figure it out. But they also say that nothing's going to happen if you don't do anything, so you have to do something in order to somehow "prepare." But at the same time, you have to do nothing, and then it's like a matter of grace. Either the grace comes down upon you and awakens you, or you have to have some kind of faith.

Andreas Müller: Yeah, yeah.

Justin Allen: So ...

Andreas Müller: So, this doesn't try to ... There is no answer to anything.

Justin Allen: But still, I don't think that the difference is only that. Because there's plenty of people that also say, "There's nothing 'I' can do," right?

Andreas Müller: But this is not what I'm saying.

Justin Allen: Yeah, but I think a lot of people would like to hear this message, actually. I think some of the spiritual people, like the seekers that have been meditating for ten or twenty years or going to these retreats, definitely don't want to hear this message. But I could imagine my father hearing this and saying, "Oh, cool. So, my whole life I haven't been trying to do anything, and I've never thought that there was an enlightenment to be attained. I also thought that life's just chaos; just whatever happens is what's happening, and there's nothing we can do about it."

Andreas Müller: Yes, but it won't really work. That person or your father would maybe just hear those two or three sentences and try to use them to confirm his theory.

Justin Allen: Exactly.

Andreas Müller: That's fine, but it has nothing to do with what I say, because he just uses his theory as a method for him as a "person" to make his way through this illusory life. So, that's possible, and of course, that's what the seeker does, or that's what the "person" does. At first, it tries to confirm its concept, maybe in spirituality or with this message or with science or whatever. But it wouldn't be what this message is saying or what I would be saying.

Justin Allen: Right.

Andreas Müller: He would immediately take sides. He would immediately think that I say something, and he would go to his wife and say, "See? I always said that it doesn't make sense. I knew it all my life." (laughing)

Justin Allen: Yeah.

Andreas Müller: Like that, yeah.

Justin Allen: "I knew nothing mattered." (laughing)

Andreas Müller: Exactly, it would be coming as a conclusion and knowledge from a personal standpoint.

Justin Allen: But also, somebody could think they could proclaim this message. Because if I read enough ... Actually, I might have read all your books already. So, if I read or listened to everything that you said, if I listened to Tony Parsons, if I listened to as many of these people as possible, I could easily conduct a talk where I just keep on telling everybody the message that you're saying.

Andreas Müller: Yes, that's true, but ...

Justin Allen: Because it's a little ... Not that it's formulaic, but it's a clear message, and one of not taking a stance, kind of not taking a side.

Andreas Müller: Yes, but then it's understood as a state of clarity. It looks clear from the "person's" perspective. But in the story, one could say that the clarity comes from the apparent death of "me." It's not repeating those words. It's not coming from a person providing a concept of non-duality. It's not coming from someone trying to be a guru or trying to save poor people. No, that's just what apparently happens; that this message or these talks with me or with Tony come out of this apparent death of the "person." And yes, that's apparently different than just repeating the concepts.

Justin Allen: Yeah, because you're saying that there's no continuity, for example.

Andreas Müller: Yes.

Justin Allen: So, if there's no continuity, there is also no repetition in a sense. Even though it's repetitive?

Andreas Müller: Yes.

Justin Allen: And ...

Andreas Müller: Like almost everything.

Justin Allen: Right, so no repetition even though your message is the same over and over again, so far.

Andreas Müller: Yeah, well said (laughing).

Justin Allen: Right? I'm good at qualifying everything (laughing). So like you're saying, if there is no continuity and only "oneness" or "noneness" ...

Andreas Müller: "Timelessness," yeah.

Justin Allen: And if there's no "me" constantly ... Well, no, you can't even say "constantly." There's the death of the "me," kind of, but you wouldn't say there's the death of "me" constantly happening, would you?

Andreas Müller: Exactly, because the only thing that lives in the illusion of happening is the "me," so you can't take an opposite. You can't turn the end of "me" into another happening. The end of "me" itself is a story, you know?

Justin Allen: Yeah, but do you feel like the end of "you" happened? I don't know if "feel" is the right word. It's not happening constantly, or is it?

Andreas Müller: Well, you know, that's all a story. But in the story, that's what seemed to have happened.

Justin Allen: One time.

Andreas Müller: So to speak, yes.

Justin Allen: Yeah, okay. So then from that time on ...

Andreas Müller: Yes.

Justin Allen: There's no more ... There's just no relationship with the "me" anymore. It just isn't there.

Andreas Müller: Exactly, it turned out that there is no one ... This is all in the story, but yes, it vanished. This experience to be something that's now here ...

Justin Allen: Just isn't there anymore?

Andreas Müller: Isn't there anymore.

Justin Allen: But you don't ...

Andreas Müller: Yes.

Justin Allen: There's some kind of recognition that ...

Andreas Müller: It's an apparent recognition.

Justin Allen: Okay.

Andreas Müller: That happens when we talk about it, but it's not that something recognizes that, and that it's a continuous state, and that recognition is liberation, no. One could say when we speak about it, it's apparently recognized.

Justin Allen: Okay, so, not that it has to, but that does mean in a sense that every conversation that you have ... Or let's say we take all your talks and somehow re-record them from whenever you started giving talks, and I would be watching it, from my perspective I would be like, "Oh, look. That talk, he's just doing the same message in this talk one year later, and one year later it's the same, and this goes on." And then I would also kind of think, "Doesn't he get bored doing that?" And isn't it boring for the other people that you see in the talks again and again? I might ask myself, "Why does this person go and get the same message ten times in a row?" But from what you're saying, if there's no continuity and no "me," then what's kind of happening is that it's new and fresh every single time?

Andreas Müller: Yes.

Justin Allen: Even though from the outside it might apparently be the same message over and over again?

Andreas Müller: Yes, exactly. It still could end at some point. Apparent boredom could come up, in ten or in five years, for example, and I would ... I don't know, but there being boredom about saying it again and again would be fresh and new as well.

Justin Allen: Yeah, or it's also possible that it could apparently evolve or change or something.

Andreas Müller: Kind of.

Justin Allen: I mean, in theory it could.

Andreas Müller: Yeah, exactly. In theory, yeah. Not really. The message hasn't really changed. The words and the concepts have changed a bit, apparently, but the message has never changed, basically because there is no real message (laughing). And in a way, even though that's a bit in the story now, it's always the same. Sun goes up, sun goes down, breakfast in the morning and dinner in the evening (laughing). In the story, everything is kind of always the same.

Justin Allen: Yeah, except that ...

Andreas Müller: But that's in the story.

Justin Allen: Yeah, that's in the story. But there's still something about that because that's the reason why people come: That they seek enlightenment or an escape from the apparent "self" is because everything does seem to repeat itself; the same routine every day, and they hate it. The "me" hates it because it thinks that life shouldn't be this way or something like that.

Andreas Müller: Well, it loves it and it hates it.

Justin Allen: Yeah, but kind of the advertisements of non-duality and spirituality are that life will still be repetitive, but you won't be there to care anymore, either way.

Andreas Müller: Yeah, but that's not really what non-duality is about. I would make an apparent difference. Spirituality provides or at least promises a way out. It tries to provide that "thing" which makes the real difference: enlightenment. Or finding yourself or losing yourself or whatever. In the end, non-duality doesn't do that, even though it may sound like that.

Justin Allen: So what do you say it does?

Andreas Müller: Non-duality is apparently ... You know, it's all in the story because there is no such thing as non-duality. It's not the answer. See, I'm speechless here (laughing) because it doesn't do anything in the end.

Justin Allen: But that ...

Andreas Müller: It's a ...

Justin Allen: But that's a major change for somebody that, from a previous ...

Andreas Müller: Yes, yes. The "person" will process that as a change and as a new something. The "person" will hear that and say, "Oh, that's the answer," or "It's like that," which is totally and utterly fine. But it will turn out that there just is no answer, and that there is no one. But see, when I say, "It turns out," seen by the "person," this sounds like another promise, like another answer. "Oh yeah, at one point it will turn out like that, for me, of course." And it just isn't like that.

Justin Allen: But what is it like?

Andreas Müller: This can't be said.

Justin Allen: Right, and then even that answer; even if you say, "There's no answer," or, "If you just do this," that's a whole different way of relating to life.

Andreas Müller: But again, yes, the "person" would see that as another way of relating to life.

Justin Allen: Yeah.

Andreas Müller: Yes, I understand.

Justin Allen: And without the "person" ... Yeah, I mean without the "person," there's no way that the "person" can understand what it's like to ...

Andreas Müller: Exactly, yes. Yes, it blows up the whole idea of "with a person" and "without a person."

Justin Allen: But spirituality does the same thing, at least the apparent goal of spirituality is to die as the "self."

Andreas Müller: Exactly. Yes, yes, assuming that there is a "self" in the first place.

Justin Allen: Right. Well, that's the illusory "self." It's not that there is a "self." It's that there's an illusion of the "self."

Andreas Müller: Exactly. They say there is a real illusion of the "self," and now we've got to work on that.

Justin Allen: Yeah.

Andreas Müller: I wouldn't go that far.

Justin Allen: Yeah, you'd say there's not (laughing). You'd say there's nothing that you can do.

Andreas Müller: There is "no one." I would say there is "no one."

Justin Allen: Right, there is "no one," so there's nothing that somebody can do or not do.

Andreas Müller: Yes, and that's already a conclusion in the end. If you say it as a conclusion, then it quickly turns into something: "I can't do anything."

Justin Allen: Oh, okay, okay, okay.

Andreas Müller: In the end, just yes, yes, yes. It's not making conclusions and saying, "Oh, you can't do that because there is 'no one', beep, beep, beep." It's not meant like that. But yes, there is 'no one', which also means that there is no illusion. And I think we talked about it the last time. All you end up with is having this religion and this focusing on dying and on killing the illusion. And suddenly you end up with religions because the "person" and the teacher and the seeker all focus on the illusion trying to make it go away. And it doesn't work, because it's already part of an illusion.

Justin Allen: But you want to ...

Andreas Müller: I think you have thousands and hundreds of thousands of people around the world right now trying to get rid of the "me."

Justin Allen: Yeah. Fuck, yeah, that's what I'm waiting around in the shadows doing (laughing).

Andreas Müller: Yes, and I think hundreds and thousands of those have been trying to do that for several years. Some people have built their whole life on the idea that they have to kill or transcend the "me."

Justin Allen: Yeah, I've lost my girlfriends because of that (laughing).

Andreas Müller: Well ...

Justin Allen: But this is an ... I think ...

Andreas Müller: You tried to lose "the one" that they fell in love with, I mean (laughing).

Justin Allen: Yeah. Like the sentence, "There is no one," right?

Andreas Müller: Yeah.

Justin Allen: And then what was that sentence that I said? I said, "There is 'no one' to do anything," right?

Andreas Müller: Yeah, but you said it like a conclusion. And because there is "no one," then I don't know ...

Justin Allen: There is "no one," therefore there is nothing to do, because there's "no one" that could do anything.

Andreas Müller: Yes, and in a way it's right, but not as a conclusion. I could say the same sentence, but I had the impression that when you said it, it sounded like a conclusion in the sense of, "You are not allowed to do something, because there is 'no one,'" and all that stuff.

Justin Allen: Yeah, as a conclusion. But that's where I see how difficult it could be, in a way.

Andreas Müller: Yes, because it's not in the words. It's not the words themselves. It's not the concepts that are provided in the end.

Justin Allen: It's like something energetic, no?

Andreas Müller: Yes, and that's the thing. You can say exactly the same sentences, and in a teaching or in a personal setup there would be "someone" saying that sentence, hoping that it will answer the personal need of the other person. This would be a teaching. It would be exactly the same sentence.

Justin Allen: This is how I kind of relate it. Maybe this is a bad example, but let's say you have a girlfriend that asks you, "Do you love me?" And then you don't know how you're feeling, you think something like, "What is love? Everybody has a different idea of what love means. I don't even know if I love somebody." So, if you were going to be honest, you'd have to say that this stuff is going on. You'd have to be like, "Well, what does it mean? I don't want to say 'I love you', because I do love you, but I also might love somebody else the next day." And then somebody has the idea, "Well, if you love somebody, you can only love one person. It's not possible that you love several persons," right? So all these things come in. And so, when somebody asks you that, generally you just don't want to disrupt their illusions of life ...

Andreas Müller: Sorry, something is missing, the picture and audio got sticky ...

Justin Allen: Well, I said that you feel uncomfortable sometimes saying to somebody, "Yes, I love you, too." But in a sense, I think a lot of times you do it as a concession to let the other person stay in their illusion.

Andreas Müller: Yes, I know what you mean.

Justin Allen: You know what I mean? And I feel like something about spirituality and these kinds of messages is that it's ... I can imagine it's really difficult to take such a kind of non-concession stance to not cater to the "self" ever.

Andreas Müller: And no, because it's not a standpoint. No, that's completely unimportant in the end.

Justin Allen: For you it is, but maybe for a Rupert-Spira-type teacher it's that they have to make concessions or that they make these concessions for that reason, to avoid being so directly controversial to the audience. You know what I mean? Because when I've seen you sitting there, you seemed to be different.

Andreas Müller: You want to save Rupert Spira (laughing).

Justin Allen: No, no. I don't. I don't want to.

Andreas Müller: No, I'm sorry.

Justin Allen: I'm just trying to play the devil's advocate.

Andreas Müller: Yeah, right (laughing).

Justin Allen: But if you say that there's "no one" ... Right?

Andreas Müller: Yes.

Justin Allen: That's like the worst thing that somebody can hear.

Andreas Müller: Yes and no. Yeah, I'd say it's in a way the worst thing the "person" can hear, but the "person" isn't real. So, for some people it's pure joy to hear.

Justin Allen: Yeah, it's pure joy, but I bet that these people are misinterpreting it (laughing) and are going, "Awesome. There's 'no one.' I'm not there. That confirms my whole philosophy of life and means I don't have to do all this hard work and all this stuff that I thought I had to do."

Andreas Müller: Yeah, I know. Yeah, yeah.

Justin Allen: But that's not true either.

Andreas Müller: No, that would be another concept. Anyway, they can't keep up that conviction for a long time.

Justin Allen: That's like when I feel there's a certain relief when I listen to Adyashanti or Rupert Spira and say, "Holy shit. I have to abide as this awareness, and how do I do that? That's so hard." It doesn't seem possible that I can just abide as this awareness all the time. And then I even question that and ask, "Well, what is this awareness?" It's also that I'm still actively trying to do something, and they're giving me the message that whenever I'm trying to act or there's an intention or an agenda, it's still the "me" operating. And then I listen to your message, which is saying that there's no one there, and the way the mind or at least my mind interprets it is "Oh, oh, this is such a relief. So, I don't have to struggle and abide as the awareness."

Andreas Müller: Yes, it's both. It's both, because yes, on the one hand the "person" will hear that sentence as another truth or as another conviction, like you just said. But of course, energetically it's exactly what's being said. This whole attempt, this whole need to do life, to find an answer, to struggle for fulfillment, to be someone, is an illusion. Of course, that's the energy of it, and this can be a huge relief. In the end, it doesn't matter if you believe one or the other. But of course, that's the underlying message, so to speak, an apparent message, but this is apparently being said all the time, of course.

Justin Allen: Okay, so then is there some way that you can kind of tell how it was for you? You were going to Tony Parsons and listening to this message that you're now giving.

Andreas Müller: Yes.

Justin Allen: And did you see anything? Could you recognize anything kind of happening to you as you were listening to Tony Parsons? How do you relate to it now, in a sense? You were on one side of the fence, and now you're on the other, so to speak.

Andreas Müller: I don't really relate to that. I know when "I" died (laughing), so to speak, which is such a story, it was a bit like, "Oh, damn it." No, not even that strong. It was a bit like, "It fucking just is like that."

Justin Allen: But do you feel that it was like the repetition of going?

Andreas Müller: I never felt like repeating, to be honest.

Justin Allen: Maybe not repeating, I don't know … I'm having a difficult time coming up with an analogy. Let's say you keep on trying to build a house on soft ground, and you keep on adding more material to the wall, and as you do so, it keeps on sinking. Because your structure keeps on getting heavier, so the house just keeps on sinking into the soft ground.

Andreas Müller: I don't get what do you mean by building up a structure? Where do I build the walls? I'm not getting the picture.

Justin Allen: (laughing) I mean, if you're trying to build a house, and you're building it on a soft ground.

Andreas Müller: Yes.

Justin Allen: And you keep on adding material to the walls. Let's say you're building a stone wall, and every time you add a new layer, the wall drops.

Andreas Müller: Yes, but ...

Justin Allen: So, your house never gets higher because it keeps on sinking into the soil.

Andreas Müller: Okay, so but ...

Justin Allen: And so because that keeps on happening, at some point you go, "I'm never going to build this wall. It's just impossible, at least on this area. I can't do it." So you stop building the wall.

Andreas Müller: Yes, and now (laughing), what does this analogy apply to?

Justin Allen: So, for me, if there was some kind of working or potential effect of your message, it's that I would keep on going to Tony Parsons or to you. I feel like the conversation will always be, "There's no one there."

Andreas Müller: Yes.

Justin Allen: Right? And I'm going to hear this repeatedly, and I might try to come up with all kinds of different avenues or arguments or ways to (deny or argue against) ... And if I keep on getting disproven over and over again, and I'm copying it, like it's sinking in to me somehow, that's where I can imagine maybe it's possible where you go like, "Holy shit. Yeah, okay."

Andreas Müller: Yes, but this would still be what apparently happens because that's the thing. The vanishing of "me," so to speak ... Now, let's stay very superficial. So why I got it, or when I got it, or "me" getting it, was just what apparently happened. It was almost like happening along the way. While I was working on "me" being alive and "me" being a happy person and all that stuff, "I" vanished along the way. That's just what apparently happened, for no real reason. It might look like, and on the other hand that was what happened, as if it was sinking in. It was wiping me out. I didn't ...

Justin Allen: Right, like exhausting your ...

Andreas Müller: You know, I wouldn't bring it so much on the "me" side, like I tried to build the walls, and it didn't work, and I saw that it didn't work. And because I saw that, I stopped seeking and all that stuff. It's not really like that. That's what I mean. While I was still trying to live my life as good as I can, I was being wiped out along the way, not noticing.

Justin Allen: Yeah, like unknowingly.

Andreas Müller: So, that's how it was for me a bit, yes.

Justin Allen: But ...

Andreas Müller: But one more sentence. There are people who have been hearing this for fifteen years or more, or there are people, not only in non-duality, who have been dancing around this idea that there is "no one" for forty years, when they read Ramana Maharshi for the first time or some Zen or whatever "kind of seeking" around this idea, and apparently nothing really was happening, in that sense.

Justin Allen: Yeah, but did you also kind of recognize a little bit that there was the chipping away of your "sense of self"?

Andreas Müller: Yes, but only looking back because ...

Justin Allen: But during it, you didn't recognize anything?

Andreas Müller: No, I recognized that things fell off, that in that period I felt better and better, and I cared less and less in a positive sense. This message didn't really give me a hard time. I had my hard time before that.

Justin Allen: Yeah, I had my hard time before and maybe still to come, also. This doesn't ...

Andreas Müller: So, but yeah, until the end I thought that whatever is falling away and whatever happens, it was still happening to "me." So, of course, I recognized things changing, but I mean, in the "person's" way, always things are changing, or that's the hope. But yes, things were changing, but in the end, until the end, for "me."

Justin Allen: And do you see ... I think I mentioned this yesterday: What the message might do to people is that it feels like it starves the kind of conventional food that you give to the "self." Maybe Rupert Spira's or Adyashanti's message also starve the ego, but at the same time they give it something.

Andreas Müller: Exactly. It's in a way no different ...

Justin Allen: It gives it a vegan diet instead of an American diet, you know (laughing)?

Andreas Müller: Yes, one could say so.

Justin Allen: It's just a healthier diet than what we're conventionally fed.

Andreas Müller: Yeah, let's stick to that. I wouldn't go to the starving thing. I mean, people eat (laughing). I mean, maybe accidentally, people starve on vegan food (laughing) automatically. But actually, I would say these messages provide "food" – apparently ... I think it's still about diet. It's still about eating.

Justin Allen: I mean, they say it's about diet, too.

Andreas Müller: Yes, they say so. But it fits the picture. I think they say they have the better diet. "This is the healthiest diet for you."

Justin Allen: Yeah, yeah.

Andreas Müller: Yeah, I mean there's nothing right or wrong with anything. It just is what seems to be happening. That's my impression of that. In a way, what seems to be happening is that, on the one hand, something is being said, and on the other hand, something else seems to happen. On the one hand, it's being said that there actually is "no one," and on the other hand what's being said is, "And now let's feed that one the healthiest diet."

Justin Allen: That's an interesting premise though, to not feed you a diet.

Andreas Müller: Yes, but the thing is that's not another idea coming from a "person," so to say. It's not about, "I don't feed you anything, because that's the best for you."

Justin Allen: Right.

Andreas Müller: Then it would just be another diet with nothing to eat, but it's not an idea. That's the important thing. It's not coming from an idea that this would serve you best.

Justin Allen: Right. It's just coming from the message that comes out of this "nothing understanding."

Andreas Müller: Exactly. In the story, it's really coming from that absence, not being able to recognize someone who could be fed with anything. It's not intellectual. It's not because I thought it all through well.

Justin Allen: Yeah. No, but that's what I think is refreshing about it; that it feels from an energetic perspective that there's almost no energy in it, or that it's an un-agenda-ically energy.

Andreas Müller: Absolutely, yes. It's that natural. It doesn't ... There isn't ... Because in spirituality, there would be an agenda about having no agenda. It would be the right intention to have no intention. No, there naturally can't be any intention in that sense when there is "no one."

Justin Allen: Right.

Andreas Müller: And yes, that's just how this energy is. Not because it's right or wrong or serves best or whatever. It's just not there.

Justin Allen: Yeah, that's what I was trying to ... I think I might get it. I might be able to express this at some point, and that's what I was trying to get at with the analogy of being with a lover. At least for me, I always recognize that I'm making some kind of a concession or saying something with a little bit of a lie or untruth to it to make a concession to myself or to the other person.

Andreas Müller: Yes.

Justin Allen: And there's a huge fear to just be really honest, you know? Or with a child, when a child is crying or something like this, and you say something like, "Just go to sleep and tomorrow everything will be okay."

Andreas Müller: Yeah.

Justin Allen: We all say that, but we all know it's not going to be okay (laughing). And that's the message though; the truthful message is to say, "I don't know if it's going to be okay. It might get worse. It could get better. Who knows?"

Andreas Müller: Yeah.

Justin Allen: But nobody ever says that.

Andreas Müller: Yes, yeah.

Justin Allen: Which is fine, maybe it makes sense that we don't. But at some point, especially if you start getting interested in, for lack of a better word, spirituality, then I do think that it becomes ... Maybe it's not dangerous, but it's potentially going to keep somebody just on another diet instead of really ... Well yeah, I don't know.

Andreas Müller: Yeah. As I said, yes, you can't really bring right or wrong in that. And, I know that wasn't really right, yeah, yeah.

Justin Allen: Yeah, you can't bring right or wrong into it, but there's still ... Well, then you can say it's refreshing to hear this message because it feels or it seems so clean.

Andreas Müller: Yes. Oh, it is, yes, yes.

Justin Allen: And it feels like there's less wiggle room for the self to grab onto something or to believe something new.

Andreas Müller: Or yes, in the end there is ... Yes, yes ...

Justin Allen: So it's like a diet of water.

Andreas Müller: Well ... Starving. It's apparent starving, but not in order to starve someone.

Justin Allen: So when you're giving a talk to, let's say, ten people, and at some point it's just an exchange between you and another person for fifteen or thirty minutes, do you ever sense that ... Are you ever able to sense that they might be grasping it? Do you ever feel some kind of energetic connection, or like something's happening and ...?

Andreas Müller: Well, I mean yes and no. Not in a directly personalized way. I can't really answer that. I mean, as it is in the talk, sometimes it's like us talking. I mean, we do that in a way, no?

Justin Allen: Yeah.

Andreas Müller: It's like that.

Justin Allen: Yeah, but at least in this case the assumption that I have is that you have recognized something that I haven't yet recognized.

Andreas Müller: No, not really, no.

Justin Allen: No, but that's my assumption that I ...

Andreas Müller: Oh, yeah. Of course, yeah. That's possible, yeah, yeah.

Justin Allen: So ...

Andreas Müller: And maybe, I apparently can recognize that.

Justin Allen: Yeah.

Andreas Müller: More or less, not that I ... Not now actually, but I know what you mean, yes.

Justin Allen: It's the same, not saying that you're a teacher, as if I were teaching somebody tennis, it's assumed that I know how to swing the racket the right way, and I'm trying to teach them how to do a forehand, and I can see that they're just on the cusp of understanding it. I can't really go there and say, "Hey, this is exactly how you do it." Somehow they have to come to it, but I might see that they're on the cusp of getting it correctly ...

Andreas Müller: Yes, yes. That apparently happens but in itself is wholeness already, and it doesn't mean anything regarding the next moment.

Justin Allen: So, there's also no attempt from you to maybe say some kind of key sentence that's going to evoke something like, "Oh."

Andreas Müller: No. There's literally no intention in that, and there's also no hidden intention, and there isn't a waiting for people to get it. Not at all. There's nothing to get, absolutely.

Justin Allen: And why do you say there's nothing to get? Just because there's "no one" there?

Andreas Müller: In the end, I say it because there is nothing to get (laughing).

Justin Allen: Okay, because that's different, I think. It's different to say, "There's nothing to get," than to say, "There's nothing to get because there's 'no one' there."

Andreas Müller: Well, in the end both go together. There is "no one" there, and there is nothing to get.

Justin Allen: Yeah, they go together, but I still think there is some subtle difference in what you just said. Because you said, "There's nothing to get." I do think that that in itself is already enough. I don't know if it's necessary to say, "Because there's no one there to get it."

Andreas Müller: Exactly, it's not necessary to say.

Justin Allen: You can say there's nothing to get, and there's also "no one" there to get it.

Andreas Müller: Yes, exactly.

Justin Allen: But you don't necessarily have to say, "There's nothing to get because there's 'no one' there to get it," right?

Andreas Müller: Yes, yes.

Justin Allen: That's a difference.

Andreas Müller: Yeah, I know what you mean. It's an apparent difference, yes, because it creates already an explanation for something.

Justin Allen: Yeah, but ...

Andreas Müller: But "there is nothing to get" is the natural reality, which is uncaused, which is not logical, which is in the end not because of something. Some would say that there is "no one" because the "I" is an illusion. I mean, me too, I probably say those sentences sometimes, but in the end, yes, it's uncaused. There is "no one," and there's nothing to get, for no reason. Not because it's right or good or better like that. No, there just is "no one," and there's nothing to get, and there is no real happening. There are no real circumstances. There is no seeker; nothing has been lost, and nothing needs to be found.

Justin Allen: Yeah, those are the starvation sentences (laughing).

Andreas Müller: Yes, because they don't try to say anything. They don't try to answer the seeking. They don't try to feed you.

Justin Allen: Right, but that's also the difficulty in being in your position to say those sentences. Those are like taboo sentences in a way, definitely for our culture.

Andreas Müller: Yes, but it's not difficult for me because I'm not in a certain position, and I'm not trying to go anywhere with those sentences.

Justin Allen: Yeah, but even that seems to be difficult. I think it's difficult to maintain that. Well, it's not difficult to maintain if I assume that there's no ego and truly no desire and no agenda for you et cetera. Then it's easy for you to stay this way.

Andreas Müller: Exactly, yes.

Justin Allen: But if somehow an ego comes in or an agenda comes in, then there's no way you can stay this way (laughing).

Andreas Müller: Exactly, and that's why you also get a lot of people who start off with that message, coming from ...

Justin Allen: Yeah, and then they want to make money or something like that ...

Andreas Müller: Or want to help. I think some people really think, "Oh, well now I know the answer, and I can help people with that." And sooner or later, after years, you end up having a personal teaching with all the ingredients of a path and a method and something that's better and something that's not so good and all that stuff. Because a "person" can't maintain it; it would start right off with some intention, with some subtle intention.

Justin Allen: Yeah, well even if you want to help somebody, sometimes you have to make a concession or a lie to get that person to kind of spend an hour with you or something like that. And then you might think, "Okay, I'm just going to kind of subtly convince them to come spend an hour with me, and then I'll start giving them the truth after that one hour." You know what I mean?

Andreas Müller: Yes, it's something else right away.

Justin Allen: Yeah.

Andreas Müller: Not after an hour. Not after one and a half hours when some teaching talk starts. No, it was right away something else.

Justin Allen: Yeah.

Andreas Müller: Yeah, energetically, yes. So yes, the "person" can't maintain it, or the "person" would have the impression to somehow form, stick to the truth and be careful to not ... Be careful. Maintain it. Have a position, a strong position. Be ready to discuss and all that, having arguments about it. Know all the becauses (laughing).

Justin Allen: Right.

Andreas Müller: Yeah, that's true. But in that sense, it's not difficult for me. It just comes out what comes out. I don't have to know it, even. I don't have to prepare myself. It's natural. It's what naturally comes out.

Justin Allen: Yeah, right now it's what naturally comes out. But can't you imagine that it would be easy to, I don't know, somehow get seduced to change?

Andreas Müller: No. No, I don't. I can't. I don't see that, to be honest, not really. I mean, I could see and understand the mechanism, but no, I don't see it happening. Because if it came to that point, I couldn't be honest anymore.

Justin Allen: Right, but that ...

Andreas Müller: And it's so different to say to someone, "Oh, yeah. Please, you should come to the talks. It will serve you." Or if you say, "Well, come or not. You are free," period.

Justin Allen: Yeah, but it's like ... I don't know. It's like you have to lie to a friend or a wife or people in your life.

Andreas Müller: Oh, but that's what's apparent ... This message isn't about personal honesty or not. I'm not ... There isn't someone in a position who thinks that he needs to tell the truth all the way, all the time. Because as you said, in the story, what is the truth? In the story, there seem to be levels.

Justin Allen: Yeah.

Andreas Müller: Do you love me? As you said, "Hmm, shall I be honest, say, you know?" But that's all in the story. In that sense, there is no truth anyway.

Justin Allen: Right, other than ... So, this is one difference. This is probably a major difference then. The message from Rupert Spira, Adyashanti and these types of spiritual people is that they always fall back on the heart, that you have to follow your heart.

Andreas Müller: Oh, yeah, exactly.

Justin Allen: Right? So then that's part of being truthful, I don't know, in life decisions like, "Where am I going to live?", Who I'm going to take for my partner?", "What job should I do?" How do you decide those things?

Andreas Müller: Yeah, follow your heart.

Justin Allen: Yeah.

Andreas Müller: Yeah, again someone which could follow something (laughing). Some orientation or direction.

Justin Allen: So, what is it like for you when you have to make a supposed important decision?

Andreas Müller: You know, there is no answer to that. I can answer with a story, and I do what I like, mostly, but I don't always do what I want to do. There is no answer to that question, how to live life, so to speak.

Justin Allen: And you also don't apparently have the dilemma of, "Should I do this or shouldn't I do this?" and turn it into a problem?

Andreas Müller: Exactly. It's not a problem. It's apparent functioning. Of course, sometimes there's also the question of, "Shall I do this or that?"

Justin Allen: Okay.

Andreas Müller: But there's no one experiencing that as a problem in the sense of ... Or not even that. Maybe it is a problem, but there is just "no one" in there who lives in the illusion that there is the need to find a conscious way through it, and that it's real and all that stuff.

Justin Allen: Maybe it's better to put it like that: There's "no one" there to take that apparent problem personally or not.

Andreas Müller: Yes, yeah, which can't be done. It's not another position. It's not a way out of the apparent dilemma of, "Should I or shouldn't I?" It's not an escape from or an answer to that. There's just "no one" in it (laughing).

Justin Allen: Okay, we're on one hour and twenty-eight minutes now. Before we wrap it up and let ourselves get on another tangent or rant, were you comfortable with everything today?

Andreas Müller: Yeah, thank you. And yeah, thanks for calling. Thanks for talking. I think it's ... I love it. It's great.

Justin Allen: Yeah, I feel positive about it, also.

Andreas Müller: Yeah, good.

Justin Allen: Bye bye.

Andreas Müller: Bye bye. See you.

November 4, 2019 Talk 02

TEACHERS & GURUS CONTINUED

Justin Allen: All right. So, I continued to read Ramana Maharshi (laughing) and wrote down some things that I thought are worth reading back to you and talking about.

Andreas Müller: Yeah, all right.

Justin Allen: So in general, some of the significant things that I pulled out from it go back a little bit to what we talked about last week: finding out about or finding out the real "I." That's the principle; that there's some sense of a "real I," which Ramana refers to as the "self," or capitalized: "Self," and then the "fake I," which is the ego or the "me." So in the question "Who am I?", "I" refers to the ego, and while one is trying to trace it back and find its source, they see that it has no separate existence but merges in the "real I." This argues for a "fake ego I" and a "real oneness I." The moment you go deeper and deeper, looking for the "real self", it is waiting there to take you in. Then whatever's done, is done by something else.

What I found interesting about this, and it goes back to what we talked about last week, was that there is a "practice" that's being proposed here but that at some point is worthless. From then on, according to what's being implied here, is that something else takes over and removes the "me", the "I" or the "fake self"; in a sense, it removes the doership.

Andreas Müller: Yes, but one could ... Again, I have to say that I don't know; none of us can exactly know what Ramana actually meant, because we can't ask him. So this is just our interpretation (laughing).

Justin Allen: Yeah, I know.

Andreas Müller: But you could read the exact same paragraph with the assumption that he's just making a description.

Justin Allen: Right.

Andreas Müller: Without anyone who has any choice in there, maybe he's just describing an apparent process that happens completely on its own (without a "me" involved), and he's not speaking to someone who has to consciously do that.

Justin Allen: Right.

Andreas Müller: My impression is that this whole paragraph gets a whole different flavor then. I don't know if he meant it in the sense of a description or a practice that "one" does. We're just assuming it one way or the other. When I speak about it, I always point out that it's a story, but when I speak about the death of "me" and all of that, it might apparently happen exactly as in this description. But again, without anyone who has any choice if this questioning even starts to happen.

Justin Allen: But still, I think a difference is that he is definitely proposing that you do something. Then in the doing of the something, at some point, the doership falls away, and something else takes over. But what you're suggesting is that even this initial doing, the trying to trace the "I" back to its source and to abide as awareness, is not even necessary, or that it's not going to help or bring you to this recognition or to the death of the "me."

Andreas Müller: Oh, yes, exactly.

Justin Allen: So, that's a clear distinction.

Andreas Müller: No, I wouldn't make a distinction here, except that this is what apparently happens. But yes, I wouldn't say that it's necessary that it has to happen like that.

Justin Allen: Right. But it could also ...

Andreas Müller: Of course, everybody who experiences her or himself as "someone" is a seeker. So before apparent liberation, there will always be a seeker story going on. There always was the impression that I'm on a path and that I (the "me") am doing something. In that sense, this paragraph would just be a description.

Justin Allen: Right, but he ...

Andreas Müller: When that happens, that happens. When the "me" is apparently doing things, that's what happens. I would use different words, but I could say that, too. When I say that there is "no one," this, again, is rather a description than something that can be done. The same could be said about this whole statement from Ramana, as I said. But if it was meant in the sense of this message, I would say it's complicated. Because it's just ... Is there someone or not? Period.

Justin Allen: But he's making this argument because he specifically says that this practice is the most direct means to eliminating the "illusory self." He's saying that this is better than meditating and all the other types of spiritual practices that you could do.

Andreas Müller: Yes, but I wouldn't say so. Well, it's an energy thing. I can imagine both, but let me repeat that I just don't know. But was it like him sitting there and giving practices, or was he just talking to someone, in a sense of, "Hey, look. Is there someone? Don't meditate, don't do all these practices, just have a look if there is someone." Again, then this whole conversation would have a totally different energy than if it were a prescription like, "First you have to look if there is someone. If you do this for ten or whatever years, then you'll see ..." You see? But yes, maybe it was just his way of saying that there is "no one."

Justin Allen: Yeah, it does seem like it's his way of saying that, at least from the way the book's reading.

Andreas Müller: I know what you mean, yeah.

Justin Allen: Some ways are better to go about it than others, though.

Andreas Müller: Yeah, I understand.

Justin Allen: Which is somewhat true to Tony Parsons. I was listening to him as well, in the sense that he admits at least that coming to these talks has a different energy and the potential to kill the "me." It seems like he might say ... He'd qualify it probably, but he might say that coming and sitting in one of his talks is potentially "better" for a seeker, energetically, than going and sitting in a room and meditating for an hour.

Andreas Müller: But even then, I would again see that rather as a description than adding this whole personal idea of a path and value. This whole liberation thing gives value to the "person" and immediately adds importance to the path. My impression is, in this story, that for people who meet those messages, in some way or the other, something apparently changes. Which is totally in the story and has no value. This doesn't mean anything; it's a description, an apparent description of what apparently happens.

It's a bit like that people who eat at McDonald's every day seem to gain weight, which just is what apparently happens, without any right or wrong, so to speak, and without anyone doing it or having the possibility of not doing it. Same with coming to the talks: First, there is "no one" who could come or not come, but something seems to be happening there. In a way, it's like everywhere; something seems to be happening, A seems to lead to B et cetera. You know what I mean?

Justin Allen: Yeah.

Andreas Müller: It's in a way undeniable that people meeting the message, in some way or the other, get "touched." But what happens out of that? Some people think, "Oh, utter crap. I never go there again." Some people are scared, other people are happy. For some people, concepts fall off, other people have no idea what happened, they just sit there and enjoy it (or not). For some people, the whole energy of the "me" collapses. Whatever it is; that's just what seems to be happening. Not because it's right, not because it's an actual goal of existence, so to speak.

Justin Allen: So, we also talked about this the last time a little bit, and I feel like I already know what you'll say.

Andreas Müller: Funnily enough, Ramana is also referring to that. I have the impression that he or maybe someone else said that, too. That it's apparently about doing the practice, but at some point, it has to be over.

Justin Allen: Yeah, that's what he basically said in that paragraph I just read to you.

Andreas Müller: Exactly.

Justin Allen: He concludes with this really interesting sentence, "Then whatever is done is done by something else, and you have no hand in it."

Andreas Müller: Yeah. That's my impression, too. I know a lot of people who come for a while and are totally in it, and at some point, it's just over. Yet, it's not replaced by something else. It's just literally the end. Usually, for people, for the "person," that's a bit like, "Yeah, I meditated for ten years, but somehow this ended; now I'm singing mantras." And five years later, "Yeah, the mantra singing stopped, now I breathe into myself," or whatever. Every method is always replaced by the next one.

I don't see that happening at the talks. People might come and go for years, but for some, it just vanishes without being replaced by another method or another concept. This is my impression at least. But still, there is "no one" in there being able to consciously do one of these things. It's not about the seeker doing it or finding something. Or about practicing or there being someone who can consciously come to a meeting. That was also my impression when I went to the meetings.

Justin Allen: You thought you were going?

Andreas Müller: Yes, but it happened quite unpredictably. It wasn't that I could do it, it wasn't even that I went all the time, because it was so obvious for me that it wasn't about going to the meetings. For me, this was totally in the air.

Justin Allen: You mean that at some point, you started to just feel like you didn't have a hand in it, that it was out of your control, and you were ...

Andreas Müller: Sometimes I went, and sometimes I didn't, yes.

Justin Allen: But you thought you were the controller behind it all?

Andreas Müller: I wouldn't go that far, I just noticed that going or not going was different from what I had planned. I didn't really feel a holy pull or something like that, it was more like, "Wow, actually I want to go, but it's just not happening." I thought for three months that I would drive there on a certain Saturday, and suddenly there was just no impulse. Boom, okay. It was not happening, not even that I waited for an impulse, but I just didn't go to the car. On other occasions, it was that one week before, I thought, "Hey, maybe I do go." Not special, but different from how I seemed to be and have lived before where I knew when I wanted to go, I would go, and stuff like that.

Justin Allen: And you didn't attribute it to anything, you didn't say, "Oh, this is 'me' finally listening to my gut or to my heart or to some other organ?" (laughing).

Andreas Müller: No, no, not really. Because I've had all this in the spiritual and "guru" thing, I've had lots of those spiritual ideals about "wholeness" and "the real" and all that stuff. And all those ideas became disappointments because I was so convinced that this is the real thing and this is about love and this is about the actual stuff. It turned out to be just another thing.

Justin Allen: I can say from my experience that I've never gone "all-in," so to speak, in anything.

I read Jiddu Krishnamurti and was really interested in it for periods of time but never convinced, let's say, to really fully believe in it. Same when I read Adyashanti and went to his retreat, and then same with Rupert Spira. Sometimes I've entertained the idea that I should go meditate or go to a month-long meditation retreat or join a monastery or something like that, but I was never convinced of that either (laughing).

But then at the same time, I'm not convinced of just living my average life (laughing). I constantly feel that something doesn't feel true or authentic; just not like, "This is it." I am searching, but at the same time, I'm not convinced that there's any point of searching at all. Then I can't really stop myself; sometimes I also think, "Oh, I'm depressed because of the searching." This constant thinking that something's around the corner or there's something better. But then at the same time, I say, "Well, you can go see a psychiatrist, you can go to a retreat (laughing), you can say, 'Fuck it all, I'm just going to live my normal life (laughing)'."

If anything, sometimes maybe what I recognize is that there's still, in every case, always a resistance. I don't know, it's like search and resistance, search and resistance. That seems to be the pattern. And it seems that sometimes people have stopped the search just out of exhaustion (laughing).

Andreas Müller: Yes and no. Because you can't "do" exhaustion. Again, it wasn't "me" melting away because "me" was in a certain condition. It just was what apparently happened, like going to retreats or meditating or whatever. In a way, again, it could be exactly what Ramana described. It's just vanishing, it's just melting away. That which is false, that which isn't real, that which never was real just melts away. I would say in the end, for no reason. Or you can't point to a reason because in every life story, you'll find an apparent story where one thing seemed to have led to another, but there are no rules in that.

When I say, for example, that seeking isn't necessary, I'm actually referring to a story. Because this question in the end doesn't arise, because as long as there's seeking, as long as there's a seeker (a "me"), there will be seeking. It will end when it ends. But yes, one could say ... Ramana, for example, would say to you, "Well, who is that? Who is exactly the 'one' who says, 'I'm seeking, and everything felt unreal, and I didn't really go into it, because right away, I couldn't really believe it or trust it'"? Ramana maybe would have said, "Yeah, but who is that 'I'? Who is that? Go see what it is." Not really addressing a "person," he could have said it in the same energy in which I would say, "But there is no one."

Justin Allen: He says, "When thoughts arise, the 'I thought' claims ownership of them. 'I' think, 'I' believe, 'I' want, 'I' am acting. But there is no separate 'I thought' that exists independently of the objects that it is identifying with. It only appears to exist as real." That sounds like it's in the same vein as your or Tony Parsons's message.

Andreas Müller: Exactly. I wouldn't call it "thought," but if you replace the word "thought" with "I energy" or something like that, then it would be basically the same, yes.

Justin Allen: And then he says, "Almost all of these identifications or 'energetic identifications' can be traced back to the initial assumption that the 'I' is limited to the body."

Andreas Müller: So to speak. For me, it would be theory that this can be traced back. But yes, as a story, I would say the same thing. The apparent root of all seeking is just the experience to be someone who is real. Every question, every seeking drive, every functioning in this dream world, based on the assumption of a real world, just has the apparent root, "I am someone."

Justin Allen: And then Ramana continues, "Discovering the unreality of the 'I thought,' this is a death."

Andreas Müller: Exactly. Yet, I would say that the discovery that there is no "me" isn't a real discovery; it's just the melting away of the "I energy." It goes together: The discovery that there is "no one" is rather a death than someone discovering a fact. It's a loss, not a finding, so to speak.

Justin Allen: He says something like, "It merges," so the "I energy" or the "I illusion" merges back into the source.

Andreas Müller: Into wholeness.

Justin Allen: Or he calls the source wholeness, I guess.

Andreas Müller: Yes.

Justin Allen: But his method or his technique is to try to separate the subject "I" from the objects of thought with which it identifies. The goal is to focus only on the "I" and not on the objects of what "I" is. In doing this, the "I" is unable to connect with objects. If this awareness of "I," without objects, is sustained, the individual "I," the "I thought," will disappear, and instead there will be the direct experience of the "self," meaning of oneness.

Andreas Müller: Yeah, well, for me, this is a story. It's a concept. It sounds logical – and conceptually, one can make up that story. However, it again looks as if there were a linear process and as if someone could do something. The apparent death of "me" is much wilder and not part of a process. Apart from there not being anyone, of course, it may happen like that, but it doesn't have to. In the end, it can be over in an instant.

Justin Allen: This is what I'm saying; this is where I see the distinction between your and Tony Parsons's message and Ramana Maharshi, maybe Jiddu Krishnamurti, Adyashanti and Rupert Spira as well.

Andreas Müller: And Nisargadatta. For a while he was making up the same story, too.

Justin Allen: Right. But at the same time, it makes sense because they have to ... Well, they don't have to, but it seems like they have to give you something. Because if you don't have something, then as a "person," you're just left to go about your life without ever ... Why would you do anything, other than eat, sleep, make mistakes and try to fix them?

Andreas Müller: Yes, but that's the goal, so to speak. And it's okay; it just is what apparently happens, too.

Justin Allen: Yeah, but even you, you spent around ten years somewhat passionately or with a lot of energy going through this religious or spiritual process.

Andreas Müller: Yes.

Justin Allen: Maybe the disheartening of that process not working is necessary.

Andreas Müller: I could say that if it was "necessary," all those years of going through this apparent process can happen like that (snapping fingers). It could just vanish within an instant, this whole apparent process which I went through in apparent years ... What we talk about is just apparent life, with the death, the melting away of the "person" in the end.

Justin Allen: Right.

Andreas Müller: There just is no rule in that. People may seek for forty years or for their whole life, and "me" doesn't crumble. I know a lot of people who said to me, because I was rather young, and I'm still rather young, "Oh my god, it was really quick for you." My impression was though that it took my whole life because I was a seeker since I was fifteen, so during all my adult life, I was seeking, which is why it felt long to me. But real long-term seekers said, "Come on, it was just a few years." Theoretically, it could happen in one year. It could happen like that (snapping fingers).

Justin Allen: This is a little bit on a side topic, but what do you say about taking psychedelics? Did you take mushrooms, ayahuasca, LSD?

Andreas Müller: Yeah.

Justin Allen: Would you say that it's equally possible that taking some of those substances somehow kill the "me"?

Andreas Müller: Everything is thinkable, but in the end, it's never really "because of."

Justin Allen: Right.

Andreas Müller: That's the thing; the "me" dies, melts away, no matter what. It could be looking out of a window, it could be taking mushrooms, it could be not doing anything. It's never because of that. So in that sense, of course, everything is possible, but there never is a real connection to what has been done.

Justin Allen: Was that also the reason or the intention for you to take those drugs?

Andreas Müller: For me, taking drugs was an utter revelation; I was so surprised that I could feel so good (laughing). This seemed to be so different from my daily experience, and I just thought, "That's what I want, I want more of that." To feel that free, period. So, this was the start of the seeking, in that sense.

Justin Allen: In your story, that was the trigger?

Andreas Müller: Yes, so to speak. But of course, even though the seeking had just started, I honestly thought that I had already found the solution (laughing).

Justin Allen: That's true.

Andreas Müller: It became a bit weird when it didn't work anymore, so to speak.

Justin Allen: Yeah, that's the big crushing disappointment, right (laughing)?

Andreas Müller: Absolutely. It was my first big disappointment.

Justin Allen: I have a sense that people in your talks don't really talk about their personal problems, but I'm always curious because there seems to be a difference, of course, between what you're suggesting and Rupert Spira's or Adyashanti's message. So, how would you respond if somebody were coming to you and saying that they're very depressed, attributing it to a relationship or to their job, or that they're not living their life how they wish they were or they're not following their dreams?

Andreas Müller: I don't have a clear way of responding to that, but yes, in the meetings, this doesn't really come up. Not because it's not supposed to come up, but the whole energy cuts it off almost immediately. In the story, one could say, "it" just immediately points back to the "source," namely that "me" is an illusion, and all those questions, in the end, come out of that "me." Like "I'm depressed, should I go left or right, should I do this or that?" et cetera.

Justin Allen: But there's this promise of enlightenment or of recognizing the illusory self or the death of the "me." There's the promise that in the death of the "me," these life dilemmas, problems or choices, which you thought maybe were the cause of your depression, vanish.

Andreas Müller: Yes, I understand that it looks like that, but it's constantly pointed out that there will be "no one" left to enjoy that. It's not really the death of those problems, but it's pointed out that it's the death of the "one" who has the problems.

Justin Allen: That's pointed out by you, yeah, but other ones, like spiritual teachers, of course, still say, "Life continues, and there are still problems. But because there's no attachment to your identity with them, then the energy of those problems is much different."

Andreas Müller: Yes. In personal teachings, there is a promise that in the end, there is "someone" who rests in that, in awareness. But as I said, in a personal teaching, there's always some work implied, something to do to keep it up, to not lose track, to not get lost in anything. It's a whole package that happens in a personal teaching, and yes, one part of that is the promise that if you behave right, if you do it the right way, you'll gain or earn a reward.

Justin Allen: That's what you're saying is bullshit.

Andreas Müller: It's just within a dream, within an illusion, yes.

Justin Allen: How do you feel after the death of the "me" about the major situational things that everybody faces in life, your day to day relationship problems, job problems, deciding-where-to-live-type problems? Do you still have all those issues, or how would you explain the difference?

Andreas Müller: Well, the apparent difference is that there is just "no one" in there being burdened by all of that. Because when there is "someone," there is always first the experience of those questions to be real, and they are always connected to the idea of personal fulfillment. That's how all decisions are burdened. It's not about, "Where do I want to live or how?" There's always the assumption attached that it will influence my future personal fulfillment. That's the burden.

It's the idea that I have to consciously choose the right thing, and if I do the wrong thing, I fuck up my happiness. That's the burden in which the "me" lives and believes. When that is no more, meaning, when the "me" is dead, these life questions and problems might still be there, but they themselves are the "self", to take one of Ramana's words, and are happening, but for and to "no one." This is just what apparently happens, and it's naturally whole already. No question and no answer to those questions needs to serve this personal seeking anymore. The "person" longs for the answer because it thinks it needs it in order to live a happy life. But that's a complete dream; that there is "someone" who lives "their" life, and that this life could be happy and fulfilled or unhappy because "I" did it right or wrong.

Justin Allen: Yeah, or with psychology and psychiatry and even with spirituality: What's often talked about and what was irritating to me, I guess, are past traumas. So, we all have past traumas, they're just relatively lesser or greater, but they say that unless you face that past trauma somehow, unless you fully process it and let it go, you're always going to be stuck.

Andreas Müller: Yeah.

Justin Allen: But you're saying that there's no need to face your past traumas or deal with them, although it might happen?

Andreas Müller: Yes.

Justin Allen: The reason why there's no need to do that is that if there's the death of "me," then the traumas would also disappear because they are some aspect of the "me"?

Andreas Müller: It doesn't matter. I don't say that facing the traumas doesn't happen. Well, "facing" sounds a bit personal, but it's just that there is "no one" able to consciously do it. There is no need to do it. And yet, what seems to be happening – but this can be rather slow, and it's not really of value – is that when there is "no one," the traumas naturally and organically fall off.

Justin Allen: You're saying that's happening after the death of the "me"?

Andreas Müller: Absolutely. It can happen before as well, but usually there seems to be a relationship going on between the trauma and the "person." In a way, the "person" doesn't really want to get rid of the traumas, because they are actually a protection mechanism, they are not a bad thing in that sense. But when there is "no one" anymore to be protected, they can at least soften. It's not even something that counts, that's the thing. It's not that there's a special focus on that.

It's the same thing with the other problems like relationships, place of residence et cetera: The actual burden is to be "someone" who wants to "do" life. As I said, being traumatized is just what apparently happens. Everybody is to a certain degree traumatized, and even there, the big surprise is that healing is not an issue.

Justin Allen: Right, because the issue is just the apparent "me"?

Andreas Müller: Yes, so to speak, the issue is just the "me." Apparently, because what's being pointed out is that there is no "me."

Justin Allen: Yeah, if there's no "me," then every single ... It radically changes everything because there's no longer a "point" to judge or look out from?

Andreas Müller: Yes. But when there is "no one," what could happen is that the traumatic behavior goes on and, over time, just softens. From the outside, it may look as if there were someone finally facing their traumas. It's very human, apparently. We don't speak about something holy or far out; even the death of the "me" is kind of human. Very natural and ordinary.

Justin Allen: Then going back to taking ayahuasca et cetera; isn't that what happens also sometimes with psychedelics? That the "me," at least for that period of time, falls away?

Andreas Müller: It's not my experience.

Justin Allen: Okay.

Andreas Müller: Well, not that it was an issue at that time if there was a "me" or not, but looking back, I was just always there. In my experience, there was always "someone" experiencing it. I sometimes even forgot my complete story, sometimes I even forgot my name, I completely forgot who I was in the story and in the world. But there was still something in there experiencing that, experiencing having forgotten everything. Experiencing that nothing is real, so "I" was always there, to be honest.

Justin Allen: Okay.

Andreas Müller: That's my experience, I did it a lot.

Justin Allen: Did you ever have any feeling like you did process some traumas, or that you did ...

Andreas Müller: Not really, no. You mean in the drug period?

Justin Allen: Yeah, because they're encouraging new research into that to treat people with posttraumatic stress disorder or addictions.

Andreas Müller: I think that can work, but I was young, that was not my

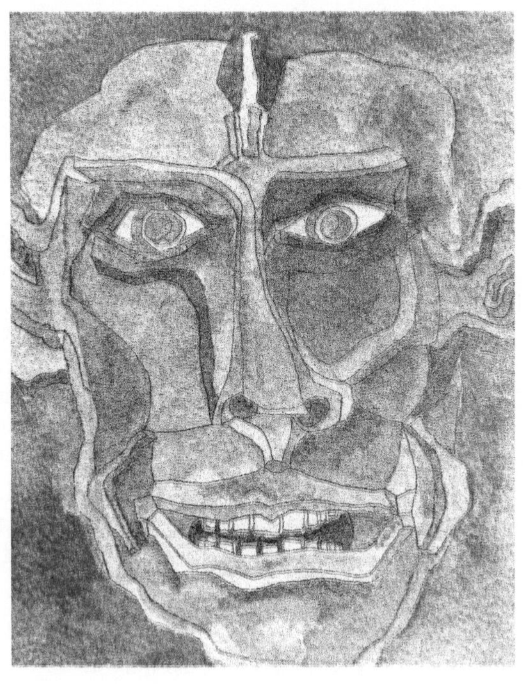

issue. I wasn't looking for that.

Justin Allen: Okay.

Andreas Müller: But I can understand how this can work, of course.

Justin Allen: From what I've read, it seems interesting, and applied to your message or Ramana Maharshi's even ... It's that some people that have severe traumas are unwilling to deal with them. They've repressed or ignored them so much; there's such a fear in confronting them. But when you take MDMA, ayahuasca, mushrooms or LSD, it could remove your identity or your attachment to your traumas, so you can process them without the huge fear component.

Andreas Müller: Yes, and you just feel well and safe at the same time, just from the drugs. So, you can open up more easily. I think that's basically what it does. I think it's not because of the identification actually; I think it's this cloud of wellbeing, just with MDMA, of warmth and love, which allows the "person" to open up more. That's how I interpret it. I think trauma has a lot to do with feeling safe. The better you feel the more open you become, so this whole stuff is allowed to soften as well.

Justin Allen: Do you have any opinion or thoughts about how ... I imagine you had notions before? For example, I had a notion from a young age that you're seeking an emotional attachment with somebody because you feel empty or that something's lacking inside. So, you're looking for it to fill that emptiness through a relationship.

Andreas Müller: Yeah.

Justin Allen: So, I always said to myself, "Oh, I don't want to be one of those people, I want to be free from that. So, I don't ever really want to get myself attached to somebody, and I don't want to put any expectations on somebody that they're responsible for my wellbeing or my happiness." And that's a notion that gets backed up by reality because it seems that a lot of relationships are totally based on that premise that there's something lacking, and they're using this relationship to conceal or fill that void.

Andreas Müller: Yes.

Justin Allen: The promise of enlightenment or this kind of searching is that when you become enlightened or when there's the death of the "me," the beauty is that then maybe you're in a relationship, but you're not dependent on it. Or maybe you're not in a relationship, and you're okay with that.

Andreas Müller: Yes.

Justin Allen: But until that happens, the reason why you're in a relationship definitely is because as the "me," you're getting something from it, thinking it's making your life better or at least ...

Andreas Müller: Yes, yes. And this is in relationship to everything because all "me" does is to live in relation with something: with people, with situations, with jobs, ... Every moment it lives in relation to the second.

Justin Allen: That's what I recognize as a torture for "me."

Andreas Müller: Yes. A lot of people seek personal relationships. I was seeking in a guru relationship. Also in women, but I thought that from a guru I'd get something emotionally, energetically.

Justin Allen: That might even be a strategy to avoid the pain of the personal relationship, which is definitely ...

Andreas Müller: But there was also the pain of the personal relationship.

Justin Allen: Yeah, so you had double pain (laughing).

Andreas Müller: Certainly (laughing). And yes, that melts away in liberation, but it doesn't leave a "person" who is free from all of that.

Justin Allen: What does that mean, it doesn't leave a "person" that's free from all of that?

Andreas Müller: Because the "person" dies, and it's not that after that you have something like, "I am someone, and I don't need that." Because the whole construct falls apart; that I am "someone" who lives in relationship to life. It's not a personal freedom. But yes, the assumption that there is something, which will fulfill you, drops, and that's freedom of course, but for "no one."

Justin Allen: But then the other fear that people have is that, for example, before the death of the "me," you're in a relationship dependent on the other person for emotional wellbeing in some ways, and then with the death of the "me," this dependence falls away. So, for the other person in that relationship, it might feel odd to be in a relationship with someone who doesn't have a "me." Because in general, the relationship is based on the fear of losing the other person or not getting the emotional satisfaction that you need.

Andreas Müller: Yeah, it can feel odd for both, by the way. But yes, of course, it can just go on, or it can change. Yeah, it can definitely be weird because, as you say, a lot of relationships are at least partly based on fulfilling this need of the other person. And of course, when that drops, this can change the whole energetic dynamic of the relationship. But still again, this doesn't really mean anything. It can be good, it can be bad, apparently good and apparently bad, of course.

Justin Allen: Yeah. So, I would like to push this "I thought" thing a little bit further: Where does it rise from? This would be a question that Ramana Maharshi, Adyashanti and Rupert Spira might ask in some form, probably Mooji as well. You come to that question, and this is a little bit of a repeat, because you recognize that the foundation of what you are, at least through empirical examination, is first to say, "I am sad." Then you say you recognize that you're just aware of the sadness, but you're not the sadness, then therefore you're the "I."

Andreas Müller: Yes.

Justin Allen: Then it goes deeper asking, "Where does that 'I' rise from? And what does the 'I' exist in?" Is that worth looking into at all?

Andreas Müller: No (laughing). I would say no. Well, there is nothing wrong with it; it just is what apparently happens. But it's a teaching, it's a theoretical thing, it's not worth anything. But of course, yes, in the end, it's a surprise that the end of all personal inquiry, namely the conclusion, "I am pure awareness," can drop, too. That there is "no one," that there is nothing, that there is no "I," that there is no awareness, that there is nothing which is aware. But it's all not theoretical, and there's no one in there who can or has to do anything. It just happens or doesn't. It's totally not spiritual; it's totally wild and not connected to a path. The concept is all right, as a concept.

Justin Allen: So, would you equate it to what they say, like, "Take the thought, 'I am sad.' Okay. Are you sad? Or are you the 'I' that's aware of the sadness?" Then you go, "I am the 'I'." So, this is one method, and then, let's say, there's another teacher that comes along and says, "Don't look, you have that thought, 'I am sad,' so what? That's part of life; you're sad sometimes, and sometimes you're not sad. There's no 'I' behind it." That teaching's equal to the other one?

Andreas Müller: Both are stories, both are suggestions to someone to behave in a certain way in order to give an answer, in order to bring about a better circumstance. This is all teaching, but there is no suggestion at all.

Justin Allen: That same premise then goes for somebody who comes and says, "Oh, I'm really depressed, I'm sad all the time, so I'm going to go to a psychiatrist." Then they go to a psychiatrist, and the psychiatrist can do two things for them basically. Maybe trying to make you look at your past in order to see how it has influenced your life. Another method is that they try to give you tools to manage.

Andreas Müller: Yes, exactly.

Justin Allen: Like deep introspective psychology or behavioral psychology ...

Justin Allen: Then another one would be to take medication.

Andreas Müller: Yeah.

Andreas Müller: It's all personal stuff. It's all assuming that they are someone.

Justin Allen: So because of that, to you, they're all equally invalid, in a sense?

Andreas Müller: In a sense, one could say they are valid as what apparently happens. But they are not valid referring to liberation, personal fulfillment and the idea of the possibility to find something in that.

Justin Allen: But then there's no valid way of doing this?

Andreas Müller: Yes, because there basically is no "doing this" in the first place. It's an illusion that there is "someone" who is doing anything. This message doesn't give answers.

Justin Allen: Right.

Andreas Müller: Theoretically, it's for everyone, but practically, it's only for those people who are interested in that. This message doesn't run around and say, "This is wrong, and that is bad, and don't do this, and don't do that, because it won't help you, and don't do therapy, because it's wrong." Not at all. This isn't trying to provide an answer to anything.

Justin Allen: Yeah, it can't.

Andreas Müller: But if I'm approached by someone who asks me about this stuff, then of course, I have to say that it's a dream. There is "no one." But not as an answer compared to everything else that's wrong. But yes, seen from the reality of finding something in therapy, in doing the methods, in doing whatever, everything is not valid. It's all part of a dream, all part of an illusion.

Justin Allen: But at the same time, you couldn't say that it's going to prevent the death of the "me"?

Andreas Müller: Not really, no.

Justin Allen: In theory, maybe it could? Or maybe it could prolong it, but you can't even say that.

Andreas Müller: Exactly. You can't really say that. That's what seems to be happening; that "me" survives on being active. But yes, that, too, is what apparently happens. "Me" dies anyway, so in the story where there is "someone," and liberation is the death of that "someone," it dies no matter what. Never because of something; "me" dies in spite of wanting to live (laughing).

Justin Allen: Just like we do, physically (laughing).

Andreas Müller: Oh, yeah. Exactly (laughing). Maybe from eating too much fat or from smoking.

Justin Allen: Or living a life of depression.

Andreas Müller: Or having been born eighty years before (laughing).

Justin Allen: They died of old age.

Andreas Müller: Yeah.

Justin Allen: What I also think is weird about your and Tony Parsons's message, and we talked about this a bit already, is that it's not really repetitive for you, because at the same time, it's a no-message. Your message is like no-answer, no-teaching and no-practice. So then, if there's a message, maybe it's just a message of no-message.

Andreas Müller: Yes. But I'm still not giving a message. I'm not emanating energetic information (laughing) or something like that.

Justin Allen: But to every single thing, whatever anybody asks, whatever situation that they create or whatever description, you literally have to always say, "But there's 'no one' there." You just have to come back to that.

Andreas Müller: Yes.

Justin Allen: There's no other way you could really branch off?

Andreas Müller: Not really, exactly. Everything that I say is that there is "no one," yes. Not conceptually; I can't explain that, and it's not coming from a concept providing the answer. But yes, there is "no one" (laughing). Everything else would be a dance around it, that's what the teachings do. They all dance around it, and then they start putting meaning to the dancing around it and all that stuff; we talked about that already. That's why it's all clever concepts, which aren't wrong, but they dance around it.

Justin Allen: Yeah, because nobody wants to fucking hear this at all.

Andreas Müller: Not at all, exactly.

Justin Allen: The only one that does want to hear this would be someone like me, in a sense, because I can say that I don't mind hearing it, at least. I would say one of the reasons I don't mind hearing it is just because it seems I've heard everything else, and nothing's been convincing. Because it all feels like it's dancing around or like someone telling you that they love you when they don't love you, showing you evidence and saying, "But I do this and that". But you still feel or intuitively know that it's not true.

Andreas Müller: I sometimes say that all the people who come to those meetings aren't coming because they want to come; it's just because everything else isn't interesting anymore (laughing). No one consciously chose to, in the sense of, "Oh, I want to go, I'm interested in this message, I want to do that." No, there's just nothing else left (laughing). It just comes down to that.

Justin Allen: The more honest or hardcore message beyond this would be where you go, and the "person" doesn't speak to you (laughing).

Andreas Müller: I don't speak to anyone.

Justin Allen: Well, words are coming out of your mouth, though.

Andreas Müller: Yeah, they don't do anything (laughing).

Justin Allen: But there are the Zen teachers, historically, who don't even talk to you. They don't; instead they point at a wall or something.

Andreas Müller: It just can very quickly become another concept; then you don't talk anymore "in order to ..." That's another thing.

Justin Allen: No, I'm just saying that's the next ... If somebody comes to you, and they still feel (laughing) like this is even too much, then where else can they turn?

Andreas Müller: Oh, it's the end. Of course, in the end, "no one" ... That's the end. It's not about listening to me, because nothing has been said. There is nothing left where anyone can go to, of course, because this whole idea of me being "someone," being able to go somewhere to get something, is an illusion. And that drops; there is nothing else to go to. It will turn out that I'm not saying anything, and that there is nothing coming from my side filling up the hole of the seeker. No word that I say does or provides anything, and no one has to see me. That's the freedom, that's the energetic dynamic. It becomes obvious that this whole seeking energy is the illusion itself, so it's just not being entertained.

Justin Allen: Imagine how desperate we all have to be to come and be willing to listen to this message (laughing). It's desperate enough to start reading Jiddu Krishnamurti and Adyashanti and meditating or working for the porsche or the best partner.

Andreas Müller: Yeah, exactly (laughing). Just desperate enough to do that, absolutely (laughing). Yeah, well, our "me" is desperate, of course. It's desperately trying to find fulfillment, of course.

Justin Allen: I'm entertaining the idea to go do ayahuasca. I've only taken mushrooms one time in my life, and that's it. And I'm to the point where I'm desperate again, that's why I'm interested to do it. I feel like nothing's working, or nothing's giving me anything. I can say for sure, there's been zero improvement, or well, there's relative improvement in my life. But I'm aware that there's still a "me" going around, experiencing everything and trying to get the best experiences out of life or hoping and everything like that. Then I just am like, "Where the fuck else can I turn? What else can I do?" And then I think, "I haven't tried that yet."

Andreas Müller: It's fine, it's logical, it's what apparently happens when there is "someone." There's nothing wrong with that. But when you said, "I am aware"; that's the illusion.

Justin Allen: Exactly. I can recognize it though, but at the same time, I recognize that there's nothing I can do about it either.

Andreas Müller: Yes. But there's still something recognizing; that recognition, that which recognizes is the illusion.

Justin Allen: Right. I can't stop that from recognizing and from still thinking, even though I know that doing this isn't going to help me or solve any problem.

Andreas Müller: Yeah, which is basically "me" beating up itself.

Justin Allen: Right.

Andreas Müller: So, it robs it even the joy of just doing it because additionally, it thinks that it won't bring joy anyway (laughing).

Justin Allen: Then you're supposed to stop, then you tell somebody that, and they go, "So stop beating yourself up about it; be gentle to yourself and forgive yourself."

Andreas Müller: Yeah. There's always an answer. In teachings, there's always an answer.

Justin Allen: Right, and then you go, "Why should I do that?" Then I'm just back on the same pattern.

Andreas Müller: Exactly.

Justin Allen: Then they would say, "Well, at least it's a more positive pattern."

Andreas Müller: It's never ending.

Justin Allen: Then the other thing that you might get told a lot is that you're an over-thinker. So then they go, "You're over-thinking everything too much."

Andreas Müller: Yes. Maybe that's right, but there's "no one" doing that. Maybe it is like that (laughing), but it's a story.

Justin Allen: Well, there's no one doing it, but at the same time, there's no one that cannot do it either.

Andreas Müller: Yes, exactly. It is what apparently happens, and it's whole and complete. Over-thinking already implies that there's something wrong; I wouldn't go there. You like thinking about things, yeah, that's what apparently happens (laughing). But there won't be an answer in there either.

Justin Allen: Right, I recognize that. I say, "I recognize that," and then in that, I recognize ...

Andreas Müller: Then you have the dilemma, then you recognize things, and then all the ideas and everything you already know comes in, then you compare that to what you recognize ... That's the seeking. It starts with the recognizing, with being something that recognizes.

Justin Allen: Yeah. I don't know. Those are what we consider the people that seem to be happier than the others; we attribute that they just recognize less.

Andreas Müller: But they still recognize something.

Justin Allen: Did you feel like ... You probably can't say the day that the "me" died for you; you can't put it into a location and time or anything, right?

Andreas Müller: Yeah, hardly. I just didn't have an event, so to speak.

Justin Allen: But did you feel a huge resistance at some point?

Andreas Müller: No, not really. Because there was resistance again and again, but I had this melting away over two years, so to speak. It was very smooth, and of course, as long as "I" was there, I thought that I'm on my way into a better future. So, I was never aware that it's actually going to die. All "me" is aware of is that it's here and alive. And that as long as it's alive, it assumes that it will be alive in the next moment as well. So, I was totally unaware that I am actually on a way to death (laughing), so to speak.

Justin Allen: I feel like I tell myself that I am on my way to my death.

Andreas Müller: Yes, which is still a story, it's still you being alive until that happens. It's still a life story, it's not a death story. It's still the set of next moments: I'll be also alive because I'm on my way to death.

Justin Allen: Yeah. But I feel like, at least I tell myself that I'm falling away. In my story, I see that I'm getting less; things that I thought were going to make me happy don't work anymore. I lose that original ambition, maybe, to do stuff, thinking that it was going to result in the proof of myself. So then you feel less motivated or less energetic, or you start to give up and think, "Why do I even do anything anymore? What's the point of it?" But I only have this idea through reading all these books and listening to these talks, and then I go, "Oh." Because they provide answers, they make it seem like that's the subtle falling away of the ego or the "I thought."

Andreas Müller: Yeah, no one knows in the end.

Justin Allen: I'm just saying that the fact of what I'm aware of right now is the story I'm telling myself.

Andreas Müller: Yeah.

Justin Allen: Even as I'm telling myself that story, I'm going (laughing), "You're just telling yourself a story; that doesn't mean anything."

Andreas Müller: Yes (laughing). Even recognizing that that doesn't mean anything (laughing).

Justin Allen: Right. It means that you're still the same as you were twenty years ago (laughing).

Andreas Müller: No, not really. It doesn't mean anything.

Justin Allen: The depressing thought that I'm living with or that I've been telling myself is how I was semi-interested in this seeking on and off around twenty years ago, and whatever crisis I had twenty years ago, and how it made me feel emotionally and how I got sad or happy or whatever. It's no different now. I don't think there's been any kind of evolution over my twenty years.

Andreas Müller: Of course, oh yeah. It's a bit disappointing, I know that. After all the doing and seeking and understanding and recognizing and maybe healing and feelings and experiences, nothing really has changed. It can be quite disappointing (laughing) and annoying (laughing). Nothing of that brought a real change.

Justin Allen: Right. I also always used to tell myself that I'm not like everybody else; I'm not going to make the obvious life mistakes as everybody else.

Andreas Müller: Oh, no.

Justin Allen: I have tried in different ways.

Andreas Müller: Yes. Absolutely (laughing).

Justin Allen: I tried to escape, but there was no escape (laughing).

Andreas Müller: There is no escape. There is "no one," and there is "no one" who's special and "no one" who can do it differently. Yes. Absolutely. Utter ordinariness.

Justin Allen: Yeah, utter ordinariness. That's the thing you want the least.

Andreas Müller: Yes. Exactly.

Justin Allen: Or at least the searching type of person doesn't want that.

Andreas Müller: Totally, oh yeah. No one wants that. That's a natural reality, ordinariness, the "real self," the natural reality. It's not something else, it's not extra, it's not special, it's not the next thing, it's not the actual thing, which will still come. And yes, no one wants that. It's unwantable; what is, is unwantable.

Justin Allen: What is, is unwantable.

Andreas Müller: Yes. It's wonderful, it's brilliant (laughing). Sorry, I have to commend myself (laughing).

Justin Allen: But what is, is unwantable for the "me"?

Andreas Müller: Yes.

Justin Allen: But for the "no me" ...

Andreas Müller: The question doesn't arise, exactly because all there is, is what is. Even then, there's nothing left that wants it; it's just everything and whole. Naturally whole, not whole in a holy way, it's just as it is, and it's naturally whole by there not being someone wanting it or wanting something else.

Justin Allen: By the way, you're going to be in Hamburg in about two weeks, no?

Andreas Müller: Yeah, true.

Justin Allen: All right. Yeah, a friend of mine told me, so I'm planning to go there unless I change my mind, like how you did (laughing). And then there are the Tony Parsons's meetings in Munich in December.

Andreas Müller: Yeah, cool. Probably I'll come for a day.

Justin Allen: So, should we end it here?

Andreas Müller: I think so, yes. I heard something move.

Justin Allen: Have a good day.

Andreas Müller: You too, thanks.

Justin Allen: Ciao.

Andreas Müller: Bye.

November 12, 2019 Talk 03

NO-POINT PERSPECTIVE

Justin Allen: All right.

Andreas Müller: All right, cool. Just to start with, I only have an hour today.

Justin Allen: Okay. So, I think what I want to try to talk about is how there's no practice and nothing you can do to liberate yourself from the illusion of "me" (laughing). But at the same time, you acknowledge that there is a "me" or the illusion of the "me" that causes relative problems in somebody's life. So, it seems like there are some people that are relatively living happier or better lives than other people.

Andreas Müller: Okay (not convinced).

Justin Allen: It seems like some people are more depressed than others. Some people take life easier, and others have a more difficult time with life.

Andreas Müller: Yes. Apparently, not really.

Justin Allen: Right, apparently.

Andreas Müller: Yes. So in that sense, I don't actually acknowledge the "self" or a real illusion of the "self," not really to be honest (laughing).

Justin Allen: It's still apparent that there are people that seem to be happier than others.

Andreas Müller: That's true, but the word "apparently" should be put before the word "people." So, it's not that there are people who are apparently more or less happy; it's that apparently there are people who are more or less happy.

Justin Allen: Okay. So but then, for those apparent people and that apparent setup, there does seem to be an apparent relatively better or worse way of living life.

Andreas Müller: Yes.

Justin Allen: So, if you're one of those apparent people that are constantly anxious about life or searching for happiness or for something to get yourself out of the apparent feeling of insecurity or instability or whatever it is, that apparently seems to be a worse life than the life of somebody that doesn't really worry about things, doesn't focus on negative thoughts, doesn't question everything or isn't constantly searching?

Andreas Müller: Yes. But to make that statement, you need a real "observer." You need someone to know this, and I would claim that the only real difference in that is made by an illusion, namely the "observer." The only thing that is able to make that clear distinction between happiness and unhappiness, between a good life and a bad life, is mainly the "observer." It's mainly someone who knows, someone who observes and already assumes there to be a life in time and space with someone in it who has or experiences a certain life. It's assuming a person which can be happy or unhappy.

Justin Allen: Right. And it seems, apparently, that through the perspective of this "observer" and "experiencer," there's relative good and bad.

Andreas Müller: So to speak, yes.

Justin Allen: And so, psychology and most of spirituality and religion is trying to address that problem to make people experience more of the good than the bad?

Andreas Müller: Exactly, yes. But always underlying is actually the assumption that there is a real entity in time and space which could have such a general thing as a life, which can be happy or unhappy. It's never really only about giving a little bit of release. It's never really only about five minutes of happiness. The underlying assumption is that there is "someone" who is working on a kind of general personal state, so all the seeking or the work of psychology, spirituality or whatever addresses that. I mean, even in economics, people want to be successful. It's always referring to the picture of there being a real person who can gain fulfillment out of happiness or out of money or out of whatever.

Justin Allen: Right, but it's also like you can't become an economist or an architect or a lawyer without going through a process of work and training.

Andreas Müller: Yes, of course. Yeah, that's what apparently happens.

Justin Allen: Right, and so it seems logical that with this kind of dilemma of acknowledging an "observer" or an "experiencer," this person would rather experience happy moments than depressing moments. So, such a training is also the strategy behind spirituality, religion and psychology, and it makes sense. It's not just guaranteed to everybody that they're going to feel and stay happy. They have to work on it.

Andreas Müller: Within the personal idea or experience, or if there is the assumption of there being a "self" or a "person," religion and spirituality are utterly logical. Same with pursuing a career or working towards anything. It's not only logical intellectually; it directly reflects the personal experience. Absolutely, of course.

Justin Allen: Because this has to happen to some degree, but it needs a "person" that's already acknowledged that they are a "person" ...

Andreas Müller: That's the dilemma of the "person": that whatever it does, whatever it thinks, whatever it imagines, whatever it tries to do or to not do in whatever story that it lives, it has already acknowledged itself to "be." Yes.

Justin Allen: And from that acknowledgement though, then they kind of have to do spirituality, religion or psychology, or they have to do something to try to increase their happiness because depression causes illnesses or suffering or whatever bad things.

Andreas Müller: Actually, the seeking only comes from this instant experience of separation. The instant experience is that this, what I experience now, isn't everything. Just energetically, because it's an illusion. But that's the experience when there is a person and a sense of presence. And out of that instantly comes the seeking energy like, "This isn't 'it,' so maybe the next moment will be 'it.' What can I do now? What can I do to make it more possible that the next moment brings fulfillment?"

Justin Allen: Yeah, but why do they feel like there isn't fulfillment?

Andreas Müller: There is no real answer to this, because this is what seems to be happening. It seems to be happening that the mere sense of presence is accompanied by a sense of unfulfillment.

Justin Allen: You're saying that automatically the identification or the acknowledgement of the one-point or person perspective comes with a lack of fulfillment?

Andreas Müller: Yes, yes. But there is no clear answer to why it is like that, because this whole presence isn't really happening. There is no real presence which is really unfulfilled, but this can't be explained. It's not logical. But yes, that's how it seems to be; that the mere sense of presence – without even doing something, without having a wrong concept or without being misled or anything – seems to be immediately, instantly unfulfilling.

Justin Allen: I mean, that's the logical reason why spirituality, religion and psychology exist.

Andreas Müller: Of course, yes.

Justin Allen: Those are the best ways to try to deal with that unfulfillment. Well, those and drugs.

Andreas Müller: Not really. Every solution seems to be good as long as it works. For most people, the solution of having a job and a family and security and earning money or more money or being a good person or being a good partner or saving the climate or whatever seems to be a much more attractive solution. But yes, for a percentage of people, I don't know, twenty, thirty percent, spirituality seems to be the solution.

Justin Allen: Yeah. I was saying spirituality, religion, psychology and drugs.

Andreas Müller: I wouldn't say so. If you look at what people generally do in order to have a fulfilled life, there is quite a bigger number who don't go into these things.

Justin Allen: Well, I mean religion ... I mean, it depends on what you say. Everybody's religious in the sense of a belief ... Like we're all Christian or Catholic or Muslim, or we are all atheists, or we believe in science or money or whatever.

Andreas Müller: Yeah, but most Christians now also seek fulfillment in having a social life and a career or whatever. I know what you mean. There are aspects of it, but I wouldn't go that far. For me, drugs and spirituality looked like the best solutions. But not for my parents, for example. Other things seemed to have worked for them. The belief in individualism in general: "I can do it. I can do and have whatever I want: cars, houses, better cars, better houses, amazing holidays." It's the same thing.

Seen from a personal experience, that's the only way to be. Seeking, in some way or the other, is the only way to be for the "person." To consciously do life, to consciously do success is seeking, in a big or small context.

Justin Allen: Right. And there's so much evidence to support it because it's the same as if I went to a university to study architecture, I got a degree and could say, "I'm an architect. I've learned something, and I've accomplished something that other people haven't."

Andreas Müller: Yes. That's the funny thing: that in a way the "person" or the illusion of a "person" only finds proof through reality. It only finds proof for its own existence. It can never find proof against that.

Justin Allen: Never find proof against existence?

Andreas Müller: Yes, never against.

Justin Allen: What would be an example of that?

Andreas Müller: Well, that's in a bigger context; when you said that life seems to be like that. "I do something and gain something from it. I have to struggle. I have to consciously do things," and all that stuff. But it's also more immediate because whenever there is "someone" who is inquiring into something, into the outside reality, so to speak, it's already the proof for there being existence. So, every inquiry comes to a conclusion within an existence. And even if I try to inquire into the question if this is real or not, my conclusion has to be real in order to be a real conclusion. So, even "me" finding out or "me" coming closer to the idea that nothing is real, in the end proves "my" existence because after inquiring a lot, "I" end up with being "me" having the conclusion or the conviction that actually nothing can be real. In the direct experience, "me" can never prove its own non-existence.

For the "me", in a way, there is no other way than to experience itself as "me" and regarding this to be everything. That's the dilemma; that with this message logic doesn't work at all.

Justin Allen: Because you're not coming from a one-point perspective. And if you're talking from such a "person" perspective, then only logic works.

Andreas Müller: Yes, but it's not really logic. It's actually based on a person's own experience, which is presence: to be something which is presence, which is really now here. That presence is the basic experience, so to speak. "I'm present as something which is now here."

Justin Allen: Well, you're like a point.

Andreas Müller: Exactly, like a center, like a point. And the proof of "my" existence is that "I" do experience myself. That's the proof.

Justin Allen: But it's like all lines come back to you, all thoughts come back to you, all experiences come back to you, all logic comes back to that point.

Andreas Müller: Exactly.

Justin Allen: So, it has to be logical. If it doesn't come back to that point, then it doesn't make sense. If there were something that couldn't come back to that point, it wouldn't …

Andreas Müller: Yes, if there were something. But in the end, this doesn't exist, because all inquiring seems to come from that perspective. So, naturally everything seems to reflect back. That's a good picture in a way. The "person" or everything only reflects back the "person."

Justin Allen: Right. That's why I'm trying to call it a one-point or person perspective because when you draw such a perspective, every line in the drawing in general has to come back to this one single point. That's your reference point to create the sense of a three dimensional drawing. Which isn't three dimensional, right, because it's on two dimensional paper. But you create the sense of 3D by using this technique of a one-point perspective.

Andreas Müller: Of course, yes. And "me," so to speak, experiences itself as the one-point, it's the center of everything "me" knows. Seen by the "me," as an experience, not as a logical thing. It's the experience. "I'm now here. I'm the center, and everything is around me. And in the end, I don't see everything. I only see my experience of everything. So, I only see my reflection in everything."

Justin Allen: Right, you see a limited view of ...

Andreas Müller: Yeah, by experience: "I'm here. I'm something that's now real. There's a computer which is now here and real." That's just a reflection of "I'm something real, and this is something real. I'm 'me,' this is not 'me.'" In a way, but actually it's part of "me" because it's what I experience. It's part of my world.

Justin Allen: And the logical message that you're giving is that the one-point doesn't exist?

Andreas Müller: Yes, exactly.

Justin Allen: That's what's not possible from a one-point or person perspective. It could never understand that because the absence of the one-point perspective immediately takes away all the lines coming back to the "one."

Andreas Müller: It not only takes away the lines, it takes away the center and with it the possibility of lines. Because it's in a way the center which starts drawing the lines. Yes, exactly. Absolutely.

Justin Allen: So, that's why it's hopeless?

Andreas Müller: Yes.

Justin Allen: The sense of the hopelessness is just the one-point or person perspective, which is already the illusion, and therefore it can't see the illusion?

Andreas Müller: Yes, exactly. And again, it's only hopeless for an assumed one-point perspective, which is already trying to draw lines here in this message. In the end, it's not even hopeless. But yes, seen by the person ... That's the hopelessness of the "person": to in the end automatically only be the "person" because that is what turns the "person" into the "person", the experience to just only be a "person" (laughing).

Justin Allen: But there is nothing you can do. And even you going out and giving your message is as valueless as a message from Ramana Maharshi or Jesus Christ or Einstein or Angela Merkel.

Andreas Müller: Yes, absolutely. That's why I also sometimes say there is no message. There is nothing drawing lines here. There isn't something in here drawing lines to you and playing this whole game of, "We get something, I'm someone, you are someone or who else, 'pure awareness,' for example. I try to give you something. I try to make you move on, on your path to the goal." No. This message doesn't do that. I don't do that. Well, it's not that "I" don't do that, just in the picture. There's just nothing there which lives in this illusion that this exists.

Justin Allen: Even though you could deny this, it still seems like there is some kind of hope.

Andreas Müller: Not here.

Justin Allen: I know, but talking to people about this and not giving them a message and telling them that this one-point or person perspective doesn't exist somehow might speak to an energy, to a shift or death. Somehow it might address the "thing" behind the "person" or whatever; the "thing" that's not the "person", and that the "person" somehow vanishes.

Andreas Müller: Yes. In the story, one could say this might be happening; that the person vanishes. But this is not a goal. Because in the end, it's the illusion of something that isn't here in the first place which may vanish. But yes, the "person" again will add its story to it and say that "me" experiencing myself as a "person" is wrong and that there shouldn't be a "person." But this idea somehow has to be turned into another personal thing. In a way, just like you described. That's very sweet actually (laughing): talking of the "thing" that's behind the "person," which I really am. That's in a way immediately installing another instance, which seems to have an advantage from there not being a person (laughing). Sorry, it's not wrong, but that's the logical conclusion.

Justin Allen: Is that the only conclusion you can draw?

Andreas Müller: Absolutely, yes.

Justin Allen: So, if we're talking about the illusion of the "me," you have to say that the "me" can only understand that with the absence of this illusion there's still something there?

Andreas Müller: Absolutely, yes. And there is nothing wrong with that.

Justin Allen: Even if it acknowledges this and says, "There's nothing behind it," that "nothing" is still "something" to the illusion of the "me"?

Andreas Müller: Exactly. No matter how well understood the concept of absence is, no matter how clear, in a way, it is what it means, it actually comes to, "How would that be?" It somehow installs some kind of instance which is aware of it and has the advantage of being aware of the absence or whatever. Nothing wrong with that, there just is no other possibility.

Justin Allen: Yeah. But still, people coming and listening to your talks for over a year or people going and listening to ... I don't know. You know Oprah Winfrey?

Andreas Müller: Yes.

Justin Allen: So, let's say there's a pool of fifty people that are constantly coming to your talks for a year, and then there are fifty people that are going to listen to Oprah for a year. There's no lesser likelihood that those fifty that go see her are somehow going to be liberated from the "me" than those who are going to see you?

Andreas Müller: Yes, one could say so. Well, yes and no.

Justin Allen: Yeah. Yes and no because apparently it seems like there'd be a higher "success rate" of being liberated from the "me" by hearing you talk because you're constantly pointing in some way to the absence of the "me," and she wouldn't be doing that?

Andreas Müller: One could say so, but that's what apparently happens. That is what seems to be happening. Not because it really is like that, not because there is a real cause and effect, not because there is someone who can choose to do A or B, not because there is something that gains anything from liberation, not because liberation is the actual goal of existence or something. No, it just is what seems to be happening, for no reason, without intention.

Justin Allen: But it seems more likely to happen to somebody going and listening to a talk from you than to someone going to listen to a talk from Oprah or, let's say, Bill Gates?

Andreas Müller: That's what seems to be happening, but you can't derive a rule from it.

Justin Allen: The same way as it could happen if somebody goes on an LSD trip, and the "me" vanishes, and then that person or their friend might conclude that he or she lost his sense of self, which has got to be because of the LSD trip?

Andreas Müller: Exactly, yes. It's all theoretical, but the friend might even ask, "What did you do? What was the latest thing you did?" "Well, I took LSD." But even then, no one really talked about cause and effect. It was just someone apparently telling a story. "Oh, I took LSD." But the seeker would immediately conclude that seeking, in this case by taking LSD, must be the price for liberation because it happened before. Well, there is always something that happened before (laughing).

Justin Allen: And that's the only example really that anybody's ever been given.

Andreas Müller: Yes, because every "me," so to speak, is seeking. So, every story of the end of "me," will tell a seeker story before, absolutely (laughing).

Justin Allen: But it is true that people say there's better ways of ... I mean, I was listening to Tony Parsons over the weekend, and he kind of directly, condescendingly speaks of Mooji.

Andreas Müller: Yes (laughing).

Justin Allen: So, he acknowledges that Mooji probably gives off some kind of charismatic energy that people are drawn to. I listened to Mooji also, and as far as I can tell, his message is the exact same as Rupert Spira's, Ramana Maharshi's and Adyashanti's. It's still acknowledging that you're the awareness, and by abiding as this awareness, somehow the "me" or the sense of "self" disappears, or else it just disappears through this kind of constant maintenance of being aware. But Tony Parsons seems to be suggesting that it's all a big facade. "Facade" is not the right word, but kind of a big show.

Andreas Müller: Oh yes, absolutely. Apparently, it is speaking to someone in order to suggest taking on a certain condition. However, it is exactly that "someone" which is not real. But what seems to be happening in most personal teachings is someone who believes in being a role model and being able to guide people to another state.

Justin Allen: But I'm just saying that because there's a distinction drawn by Tony Parsons himself between his message or what he's saying that also plays into the seeker feeling like, "Okay, I have to pick one of these. I'm seeking. I can't stop myself from seeking. I have to pick somebody to listen to, so who's the one that can help me die?"

Andreas Müller: Yes. Of course, the seeker will go on living in a story, with this message as well as with any other message. And the distinction that is drawn is apparent. There's not a real distinction.

Justin Allen: Right. But if you have been listening to gurus and think, "Okay, I've been going to these teachers for five or ten years and still have the same sense of self that I had when I began. It hasn't gone away. Maybe I've noticed some change or improvement or some lightness in my life, but I know that I still feel like I am here." Then you listen to Tony Parsons criticize gurus ... Well, not necessarily criticize, but you hear him say that this is all a joke, the message. And then you think, "Oh, I've been listening to the wrong guy. Now I have to start listening to Tony Parsons."

Andreas Müller: Well, yes. The seeker may have that conclusion.

Justin Allen: I mean, it would be logical because the "me" is stuck in that logical experiential path.

Andreas Müller: Yes, that's true, and it's totally fine. But in the end, nothing really changed so far. It's still the seeker thinking they have to follow someone. So, the situation didn't get worse so far, it just didn't get better (laughing).

Justin Allen: It didn't get better, and you're running out of options (laughing).

Andreas Müller: Yes. But in the end, a totally different energetic dynamic seems to have happened. Which isn't better or right, that's not the point, but something else seems to be happening.

Justin Allen: Right, but it could also happen ...

Andreas Müller: Sorry, one more sentence. And I think the misconception is that life happens in the end because of what the seeker thinks. So in the end, then seeing Tony Parsons again doesn't really happen because there was someone misled by their stories. In the end, again it would just be what apparently happens. As it was with following gurus for ten years. So yes, the seeker would live in the story, but going to Tony Parsons or staying with their guru or whatever will happen or not anyway.

Justin Allen: And the same could happen in reverse; that somebody goes to Tony Parsons for five or ten years and listens to him over and over, and then they still say, "Well, it's not working, because I still have this sense of self. I'm going to go listen to another guru now."

Andreas Müller: It's thinkable, but it's hardly happening actually.

Justin Allen: Right, but I'm just saying that it totally could happen.

Andreas Müller: Yes. What usually happens is that people listen to Tony once or twice, then go to a guru like Mooji for ten years and then come back (laughing). But yeah, of course, in a way everything is possible.

Justin Allen: You have to acknowledge. By acknowledging that this whole one-point or person perspective is the illusion itself and that in this illusion there's no control, there's nothing that actually can happen or not happen. And it's just as likely that you could be liberated from the illusion of the "me" sitting down listening to a guru like Mooji or Rupert Spira as it could be sitting down listening to Tony Parsons.

Andreas Müller: Absolutely, yes.

Justin Allen: And if I went to listen to a certain guru tomorrow and came out and said, "I'm finally liberated," and people agreed with me, then they would attribute it to my constant years of seeking and eventually going to talk to this guru.

Andreas Müller: Yes. But no one becomes liberated. But yeah, when there is "no one," to be honest there would be no possibility to draw a connection to the guru.

Justin Allen: Right, or to Tony Parsons or anyone.

Andreas Müller: Exactly. I can't really draw a connection to Tony Parsons. And he would totally agree with that, whereas a guru maybe wouldn't (laughing).

Justin Allen: Yeah, he probably wouldn't. Yeah, he definitely wouldn't, because he basically says he's going to get you enlightened.

Andreas Müller: Yes, that's his role, and the role is assumed to be real, and there's real gain going on in all of that. Yeah, okay.

Justin Allen: But looking at this from the outside, especially if somebody writes a book about you or if you go to an interview and somebody asks you about your life story, everybody's going to conclude to some degree, "Okay, Andreas somehow started seeking when he was fifteen, and then he went and did this for a few years, and then he went and did that, and then he followed this person for a while, and then he became disillusioned with that,

and then he discovered Tony Parsons, and then somewhere in there he was liberated." And so, everybody's going to be like, "Why waste my time doing everything that he did? I'm going to go directly to Tony Parsons."

Andreas Müller: Yeah, very good (laughing).

Justin Allen: But even from your message, Tony Parsons has nothing to do with it.

Andreas Müller: No, it depends on if you go into the story or not. In the story, that was what apparently happened; that I did see Tony Parsons and not Oprah Winfrey. And accidentally, automatically, innocently, at the side, I died.

Justin Allen: Right, but it's extremely apparently that you would attribute it to Tony Parsons because it could also be the LSD trip you did twenty years ago that took twenty years to finally take full effect (laughing).

Andreas Müller: Oh, yes. So, you can have two stories. Either you say everything lead to my death. Life leads to death, so to speak. So, either it was everything; it started when the universe started. Or it was nothing, which I prefer because if you take the whole, then you are pretty much into a big story of existence. But in the end, nothing specific lead to that. Because in itself, all that is the story, that's the other thing. Nothing lead to that, because the birth of "me" and the end of "me" is a story already. But in the story, there is no real cause and effect. That's why I like the concept of death so much. The death of "me" or the end of seeking is just the end of seeking for no reason, not by successfully having walked a path. In that sense, it could just end any time.

Justin Allen: Yeah, because there's no reason for anything because there's no point, referring to the one-point or person perspective.

Andreas Müller: Nothing has to be accomplished first, but the whole thing of the seeker is this path thing. And that's what's funny. From that story, from that conclusion that you just made, the seeker draws the only conclusion that it can draw. Namely, it's good to be here, and it's good to seek. Which is kind of the complete opposite to what this message points at; that there is "no one" and there doesn't have to be seeking (laughing). The "person" immediately says, "Yeah, but you were also seeking, so I, too, have to seek," again proving its existence as the only possibility, again taking the story to prove the need to "be" and the need to seek. It's gorgeous (laughing). It's gorgeous, but somehow the complete opposite of this message. The seeking can drop. There is "no one." Immediately, nothing has to be found. Nothing has to be fulfilled. There doesn't have to be another ten years of listening to Mooji. There doesn't have to be another ten years of listening to Tony Parsons. "But you were also seeking," someone might say or think. It's not wrong, of course, but it's not the message.

Justin Allen: And the message is also that there's not a right or a wrong way to seek?

Andreas Müller: Absolutely, because this would immediately imply that there was someone who could choose and that there was a real goal.

Justin Allen: But still, if somebody's seeking, and then they're beating themselves up about it, you would want to come in and kind of console them. Wouldn't you?

Andreas Müller: Yeah, in the story apparently. Not really, because the beating up of themselves is what apparently happens, too. But I'm a nice guy, yeah, maybe I would (laughing). In the story, apparently I'd try to console them (laughing).

Justin Allen: But I mean, it is also kind of consoling somebody by saying, "You're not there. There's nothing that you can do. There's not a right path. Even beating yourself up and being depressed isn't really happening."

Andreas Müller: Yes, oh yeah. In the end, looking directly, we can give two messages. One is, "There is no one," and the other one is, "You can't do it wrong anyway." The second one would be consoling the "me," and the first one would just be nothing or silence. It's getting a bit picky now, but if you just take the words ...

Justin Allen: Yeah. But it's also such an odd thing if we assume right now that the "me" ... I mean, you don't acknowledge the "me" from your perspective, and I acknowledge the "me" from my perspective. So right now, everything I'm saying is coming from "me" and a one-point or person perspective, and everything that you're saying ...

Andreas Müller: That's what you're saying.

Justin Allen: Right. And everything that you are saying isn't coming from a one-point or person perspective. So, that's our assumption, that's what seems to be happening between us right now.

Andreas Müller: Yes, but I wouldn't regard you as coming from a one-point perspective.

Justin Allen: Right, but you're aware that I regard you as not coming from a one-point perspective, even though I can't ...

Andreas Müller: I'm not aware of that, but you are telling it to me. Yes. That's the only hint I have. You are saying it to me. I don't assume that.

Justin Allen: And same for me, I have to assume that you're missing your one-point or person perspective because you tell me that you are.

Andreas Müller: Yes.

Justin Allen: Same with Tony Parsons and Mooji, they somehow claim that they are this, and otherwise they would just be normal people on the street.

Andreas Müller: Yeah, yes.

Justin Allen: What I also think is that if I assumed and we all assumed that you're missing the one-point or person perspective and I have it, and let's say that somehow it's reversed, that your way is an undesirable way to view and live life, and my way is the desirable way, how would I be trying to teach you or give you a message so that you view life from a one-point perspective?

Andreas Müller: Well, that's impossible because there is no one-point perspective. Even in your position, there is no one-point perspective. It's an illusion. But you would need to tell me the same thing the "me" does say: "You are someone," "You can do it," "Pull yourself together," "Be aware."

Justin Allen: That's what I mean. I think it's kind of interesting ...

Andreas Müller: Yeah.

Justin Allen: It's an interesting thought experiment because that is essentially what you do to a child.

Andreas Müller: Yes.

Justin Allen: So, for a child ... At least we all kind of acknowledge and assume, even though nobody knows, that the baby hasn't yet developed a sense of "me." So even biologically, it can't develop a sense of "me" until the brain develops to a certain point (Andreas expresses visual signs of doubt). I'm just saying that's the current ...

Andreas Müller: That's what apparently seems to be happening, yes.

Justin Allen: And then either the baby on its own develops its own one-point perspective somehow ...

Andreas Müller: This would be my (a) story, yes.

Justin Allen: Yeah, or the parents give it that one-point perspective.

Andreas Müller: Nope, I wouldn't say that.

Justin Allen: They definitely reinforce it.

Andreas Müller: I would say from the moment self-awareness seems to be happening in the child, it gets reinforced. But without there being something that feels addressed, you can speak to a person as long as you want; it doesn't make the "me" be born, so to speak. People address me all the time as someone, but there is nothing that feels addressed by that. But of course, as long as there is someone here, I felt spoken to immediately, all the time.

Justin Allen: But when you speak to me, I feel like you are speaking to my "one-point perspective self."

Andreas Müller: That's the assumption, yes. It might become obvious for "no one," but it completely isn't like that. But yes, the one-point perspective starts drawing lines and tries to experience it like that. Yes, that's true.

Justin Allen: Well, it doesn't try to experience it like that, that's the only way ...

Andreas Müller: I know, that's its only way, yeah. But that's also what it assumes and expects and what it's looking for. That's what I meant with "trying." Of course, on the one hand, that's all it can do. But on the other hand, that's all it wants to see in a way and wants to have confirmed. Not consciously, it's all a bit ... (hand gestures from Andreas indicate ambivalence or complexity to further illustrate his point of mystery)

Justin Allen: But if I believe that you're missing the one-point or person perspective and I say to you, "You can't live life that way. That's a terrible way to live life. You need to somehow develop this one-point or person perspective, so you can really say that there's a you that's hungry when you say 'I am hungry.'" And I would have to try to train you. I'd have to try and say stuff like, "Look, you have to go read books and meet people, and when you interact with them, you have to identify yourself and say, 'I'm Andreas, and you're Justin.'"

Andreas Müller: Yeah, I just wouldn't see the point in it, because there would be no need for another circumstance. Not because there is someone who has happily found and dwells in a joyful state, no. There would just be no resonance with this promise at all. It just wouldn't be promising.

Justin Allen: No, I just mean it in the sense that I could, from my one-point or person perspective, kind of have a clear way of how to try to train you and "convert you back". Okay? But you don't really have a way to train me into your no-point perspective.

Andreas Müller: No, because this isn't even recognized as another perspective. That's what I mean. Seen from the personal perspective, these are two really different perspectives. I don't see that. There is no one-point perspective which is really different from what's going on here.

Justin Allen: Yeah, that's what I'm saying. That's actually the only thing that you can say; you'd have to keep on telling me, "Your one-point perspective doesn't exist, man."

Andreas Müller: And I don't even tell it to you, it's rather that when you come to me from this one-point perspective, I'm sitting here having no clue what you're talking about, and I'm just answering that. It's not even to make you see that there is no one-point. And then, all I can do is say, "What are you talking about? There is no one-point perspective." But not to make you see that, not to bring you to something better. I don't think that I'm in a better situation than you are, not at all.

Justin Allen: Yeah. That's what I mean, but it's the same as if I were a happy person and didn't dwell on things, and then you came to me with your depression and because I didn't understand your depression, I would just be like, "Just don't be depressed, don't have negative thoughts, only have positive thoughts."

Andreas Müller: Yes. You would assume that there is someone who could do so.

Justin Allen: Right. I mean, I'm just comparing. It's the same as you not acknowledging that there's a person. So, when a person comes to you and says, "How do I lose my sense of self?" you can only say, "There is no sense of self actually, that's an illusion." But they can't understand it. The same way as if I were depressed and you were not, and I talked to you about my depression and you said, "Just don't focus on your depressing thoughts and you'll be fine." And then I said, "I can't though. I can't not have depressing thoughts." And then for you, because you didn't experience depressing thoughts, you couldn't really relate to me.

Andreas Müller: Yes. I know what you mean. But for me, this picture doesn't really work, because there are many possibilities. You give the advice, then the other says, "Yeah, but I can't let go of my depression." Then the other one either becomes impatient and says, "Okay, then leave me alone. Fuck off. I'll remain 'me' being happy, and I don't care about you." Or they would go, "Okay, you can't do that, so let's think about other ways of making you feel happy." It just stays in the "person," which is fine. Not that there was anyone being able to do it differently, but I would say from the energetic setup, it's different, apparently.

I mean, listening to the message doesn't do anything. It's just what apparently happens. But on the other hand, there is also no one who could consciously buy that. I don't, not really.

Justin Allen: But it's a difference of describing ... You could kind of describe to me, and Tony Parsons does it to some extent and also Mooji, what it's like to be liberated.

Andreas Müller: But for no reason. I'm not describing it "in order to ..." No, it's just what happens. Sorry, it's just coming out when it's addressed. It can't even be described.

Justin Allen: Right, but same with when I come to you and tell you my problem or how I've been seeking, and then you say, "But actually there's no one there to seek." And then I say, "Yeah, but I'm still seeking." And you say, "Yeah, but you're not there. It's not happening." So, you're describing to me something that I can either experience or not. No, I don't experience it. But it either happens to me or not.

Andreas Müller: In the end, I would say it's just replying, it's not even describing "in order to ..." And of course, admitting that there is no use for the seeker in that. That it's not useful or valuable for the seeker at all. I can freely admit that.

Justin Allen: Yeah. There's nothing useful or valuable to the seeker.

Andreas Müller: Exactly. And I don't admit that with another hidden intention, to create some paradox or anything. No, it's honestly without value for the seeker.

Justin Allen: Even in the sense that it might relatively be better for the seeker to vanish? I just want to make this distinction because I think it's important. If you see some seeker really struggling and being really depressed and not getting anywhere, and then there's another seeker who seems to be getting benefits from seeking. They feel like, "I'm getting closer and closer and closer." Right? And then there's the seeker who is seeking the same amount as the other one but is going, "God, none of this is working. This is so depressing. I've tried everything."

Andreas Müller: Wonderful.

Justin Allen: You wouldn't say one's better than the other? That's what I mean.

Andreas Müller: No, of course not, no.

Justin Allen: Tony Parsons does this too, he says "wonderful" to the person who seems to be coming to the point of giving up more so than to the person who seems like not giving up, who still feels like they're on the right track.

Andreas Müller: Yes.

Justin Allen: But don't you acknowledge that somehow the one that seems like they're giving up and discovering the futility is somehow more in line with your message than somebody who sees the point in everything but still thinks that there's hope and they're on the path and in another year they're going to get it?

Andreas Müller: Yes and no.

Justin Allen: What would be the yes (laughing)?

Andreas Müller: Well, I know what you mean, but it's more direct because it's not coming from a concept. It's not coming from a general idea, but usually, the people who come to those talks just are so exhausted by seeking. From the seeker's perspective, it's always like, "Damn, I don't manage. I'm trying so hard, and I can't do it." And they feel bad and get depressed. But actually, that's beautiful.

Justin Allen: Right, but why is that more beautiful than somebody who's like, "Awesome, this is my fifth talk. I'm going to get it this time. Today's going to be the day."

Andreas Müller: Well, it is not really more beautiful. Both are wholeness, and both are beautiful in their own way.

Justin Allen: Yeah. It seems like for the person that's exhausted and at the end of the road of seeking is better off so to speak ... I mean, you can't really say "better," because now you qualify it, but it does seem like they're denying the sense of self more than somebody who thinks that they're on the path and going to get it.

Andreas Müller: Of course, because that is what the "me" wants. Of course, that's just someone who experiences themselves to be a person. I mean, that's the thing. "Me" feels totally happy as long as it thinks that it's on the right path. As long as I believe, let's say, that I will be enlightened at some point within the next hundred lives, I can be happy on the path. There's no problem with that for the "me." That's all "me" wants, so to speak: to know that it's on the right path, having this big promise ahead. I will get it at some point. I, too, will be sitting on the throne one day.

Justin Allen: One day. All right, well it's been a little more than an hour.

Andreas Müller: Yeah. It's lovely though.

Justin Allen: Have a good day and thank you for the talk.

Andreas Müller: Yeah, cool, thank you. You too, have a good day.

Justin Allen: Bye.

Andreas Müller: Bye.

November 17, 2019 Talk 04

MY NAME IS NO-ONE

Justin Allen: I went to your talk last night in Hamburg (smiling).

Andreas Müller: Yeah (laughing).

Justin Allen: Why are you laughing?

Andreas Müller: Because you are laughing. You started laughing.

Justin Allen: Well, there were fifteen people there. And I thought, "So, this is how you start off basically – 'no one' is there." And you're doing this almost every weekend or how many weekends out of a year?

Andreas Müller: Well, I don't really know. Almost all weekends, I would say.

Justin Allen: Well, not fifty-two weekends a year?

Andreas Müller: Yeah. I mean, there's Christmas, and now and then there are weekends where I don't do anything, so maybe it's six or seven weekends less.

Justin Allen: Okay. That's a pretty intense schedule in a way.

Andreas Müller: Yeah, that's true. It's quite covering in a way.

Justin Allen: And then I was just thinking, "Okay, so every weekend you basically repeat the same thing." You sit there in front of the people and more or less say the same thing. And then I also noticed that the questions ... I mean, I was only there once, but the questions seemed to really focus on what it's like for you (laughing). That's what people really wanted to know.

Andreas Müller: Yeah. It's not always like that, but it may become like that in some talks.

Justin Allen: And then I also noticed that you seem to get more animated in a way. Maybe you got a little bit more excited talking about it. I don't know how to describe it exactly, but I can't judge you and say that you were bored. Anyway, it seemed like the questions where people are trying to ask what it's like for you aren't as intrinsically interesting to you as maybe a more challenging kind of question.

Andreas Müller: Oh, yes. Because it's basically boring how it is for me. Well, not boring, that would also be wrong. It's all wrong what I say, in a way. But yes, because that's totally not the point. In the first place, there is no real "how it is for me." People just assume that there is a certain state like being "no me," and so they ask how it is for me, but there is no state for "no one," so to speak, and there is no state of being "no me." So, there is no answer. And not that there is a real point in these whole meetings, but that's also one thing which definitely isn't the point. If I feel good or bad or if I see things like this or like that or if I get angry or not angry – I mean, exactly that's not the point. So, that's kind of ... I can understand in a way why people ask that because usually, if there is someone, people think that it's about happiness. How do I feel, how do I behave, what do I think and all that stuff. But it's just totally not the point. It's not about me. Not at all.

Justin Allen: That's where I thought maybe we could start because we kind of broached this theme a little bit last time. And maybe we'll start off slowly just because I want to make sure we get on the same page, which might mean that we have to make some concessions in language. So, we started off last time with me confessing that I'm coming from what we started to call a one-point perspective. So, I'm addressing the world, and I feel like there's somebody here. I feel like I'm my body, and I'm trying to understand things for me and make my life better et cetera. So, I'm coming from a one-point perspective where

I think of myself as the center, or in other words, I'm coming from a "me" perspective.

Andreas Müller: Which is the same, I would say.

Justin Allen: Right. Just two different ways of saying the same thing.

Andreas Müller: Yeah.

Justin Allen: And you, there is no "you." Right? (laughing)

Andreas Müller: Exactly. Which already is a contradiction, I mean making an opposite out of it. But yeah, go for it.

Justin Allen: So, for "you," for that which "you" feel from the other side of this conversation, there is no "you," and there's a no-point perspective or a no-me perspective?

Andreas Müller: Yes. But may I already say something, or do you want to first describe?

Justin Allen: No, you can say it.

Andreas Müller: But the only thing that can state that is the one-point perspective.

Justin Allen: Right.

Andreas Müller: I can't state that.

Justin Allen: Right. And you address "me" as though I were a no-point perspective because you don't even recognize ... Not that there's a "you," but if there were a "you," "you" wouldn't be able to recognize a one-point perspective, because it doesn't exist?

Andreas Müller: Exactly. Yes.

Justin Allen: And that's the paradox ... Well, I don't even know if it's a paradox. But that's the dilemma as you say, or that's the frustration – that you can't avoid seeing ... Not that you're there, but you can't avoid seeing the world from a no-point perspective. And in a sense, even though I'm equally not there, I'm somehow convinced that I'm here (laughing).

Andreas Müller: Yes. Exactly (laughing). That's what apparently happens. But "no one" knows that.

Justin Allen: Right. So, that's the thing that's really challenging for all of the "me's" that don't exist but think that "they" exist, somehow (laughing) ... And it's "somehow," right? There's no explanation why?

Andreas Müller: Yes (laughing).

Justin Allen: So, I don't really exist, the "me" doesn't really exist, but somehow it seems like it does, and I'm convinced that it does?

Andreas Müller: Yeah.

Justin Allen: And you're calling that an illusion, which you can't even really call an illusion, because for an illusion to happen there has to be somebody there to experience an illusion?

Andreas Müller: Yes, exactly. There would have to be something which recognizes itself and the illusion to be real.

Justin Allen: So, this is where my problem lies because you also call it the dream.

Andreas Müller: Yes.

Justin Allen: And then I say, "Yeah, but there has to be somebody there to dream a dream."

Andreas Müller: Yeah, but it's the same thing like we said about the illusion.

Justin Allen: I know, but that's the ... You know what I mean? Even though you can't say this, but if I say you're liberated, and you're over there on the other side of this conversation having a no-point perspective in the world, and I'm not liberated, and in the case of the audience last night there were fifteen of us that were, in theory, not liberated and coming from a one-point perspective ... And on the other side of the audience there's one person that's coming from a no-point perspective, and we're trying to understand what that's like. And we're trying to understand how that shift happens. But at the same time it can't happen, because ... And that's what's not possible to grasp.

Andreas Müller: Totally. Yes. Exactly. And I can understand, so to speak, the story and how it is possible that it ... Or I can understand apparently that for the individual it looks like that. And in a way, it can only draw those conclusions and make up that story. With variations, of course. But it's not what happens, so to speak, in a way. But yeah.

Justin Allen: That's why the cleanest way to try to talk about all this is ... For example, you were going through your life ... I mean, even this you can't say. But in the story you're going through your life from a one-point perspective, and then at some point the point drops away.

Andreas Müller: Which would be a story because there never really was a one-point perspective.

Justin Allen: But that's the cleanest way that you can try to say this.

Andreas Müller: Yes and no. I mean, some people would say the cleanest way to say it is to say nothing. There just is no clean way to say it.

Justin Allen: Well, there's cleaner ways to say it.

Andreas Müller: Apparently. Yes. I know what you mean, but it's ...

Justin Allen: But that's kind of how you say it, and that's kind of how Tony Parsons says it. You're sometimes using the word "melting" or "death."

Andreas Müller: Exactly. In the story this is something that seems to be happening or seemed to have happened. Yes. But there is "no one" left who lives in that reality.

Justin Allen: But there was "no one" in the first place?

Andreas Müller: Yes. Absolutely.

Justin Allen: That's the thing that I think has to be constantly said. It's the same as ... You know how people made the mistake last night, and they do so at Tony Parsons's meetings, where they go, "So, there's nothing I can do." And then you have to correct them and say, "No, I'm not saying that there's nothing you can do. I'm saying that you don't exist. Or you're not there." Because you're saying all the time, "You're not there, you're not there," but then people interpret that and say, "Ah, so there's nothing I can do."

Andreas Müller: Yeah, but it doesn't matter how often I say it. One could say as long as there's the illusion of "me," apparently, something will be understood. So, it's really hopeless.

Justin Allen: One of the things that I wanted to try to ask last night but couldn't find a way to ask, and I might not be able to now either, is that apparently there's the apparent illusion of a "me" that I'm experiencing.

Andreas Müller: Yes.

Justin Allen: And if the illusion were to die or disappear or vanish or whatever, then I could say that instead of "me" experiencing sadness, maybe there would be sadness.

Andreas Müller: So to speak, yes.

Justin Allen: But even that you can't say, because sadness is still dependent on happiness or comparing from a point of view?

Andreas Müller: Exactly. One can't really understand or know what this means when it is said that there is sadness for "no one." This can't be understood. And yes, there isn't anyone knowing what sadness is. But everything, also sadness, doesn't need the knowing or the experiencing of itself in order to be there or in order to be sadness. It's just not knowable how it is. How this feels, how this really is can't be known at all. Which, again, refers to everything. "What is" how it actually is can't be known.

Justin Allen: Yeah. And that's true even from a current me perspective and current science, religion, spirituality – whatever we have available to us. Even with that, you can't really know.

Andreas Müller: Yes.

Justin Allen: If you take everything into consideration, like your blood is working without you doing anything, cells are dying and emerging, et cetera ... If you listen to the scientific explanation, it is that you're smelling something, you're feeling something, there's all kinds of endocrine and nerve system things that are going on over which you have no control. So, even in that sense you don't really know what's going on at all.

Andreas Müller: Yes, but this one statement is believed to be known.

Justin Allen: Yeah.

Andreas Müller: Yeah. There is still something that can be known. It's philosophy. "I know that I don't know."

Justin Allen: Right. But then you're going deeper ... But I'm trying to keep it more superficial and just say that you can't even know that the world is a sphere.

Andreas Müller: That's true. I'm just making this apparent difference because it sounds like as if it were almost the same sentence and as if there were some connection between "me" understanding that it actually can't know and there being "no one" to know anything. It sounds so close, but there's no connection at all. In a way. Apparently.

Justin Allen: So, back to how I wanted to try to ask and phrase this one question: From my one-point or me perspective, I am apparently in the illusion that a "me" exists and that there's a point to perceive the world from?

Andreas Müller: Yes.

Justin Allen: And that the world even exists. This is my illusion, and it's an apparent illusion, and if this illusion were to die or disappear or vanish, then wouldn't you still say though that apparently there's no illusion anymore? When that happens isn't it still that whatever's happening is still apparently happening? (laughing)

Andreas Müller: Yes, absolutely. Of course. There is no real illusion, and there is no real absence of the illusion.

Justin Allen: Right. There's no real un-illusion either.

Andreas Müller: Yes, exactly. But of course, the "me" loves this idea of an un-illusion state of clarity and knowing and seeing the truth and all that stuff. No, no. Those, too, in a way just don't really exist. Illusion or un-illusion. Or the state of blindness and the state of clarity. No, no. Or yes, absolutely: They're already an illusion.

Justin Allen: So then, there's no illusion, right?

Andreas Müller: Yes.

Justin Allen: And hypothetically, if we say there's no illusion, you assume that that means that there's the alternative of seeing truth or seeing things as they really are. So right now, I'm only assuming this in a way because you exist in a way and Tony Parsons exists and all these other spiritual teachers or philosophers or thinkers or however you want to categorize that constellation of people. That's the only reason why I think that I'm living an illusion and maybe have some kind of feeling that this isn't right.

Andreas Müller: Yes. The story of the illusion in a way seemed to be provided ... Or you seem to have met this idea of there being an illusion from those people you just referred to.

Justin Allen: Right. Or from your own life experiences where sometime something happened and you had "a moment" or "a glimpse."

Andreas Müller: For example, but as soon as there is a "person," there is somehow living in a story about oneself.

Justin Allen: But even with that sentence, if there is a "person," there's the seeking and the illusion.

Andreas Müller: Well, in a way the experience to be a "person" is the illusion.

Justin Allen: Right. It is the illusion and the seeking?

Andreas Müller: Yes. But it's not really someone living in an illusion. Someone itself is the illusion.

Justin Allen: Right. And when that illusion disappears, the "person" disappears?

Andreas Müller: Exactly. Because it's the same. It's not that I'm a "person," and at some point for "me" the illusion disappears, and then I'm an un-illusioned person. That does not exist. But of course, that's what the "me" is working on in religion and spirituality and all that stuff. Hoping to survive its disillusionment.

Justin Allen: Right. Because it still wants to be there to enjoy the gifts of it?

Andreas Müller: Yes.

Justin Allen: But what you're saying is that no people, no "persons," no "me's" exist or have ever existed?

Andreas Müller: Yes. And no "persons" have reached or gained anything, a true state or something like that. Because the state itself is the "me," so to speak. It's living in states.

Justin Allen: But because you're not responsible for that illusion, and I'm not responsible for that illusion, and for you then ... I'm using "you" in the spirit of the concession. For "you," the illusion's gone, so there's "no person" there, and you're also not seeing other people as "persons"? But as for me, I am?

Andreas Müller: So to speak, yes.

Justin Allen: And if the illusion for "me" disappears, then I would also be "nobody," there would be no experience of a "person," and I would be seeing no people as "persons"?

Andreas Müller: Yes. But this can't be really stated to oneself. It's not that "one" now tells another story about "oneself." There's just nothing there anymore. But yes, it wouldn't be possible anymore to state that there is a "person."

Justin Allen: This is where I have a problem because if before ... Let's just assume that you're born and there's no "person" yet, and then at some point there's the "illusion," and the "person" is created in the illusion.

Andreas Müller: Sorry. If you want to speak longer, that's fine. But the person is never really created.

Justin Allen: Right. But the illusion is.

Andreas Müller: Yes. Well, as we said, not even the illusion is really created; it rather never happens. The creation of a "person," even in the illusion of being a "person," never happens.

Justin Allen: Right. But the illusion happens apparently, and it's the apparent "person" or the sense of being a "person" or whatever?

Andreas Müller: Yes.

Justin Allen: But that happened without anybody doing anything to make that happen?

Andreas Müller: Yes. Oh, absolutely.

Justin Allen: And then the disappearance or the death of that illusion also has no correlation to somebody doing it or it happening because of A, B, C or D?

Andreas Müller: Yes.

Justin Allen: But then it's totally possible that you started off, let's say, at the age of one where your sense of self, your illusion, developed, and then at the age of thirty or whatever you lost your sense of illusion?

Andreas Müller: Yes.

Justin Allen: So, it could also happen that you gain or re-gain your sense of illusion (laughing)?

Andreas Müller: Not really. That's the thing. Because it turns out that this whole gaining and losing ... I mean, I totally agree that it's not logical. But in liberation, which is not some experience of the "me" coming and going and dancing around the idea that maybe "me" isn't real, it never happened.

Justin Allen: Right. But it apparently happened once. Let's just call it the birth. The birth of the illusion apparently happened once, and then the death of the illusion apparently happened once.

Andreas Müller: Not really. No. That's the big surprise: When the illusion drops, so to speak, nothing drops. And it's in a way obvious, but not by someone looking, that nothing happens. That all of that was already it. With no concession. Seeking, going to the gurus, feeling how I feel, being how I am (apparent struggling for words). That's the dropping of the illusion, that honestly there never was an illusion. And in that sense nothing really happened. This is not logical. But I don't know what could come back or how that would look like and how it would be really different from how it is now. In the story, this would be seen as the worst case scenario, so to speak. If you think that I'm in a state of being no one and promoting it all the time, to become someone again would kind of be the worst case (laughing). But I don't see a difference. I don't know what would be the worst case that could happen and still wouldn't be what apparently happens.

Justin Allen: Yeah.

Andreas Müller: It's impossible.

Justin Allen: Yeah, that I can't grasp it.

Andreas Müller: Absolutely. And when I'm in the talks and say that I don't see a difference and there is no advantage here and no disadvantage there, it's a story, but I do mean it like that. It's not some, "Well, don't bother, I know you're in a bad position, but it's not that ..." No, no. It's an utter illusion that there is something which is not wholeness, which is not okay. And it's not logical. I can't explain that. And there isn't a real reason why it is like that. You know, something like, "Hmm, true, it must be like that because I understand it must be all wholeness or all that." No. And it's not about me having reached somewhere or me feeling good or me being in an opposite state of you or of the people sitting in the talks. Not at all. There's no experience of that here.

Justin Allen: But then, don't you think that liberation's a bad word to use?

Andreas Müller: Everything is a bad word.

Justin Allen: No, but I mean specifically that's a bad word because it automatically implies a before and after.

Andreas Müller: Seen by the person, every word would imply a before and an after. I'm sorry. I can't do it right. No matter what I say, "me" will try to read something out of it, which can't be prevented from happening. But it's not wrong either, because it's not a teaching anyway. I'm not really ... There is "no one" working on something. Honestly, so to speak, it's not a hidden method. There isn't a hidden intention going on to bring about insights or enlightenment or even the death of the "me" or something (laughing). So, the possibility of people misunderstanding is totally what apparently happens. Which is the "person's" life anyway. To live in stories about what's going on, not knowing what happens. One could almost say all that the "person" experiences with this message or in the talks is its life experience anyway.

But there is nothing which thinks that that's wrong or that that should change or that there is honestly, literally a better alternative. No. Neither in the talk setup nor in a bigger sense if you assume a world and there being seven billion people thinking they exist. No, that's absolutely one hundred percent what apparently happens. No solution. No solution needed. No problem recognized. But also not nothing discarded. I don't know if "discard" is the right word. It's not about denying anything in that sense. But not about accepting everything either.

Justin Allen: But you might start off a talk by addressing the kind of standard life of the "me," which apparently wants the car, the relationship, the house, the good job or the good location, and then you're talking about that in the sense that you understand what it's like being the "me" for me and the audience?

Andreas Müller: Yeah.

Justin Allen: And you're talking about it in the sense that it's not the case for you?

Andreas Müller: That's how it looks like. Yep.

Justin Allen: And that's kind of the attraction for me or the audience in one of your talks. Even though, as compared to a talk from teachers like Mooji, Rupert Spira or Adyashanti, it might be different, but the people are going there with the same kind of dilemma.

Andreas Müller: Of course. Because the people themselves, so to speak, are the dilemma.

Justin Allen: Right. And what's being offered basically is evidence like, "Yeah, it's true, you're in a dilemma," or, "You are the dilemma."

Andreas Müller: I would say that's what apparently happens, but it's not what I offer in order to bring something about. It's not a conscious offering.

Justin Allen: Yeah, but you're confirming the dilemma.

Andreas Müller: Yes and no. In a way yes, but at the same time it's being said that there is no dilemma.

Justin Allen: Right.

Andreas Müller: One could say that apparently it's a confirmation of what apparently happens. It's saying yes to what apparently happens, but at the same time it's saying that it's not real. Which also is what apparently happens. One could also say, and this sounds a bit spiritual, that what apparently happens is pointing to itself.

Justin Allen: What apparently happens is pointing to itself?

Andreas Müller: Yes. What apparently happens is oneness talks with Andreas constantly saying, "All there is, is oneness talks with Andreas." And if this includes people experiencing themselves as someone, there's constantly a pointing to, "Yeah, that's what apparently happens. Yeah, that's what apparently happens. Yeah, that's what ..." "But I feel bad." "Yes, that's what apparently happens." "But I think I feel like I'm a person." "Yes, that's what apparently happens." "But I can't get out of it." "Yes, that's what apparently happens." Just saying yes constantly. Not for a reason. Not in order to make it into a yes. Not in order for people to be able to say yes to it from a "person's" standpoint, in the sense of accepting and not resisting what is. No, the yes is imminent automatically. But what seems to be happening in the talks is this pointing to itself for no reason. Not because it's needed, not because it's right or better. There is no story around it being special or holy or important or anything. It just is what seems to be happening.

Justin Allen: Right. That's the same if the illusion dropped away for me. This is all theory and conceptual, but then my realization in a sense would be that I don't exist, I never existed, and even that didn't happen. It would be absent a point of view and absent a reference to even compare from before and after because then you'd be ... You can't experience a before and after in a sense, but that what you would be experiencing would be ... Or you'd be experiencing the absence of experience without the experience of it somehow.

Andreas Müller: Yeah, exactly. Yes. And this is not intellectual. This is not a realization even. Nothing becomes realized in that, in a sense that this is what is being hoped or looked for or assumed to be. Not at all.

Justin Allen: Would you say that there's any kind of symptoms that lead to this?

Andreas Müller: No. Not really. I mean, there are all kinds of symptoms, but it's always unpredictable.

Justin Allen: But Tony Parsons talked about how it's different for different people.

Andreas Müller: Yeah. That's why it's unpredictable. In a way death, so to speak, is very individual. Everyone dies differently. Apparently.

Justin Allen: So, a car crash, which is accidental, couldn't be predicted. That would be like a person who is just walking down the street one day, and all of a sudden the "me" disappears.

Andreas Müller: Yes. One could say so. Exactly.

Justin Allen: And the one that dies of some kind of chronic illness where it takes them ten years to physically die would be the person that has a glimpse of the "no me," but then comes back to the "me."

Andreas Müller: Yes. And nothing means anything. Even this meaning and being thing doesn't mean that it's like a process in a way the person would assume it. Looking back, there seemed to have been ... Well, it's just a story. Like you said actually. It can be an accident. It can be a fading out. It can be fighting. It can be harmonious. It can be fighting at times and harmonious at other times. Anything. Apparently. But while there is all of that, it's always a life experience. The "person" in the end, even if the direction in the story were towards death, would always assume that it's on a path towards personal gain. And even if there were predictable signs, so to speak, "me" would use those signs again to confirm itself being someone who is on the right path, waiting for arriving at the goal.

Justin Allen: Yeah. I mean, there are so many things in life that validate or reinforce that.

Andreas Müller: Only seen by the "me." Nothing validates the absence of "me." The only validation for the "me" is "I am."

Justin Allen: Right. No, I mean if you have a health problem, you go to the doctor, and they explain it's because of this or that.

And then sometimes when you have a mystery illness, they blame it on stress or on something where they don't have a proof in form of a blood test, for example. Ten years later, they're maybe able to prove that with some new technology, and then they can say, "Now we've identified what that is. It's such and such."

Andreas Müller: Yeah.

Justin Allen: But still, even with the common cold, they say that you get that from other people. But ultimately, for every single illness that you get, there's no real reason for it, either scientifically.

Andreas Müller: Yeah. Okay.

Justin Allen: But that's what you always want to do; you always want to find the reason.

Andreas Müller: Exactly. In order to do it, in order to be able to make it oneself.

Justin Allen: Well, I mean, in the case of health you want to do it in order to know and then improve yourself or fix yourself at least.

Andreas Müller: That's what I mean, you want to know "in order to ..." "What's my approach, how can I do it then? If I know where it comes from, I know how to treat it."

Justin Allen: Right. And the most painful illnesses that people have in a way are the ones where there's no explanation. They can't figure it out. And that's what spirituality seems to be: It's an illness that people have; that they want to become enlightened or figure out the meaning of life or figure out who they are. And it's an endless search.

Andreas Müller: Yes.

Justin Allen: The same way as if you had a health problem, you might go down the rabbit hole of going to different doctors trying alternative medicines, trying different diets, trying this and that, and it doesn't help your health at all.

And the same with spirituality: People go to ten different teachers and try meditating for ten years.

Andreas Müller: Yeah. Or when there is "someone," same with life in general. You have a partner, and when this doesn't work, you go to the next partner. Then you say that partnership is completely bullshit, then you work for ten years only. Then you notice that money is no good. Then you go into spirituality. After ten years of spirituality you think it's such crap, I go back to earning money. Or some people just have one method which seems to work for them. They just have one partner and keep the same job, and they just do it for them. It's all possible.

Justin Allen: And that's all just apparently what happens.

Andreas Müller: Yes. Exactly.

Justin Allen: And to the "person," it all apparently happens that way, but what you're saying is that that "person" doesn't exist in the first place?

Andreas Müller: Yes.

Justin Allen: And that even if that "person" didn't exist in the first place, they still might go and do all those thousands of different ways of living life?

Andreas Müller: Yes and no. Because you can't really separate the illusion of a "person" out. Because the illusion of being a "person" happens for "no one," but what apparently happens is that to experience oneself as a "person" has apparent consequences. Like seeking. So, you can't in a way really cut the illusion to be "someone" out and say, "But the same thing would happen."

Justin Allen: So, we know the apparent things that happen when there's an apparent "me," and there are apparent consequences of that apparent "me" existing. And when the apparent "me" dies, there also should be apparent side effects?

Andreas Müller: Yes, one could say so. But it's rather the end of the consequences of seeking than a new state with new consequences of not seeking. I don't know if that was clear. But that's why it's hard to describe. It's just a lessening of the consequences of being a "me."

Justin Allen: It's not creating a new state?

Andreas Müller: It's a bit like when you stop smoking. In a way, it's not that something totally new happens then. It's in a way coming back to what's normal, so to speak. It's not that you get extremely healthy like superman. It's just that you don't do unhealthy stuff anymore when you stop smoking. You can still get sick, you can still get cancer, you can still get anything. But there may be consequences. It's a bit like that, I would say. Which can't be really described. This doesn't really say anything about how it looks in a certain story for anyone. You know what I mean?

Justin Allen: Yeah. But with the way that you say that or the way that I interpret it, it puts the pressure back onto the illusory "me" going, "Oh, my god, I really have to get out of this illusion of the 'me' because of all these bad consequences that are happening to 'me.'"

Andreas Müller: Again, I understand that this is the picture the "me" gets, but it's not really what's being said.

Justin Allen: But that's the reason why there's an audience to this kind of message because in general the "persons" are at the end of the road of seeking, so to speak. They're deep in the rabbit hole and realizing that it's bad for their health or bad for their psychology or whatever, and they want a way out.

Andreas Müller: But again, this is how the "me" lives anyway. The whole seeking energy is because of that. That's the "person's" experience.

Justin Allen: Right. But in general, probably the people that are coming to you or Tony Parsons or even to gurus are people that are in or have gone through some kind of a crisis.

Andreas Müller: Yes and no. But in a way, "me" is the crisis, and so everybody has this crisis. And in the talks, especially as compared to the satsangs of gurus, there are relatively a lot of so-called stable people who have a regular job, earn good money, are kind of happy in their relationship and all that stuff. But yeah, there is some interest in this "me" thing. But I would say that that's already there, no matter if the people are in a crisis or live a stable life.

Justin Allen: Yeah, but the attraction is that we feel that if the "me" vanished, this constant searching would disappear. This constant striving to figure things out, to live life the right way et cetera.

Andreas Müller: Yeah, but I'm not sure if that's really the drive. I would say that's the reason why the "me" thinks it goes there. I'm totally there. But in a way, coming to the talks or the attraction is what apparently happens anyway. It's not about ...

Justin Allen: There's no real reason, but there's an apparent reason, which is that my life sucks or something's not right or it could be better.

Andreas Müller: Yeah, but that's what I mean. That's what happens anyway. I think in the talks, there can be attraction, but only for a few people. You can't generalize it. But there are just a few people who seem to be open to the possibility of total failure. Of "no way out." Of "me" being not real.

Justin Allen: Yeah. But that I think is the ... Even if they're going there without that attraction, that is the attraction.

Andreas Müller: Oh, yeah, of course. That's what I mean, yes.

Justin Allen: The fear comes when you say something like, "You don't exist." Then they might resist.

Andreas Müller: Oh, that's the attraction, but the attraction is different than the story that runs in their head. Because the story is, "Oh, yes, I go there, and I may become 'no one,' and when I see that, I will be fine, and this is the answer," and all that stuff. But I would doubt that this is the actual resonance. It doesn't matter in the end, because, as we said, it just is what happens anyway.

Justin Allen: But also when you're talking to me and to your audiences, you're talking to them as if they didn't exist (laughing). You're talking to them as if they were not coming from a me perspective in a sense.

Andreas Müller: Yes.

Justin Allen: And they've never been talked to like that. If I'm sitting in the crowd and start talking to my neighbor, we're both in a sense reinforcing the illusion of the "me."

Andreas Müller: Yes (laughing). Apparently. Yes.

Justin Allen: And then, when we turn forward to face you and talk to you, you're talking to us without reinforcing the "me."

Andreas Müller: So to speak, yes.

Justin Allen: When you say that you're trying to communicate or that in your talks something gets touched or addressed ...

Andreas Müller: Yeah, sometimes.

Justin Allen: You say that it's not the "me." You're not essentially communicating to the "me," because you don't even recognize the "me"?

Andreas Müller: Yes. In that sense, I'm not even really communicating something.

Justin Allen: Well, there's no "you" communicating something. But communication is happening.

Andreas Müller: Apparently, yep.

Justin Allen: So if there were a point to the talks or a point to there being an audience that is in front of you, it would be ... Not that it exists, but it would be that the un-illusionary "me" might hear the message. Like if we just pretend for a second that there were a "me" that's here, that sees the world and generally gets talked to, that somehow you're communicating through the hands (a veil) to the actual. And that if the actual thing hears it, it can be like, "Oh, just move the hands (the veil) out (away), and now ..."

Andreas Müller: That's a very personalized picture, which is fine.

Justin Allen: But isn't that kind of what you or Tony Parsons says; that when you're addressing the people in your audience, something might hear this message or that the ...

Andreas Müller: Something might happen, yes. But rather as a description than as a goal or an intention or a necessity or a valuable thing. It's just what seems to be happening: that in the story, so-called people seem to be touched by this message in all kinds of directions. I mean, ninety-eight percent of all the people would say it's bullshit. They wouldn't even listen to it. They would think that's something weird. One percent listens to it and is totally scared and never comes again. So, one percent is left. I don't know about the numbers, they are made up. So, let's say, one percent is left and even within this one percent, it's totally unpredictable how they react. Some people may go into a strong seeking phase for many years with desperation. It's totally unpredictable. And it's not about touching people, it's not about creating effects. But that's what apparently happens, yeah.

Justin Allen: Right. But I'm trying to make a distinction between you addressing the illusory "me" and addressing the un-illusionary "me." You know what I mean?

Andreas Müller: No. Because there is no "me." It's not trying to talk to "who you really are" or something like that.

Justin Allen: Not to "who you really are," but like to what you're not. Or is that still too ...

Andreas Müller: Yeah, because there isn't the experience of addressing anything at all. Sorry, it's not ...

Justin Allen: But if I don't exist, here is a point, right?

Andreas Müller: Yes.

Justin Allen: Then I don't exist, period, and all that there would be is nothing - a no-point perspective.

Andreas Müller: Or you don't even know if there's nothing, but yes.

Justin Allen: What else would there be?

Andreas Müller: Now you start thinking already from the one-point perspective.

Justin Allen: Well, I mean the no-point perspective: If there's no point, then, at least in using language, that's indicating that there's nothing.

Andreas Müller: Nothing specific.

Justin Allen: Yeah.

Andreas Müller: Yeah.

Justin Allen: But you could be communicating with that nothing. Because if you're nothing ...

Andreas Müller: The communication is this nothing.

Justin Allen: Right.

Andreas Müller: It's already no-point perspective. This is already no-point perspective.

Justin Allen: Right. I'm just saying, you're a no-point perspective, I'm a no-point perspective. The wall behind you is a no-point perspective. The computer's a no-point perspective. But there's the illusion of a one-point perspective, which is apparently happening to this body here where "I am."

Andreas Müller: Yes, but actually only to itself. It's not really happening to the body. The body doesn't know that. Yeah, sorry.

Justin Allen: So, when you're communicating to me, you're not communicating to that illusion of a one-point perspective? You're communicating to the no-point perspective?

Andreas Müller: That's the problem because then the word "communication" doesn't really work. No, because there's absolutely no ... It's just happening. Questions, answers are happening, but I'm not speaking to "you" energetically. I don't want to create any reaction in you. I'm not saying something "in order to ..."

Justin Allen: I'm not saying that you're trying to do anything. I'm just saying the nature of what you're explaining to me sounds like all you can do is ... Well, first of all, there's no "you" that can do anything, but the no-point perspective which, at least in this conversation we're having, is apparently coming from your body and your mouth and whatever you are on the other side of the video talk.

Andreas Müller: Yes, yes. I know what you mean. But not only in the talks. All the time, so to speak.

Justin Allen: All the time. And everything that comes out of you is a no-point action or a no-point perspective.

Andreas Müller: Yes (reluctantly).

Justin Allen: It's nothing. Nothing happening basically.

Andreas Müller: Yes. But this doesn't only ... This also refers to the computer, to the trees, to the wall and also to you, of course.

Justin Allen: But the difference of me and the computer and the wall and you is that I apparently think that I am a person or a one-point perspective.

Andreas Müller: Yes.

Justin Allen: So, I'm just saying that when you're apparently communicating to me, you're apparently communicating not to me actually, but to the nothing.

Andreas Müller: Yes, exactly.

Justin Allen: If we make the concession that there's an illusion or a veil or something like this around the nothingness that I apparently am, then maybe the nothingness kind of awakens to itself and ... I'm just making this up. But that then the illusion drops away.

Andreas Müller: Yeah, but these are ... I know you don't mean it like that, but these are all those spiritual pictures. As if nothingness needed to awaken to itself in order to be and all that stuff. It's not like that, because it already is completely itself.

Justin Allen: Well, that's what's so fucked up because it is itself, but then what the hell is this illusion?

Andreas Müller: Exactly. In that sense, that's where we started. There is no real illusion even.

Justin Allen: Yeah. That's what's so weird. How can there not be an illusion?

Andreas Müller: Yes.

Justin Allen: How can there not be an illusion, but this apparent problem exists?

Andreas Müller: That's the dilemma. There is no answer to that. There is no answer to the question, "But why am I 'me'?" There is no answer to, "Who am I? Why am I?" This is all the same question in the end, coming from this one-point perspective asking, "Why am I? What's this about? What is the meaning or purpose of my existence? Who am I? Where do I come from?" It's all the same question. And it remains unanswered.

Justin Allen: And there's also nothing that ... You know how a lot of times, especially in spirituality, somebody says, "I'm never going to get enlightened." And then the teacher says, "That's the biggest hindrance," or something like that. Have you ever heard that? Where they say that's blocking you from getting enlightened.

Andreas Müller: Yeah, but it's superficial because in a way ... I can't say it like that. It's not a teaching, it's not a story. But of course, you assuming yourself to "be" in this instant is blocking you from not being.

Justin Allen: Right. But there's also nothing you can do about it?

Andreas Müller: Exactly.

Justin Allen: That's the fucked up thing with saying that sentence. Like you constantly reflecting back and making yourself exist is the thing that's blocking you from ... And then you go, "Oh, so all I have to do is stop doing that or all I have to do is ... whatever."

Andreas Müller: Exactly, yes.

Justin Allen: But you can't not do that?

Andreas Müller: Oh, absolutely. Yes. Yes. Yes.

Justin Allen: But that's the difference. That's again ... We went through this in most of our talks, I think. That's the distinction again between you and spiritual teachers.

Andreas Müller: Totally.

Justin Allen: They're definitely saying this.

Andreas Müller: Yes, at least it seems like a prescription rather than a simple description.

Justin Allen: And that's what's so stressful, I think, about going to them: realizing that I have to do so much work.

Andreas Müller: And again, the difference is exactly why I thought about that already before. When we talked about this knowing thing, it's exactly that difference. You remember when I said, "Nothing can be known," and you said that this can be somehow understood even by the "person." And it sounds so close: Saying that nothing can be known because there is "no one" and a "person" knowing that it can't know everything. It sounds so close, but it's two completely different things, which don't meet at all.

Justin Allen: Yeah, so for clarification, how would you say it then?

Andreas Müller: And that's the same with spiritual teachings and this message.

Justin Allen: So, the spiritual teachings can basically come to the point where they say, "There's nothing to be known, and there's no knower."

Andreas Müller: Actually yes, but it's only conceptual when in the same breath they say, "Yeah, actually there is no one, and actually nothing can be known, but do this, do that, you are someone, there is a goal. Know all the tricks, know all the traps. Be aware. Work yourself through. Be attentive. Do all you can, although there is no one. But use your chance," and all that stuff.

Justin Allen: So if they didn't have the qualification, would it be a similar message to yours? If they just said that there's nothing to be known and no knower, and they just ended right there?

Andreas Müller: Yes, but they just don't seem to end right there. Well, I don't know anything. And of course, also there, "no one" will be found who does it like that. Even in a personal teaching you will never find a "person." There is "no one" there either. That's important. It's not saying that there are people who are wrong. No, there isn't anyone as much as here isn't anyone. But as I said already, I don't even claim one is better than the other or one is right and the other wrong. But when there is "no me," it would just be impossible to make that whole thing up. To say that you should spend your time looking if there is really a "me" or not, it would just be lying. We already talked about that when we talked about Ramana. At least, I have no idea how this could ever come out of my mouth (laughing). Maybe as part of a talk I might say to you, "Yeah, look, is there someone?" But not really ...

Justin Allen: But the thing is, when somebody asks that question, "Look, is there someone?" and the answer's always like, "Yeah, there's fucking somebody that's looking, somebody that's aware of stuff."

Andreas Müller: Yeah. But some people say, "No, actually there is 'no one.'" It can also be seen, but yes, there is still someone being aware. That's the dilemma: that every inquiry leads to "me." Every inquiry of the "me" ends up with, "Well, I am, that's all I can say. Everything else, I'm not sure about, but when I have a look about what is, for sure I am."

Justin Allen: Yeah. That's also the distinction that you make: You say that that's not there.

Andreas Müller: Exactly, yes. In a way, this is the only thing that can be said, but there is no one saying it to oneself. But this can only be said when it has dropped. Before that, it remains a concept that you can maybe read in a book. But it's impossible to know that, because that which is aware can't un-experience itself. It can go there conceptually, but it doesn't really know the possibility how that is, so to speak.

Justin Allen: And the "me" can't be dropped either (laughing)?

Andreas Müller: Yes, exactly.

Justin Allen: And when you have these talks, you have to be so diligent and qualify every goddamn thing you say because it's like ... It's not a critique, I'm just saying I can see the challenge. Because you just said kind of casually, "When the 'me' drops, then ..." And it's like, "Yeah, but the 'me' doesn't exist, so it can't drop away." That's the constant dilemma ...

Andreas Müller: Oh, yes, exactly. Our every sentence is wrong. Every sentence seems to contradict itself. But again, that's the "person's" experience anyway. This whole message contradicts the experience of a "person." In a way, the whole life is a contradiction to the "person."

Justin Allen: In what way?

Andreas Müller: Or the other way around: The "person" only confirms its existence, but nothing confirms the existence of a "person" in that sense. Nothing else does that.

Justin Allen: What do you mean by, "Nothing else does that?" Do you mean that a table doesn't do that?

Andreas Müller: Yes. No tree, no computer, no table, no animal, no planets, no stars, no thought, no feeling. Not even the body confirms a "me." It's still "me" confirming itself in the body.

Justin Allen: So, nothing else confirms itself, like a mirror in a sense, like the "me" does? So, the "me" is the only self? That's what we then basically call self-awareness or self-reflection.

Andreas Müller: Yeah. Yeah.

Justin Allen: And that "me" is the illusion? The apparent illusion? It doesn't exist?

Andreas Müller: Yeah. We were jumping over a point, but I don't find the right words right now with the contradiction thing. We overleaped that a bit, but that's fine.

Justin Allen: It is incredible to think. I think there's something kind of ... I don't want to use the word "important." But there's something important in this last one or two minutes of talking.

Andreas Müller: I mean, it's just very interesting. Even for the "me," so to speak, it's kind of interesting to think about it. Because it's so convinced about being itself, and it gives itself so much importance. Seen by the "me," "me" is everything. And everything is about "me." My whole life is about "me." Every moment is about "me." It's all about "me." If I inquire into what's real, again it's "me." So, the highest thing in the world is "me." The crown of evolution is "me." The highest spiritual goal is "I am." The highest goal is "I am consciousness." All there is, is consciousness. And all that stuff. "Me" is constantly saying "me." But nothing except the "me" even knows about the existence of "me" (laughing). That's brilliant.

Justin Allen: Well, all the "me's" also help reinforce all the "me's."

Andreas Müller: Which in a way, if you put it in a bigger picture, which isn't really there, is again just "me" confirming "me" (laughing).

Justin Allen: Like using another apparent "me" from somebody else to confirm your "me"?

Andreas Müller: So to speak, yes.

Justin Allen: Or even like this idea of finding your soulmate where two "me's" merge into one "me." That really gives your "me" such a strong sense. That's why it's so attractive to find your soulmate.

Andreas Müller: Yeah. Or to find the "true self," all that stuff. With the soulmate it's interesting because it can be "me" and still meld into something bigger. It's trying to fulfill the idea of being "me" and being one with something else (laughing).

Justin Allen: Right. But that's what I mean. That, in a way, even gives you a stronger sense of "me" because you feel like you've connected. You've exploded your "me" a bit, you've made it bigger.

Andreas Müller: That's the intention anyway: to be "me." And "me" is always the answer. "Be present," is like saying, "I'm the answer. What's the problem? I'm the answer. Be present in the moment."

Justin Allen: I mean, don't you think everybody's experienced moments in life when there's no "me"?

Andreas Müller: Yeah. "No one" knows. But yes, that's quite possible.

Justin Allen: You know, when you're in deep sleep?

Andreas Müller: Yeah.

Justin Allen: Or sometimes in sports or when you're super busy working.

Andreas Müller: Or maybe just during the day when nothing special happens.

Justin Allen: Right.

Andreas Müller: But these times are just overlooked. Even deep sleep.

I mean, the "person" can in a way deal with that idea, but what happened in deep sleep has absolutely no importance itself. It's so unimportant. It so much doesn't matter that there was "no one." This information is so useless for the "person." It's interesting to think about it for ten seconds (laughing).

Justin Allen: Couldn't it be possible that somehow there's a chemical, maybe an antidepressant, that you could take to get rid of the "me"?

Andreas Müller: Yes and no. I don't know. But again, just from the picture you would still state there being a "me" in the first place. But yeah, there may be all kinds of chemicals which bring about all kinds of feelings and reactions. Everything is thinkable at least, but not knowable.

Justin Allen: This is really crazy to me. I mean, it's so clear ... I don't know if it's been clear my whole life, but I feel like somehow it's been clearly intuited and that the "me" ... I always felt like as long as there's ... I'm going to call it a "me" now. I don't think I called it a "me" my whole life. But as long as there's a "me," I knew there's going to be problems for my whole life. So, my goal always was to escape out of the "me."

Andreas Müller: Oh, yeah, of course.

Justin Allen: But this seems to be the only message that says that there is no "me" in the first place. Because generally, all messages seem to address a "me."

Andreas Müller: Yeah, totally. I would say so. I mean, it's not just "me" as Andreas, but ... Not that this were the only measure, of course. But yes, the message which says that there is no "me" is rare. Let's say it like that. And a lot of teachings in spirituality and religion, so to speak, dance around the idea that there is no "me." But they are coming from a personal experience and are always pointing to the "person." So yes, this is very rare. Not better or anything, but rare.

Justin Allen: And there's a certain logic, an apparent logic to the "me" also. Because the people that get super identified with their "me" or give it way more attention seem to suffer more than the people that ignore the "me."

Andreas Müller: It depends on how the story goes. If you have a nice story and a successful life, then "me" feels very good in that successful life, both in an economic and a spiritual sense. One example is a guru who is a very successful "me," who looks good, who looks quite happy, gets all the money, and people throw roses before their feet and all that stuff. It's still "me," and there's still kind of doing and seeking and suffering going on. But the "person" probably wouldn't say so. Because the story is that I made it. "I am someone, and I made it."

Justin Allen: This is something that's maybe unrelated, but I thought of it today and did want to talk about it. We're running out of time though ...

Andreas Müller: We can still go on if you want.

Justin Allen: Are you familiar with Odysseus, the Odyssey?

Andreas Müller: Uh, the Greek who did the boat trip (laughing)?

Justin Allen: Yeah.

Andreas Müller: Briefly.

Justin Allen: So, the author is Homer, and he wrote ***The Iliad and The Odyssey.*** The Iliad is about Achilles and the Odyssey is about Odysseus.

Andreas Müller: All right, yeah. I don't know much about it (laughing).

Justin Allen: Well, Achilles is the great warrior who's powerful and strong and great at battle. And also intelligent but more in the sense of brute warrior strength. Odysseus is also a great warrior but more of a strategist and an intellectual type.

Andreas Müller: Mm-hmm (affirmative). All right.

Justin Allen: The Odyssey though is about him returning home after the war, and he goes through all these obstacles, one of which is he being on an island with his men where they are captured by Cyclopes, which are giants with one eye.

Andreas Müller: Yeah. Yeah.

Justin Allen: And I'm probably telling the story a little bit wrong, but they're trapped by the Cyclopes and can't really defend themselves against them, because there are too many of them. When the Cyclopes ask their names, Odysseus ends up telling one of them that his name is "no one."

Andreas Müller: Yeah, okay.

Justin Allen: And he does this strategically because he knows that at some point they will manage to attack and kill one of the Cyclopes, but probably only one, not three or five of them. So, the other Cyclopes go away, and then Odysseus says, "Okay, guys, let's kill this single Cyclops." And they start attacking him knowing that it's going to take a while. Meanwhile, there's noise going on, and the other Cyclopes ask the single guard, "Hey, what's going on? Are you okay?" And he goes, "No one is trying to kill me."

Andreas Müller: Yeah, yeah.

Justin Allen: So, they don't come to help him.

Andreas Müller: Yeah.

Justin Allen: Just from our last talk about this no-point perspective I was thinking about that a bit and about how freeing it would be and literally, in that sense, it frees them by identifying as "no one." That's the only way they were able to escape from being killed by the Cyclopes.

Andreas Müller: Yes.

Justin Allen: This, or at least this general interest, is to talk about "no one." Like "no one" being there.

Andreas Müller: Yes.

Justin Allen: And that's what you don't want to ever ... I mean, in general the "me" can't ... It can't even allow that to be addressed really.

Andreas Müller: Oh, totally. Yes.

Justin Allen: And so it just makes me think about the futility of it. But at the same time ... I don't know. Of course, there's something beautiful about that.

Andreas Müller: Yes.

Justin Allen: It's such an impossible thing.

Andreas Müller: Yeah. Which is the beauty also.

Justin Allen: Do you ever entertain the idea ... Let's assume for the sake of this, the "me" in "me" ... I don't know if I should say it like that, but the "me" that I think that I am is in a sense an illusion, even if it's not really an illusion. It's like a person. It's like a created entity.

Andreas Müller: That's how it feels. And it consists one hundred percent of that impression: to be something which is alive and which is everything that is known and valuable, although it doesn't have any substance at all. It's not "me" having some illusion, and when that will be cleared out, I'll stand there clarified or anything. No. It's exactly that sense. As I said, that's what the "me" consists of. Undoubtedly, in a way.

Justin Allen: And anything that would threaten it somehow, it would want to resist or survive, so it would do whatever it would take. The same way, if somebody came to attack you right now, you would physically do whatever you could to survive.

Andreas Müller: Yes. It doesn't have to be like that, because it sounds a bit too much as if it were a separate entity, which it actually isn't. But exactly. If it would be a separate entity, it would do everything to fight against that attack. That's the ultimate attack; to say you don't even exist. To say, "One day you will become 'no one,'" is a safe place for the "me." It can survive from that. But not from this energetic, immediate attack, which isn't an attack, it just feels like that. I don't attack. And this message isn't attacking. It's just around, so to speak. "Me" feels automatically attacked. All the time, in a way, not only by this message. It's attacked all the time because all there is, is nothing. So, it constantly has to create itself and be active and fight for its existence. It's already fighting for its existence.

Justin Allen: Like that sense of being worthless. Like that, in general, the Western population all has low self-esteem. And this sense of being ... You know the word "worthless," right?

Andreas Müller: Yes.

Justin Allen: Because if it's an illusion, it is nothing.

Andreas Müller: It is worthless.

Justin Allen: So, it has to try to prove itself that it's not worthless; to prove that it is not an illusion.

Andreas Müller: Exactly. Oh, that's also why there are all these stories about how great consciousness is, for example. It's all coming out of trying to add value to that. Also spirituality. It's constantly saying, "I'm consciousness, I'm everything." It's great. It's the absolute. There's the constant need to make itself valuable and important.

Justin Allen: Except that you have to make a distinction because in spirituality, they're not giving "me" the value, they're only giving consciousness, which isn't the "me," the value. Is that what you're trying to say?

Andreas Müller: No. Well, it's still the experience to be conscious. When they say, "All there is, is consciousness," most ...

Justin Allen: Not the experience, but they're also denying the "me." They're also saying the "me" is an illusion and that you have to ... You don't have to do something about it, but they are saying ... They call it the "me" or the ego and are saying that that's an illusion and that that somehow

...

Andreas Müller: Yes. But they don't understand that the experience to be conscious is the "me."

Justin Allen: Right. That's the distinction.

Andreas Müller: That's what they don't get, of course. They think of the "me" as something else. The conditioning, the story, the ego.

Justin Allen: Yeah, they call the "me" a collection of feelings, emotions, thoughts. And then consciousness is something that's aware of all of that.

Andreas Müller: Exactly.

Justin Allen: What you're saying is that the consciousness is actually the "me"?

Andreas Müller: Yes.

Justin Allen: And so for you, thoughts aren't a problem, feelings aren't a problem?

Andreas Müller: No, it's working on a problem which isn't a problem. That's why that never ends. That's why they say you have to be consciously aware your whole life to not go in the story. It's a lifelong task.

Justin Allen: No, I think what you said was really interesting ... Maybe I misunderstood, but you said earlier that thoughts don't confirm the "me," feelings don't confirm the "me," only "me" confirms the "me."

Andreas Müller: Yes. One could also say "me" confirms itself in anything. Because I think thoughts don't seem to confirm "me." Still, it's just "me" confirming itself by thinking thoughts. By feeling feelings. By experiencing a room.

Justin Allen: So, I had this experience once while I was meditating ... I can't even call it meditating. But I was lying down and heard birds outside and a car go by and people talk. And then I was aware of my breathing. And then I was aware of my thoughts. And then all of a sudden I felt like everything's equal. So, I felt, "Okay, the same way that I'm aware of my thoughts is the exact same way that I'm aware of the bird outside." And for me it felt like an insight. The way that I turned it into an insight was by saying, "Oh, wow, for my whole life I've only been identifying with my thoughts, thinking that I'm my thoughts. But I never ever thought I'm a bird, I never thought I'm a car passing by." But as to the experience of awareness, I was equally aware, and the place where I was aware of my thoughts is the same place where I'm aware of the sound of a bird.

Andreas Müller: Yeah.

Justin Allen: So, what that did for me is it took away ... Not really, but for that moment it seemed to have taken away "thought" as being so precious and important. Or you could say it made the sound of a bird as (or equally as) important (unimportant).

Andreas Müller: Yeah. And it brought you to the conclusion, which sounds very spiritual, that everything is the same, so to speak.

Justin Allen: Looking at it now, where you start to call that thing that was aware of the thought, the bird, the car et cetera the "me" ... That changes everything actually.

Andreas Müller: Oh, totally, yes. It's such a game changer (laughing). That's true.

Justin Allen: Because you don't think that the "me" is that for whatever reason, or at least I didn't.

Andreas Müller: Yeah, "me" doesn't really see itself. It identifies all kinds of problems and hindrances: "What I should see," or, "What the problem is." And when it thinks about the "me" from all those teachings, it thinks about exactly that: the personality, the thoughts, that what those teachings provide. But it never really comes back to itself. And also those teachings don't do that. They don't go there. It seemed to be always about "me" and there being no ego and no person. And suddenly I found out ... It's in the story now. Suddenly I found out that they actually never go to the "no me" ... You know, there is no actual "me."

But they don't actually come to the point, not at all. They all meander around those ideas about thoughts and feelings and being aware and trying to not be that and that it's better to not go into the story too much and all that stuff. They're all circling around this idea having no idea what they are talking about. Sorry, I don't want to be mean. It's not that there is someone who could do differently and who's bad or so. I don't mean it like that. It's very sincere. And it's all fine. But I was and still am surprised. I still can't believe it in the end. But again, not that there is someone who could do differently. It's all according to what is being believed and experienced and all that. It's all fine. It's all okay. But it's so different in a way.

Justin Allen: So, this "me" is consciousness?

Andreas Müller: The experience to be only consciousness and self-awareness, yes.

Justin Allen: And a thought doesn't confirm self-awareness, but consciousness uses thought to confirm itself?

Andreas Müller: So to speak, yes. But it naturally happens like that. The word "use" is already too much.

Justin Allen: Okay.

Andreas Müller: Because by only experiencing, by being separate from the thought and only experiencing it, a confirmation happens like, "Well, I'm separate. I must be separate in order to experience thought."

Justin Allen: I'm just going to use the word anyway. So, it "uses" thought to confirm itself?

Andreas Müller: In the end, to confirm everything.

Justin Allen: Right, right. But I want to do it slowly. So, it uses thought to confirm itself in the same way it would use a feeling or an external noise to confirm itself?

Andreas Müller: Yes, exactly.

Justin Allen: And so if that "me" disappeared, then there'd still be the thought, but for "no one." There'd still be the feeling, but for "no one," there'd still be the external sound, but for "no one"?

Andreas Müller: Yes. But it can't be known or explained how that actually is.

Justin Allen: There'd be "no one" there to then explain it or confirm it or ...

Andreas Müller: Yes, exactly.

Justin Allen: And we think always that "me" is necessary for survival and for everything, right? And that's always the question that everybody asks. Not just to you, but also to teachers like Adyashanti and Rupert Spira, for example. They always go, "Yeah but then, what do I do then? How will I drive my car? How will I eat?" In this scenario that we just created, the "me" isn't necessary to do all that stuff?

Andreas Müller: Absolutely. Yes. It's a big surprise.

Justin Allen: That would be one of the things ... If we pretend that the "me" is a character, like an entity of its own within you or something, it would want to convince you that it's necessary for you to survive so that you don't discard it. Because if the actual you, which I know doesn't exist, ever realized that consciousness, the "me consciousness" isn't necessary for anything, it would just "let it" die, but it wouldn't want to die, the same way that any organism doesn't want to die. Does it bother you saying it that way?

Andreas Müller: I didn't really get if there was a question.

Justin Allen: No. It's not really a question.

Andreas Müller: Yes, of course.

Justin Allen: It's just that it can be said that way?

Andreas Müller: Yeah. Yeah.

Justin Allen: Holy shit.

Andreas Müller: Yes, absolutely (laughing). Yeah. Who's going to do life, if not "me" (laughing)?

Justin Allen: Exactly.

Andreas Müller: Who the fuck takes care of things, and who will become enlightened? Who will survive in order to become enlightened?

Justin Allen: You really think that without that, you're going to be a vegetable or you're just going to ...

Andreas Müller: Yes. End up under a bridge and not earn money and starve. Who would even get out of bed in the morning?

Justin Allen: But that "me" doesn't even exist?

Andreas Müller: Yes. See, that's the burden the "me" lives in, which is completely illusionary: "I have to do it. I am needed. I have to be there. I have to be aware, attentive, think it through, do everything." Well, not at all.

Justin Allen: But that's not its burden, that's its sustenance.

Andreas Müller: Sustenance, I don't know.

Justin Allen: Like food, water and oxygen for the body. Those are necessary for physical sustenance. Things that you need to survive.

Andreas Müller: Yes, but seen by the "me," it's only survival in order to be able to come to the actual thing. It always has a goal, so to speak.

Justin Allen: Yeah. But I mean, if it doesn't do it then, it's like an employee that you don't need.

Andreas Müller: Yes, exactly.

Justin Allen: That employee realizes at some point, "Oh, I'm not necessary, so I better keep busy so that the boss doesn't realize that I'm not necessary."

Andreas Müller: So to speak, but the "me" never really comes to that point.

Justin Allen: You don't think so?

Andreas Müller: No, I don't think so. Well, it can have those glimpses, but in a way it will turn even these glimpses into being a good thing, so to speak. In order for "me" to recognize that I'm not needed, it's still good that "I" recognized it. It's good that "I" was there to recognize it. So, yes and no.

Justin Allen: That's where I feel like my "me" goes, "Get the best job and earn the most money." And so the "me" helps "me," or at least it seems like it helps "me" do everything possible to get the best job and earn the most money. And then, when I have accomplished that, in a sense the "me" could be like, "Oh, I'm not necessary anymore, we already met our goal." So then "me" would have to come up with another goal in order to sustain itself. And then it would say, "Okay, now I want to give money to charity."

Andreas Müller: Nah ... You can say it like that, of course. But I would tell the story a little bit differently. "Me" doesn't really want to have a good job and a lot of money. It hopes that somewhere in having a good job and a lot of money, there is fulfillment. Somewhere in that is something that gives "me" something.

Justin Allen: Right. But I'm saying that as soon as "it" gets fulfilled, the "me" is basically superfluous.

Andreas Müller: No, because the dilemma is that it never is fulfilled.

Justin Allen: Exactly. That's what I'm saying. That's how it sustains itself, by constantly searching, by constantly not being satisfied.

Andreas Müller: Yes, but it doesn't sustain itself by feeling useless. It sustains itself by, "Oh, I'm still needed. I have to move on to the next thing."

Justin Allen: Right. Because since it knows that it's useless, it has to constantly ... That's what I'm thinking.

Andreas Müller: Okay. But no, at least I thought that because the job and the money didn't bring fulfillment, the conclusion would be, "Oh, fuck, my task isn't done yet. I thought it would be done afterwards, but it isn't, because I'm still not fulfilled."

Justin Allen: All right. So, somehow that "me" comes into being in a sense?

Andreas Müller: The illusion of "me" apparently comes into being.

Justin Allen: And that's what we think we are. We think that there's seven billion "me's" on planet earth?

Andreas Müller: Yeah.

Justin Allen: I was thinking about that in our yesterday's talk, too. I couldn't come up with the right example, but I was thinking about a computer. A computer or a chair doesn't have a sense of "me," at least as far as we know. And animals probably don't, at least not the same way that we do. But then I was thinking, "What if you – and that's kind of the goal with artificial intelligence – somehow put a 'me' into a computer?" You know?

Andreas Müller: Yeah. To make them self-aware. Yeah, I know.

Justin Allen: Yeah. And then I thought, "So what if they did that?" Imagine the computer was already built, and then they found a way to kind of embed a "me" into that existing computer instead of manufacturing it from the very beginning with a "me." That computer wouldn't recognize anything, because now, as soon as that "me" was put into it, it would recognize itself as being a "me"?

Andreas Müller: Yeah.

Justin Allen: It would still have all those functions that it had before: pressing the keyboard and the commands would go on.

Andreas Müller: "Don't hit me so hard (laughing)!"

Justin Allen: Yeah. "Stop typing so much (laughing)!"

Andreas Müller: "Bloody idiot!"

Justin Allen: And then it would be fucked. And if it ever wanted to go back to how it was before that "me" got embedded in it, it would have to somehow short-circuit its system or something.

Andreas Müller: Yeah, it would feel trapped in this I box, in the computer. "Why is this fucking guy typing so hard, and I can't go out (laughing)?"

Justin Allen: Yeah. And the only way that "me" could get rid of itself were if the person that put it in took it out. Right?

Andreas Müller: Yeah.

Justin Allen: I was thinking about that (laughing). Somehow that's an analogy: that you got stuck with this "me," and you can't think anything other than from the perspective of a "me."

Andreas Müller: Yes. And it's not even attractive to be not "me." That's the thing. You ask the computer, "Well, I can destroy your 'me,' but then there will be no 'me.'" And the computer, respectively the "me," might say, "Hmm, I know. It's pretty shitty in here, but I better stay. Who knows, maybe there's a solution one day." That's the dilemma. No matter how fucked the situation is, "me" hardly ever says, "Yeah, kill 'me.'" Because maybe it gets better one day. Who knows.

Justin Allen: Even saying that doesn't do anything?

Andreas Müller: Yeah, of course.

Justin Allen: Wanting to kill the "me" doesn't help you kill the "me," because you can't kill the "me."

Andreas Müller: Exactly.

Justin Allen: You can't kill the "me," because it doesn't exist in the sense of a chip or a USB that you plug into the computer. Or at least, as far as it seems, it's not something physical that you can mess around with.

Andreas Müller: Yeah. That's the thing. In the end you can't kill the "me," because there is no "me" in the first place. But seen by the apparent "me," it would absolutely be ridiculous to want to kill the "me" in order to be something that's free from the "me."

Justin Allen: Right. And that's all it knows because knowing is the naturalness of the "me."

Andreas Müller: Yes, which is basically experiencing, which is knowing though. So, yes.

Justin Allen: Basically your life is only that?

Andreas Müller: Yes, exactly.

Justin Allen: Because again, right now in your physical body there's so many things happening that you're totally unaware of.

Andreas Müller: Absolutely.

Justin Allen: But because you're unaware of it, it doesn't do anything for you.

Andreas Müller: Yes.

Justin Allen: So, the only thing that does things for you are things that you're aware of?

Andreas Müller: Yes. That's the hope. Exactly. Which is, in a way, logical ...

Justin Allen: That's not the hope, that's the thing that's so fucked up about it because the illusion is that that's all that you know?

Andreas Müller: Yes.

Justin Allen: And that's all that you can know. You can only know the illusion.

Andreas Müller: Yes. Absolutely (laughing). "Me" only knows itself or lives in the illusion of knowing itself.

Justin Allen: But anything that it could know would always be an illusion?

Andreas Müller: Yes. Because in order to know it ...

Justin Allen: The absence of knowing is no illusion?

Andreas Müller: Yes. Which is unknowable.

Justin Allen: Right.

Andreas Müller: Yes (laughing).

Justin Allen: Sometimes I do feel that I don't get this. You know (laughing)? And I can also feel the resistance all the time, like when the knower or whatever comes back. All right. Should we end there?

Andreas Müller: I think so, yeah. Let's do it. It's lovely though.

Justin Allen: Bye-bye.

Andreas Müller: Bye-bye. See you.

"YOU WILL NEVER BE FREE"

Justin Allen: I read through your book *You Will Never Be Free*. I've been reading it on my iPhone, and then I'd take pictures of the pages that I thought hit me in a certain way. I typed them out here so that I can reread your ... (laughing)

Andreas Müller: What I said, what I already said (laughing).

Justin Allen: Yeah, and actually, what you already said in *You Will Never Be Free* is also what you've already said in our past four talks, but in the book, I think, it's very edited and really crystal clear. Whereas our talks have the nature of a real conversation with the errors and the pauses and all kinds of different words, right?

Andreas Müller: Yeah. Absolutely. Of course. This book, *You Will Never Be Free*, is edited.

Justin Allen: Right. Well, for sure. It's really polished in a way.

Andreas Müller: Yes, yes, but what I've noticed when I went through our text is that ... I should say that's just in a way how it is, but some things seem a bit confused or confusing because I think there is much more unspoken in the air.

Justin Allen: Right, but I think that's good because even when it's really clear, it's still not really clear. You can write the most perfect text, and it doesn't mean anybody is going to get it.

Andreas Müller: Absolutely. Oh, for sure, yes.

Justin Allen: I think that's the same as when you go out with a friend to a café and talk. You don't necessarily remember what you said, and you definitely didn't record it, but you're left with a different energy or with something that was there in the exchange that you can't grab and print. I think that's what happens in our talks as well because of those confusing moments. I think people would read that and say, "Oh, yeah. I might not know exactly what's going on (laughing), but I've sensed something."

Andreas Müller: Yes (laughing).

Justin Allen: It's actually probably good for it to be vague, for there to be ambivalence or ambiguity because that's the nature of this topic in a way.

Andreas Müller: Yes. That's the vagueness of it; that there isn't a real topic. That's in a way the vagueness or this hole or everything not being quite real.

Justin Allen: It's also something that you can't really ... Even the ungraspableness of it ... I think it's good to not have that either because you can't ... That's what I'm saying is there in *You Will Never Be Free*. It's as cleanly and polished and refined as you can make it.

Andreas Müller: Yes. Absolutely.

Justin Allen: Still, you're unsatisfied because you can't get it like you want. So, then before I read some of these texts from your book, I want to say that I've been thinking more and more ... I don't know. We've had the four talks already, and I also went to your Hamburg talk, and then I was at the Zoom talk. Sometimes I'm thinking, "I don't know. At some point, it feels like I don't know if we could even keep on doing these talks."

Andreas Müller: Yes. Yeah.

Justin Allen: I can also see, while I'm going over our previous talks, what my preconceptions were in a way or what my interpretation was back in talk one, and then I can see it getting adjusted in a way.

Andreas Müller: Yes, one could say so. That's what apparently happens. Yeah.

Justin Allen: Basically, your message can be boiled down to this one sentence, in variations: "There is no one." "There is no me." "There is no person." How I understood that before talking with you is wildly different in a way than how I understand that now.

Andreas Müller: Yeah. I guess so. Yeah (laughing).

Justin Allen: Still, I'm sure that I'm not getting it like how you might get that sentence, but it is starting to ... I don't know. The only way I can say it, and I'm going to say it from a perspective of the story, is that I'm still aware that if there really is no me, there is "no me" (laughing), and then it makes everything so pointless. So, there's nowhere left to go. You know what I mean? Because everything is always coming back to that misperception in a way.

So, if you really come to that conclusion, "Oh, yeah. There is no me," then what is there left to talk about?

Andreas Müller: Yeah. It deletes it all. Exactly.

Justin Allen: So, it made me think if we assume that it is a fact that you have no "me" or that there's no "me" there (there where you are), and no "me" by me as well ... So, if there's no "me" by you, and there's no "me" by Tony Parsons, and you and Tony got together and had a conversation, it would really be just mundane or ... I wouldn't imagine that you guys sit around there and talk about ...

Andreas Müller: How nice it is to be no one (laughing).

Justin Allen: Well, or how the big part of "me" is there or not or what's consciousness or something like that. So, if you met, it would be talking about the weather or talking about whatever.

Andreas Müller: Yeah, but it could also be talking about consciousness, but it would be as mundane as talking about the weather.

Justin Allen: Because there wouldn't be the energy from "somebody" trying to figure something out from or with the other person?

Andreas Müller: Yes, or passing on knowledge or something like that. Exactly. Yeah.

Justin Allen: I don't remember our last talk. I don't remember it that well. That's something that I can also say; I don't know if that has anything to do with this, but I generally always have a really good memory of things that happened to me. I place such a value on that and on being able to recall it. Now I notice I don't care that much about recalling ... It's the same as when you get into an argument with your girlfriend or wife or even a friend where you might go, "You said such and such," and then you can repeat exactly how they said it, and you put so much value on what they just said five minutes ago (laughing). I feel like this is fading out for me, not that I'm attributing it to whatever is going on here, but ...

Andreas Müller: I mean, in the end, it is like that, nothing has been spoken. The "me" would say, so to speak, or the assumption is, "Okay. If nothing can be said, I should shut my mouth," or there shouldn't be words coming out of that mouth. The interesting thing is in a way that, while speaking, nothing is being said. No facts are provided ever, and there is "no one" who has to stop talking, but there's also "no one" who needs to talk in order to pass on information, but that's the thing. We can speak for an hour or forever, but no real fact will be spoken, no truth will be spoken. The only "truth" is that these words, which only have an apparent meaning, are coming out of our mouths.

Justin Allen: Seen by the "me," or if the "me" still believes that it's there, it will think that all that was spoken could be very, very important and have a lot of value and needs to be ...

Andreas Müller: Exactly. That's the hope at least; that it's important or could be potentially important and meaningful.

Justin Allen: The "me" has to think all the time that whatever is being said is important because of its point of view.

Andreas Müller: So to speak. Yes.

Justin Allen: That is because the "me" is existing through this reflection of ...

Andreas Müller: That's one method, actually, to assume truth in analyzing.

Justin Allen: It's not even that. It's also assuming that I exist and analyze.

Andreas Müller: Oh, yeah, of course.

Justin Allen: Just the analysis is proving my existence.

Andreas Müller: Totally. Of course.

Justin Allen: So, the past conversation or what I said five minutes ago – I think that I can go back to where I was five minutes ago and that's proving my existence.

Andreas Müller: Also all the time, along the way, so to speak. Whatever "me" does or believes to do is automatically confirming its existence.

Justin Allen: Right. That energy which is the illusory "me." So, that's why this is "me" telling my story and trying to still the "me" by trying to find a correlation or trying to explain what's happening or what could be happening. And I'm noticing that this is not so important to me anymore. It used to feel so important to have a past and be able to recall it and put significance into everything that had already happened.

Andreas Müller: Yeah, but there are two things going on. Only apparently, not really, because all of that is what apparently happens. There's a reporting happening on the one hand, and then maybe the illusion of "me" on the other hand, thinking that it's a real happening that happens to you and means something.

Justin Allen: Yeah. Exactly.

Andreas Müller: Yes, because you saying that you don't think about it that much anymore is just an apparent report of what apparently happens. That's wholeness as that. That's what seems to be going on. "I'm sad." "It seems I don't think so much anymore." That's wholeness as that, but, of course, as long as there's the illusion of "me," so to speak, apparently, it feels as if this were really happening to "me" and meant or might mean something.

Justin Allen: Exactly. Even that, I find it's being weaker, but that's always the case when things have dropped away. Or let's say I've had some drive before. I've had some ambition before, and then all of a sudden you wake up, and you're like, "Oh, I don't care so much about this, and I used to care so much. What's wrong with me?"

Andreas Müller: That could be, yeah.

Justin Allen: Then what if that question that comes in and says, "What's wrong with me?" drops away and doesn't come back? It's just like, I don't know, treating it like air. So, from your text, I don't think it's that important, but I have the pages marked anyways. So, on page 216, this is all out of context a bit, but the person asks, "But who knows that?" and then you say, "No one does. Oneness seems to see everything – actually it's everything – and yet remains completely blind. It's wonderfully ignorant by not recognizing anything that's not it, even the illusion of being a person. Oneness doesn't recognize 'me' as such. 'It' just is it."

Andreas Müller: Yes. Wonderful (laughing). Sounds a bit polished (laughing).

Justin Allen: It's really polished, yeah. So, the things that stand out to me are that "oneness" seems to be everything, and that you mean literally everything as in tables, chairs, birds, trees, people?

Andreas Müller: Yes. Absolutely.

Justin Allen: Then thoughts and feelings, also.

Andreas Müller: Yeah. I mean, the concept of "oneness" actually isn't really helpful here, because it may sound like it were not tables and chairs. Like it were actually something "else," namely "oneness," but that's not how it is meant. All there is, so to speak, is what apparently happens. Without any meta-level. Without some hidden absolute essence which would be separate from chairs and stuff like that – that would just be another idea that comes up in or as what apparently happens. It's all there is; everything is what apparently happens. It's almost plain and superficial; everything just being itself. There is no hidden mystery in anything or no additional thing to be seen or no hidden truth to be discovered.

In that sense, everything is "oneness," or everything is whole without ever becoming something else. It's not that the relative actually is something "else" than the absolute. It's really just the same.

Justin Allen: All right, to just stay on that, I'm going to tell you my interpretation. So, I think in a way you're using "oneness" in this certain train of thought. "Oneness seems to see everything." The only thing that we attribute to seeing things is ourselves in a way?

Andreas Müller: Yes.

Justin Allen: So, here it seems like you're saying "oneness" as consciousness or as the person seems to see everything, meaning chairs, tables, other people, thoughts, feelings. Actually, it is everything. Meaning, I am also my thoughts, my feelings, the chair, the table, everything and yet remain completely blind. So, I interpret "completely blind" in the sense that I am unaware in a way.

Andreas Müller: Yes. Exactly.

Justin Allen: So, right now my experience, though, is that I'm here as separate, and I'm aware of everything that's not "me," and what you're saying is that I'm here, aware of everything, but I am everything, and I'm not aware that I am myself or myself as separate from everything?

Andreas Müller: Well, I would say this awareness just is what apparently happens, but it's just not everything, so to speak, not in the sense of, "I am only awareness," or, "'what is' is only awareness," whatever "what is" means – no one knows even what that means. There just is no awareness of wholeness about itself, in the sense of a meta-level.

Justin Allen: Yeah. I mean, really, what this sentence is saying is that there's "no awareness" in what I think. There are just thoughts coming up?

Andreas Müller: Yes. Exactly.

Justin Allen: I'm just trying to explain it from the perspective of somebody that still thinks and goes about the world as if they were aware, referring to "me," myself. So, from that, it seems that knowing what it would be like to be blind in the sense of not being aware seems impossible because ...

Andreas Müller: Of course.

Justin Allen: Right. We've talked about that. That's literally the dilemma; that as awareness, you can't understand "no awareness," which in this context also means blind.

Andreas Müller: No. Exactly. Well, yes, but not because of the concept. One can understand the concept, but it's just impossible to experience that.

Justin Allen: Right. As awareness, you can't experience "no awareness," because ...

Andreas Müller: That's what makes it so incomprehensible.

Justin Allen: It's the same as trying to understand what it's like to be blind. If you have vision, you can't understand blindness.

Andreas Müller: Well, in a way you can because you can follow the experience of blindness by just closing your eyes and then experience how it is to be blind.

Justin Allen: Sort of.

Andreas Müller: Sort of, yes. That's what I mean. In a way, "me" can almost imagine everything in the "me" world because it somehow can refer to an experience of it. "Me" can experience or assume how it is to be really sad. "Me" can experience or assume the experience of how it is if I lose a child without having lost a child because it's somehow possible to project itself into that imagination, but the only thing that can't even be imagined how it feels like, not as a concept, but how it really feels like, how it may be, is absence. That's incomprehensible.

Justin Allen: Right, because there would be "no one" there to be measuring things. There'd be no one there to be seeing things. There'd be no one there to be aware of that ...

Andreas Müller: Exactly.

Justin Allen: This is another dilemma: that it's true that you can kind of imagine what it would be like to literally be visually blind or what it would feel like to lose a loved one. You can imagine, "If I lost a loved one, it would be so terrible and painful."

Andreas Müller: Exactly. Yes.

Justin Allen: Then there's the other thing ... The person that is blind would say, "You don't know what it's like. You say you know what it would be like to be blind, but you can't understand what it's like to be me."

Andreas Müller: That's true. Of course.

Justin Allen: I think that people say that it's also like if I lost a loved one and you haven't and I'm crying and you're telling me, "Oh, I feel for you," and then I yell at you, "No, you don't know what it's like!"

Andreas Müller: Yeah, of course. That's true.

Justin Allen: I think that people do that because yes, the other can somehow understand what it would be like to be blind because they can close their eyes and imagine that they'd have to stumble around and feel for stuff. But when it actually happens that you are blind, there's the whole psychological pain of, "I used to be able to see, now I can't, how do I deal with this?" That's what I always think that people are referring to: the psychological element of that transition, right?

Andreas Müller: Of course, but I just meant that seen by the "person," it seems at least to be some kind of comprehensible thing, knowing that it might not be exactly how it is, but there seems to be some possibility of an approach to how that might feel.

Justin Allen: I still think that maybe there's some way of sensing how it is. Even though you're saying it's impossible with this "me" and "no me" situation, everybody's question to you is the same as if you were blind and I asked you, "Yeah, but what do you see? You must see something," and you might be like, "No, there's just blackness. There's dark red." I mean, you couldn't even say, "dark red," if you were born blind, but you'd be describing what it's like in a way.

The same with a question that people asked at your Hamburg talk: "Yeah, but if you're not there, then why do you wake up in the morning? Why do you go eat breakfast?" Right?

Andreas Müller: Yeah.

Justin Allen: You're trying to describe it, and it's definitely not the same, but it's still ... It just makes me question it. Maybe people do have the experience of absence or of "no me."

Andreas Müller: One could say so. Oh, yes, absolutely.

Justin Allen: There's some taste that everybody ...

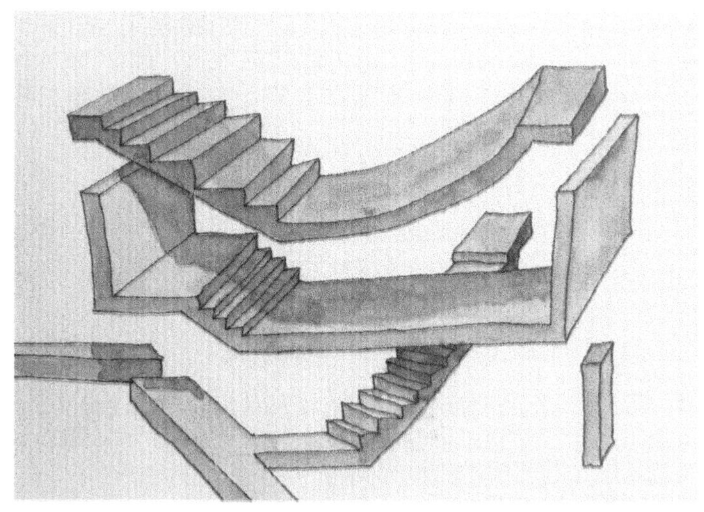

Andreas Müller: Oh, yes. One could say so, because there is "no one" anyway. Absolutely. Yes, but in a way, it's never about who asks really, so to speak. The question just arises in either case. The other thing is that I'm not even really able to describe how it is. There are just words coming out, which is an apparent description, but there's no attempt to show how it is for me, because there literally is "no me." It's still different than a blind person experiencing themselves to be blind and being unable to explain it because of a lack of words or a lack of possibility because a blind person by birth doesn't know colors. But, yeah, kind of.

Justin Allen: The similarity of a person who is blind and is trying to communicate what it's like to be blind to somebody that's not blind is that they're still sharing something: Both have a "me."

Andreas Müller: Yes. Exactly.

Justin Allen: The blind person is explaining what the experience of being blind is to the "me" perspective, and that's how I can relate to and understand it ...

Andreas Müller: Exactly. Yeah. One can say so.

Justin Allen: You're trying to explain, basically, a "no experience" of a "no me" to "somebody" that is a "me" that only is familiar with experiencing?

Andreas Müller: Yes, but because there is "no one," there isn't even a way of a description coming from another standpoint, because in a way, when I describe, apparently, I also include the other one. It's already included. It's not that for you it's like that and for me it's like that and I try to tell you how it is that you can do something with it or that you can understand it or something. In a way, my description, my apparent description, includes the other one because that's also what apparently happens and there also isn't really someone.

Justin Allen: Yeah. Right.

Andreas Müller: That's the dilemma, the apparent dilemma.

Justin Allen: So, back to the sentence, "Oneness seems to see everything – actually it's everything – and yet remains completely blind. It's wonderfully ignorant by not recognizing anything that's not it": It means that I recognize everything that's not "me"? That's how I'm defining myself constantly; by what I'm not, in a sense?

Andreas Müller: Yeah. It's both. Of course, you also define yourself as what you are, or at least, that's the attempt. I mean, in spirituality, they all try to find "themselves" or what "they really are," and the outcome is awareness, but it's just this dual setup in which there is something that one is and something that one isn't that's somehow constantly confirming itself in both ways, so to speak. It all has to do with knowledge, which is based on experiencing, knowing who I am, knowing where I am, knowing when I am, knowing what everything else is, what role it plays, what meaning it has for "me." It's all about knowing, experiencing, positioning and based on division. "Me" is that which recognizes and makes the division. It's the divider and the division. It's the only thing that divides itself from everything else, in the sense that it wants to somehow oversee life.

Justin Allen: I don't know. There's some real value in this. Well, I don't want to say "value," but "it's wonderfully ignorant by not recognizing anything that's not it." So, if you break that apart, what would be an example of recognizing something or anything that's not it?

Andreas Müller: Well, that's the thing. There isn't such a thing.

Justin Allen: That's the thing, so it would be non-recognition, basically?

Andreas Müller: Yes, which is seen by the "me" and the absolute opposite. One could say blindness in that sense is the natural reality. Not recognizing ...

Justin Allen: Blindness as a natural reality just means it's blindness in the sense that there's no awareness, so in that sense, there's really no seeing, because the seeing that we're or I'm familiar with is always a seeing from a point. It's always an overseeing.

Andreas Müller: Yes. Exactly.

Justin Allen: So, if that point vanishes or doesn't exist in the first place, it doesn't necessarily mean that the tables and the chairs and everything like that vanish?

Andreas Müller: No, not at all. Exactly.

Justin Allen: It means the recognition, the separation of me being a point and everything else being no point – this is what vanishes?

Andreas Müller: Yes. So, not the table and the room and feelings and thoughts are the illusion. That's the natural reality. That's what apparently happens. The illusion, so to speak, is the experience and the recognition of it from a separate stand-point (a separate one-point) which turns chairs and the room and the computer and feelings and thoughts and your own body into separate and real things.

Justin Allen: Right, and that's knowledge, and then ignorance would be the absence of that knowledge?

Andreas Müller: So to speak. It is the absence of the experience of it. Knowledge in that sense is already the outcome of experience, or experiencing is knowing, so to speak.

Justin Allen: You also said at some point in our talks that ... What was it?

Andreas Müller: That's why, sorry, I don't want to interrupt your thinking, but that's why I wouldn't say that everything is an illusion. Some people say that. I mean, even in the awareness teachings they would say that: "I'm the only thing that's real, and everything else is an illusion or appearance or something." In a way, chairs and trees and you and the body and feelings – that's just what apparently happens.

That's it, so to speak. It's feeling the unrealness of it, but it's not discarded as, "That's not it." No, no, not at all. It is it. The only illusion, so to speak, the only apparent illusion in the end, is the experience of it. "Me" is the only illusion, nothing else, so to speak.

Justin Allen: That is what you said before: that when that happens in infancy, when somehow the "separation" occurs, that when, in a sense, the seeker and everything "else" is born, everything after that point or everything ... Yeah, that's a good way to put it: Everything after that point that comes into existence is seeking some kind of fulfillment, and this is where you say there's no reason why, there's no explanation for why that happens, for why that point isn't already fulfilled? Wouldn't it be totally unfulfilling to become something (else) when you're not something (else)?

Andreas Müller: Well, that is the apparent unfulfillment of the "person." In a way, it's experiencing, which does not exist, itself and the real world.

Justin Allen: It's missing the natural order. It's missing the reality.

Andreas Müller: Constantly. That's one way of seeing it.

Justin Allen: It's the same as when you have ... That's why people search for their soulmates, or when their partner leaves them, they feel that sense of separation because something disappeared which you felt you identified yourself with as being connected or something.

Andreas Müller: Yes, exactly. Something which was covered before by a sense of "we."

Justin Allen: Right, but you were born already in the natural order. You're born already with an automatic "we-ness" – I mean wholeness or fullness; "fulfilledness" – or with an automatic "no we-ness" with another thing. I just mean "we-ness" as in "oneness" where it's whole and you are everything already.

Andreas Müller: One moment, please, I have to go to my son. I'll be back and say something to that. (Leaves and returns) Okay. I'm sorry. Yes. One could say so. One could say "unseparateness" or non-duality is the natural reality, but there is no sense of "we-ness" or "wholeness." Every separation as in trees appearing as trees and not as tables or human bodies and even every sense of separation, the "me," is already whole, too.

Justin Allen: Right. But I don't mean that. I mean, there's the starting off with "unseparateness," and then as soon as a point is somehow created (as an illusion) that "separates" out of that "unseparateness," it would be logical that you would have to spend your whole life trying to get back to that "unseparateness."

Andreas Müller: Yes.

Justin Allen: The only problem in a way is the way that we do it. I mean, not that there's any other way, but the way that you go about it.

Andreas Müller: Well, the thing is that the only thing how the "me" can process this need for wholeness and this seeking energy is, in a way, that the solution to that need, the solution to the feeling of lack, must be an answer, must be another "experienceable" thing. That's how "me" could process it. "Whatever my fulfillment would look like, whatever the end of that seeking drive would look like, whatever the end of that feeling of lack would look like, it must be something that I can consciously experience."

Justin Allen: Yeah. So, let's say I started off as "unseparateness," and now I've somehow created a point that dislodges itself as an illusion from this "unseparateness."

Andreas Müller: I would say to explain it is almost the same thing like waking up in the morning. Suddenly, there is something there in the morning. That's the apparent birth of self-awareness.

Justin Allen: Right, but nobody knows the mechanism of that, right? So, then you wake up as "separate," and then something doesn't feel right about that, or there's some kind of dissatisfaction or longing or lack or whatever. That's recognized only because of waking up to this separateness?

Andreas Müller: Exactly. Yeah.

Justin Allen: So, then it's already talking to itself in a way because it's already saying, "Something's missing." Then this is what I don't get ... So, even just from that sentence or that feeling or that sense that something is missing, it creates further separation in a sense, or it just keeps on validating its separation or this feeling, or it keeps on having to try experimenting basically?

Andreas Müller: Yes. Exactly. "What could make me happy? What could give me ... What could end that ... What could satisfy that need?" Yup.

Justin Allen: Even not that ... It's like when you watch those nature shows or animals outside: There's no explanation really why an insect flies to honey and then goes back to the queen bee or something like that. They're just naturally doing what they're ... And these are still only our explanations. Same with science, which says that from an evolutionary perspective, every single thing you do is just to procreate in some sense. So, the nature of separateness also is to try to be non-separate?

Andreas Müller: I wouldn't say so. Yes and no. One could see it like that, but the experience of separateness or the separate thing, or in the story: the hope, is to rather survive and find fulfillment.

Justin Allen: Right, but even though you might project it on a job or a house or a lifestyle, ultimately the fulfillment is trying to get back to "unseparateness"?

Andreas Müller: Yes and no, because there is "no one" in "unseparateness." So, it's actually not really what the "person" wants. I know how you mean it though.

Justin Allen: Except that it will never be fulfilled unless it doesn't exist anymore in a sense?

Andreas Müller: Yes, but then also, it will not be fulfilled.

Justin Allen: Right, because there's nothing there to have fulfillment.

Andreas Müller: Exactly. Of course, one could say that the natural reality is fulfilled, but that's not something that works for the "me." It's not really comforting to "me." You can't really say to the "me," "Yes. Afterwards, there will be fulfillment anyway," but absence is not really what "me" wants, so to speak.

Justin Allen: Right, but it is the only ending of the seeking?

Andreas Müller: Yes. Exactly.

Justin Allen: So, to repeat the sentence from your book again, "... and yet remains completely blind, it's wonderfully ignorant by not recognizing anything that's not it – even the illusion of being a person." So, here, you're just saying even the illusion of being a person isn't "it"?

Andreas Müller: No, the illusion of a "person" isn't recognized as something that's separately happening.

Justin Allen: Right, but that is actually the only illusion?

Andreas Müller: Yes, but it's an apparent illusion because there isn't anything which experiences the illusion of being "me" to be something that's really happening. It's only again the "me," which experiences itself to be, but exactly that self-experience is an illusion.

Justin Allen: Right. So, the separation doesn't actually exist. There's only "unseparation" or wholeness or oneness or whatever. The separation is the illusion because it doesn't exist?

Andreas Müller: Yes, so to speak.

Justin Allen: So, then the final sentence is, "Oneness doesn't recognize 'me' as such. 'It' just is it."

Andreas Müller: Yes.

Justin Allen: So, that's just saying that all there is, is "unseparateness." All there is, is wholeness or oneness or no-thing-ness or non-duality, however you want to put it, but also the illusion of separateness is wholeness?

Andreas Müller: Yes. Exactly.

Justin Allen: So, that's basically something that you're saying over and over in different ways?

Andreas Müller: Yes.

Justin Allen: That's the thing that's not really manageable to comprehend.

Andreas Müller: No, which is also perfectly whole.

Justin Allen: Right. And that's what you mean with this sentence from the book, "Oneness doesn't recognize 'me' as such. 'It' just is it."

Andreas Müller: Yes, but it's also in a way ... In the story one can say that it's also "me" not being able to recognize that it is whole and complete.

Justin Allen: Right, because everything is whole and complete.

Andreas Müller: Yes, for "no one."

Justin Allen: Right, but for "no one" is the same as ... You can also say, "but for someone"?

Andreas Müller: No, that's how the "me" would hear it, like there being a person running around with a sense of having found completion. Actually, it's blindly whole and complete. "For 'no one'" is another word for "blindly."

Justin Allen: Right, but "no one," in this context, is equal to "someone" because they're both equally oneness.

Andreas Müller: Yeah. Okay. I know what you mean. Yes.

Justin Allen: I mean, that's the complication of semantics, in a way.

Andreas Müller: Yeah, but in a way, there is never a real someone.

Justin Allen: Exactly, but still "someone" is also just what is.

Andreas Müller: Yes, which is also whole and complete for "no one."

Justin Allen: Exactly.

Andreas Müller: Yeah. Oh, absolutely.

Justin Allen: So, then on page 22, you give an answer to a question. You say, "Oh, yes. There's nothing to get. The whole setup of experiencing doesn't exist. The first element of it – you – seeking in the second element – what you experience – is a dream reality. All results of that seeking are part of that dreamt reality as well. There is no fulfillment in there." So, the whole setup of experiencing doesn't exist. At the same time, it does exist (laughing).

Andreas Müller: No.

Justin Allen: The illusion of it exists, though.

Andreas Müller: Yes. One could say so. But well, even that ... (laughing) The illusion of it is what apparently happens: that you might assume that you experience a real world is what apparently happens if that is what apparently happens.

Justin Allen: Yeah, but the definition or the logic of an illusion means that illusions don't exist.

Andreas Müller: Yeah. That's the thing. When I mean it's an illusion, the "me" turns exactly this into another thing that's real. "Me" isn't real, but the illusion is real. That's not completely how it is meant, because when I say "me" is an illusion, it's rather saying that there is neither a "me" nor an illusion, so to speak. This is not really logical.

Justin Allen: Yeah. I just wonder if there's another way ... If we take the personal experience: The "person" feels like they're conscious, and if they listen to the personal teachings of the spiritual teachers, they feel like they're moving out of the illusion because the teachings are constantly pointing out that you are the awareness. The way that they do it is, again, by saying that you're not your thoughts and not your feelings and not your senses, right?

That's something that a "person" can relate to and understand because it's their experience. But before they even understand that they're supposedly awareness in general, it seems like most people are going around in the world thinking that they are their thoughts and their feelings.

Andreas Müller: That's true. They think they are their story, at least.

Justin Allen: That's one difference between the kind of conclusion of spirituality and what the normal day-to-day life is for the "person."

Andreas Müller: Yes. Absolutely.

Justin Allen: Within that "person" and that experience, they can see, "Oh, yeah. I'm not my thoughts, and I'm not my feelings. I'm this thing that's aware of those thoughts and feelings."

Andreas Müller: Which is an illusion.

Justin Allen: It's also that all this is doing is replacing one illusion with a more subtle illusion.

Andreas Müller: It's not even really more subtle. It just feels like that. I would say it's equally strong ... So, for me, it's the exact same thing.

Justin Allen: Right. I'm just saying from that personal experience where you have that aha moment when you go, "Ah! Oh my! My whole fucking life I've been thinking I'm my thoughts and my feelings and my story, and I'm not. I'm actually this awareness!" Maybe it doesn't feel more subtle, but more sophisticated.

Andreas Müller: Yes. For some people, this is such a big impact that they think that this is enlightenment. "This is so overwhelming and breathtaking that I'm not my story. It feels so different and enlightening!"

Justin Allen: Right, and they get to experience it still.

Andreas Müller: Yes, for a while.

Justin Allen: That whole setup of experiencing just doesn't exist. That's like if you just read that sentence and then put it into the context we just talked about, I might go, "Ah, I know what Andreas is talking about now because me, too, I used to experience myself as my thoughts and my feelings and my sensations, and now I don't. That's what he's talking about. That whole setup of experiencing doesn't exist. That's true." They're saying it, though, from still being the awareness that gets to experience that they're not their thoughts and feelings and sensations anymore.

Andreas Müller: Yeah.

Justin Allen: So, but here, when you say that the whole setup of experiencing doesn't exist, this is talking about consciousness and the whole structure of experience?

Andreas Müller: Exactly. Yes, yes, yes, yes.

Justin Allen: Then "you" become the first element of it; the "you" gets created when you transition, in a sense, from "unseparateness" to separateness and are then seeking in the second element. So, that means once you've separated from "unseparateness," then the second stage or the thing that you're stuck doing for your whole life is searching: You are seeking, and then what you experience is a dream reality. So, as soon as you're separate from "unseparateness," then everything is a dream reality?

Andreas Müller: Yes, because that separation already, that first separateness, so to speak ...

Justin Allen: Is the dream?

Andreas Müller: Is an illusion already, an apparent illusion. The rest comes out of it, so to speak (laughing).

Justin Allen: Then you write, "All results of that seeking are part of that dreamt reality as well."

Andreas Müller: Exactly.

Justin Allen: There is no fulfillment in there?

Andreas Müller: Exactly. No fulfillment in money, no fulfillment in noticing that one isn't the thoughts, no fulfillment in recognizing oneself as, "Oh, actually, I'm awareness," no fulfillment in living with a partner – whatever.

Justin Allen: No fulfillment, period, because it's all the seeking dream?

Andreas Müller: Yes. It's all within a dream, and it seems to be that the mere cause of unfulfillment is self-experience. So, whatever you experience, so to speak, the actual cause, which is separation in the first place, is never removed.

Justin Allen: Yeah. Exactly. So, that's the trap. That's the no-way-out scenario?

Andreas Müller: So to speak, yes. "Me" can't be anything else than "me." That's what "me" defines to be "me": to experience something as present. There's something, which experiences itself as present.

Justin Allen: So then, after you said, "There is no fulfillment in there," a questioner, quite understandably, asks, "But where can I find fulfillment then?"

Andreas Müller: Yeah. Where is it then?

Justin Allen: Yeah. Then you have to repeat: "Nowhere. You can't find fulfillment. In fact, there is no such thing as fulfillment. What you're actually seeking is an experience of fulfillment."

Andreas Müller: Yes. One could say that the "person" doesn't really care about fulfillment. It's not interested in fulfillment. All it's interested in is seeing it. It's not interested in what fulfillment actually is, so to speak. It's interested in, "Yeah, I don't care, but I am whatever it is. I have to fucking see, which means experience, it."

Justin Allen: Yeah. It has to experience it.

Andreas Müller: Exactly. Yeah.

Justin Allen: So, what you're seeking is an awareness of fulfillment, and exactly that doesn't exist?

Andreas Müller: Yes.

Justin Allen: Like you say in the book, "The apparent me believes that liberation is replacing the experience of unfulfillment and seeking with an experience of fulfillment and having found."

Andreas Müller: Yes.

Justin Allen: "It thinks that the experience of presence is replaced by an experience of absence."

Andreas Müller: Which would still be an experience of presence.

Justin Allen: Right. So, the fine distinction here is to say that the experience is the illusion which, in a sense, doesn't exist. You can't experience presence, and you can't experience absence, because there's "no one" there; there's no "me" there to experience anything?

Andreas Müller: Yes. Exactly. In a way, that's the illusion. Experience actually means the same as presence, but exactly, that's the illusion. The experience of absence is absurd. It's a contradiction because experiencing already means that there is something present.

Justin Allen: Right. It's the same as that everybody can kind of understand in a sense that you can't experience physical death. At least, logically, you can say, that you can't experience physical death, because if you accept that death is the end, then there's nothing there afterwards to know what happened, right?

Andreas Müller: Yes.

Justin Allen: If there were something afterwards that goes, "I just died," then you wouldn't really be dead.

Andreas Müller: Yes. Exactly.

Justin Allen: Same with birth. There's no birth in the sense that for there to actually be a birth, there would have been a "before," which means that you were already something, and then all of a sudden, you're born and go, "Ah, before I was that, and now I'm this."

Andreas Müller: Yes, but now, if you really want to know, if you really start thinking about how it actually feels, how it actually is then, you realize that it's just impossible. You can't go there. It's impossible to go there.

Justin Allen: So, then in the book it goes on, "However, in liberation the whole setup of experience turns out to be non-existent." So, that's what we just said. And the sentence continues with, "but it doesn't get replaced by anything." That, of course, from the "me" perspective, is torture. It doesn't want to hear that. It's the same as why we avoid death because out of the fear of physical death, we created heaven, myths or whatever.

Andreas Müller: Yes, and the next life and stuff like that. Of course, that's what I mean when I say that what separateness actually seeks is to become unseparate again. Then I say, "Yeah, one can see it that way," but actually, if it comes to what that would mean, it's torture, it's death, it's the last thing it wants. It's the most unattractive scenario. "Why on earth should I want that? Why my whole life have I been working towards this conscious event of becoming fulfilled or hoping for the point when my whole seeking served its purpose and I've actually arrived there? Why on earth should I want to become absent before that happens?"

Justin Allen: Right, but as far as the story goes, that "unseparateness" is the reality?

Andreas Müller: Yes, anyway.

Justin Allen: It is the reality anyway, and then the illusion is separateness. It's almost like separateness is like an organism or a fake life that's been created that also wants to survive, the same way as if you had cancer or some illness or bacteria or whatever; it would want to survive also. It wouldn't want to die.

Andreas Müller: Yes and no. Well, one could see it like that, but in a way, cancer is just what naturally happens, without there being an agenda. The cancer doesn't have an agenda like, "I have to survive in order to become fulfilled cancer."

Justin Allen: No, but I mean that the nature of cancer is to survive, the same way as the human body wants to survive.

Andreas Müller: Yes. Absolutely.

Justin Allen: So, they're in a battle against each other: The human body wants to live, and cancer also wants to live. I feel like I'm just putting this in a story in the sense that "unseparateness" is the reality, but separateness is the illusion that comes in and has its own will to survive.

Andreas Müller: Apparently. Yes. One could say so. It is what it is. That, too, is what it is, and apparently, it does what it does. Yes.

Justin Allen: I even think that the illusion somehow recognizes that it is an illusion and that there is a reality of "unseparateness," and in order to sustain that illusion, the actions have to be the seeking, and it has to be constantly verifying itself through experience and presence and existence. Somehow it knows that if it stops doing that or if it sees through the veil or whatever, it could disappear.

Andreas Müller: Yes. I know what you mean. But the illusion doesn't recognize that it's an illusion; that's impossible. The illusion might disappear, which might then apparently reinforce it, so it starts to fight.

Justin Allen: That's what feels like the fear all the time or ...

Andreas Müller: Yes.

Justin Allen: I mean, that's the fear even when you meditate where it might feel like you don't exist, and then you go, "Oh," and then somehow you use a defibrillator and bring yourself back (laughing).

Andreas Müller: Yes, yes, as fast as possible. Absolutely. I once had a talk were just two ladies came. It was in a small spiritual center, and they had spent the whole day there. I was the last event in the evening to happen, so to speak. I was literally the bouncer (laughing). I think before my talk there was something with holy colors or the energy of colors, and they just stayed. I started and then noticed that they became more and more uncomfortable. So, after twenty minutes, we made a break already. They were both saying to me that they wanted to go. We talked a bit, it was nice. Then they said, "Oh, sorry. This scares us really. We want to end that and go home now."

In a way, it was immediately recognized what it was about. That is just what happens, but they were totally honest about that. They said, "Whoa! That's too scary for us. We don't want to hear that. We don't want to be there." So, they had never been to such a meeting, and they were never reading Ramana or stuff like that. They didn't know anything of it, but in a way, they caught it immediately. Right after five minutes, it was in the air, so to speak. "Oh, fuck! It's about life and death here!"

Justin Allen: Yeah. It is. That's the fear (laughing).

Andreas Müller: That's the fear, yes (laughing).

Justin Allen: So, then you go on to say, "What's left is naturally whole and full." So, "what's left" means when the illusion vanishes, when awareness vanishes, when presence vanishes, "what's left is naturally whole and full, yet, there is no experience of being it"?

So, this is, as far as I can tell, the most critical point of the message or one of the most critical points: this "no experiencing of it." Because even I am recognizing that you can't talk about this without there being a replacement, without there being some substitute that comes in, because you just can't comprehend "nothing." You can't comprehend there not being awareness. Same way you can't really comprehend or talk about physical death. It's impossible.

Andreas Müller: Yes, same way. Oh, yes. Seen by the "me," liberation is the same as this. It looks like the same thing.

Justin Allen: So, then you go, "Of course, seen from the perspective of the apparent me, this can't be comprehended," which we just said. "All the 'me' knows – and all it exists in – is to experience, and all it has been working on for its whole life is that replacement." So, that's what we just said, too. "Yet, nothing has to be seen. Nothing has to be replaced and nothing has to be experienced. This 'I have to find it' is an illusion meaning that it just isn't true. Nothing can and has to be found."

Andreas Müller: Yes.

Justin Allen: But, you can't stop trying to find it (laughing).

Andreas Müller: Yes, yes, yes. I know. It's a bit of useless information in the end because you can't do differently. The "me" in its experience is so convinced that it has to find something or that the solution lies in finding something, and all the effort, of course, goes into that.

In a funny way, even that need is an illusion. In a way, "me" can understand to some degree that it will never find, and that it's all useless, but it still is left with that fucking need that seems to be so real. In a way, the most revolutionary part of that message is, "Yeah, of course, you can't find, but who cares?" Because there's nothing that's needed.

Justin Allen: Yeah, but what does that mean, "There's nothing that's needed"?

Andreas Müller: The dilemma is that the "person" might end up with a Buddhism saying, "Oh, you should learn to not want anything." That's the bad thing about that.

Justin Allen: What does that mean? "Nothing is needed," just means that everything is as it is, everything is fine and full and whole as it is?

Andreas Müller: Yeah. "Nothing is needed," refers to the illusion of unfulfillment. You trying to find something is already wholeness, even if it feels unpleasant and not whole at all.

Justin Allen: Yeah. Then the problem is that you're saying it as if you were speaking to the "no me," but to the "me" that hears it, it doesn't do anything.

Andreas Müller: Oh, it's useless information, but for the "me," this whole message is useless information.

Justin Allen: Right. Other than my theory that by hearing this information that is confirming over and over and over and over again that there's no "me" and that it's an illusion, the illusion could be killed?

Andreas Müller: Yes. That can be ...

Justin Allen: Tony Parsons calls himself the killer or something like that.

Andreas Müller: No, I think it's not him; he's been called like that (laughing). But, yes, that's what apparently happens. Again, not because the "me" grasps the concept. It wouldn't still be because of the understanding of the concept, so to speak.

Justin Allen: Right, but that is in a sense the goal of the techniques and the trainings and the ideas behind all spirituality. It's as if somebody gave you the task to dig a hole and then fill it up again, and then dig another hole and fill it up again. Maybe you'd lose the "me" then because you'd see the pointlessness of that exercise or of life in general. Same with a Koan where a question is asked which can't be answered loud and clear. There's no logical answer, and through that, it fucks up your normal trance or whatever, right? That is the theory behind all these games in a sense.

Andreas Müller: Oh, no, of course not. I mean, yeah, that's the theory behind it, but that's why they all end up in awareness, even the Koan stuff. One could say this message is a natural Koan, which means that it is neither an exercise nor a message.

Justin Allen: Right.

Andreas Müller: It's not given in order to create or bring something about.

Justin Allen: Yeah. I mean, even talking about death would be a natural Koan because there's no ... I mean, anything where there's no answer (laughing). So, then another question in the book is, "What's the 'me' actually?" and then you say, "There is no answer to that question, simply because there is no 'me' around. So, we would be talking about an illusion. There is no 'me,' no soul, no presence, no self-awareness and no self-consciousness. Isn't that interesting?" And the questioner goes, "But why do so many teachers, religions and traditions emphasize that consciousness so much?" And you answer, "Oh, just because these are personal teachings. All the person does is to uplift its existence. All the 'me' has is its existence – that's what it consists of. And exactly that existence has to be pumped up artificially with meaning and greatness in order to make it worthy. All the 'me' knows is 'me,' so 'me' must be God. What an arrogance. An apparent arrogance, of course."

So, here, I just wanted to say, "All the person does is to uplift its existence." This critique doesn't matter other than it's not that it uplifts its existence, it's that it has to confirm its existence, I would say.

Andreas Müller: Yeah, but I have the impression that in many religions and traditions, it's already a method because suddenly, you don't end up with, "I'm consciousness because consciousness is all there is." Usually, you end up with, "I'm consciousness, and that's God, that's divine, that's what we really are, that's all the soul, the soul is pure et cetera." And that's already a method because it actually senses lack, but it has to uplift itself to being the crown of evolution and all that stuff. It has to give itself meaning and importance and holiness. Man is above everything else because of self-consciousness. That's what I meant.

Justin Allen: Don't you think that a sentence like, "Just be yourself, man," that has gotten so much power and significance in the last twenty or thirty years has a certain value, so to speak? I mean, it's being used in marketing and in

Hollywood, but still ... It's because people are upset or dissatisfied now with religion and this promise of uplifting and this striving and trying to behave, and there's a resistance against this now. It sounds like such a much more relieving message when somebody goes, "Just be yourself." Even though that's not really understood, and who knows who started saying that, but ...

Andreas Müller: If you try to be yourself, it can become as weird as a religion (laughing). But yes, seen by the "me," it seems to have a certain value when you give yourself permission to be more authentic, so to speak.

Justin Allen: Right. That's the new dilemma, and it's the same with mindfulness. Meditation and mindfulness are trending now in the Western world more and more, but it's just part of the same run. It's like the workout routine now of self-betterment, but still even this message is also saying that in a sense, right? Fundamentally, it is saying, "Just be yourself," but what yourself is isn't actually a self?

Andreas Müller: Yes. Well, one could say, "Be yourself," but even that is nothing that you can or have to do, because it's already what happens. There is no way of not being yourself, however this might look like.

Justin Allen: Then just to come back to this point, even though we've talked about it before: "There is no answer to that question" – of what the 'me' actually is –, "simply because there is no 'me' around." So, we would be talking about an illusion. So, that's all that you can talk about (laughing)?

Andreas Müller: One could say so, yeah.

Justin Allen: Yeah, because whatever you're talking about in this context, or not only in this context but anything you talk about, is an illusion, right?

Andreas Müller: It's a story. It's at least not something that's real. Yes.

Justin Allen: But even for you, even if you don't have a "me," isn't it like there has to be a "me" for you to be able to talk?

Andreas Müller: No.

Justin Allen: Yeah. I don't mean like ...

Andreas Müller: No. No. It's just functioning. Thoughts, speaking, understanding, ... That's what apparently happens.

Justin Allen: So, even for me ... If we made a distinction between you and me, the only distinction would be that there's no illusion of a "me" on your side and for me, there is the illusion of "me"?

Andreas Müller: So to speak, yes.

Justin Allen: So, anything that I say, think, feel or experience I think that I'm experiencing it and you don't, but the reality is that I also don't?

Andreas Müller: Exactly. Yes, of course.

Justin Allen: So, I just mean everything that I'm talking about and you're talking about to me at least is an illusion inasmuch as we're both talking about an illusion.

Andreas Müller: We are both talking about things which aren't things, yeah. There's just talking happening, apparently, and it's whole and complete and empty. And there's an apparent referring to circumstances which don't exist as such. It's just wholeness. The conversation is just itself. It's whole and complete and empty and for nothing, yes (laughing). Which isn't bad; it's just how it is.

Justin Allen: Yeah, but it would be bad or good seen by the "me"?

Andreas Müller: Then it looks good or bad or useful or useless or whatever. But then still, it wouldn't really "be" good or bad or useful or useless. It would still be whole and empty and for no one, and it would still be whatever it appears to be. That's what I mean. And it includes you as well. It's not my perspective, so to speak. It already is like that, also on your side. But yes, there may be the idea running that it's bad for you because you thought it's about something particular, something pleasant or uplifting or whatever. But this is empty and whole and doesn't disturb anyone, nor is it right or wrong or whatever. It, too, is exactly that, empty and whole, and complete already with no gain for anyone, but no one loses in there either. That's the thing. It's nothing that is being seen by me or some other people only; it's not my way of viewing things. No; it's the same for you in a way. Wholeness appears as you, exactly as you are.

Justin Allen: Yeah. I was talking to a friend about this a little bit. Before I start talking to people about this, I usually say, "Well, let's not talk about this, because it's a rabbit hole." You know that saying of a rabbit hole?

Andreas Müller: Yeah.

Justin Allen: Then they might push me, and then I start hearing myself say what you say, "Yeah, but there's no one there." So, I end up saying these sentences that I hear you say. Then I can see the other person trying to wrestle with that. They come up just like how I would, with another way of trying to be, like, "How can that be? If there's no one ..." You see how impossible it is when you reverse the roles? Even if I'm trying to paraphrase what you say to another person that hasn't heard this message or never even has been involved in spirituality or something like that, you just see how incomprehensible it is.

Andreas Müller: Yeah. Absolutely.

Justin Allen: The last thing that I have here is you saying, "All 'me' knows is presence." All "me" knows is illusion?

Andreas Müller: Yes. All "me" knows is itself. All "me" knows is presence. All "me" knows is the dream because it is the dream.

Justin Allen: I also like to say that all "me" knows is awareness, just because "awareness" is such a buzz word.

Andreas Müller: Yes, awareness is presence, but there's something which is there which is aware of its presence, at least. It doesn't need to process something. It doesn't need to have thoughts and all that stuff, but there's a sense of presence which is aware of its presence, so to speak. It's in a way almost the total opposite of what "me" thinks what awareness is: like floating above everything and how beautiful and sublime and holy this is; all that uplifting stuff (laughing).

Justin Allen: Yeah, because the message is, if we change the wording around a little bit, that all "me" knows is awareness, or all "me" is, is awareness.

Andreas Müller: Exactly. Yes.

Justin Allen: All awareness is an illusion, meaning the sense of being a "me" or the sense of being presence or the sense of being awareness is the illusion?

Andreas Müller: Yes. Exactly.

Justin Allen: That's new as far as I know of. I've never heard that said before.

Andreas Müller: Yeah. It's an absolutely rare message.

Justin Allen: All "me" knows is "me," right?

Andreas Müller: Yeah.

Justin Allen: So, all that it could know is the illusion?

Andreas Müller: Yeah, while it thinks that that's the real thing.

Justin Allen: Yeah. So, by personal investigation, all I can do is to find out that all there is, is consciousness or awareness, but this finding is an illusion, although it can't really understand it as an illusion as such?

Andreas Müller: Yeah. Exactly. Every inquiry will end with itself. "Me" inquiring into what's real, into how it is actually – with the best intentions, of course –, will end up with itself. "Well, all I can really say is that I am. All I can really say is that there's awareness. That's all I can know; that everything else is unreal." That's the conclusion out of that.

Justin Allen: Right. So, all it can do is to find out that all there is, is consciousness, which means nothing else other than, "All there is, is 'me.'"

Andreas Müller: Exactly. Yeah.

Justin Allen: And you're saying also that this is what spirituality is all about, where ultimately you come to that conclusion. "All there is, is 'me,' so therefore, I'm God, or therefore, I'm everything."

Andreas Müller: Exactly. "Therefore, I'm the only thing that's real. I'm the only instance. I'm the absolute."

Justin Allen: It's still very similar in a way to what you're saying in the sense of where we started off in the very beginning. I'm aware that it is very different also, but subtly different.

Andreas Müller: One could say that this – "I am God, I am everything" – is a oneness teaching and what I speak about is a noneness teaching. If you want to use the word "teaching," but of course, it's not a teaching. In the oneness teaching, there is one thing left. Actually, it's still two things left, but one of those two things is considered to be "the real thing": the awareness or the subject that is aware of the objects.

Justin Allen: You say, "Oneness seems to see everything – actually it's everything – and yet remains completely blind." So, there is no "me"? "All 'me' knows is 'me,' so, by personal investigation, all it can do is to find out than all there is, is consciousness, which means nothing else than, 'All there is, is "me."'" By that it means, "I'm God," or, "I am everything," which is what the oneness message is also saying in the sense of, "All there is, is everything and what is." But the difference to your noneness message is that it is for no one. There is no one there to experience or to be oneness or everything or God?

Andreas Müller: Exactly. And the illusion is that if you manage to be convinced of being that, if you are able to be present or constantly experience yourself as that, then you are free. That's when the method comes in and all the work to consciously keep up that state.

Justin Allen: That's where you say it's absolutely amazing how "me" turns this message into an utterly personal message?

Andreas Müller: Absolutely. I mean, in a way, it's all it can do, but it's amazing.

Justin Allen: Right, and you say, "'I'm here now' is the dream. 'I'm conscious of being here now' is illusory. That which experiences itself as present can't know its absence. There is no true self to be known. There isn't something that is here. That's why I say that liberation is death. It's not something that happens to someone. It's the sudden and final death of the illusion of being someone. Nothing is left. Everything is left. It's free and it's total."

Andreas Müller: Yeah.

Justin Allen: So, I think it is similar, but the huge difference is it really is the death of experience. The death of an experience or the death of the "me," the death of a point, the death of awareness, right?

Andreas Müller: Yeah. My impression, which is a bit superficial now, is that the awareness teachers try to squeeze that message into an awareness teaching. They think around that and draw conclusions. When you look at it closely, there is a lot of experience, but there's always some mental "conclusioning" going on, some mental processing of it to make it right, to make it fit. They come up with the same sentences that I'm saying, but you see that at one point they use a trick, so to speak. They make one logical conclusion, which isn't experience anymore.

Sorry, we have to end soon. So, they try to squeeze it in those sentences, one of which is, "It's all whole, and it's everything," and I don't know what the other sentences are right now, but there are some more. Anyway, it's something completely different, but it sounds so similar.

Justin Allen: Yeah. I feel you. Go ahead.

Andreas Müller: If you look at it closely – not that one could or had to –, you see that it's coming from a completely different angle, and at one point you notice where the concept comes in, which still looks logical because it's thinkable, but at one point, it's not the actual experience anymore of oneness and all that stuff. It's interesting.

Justin Allen: Yeah. I mean, I find that in myself, too, it's the same as whenever ... Let's just pretend that there is some kind of coming close to the precipice of dying, and you don't want to die. So, you change the story to still keep yourself alive (laughing).

Andreas Müller: Well, I would say it is being done with best intentions. I mean, they really want to do it. It's a sincere attempt. So, the question is, how could that fit my experience? What could that mean?

Justin Allen: Right, to still somehow stay alive, though.

Andreas Müller: Exactly, because everything else, again, isn't logical or "processable." It's absurd to not stay alive, of course.

Justin Allen: Because they also speak of death. It's like a death or a death of "me," even with these teachings where they say that you or the self needs to die, right? The little self or the ego needs to die in order to meld with the higher or real self – which, of course, means that the awareness survives. That's what I think is disappointing or still unsatisfying about these teachings: You sense that they're really bringing you close to the precipice, for sure. I think they're bringing you close to the death of the "me," but then there's a gymnastics move which tells a whole different story and puts the "me" in a whole different context from what it's familiar with, but it's still there.

Andreas Müller: Exactly, because in the end, the whole idea is that you are not your personal story, which, of course, can be very energetic and quite a game changer, but this pretty quickly turns into something like, "I shouldn't be angry. I shouldn't be jealous, I shouldn't have desires, I should be more open and more loving," et cetera. In the end, it turns out actually, "I shouldn't be my personality." And it's almost or actually totally like a religion where you should do certain things and shouldn't do others.

So, whenever there is some personality thing going on, it's seen as wrong. You should come back to you actually being "pure awareness." It's so much based on separation, but I know what you mean. It seems to be close to the "death thing" because so many ideas about you get challenged, about the personality and if you really are that and how real the world is. But in the same breath, it's confirming separation as much as any other experience and turns all your personality things into something that's wrong or inferior.

Justin Allen: Yeah. Although some of them don't turn your personality things into something wrong.

Andreas Müller: Yeah, I think conceptually, they don't. But the actual experience is always a dance between getting lost in the personality and in the story and the need to come back to "pure awareness." So, in the actual experience, that's my assumption, and it's a story now, but the actual experience again becomes a struggle against something.

Justin Allen: Right. But that's why I think it's satisfying at least for the person that is religious or spiritual or soul-searching or whatever because, if there are levels or hierarchies, it is getting closer to the death of the "me," but it's still letting you live, it's still letting the "me" exist. That's why I think it's more and more attractive because it's still not a real death.

Andreas Müller: Oh, yes, of course, I know what you mean. But for most people, the turn out is that "me" gets just as confirmed as in any other setup.

Justin Allen: Right, but there's this trick where the "me" seems to not be there. Same as I said, if you have that awakening moment where you go, "Ah! I'm not my thoughts, I'm not my feelings, I'm not my sensations. I thought my whole life that I was this guy with this life, and I'm not that."

Andreas Müller: Yes.

Justin Allen: "I died. Now, I can take on a new name. I can change my name and start my life as this other person."

Andreas Müller: Yeah. That's it. Exactly. It is seen like that. That could be the story. "Oh, my ego has died. I died. I'm not the person anymore. I'm pure awareness."

Justin Allen: Exactly. Well, I have to go, too (laughing).

Andreas Müller: Yeah, all right. By that – becoming another person who feels separate from everyone else, who is special, who is now ahead of all those unconscious agents out there and all that stuff –, the oneness message turns into the same "me" stuff again.

Justin Allen: Okay.

Andreas Müller: Yeah. Okay.

Justin Allen: Thank you. Do we talk on Monday again?

Andreas Müller: That won't work, because I'm traveling now in the US, and on that Monday, I'll be flying. So, maybe we have to have a break for a week.

Justin Allen: All right.

Andreas Müller: Thanks for talking.

Justin Allen: Thank you also.

Andreas Müller: Yeah. Bye.

Justin Allen: Bye-bye.

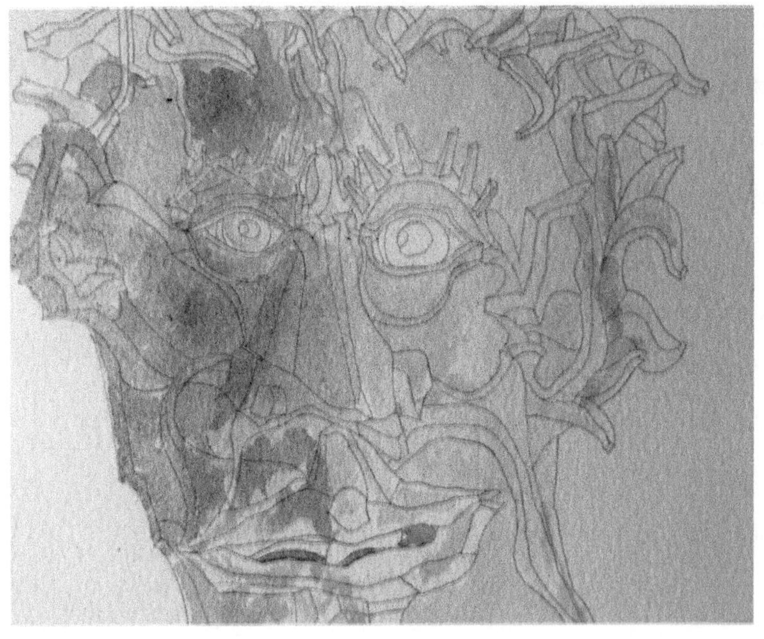

December 9, 2019 Talk 06

ROMEO

Justin Allen: So, I went to the Tony Parsons weekend in Munich.

Andreas Müller: Yeah.

Justin Allen: You were there on Saturday?

Andreas Müller: Yes.

Justin Allen: I was there on all the three days. Friday was the most verbal action.

Andreas Müller: All right (laughing).

Justin Allen: Sunday, it was dead (laughing). It was like eighty people sitting in a retirement home auditorium, not talking (laughing).

Andreas Müller: Yeah.

Justin Allen: So, there are some things that I wanted to ask when I was there but didn't, because I thought it would be better to ask you since we have the potential to spend more time talking about things. Tony gave this example on Saturday that was something about how he would get out of his chair and would say, "You can't imagine or you can't comprehend or understand what it's like to be walking down the street one day, and you're looking at the road. And you're there, you feel you're there, and there's the road, and then all of a sudden, there's just road."

Andreas Müller: Yeah.

Justin Allen: So, it's like there's "the road," and then there's "just road." And what I think he meant by that is that when you're walking, and there's the road, that means that there's you and the road, which means there's separation?

Andreas Müller: Exactly.

Justin Allen: And then, when there's "just road," he's saying that there is no separation?

Andreas Müller: In the end, yeah.

Justin Allen: Right. And that's like "just road" happening, "just walking" happening? Because there's no separation, it's everything all at once?

Andreas Müller: Yeah.

Justin Allen: So, that's somehow how he was trying to give that sense or that energetic feeling of the apparent difference of there being separation or no separation?

Andreas Müller: Yeah.

Justin Allen: And so, then I thought I'm going to read what I've written as a question for Tony for you. I might have to change it around a bit. I said, "Could one also equate your example of the road with sleeping? Every night there is apparently sleep happening, but there is "no one" there that experiences sleep, or at least it seems that way. You can't even say that sleep happened or that sleep is happening. It's clear that sleep seems to happen, but it's not known in the same way that eating happens, because when I eat food, I experience that. There is knowing of what I'm doing."

Andreas Müller: Yes.

Justin Allen: And the question goes on, "So, could one equate there just being apparent road without a knower of the road with sleep apparently happening? So, there is apparent sleep happening, but no sleeper?"

Andreas Müller: Oh, yes, absolutely.

Justin Allen: Go on.

Andreas Müller: Yeah, one could say that ... But you say first.

Justin Allen: So, I'm just curious. For example, there is the Big Bang theory in science, where they say that life started with this incident. But nobody knows what happened before the Big Bang or how there's no explanation for that (laughing). And that just made me think about some of our previous talks where somehow we got on a thread of thought about sleep and about how you wake up every morning and you're there. And that's the separation that's kind of happening every morning as long as the "me" is there. And maybe we could say that's like a moment of the Big Bang because every morning you wake up and you're like, "Ah, I'm here." And you don't know where you were before. You put a story together about where you were before and everything that's happened to you before, but you don't really know.

Andreas Müller: Yes, exactly.

Justin Allen: Right. And back to this example of walking down the street one day, and then all of a sudden the "me" collapses or drops away or disappears: Then somehow you're not there anymore experiencing anything. But everything's still happening regardless?

Andreas Müller: Yes and no. Apparently.

Justin Allen: So, that's what every single person goes through every time they fall asleep in a sense?

Andreas Müller: Yes, absolutely. One could say so. It's still a story, and I'm lacking a word here now, but what happens in deep sleep is, in a way, what happens in liberation; it's the absence of an experiencer. Deep sleep is not liberation, but this aspect is something that's similar because in deep sleep there is no experience of something. There is no experience of anything. So, one could describe liberation as being in deep sleep during the day.

Justin Allen: Yeah, or awake during deep sleep somehow.

Andreas Müller: Exactly, but not as a state of awakeness. And this is something that the "me," so to speak, cannot comprehend at all?

Justin Allen: Right. It can't comprehend it, but it happens "to it" – although in this message "it" or "me" is not there – every single night when "you" fall asleep?

Andreas Müller: So to speak. Yes.

Justin Allen: So, it still is something that, in a sense, every body or everybody goes through: The "me" in a sense is dropping or collapsing every time somebody falls asleep?

Andreas Müller: Yes, one could say so. But of course, one could say that the whole concept of there being something like deep sleep again is only processed afterwards when there is "someone" awake again. But yes, one could say so. But the other thing is that it's not really the "me" that goes through deep sleep, there just is no "me."

Justin Allen: There's no "me" for me right now, but I still think that there is. But when I'm sleeping, I don't think that there's a "me," the same way that you don't think that there's a "me" or that there's "no me" happening for everybody?

Andreas Müller: Yeah. I'm just saying it's not something that happens to someone in the end.

Justin Allen: Right. And the same with when you become liberated?

Andreas Müller: Yeah, totally.

Justin Allen: Same. Nothing's happening in that case, either?

Andreas Müller: Yeah, of course. Absolutely.

Justin Allen: So, I feel there's something really dynamic or interesting about that statement because for sure it's the closest thing that the "me" can kind of get its head around.

Andreas Müller: Yes, I understand. It can get its head around the concept of it. But still, how it actually is can't be comprehended at all.

Justin Allen: But it's like physical death: The same way that you can't comprehend physical death you can't comprehend sleep?

Andreas Müller: Yeah.

Justin Allen: But in physical death, you're done (laughing). Physically, at least. And in sleep, apparently you're not?

Andreas Müller: Yes.

Justin Allen: Sleep in a sense is like being reborn and dying every day?

Andreas Müller: Yes.

Justin Allen: So, that also made me think about something that Tony Parsons said, but also spiritual teachers. They also talk about the awakening phase.

Andreas Müller: Yeah.

Justin Allen: So, if there are stages of liberation, the first stage is the awakening phase. Tony described it as when you have glimpses of "no me," or the "me" collapses, but then it comes back, and then it collapses and comes back again. And I've mentioned this also; that there have been times when I have been, for lack of a better word, meditating or just sitting or lying around by myself and not really doing anything. Where it does feel like I'm on some kind of a precipice or entering into nothingness. Like all of a sudden getting sucked into a no-ness place or something. It feels like you're going to die, and then you want to resuscitate yourself and bring yourself back, and then the story comes back, and you're talking about it all again. But before that, there was a moment where the story was either dying or not happening.

Andreas Müller: Yeah.

Justin Allen: And it's the same that happens to me when I fall asleep sometimes. And of course, I don't know what any of this really is. But sometimes when you fall asleep, right before you kind of jerk, your body jerks. I think this happens to everybody. Sometimes I think that's a resistance. Putting it into this context, it would be the "me" confronting sleep the same way that it goes to one of your or Tony Parsons's talks where it is hearing that it doesn't exist. And it doesn't want to hear this message as this is the worst message. Same with sleep: It would be one of the worst conditions of the human experience, so the "me" would want to resist it, even though there isn't really something there that could resist or not resist?

Andreas Müller: Yeah, but "me" actually goes to a meeting like going to sleep. It does exactly the same thing. It goes there with the total conviction that it'll survive it anyway. And that's how it goes to sleep also. It goes to sleep happily because the conviction is, "Oh, I'll wake up tomorrow anyway. I can easily let go, I can easily go to sleep because tomorrow my life will go on (laughing)." But of course, all this is not done by the "me"; it just happens like that.

Justin Allen: Some people maybe can do it like that, I can't let go (laughing), so even sleep is a dilemma for me (laughing).

Andreas Müller: Most people do it like that. They just go to bed and think tomorrow there'll be another day.

Justin Allen: I have to think that some children must be afraid of going to sleep though.

Andreas Müller: Actually, there are. I know some people who had panic of dying, in a very early time as kids and out of the blue.

Justin Allen: I feel like I have that as an adult (laughing).

Andreas Müller: Yeah. It can always happen, of course. I mean, death is always around the corner or even closer. Totally. Actually, last week someone said to me, "It wasn't fear of the process of dying. It was fear of no self."

Justin Allen: Yeah, that's what it is for me. Also, when I "do-nothing," it's so clear to me that it's an existential crisis. As soon as I seem to be confronting the "no me" or the absence or the potential of absence, I'm literally taking a "me-defibrillator," whatever that would be, and I'm ... (with hands suggesting using the defibrillator on himself).

Andreas Müller: Totally. Yes.

Justin Allen: Bringing me back to life. So, this is still something that is kind of weird, and I guess you wouldn't have an answer, but sleep then is the absence of the "me"?

Andreas Müller: At least it seems that in deep sleep there is "no one" experiencing, yes.

Justin Allen: Right.

Andreas Müller: That's what apparently happens.

Justin Allen: But also feelings don't happen, or at least they don't seem to be happening. Thoughts don't seem to be happening. Objects don't seem to be there. Nothing seems to be present. But in the waking state or during the day for you and there being "no me," things are still happening?

Andreas Müller: Apparently, yes.

Justin Allen: But apparently when you're sleeping, those things aren't happening?

Andreas Müller: No, they aren't. That's why I wouldn't say that deep sleep is liberation.

Justin Allen: All right.

Andreas Müller: It's even far less comprehensible how it is in daily life when there is "no one." Because obviously it's not the thoughts and the feelings and that stuff which need the "me." That's why the concept of there being no experiencer in deep sleep is kind of easy to comprehend from a personal viewpoint. But how is it in daily life when there is "no one"? That's even weirder to think about. Because there are so many things (and things apparently happening) ... Not that it has to, not that anyone has to discriminate, but the character just in the end can't discriminate anymore what's personal and what's not, what's part of the dream world and what's not. Is the feeling of sadness there because I'm there creating the sadness, or is sadness just apparently happening for no one?

Justin Allen: Yeah.

Andreas Müller: That's what I mean. "Me" can only imagine what it would be like.

Justin Allen: Just for the sake of this discussion, let's say that there's the "no me" during the day when the character is awake, so there's the "no me" awake situation.

Andreas Müller: Yeah (laughing).

Justin Allen: And then there's also the "no me" sleep situation?

Andreas Müller: Yes, but the interesting thing is when there is "no one," there is no real difference between those two.

Justin Allen: Except that there's an apparent difference because in the "no me" waking situation, feelings, walls, animals, other people et cetera are apparently happening. And in the "no me" sleep situation, there's apparently nothing, literally nothing. There are no walls, no objects, no people, no feelings. That would be a distinction as far as we can tell?

Andreas Müller: Yeah, but I cannot make this distinction. That's the thing; of course, you can always say, "Yeah, but it's apparently different." And when the "person" hears this, it's subtly being implied, "Oh, but there is a difference." And of course, I understand the concept you come from and why you are saying that there is a difference, an apparent difference. But there is no experience of there being a difference.

Justin Allen: Okay. But you wouldn't know that either (laughing)?

Andreas Müller: That's what I'm saying. Or you could say the only one that knows the difference is that which seems to wake up in the morning.

Justin Allen: You know the difference between a "no me" entity and a "no me" Andreas Müller?

Andreas Müller: That's what I mean, I understand the concept. I understand where you come from.

Justin Allen: But I mean you understand that right now? I'm visually happening to you. And talking is happening.

Andreas Müller: Not really, of course. But apparently yes.

Justin Allen: But when you close your eyes, then I'm not visually happening anymore.

Andreas Müller: That's true. Apparently.

Justin Allen: Right. So, that's the difference that you can tell with knowing and with a certain amount of certainty right now, but you can't say that when you sleep, literally nothing's happening?

Andreas Müller: Again, I understand where you're coming from, but no. It's both blind.

Justin Allen: Okay.

Andreas Müller: There is no more certainty about that I now see you than there is about anything in deep sleep or in whatever. No.

Justin Allen: I was trying to make the argument or the case for using the word "liberation": So, the liberation of the "me" to the "no me" can occur during the waking situation, but not only then. However, deep sleep isn't liberation.

Andreas Müller: Exactly.

Justin Allen: But it makes me think there's a case for saying that deep sleep isn't liberation, and then I want to object that there's actually nothing in deep sleep to liberate from – because the "me" has temporarily collapsed –, but during the wake situation, there apparently is something to liberate from. You know what I mean? In deep sleep it's the default situation that there's "no me." And the default wake situation is apparently that there is a "me."

Andreas Müller: Yeah, I understand where you come from. But you can't really do that, because it's just very theoretical. That's all. Again, I understand the concept, but deep sleep in that sense isn't liberation. Liberation itself is a story. So, you can't take all of that too literally, because deep sleep in a way isn't liberation because usually it is being survived, so to speak. And in a funny way, deep sleep isn't like an awakening. Because when you take the story of awakening, it's something that happens during the day, so to speak.

Justin Allen: But it also can't be an awakening, because the default situation is automatically that there's nothing that could awake or change. There is nothing that can happen by default in the sleep situation.

Okay. So, Tony Parsons started off the talk by explaining how this whole setup of the "me" apparently happens; that it happens sometime between one and two years old, although he said he didn't know if that's true. It's just a theory basically. And then he said, "This is it," like this is what is, the wall, the floor, feelings, thoughts. This is all just apparently happening to "no one." Okay?

Andreas Müller: Yeah.

Justin Allen: So, then I asked him, "Okay, so feelings happen." And he went, "Yeah," just like you would say. "Yeah, feelings happen." "And then walls happen. And then thoughts happen also." So, feelings happen, walls happen, thoughts happen, but also the "me" happens.

Andreas Müller: Is this a question now already (laughing)?

Justin Allen: Yeah. That's a prelude question (laughing).

Andreas Müller: All right. Now if you want to go that far, then I would say the illusion of "me" is happening.

Justin Allen: Right. But then you have to go back and say that the illusion of feelings is also happening?

Andreas Müller: No.

Justin Allen: Okay. So, isn't that something different? I haven't heard or read something like that before.

Andreas Müller: Oh, yes. Tony also sometimes says that the only illusion is the "me."

Justin Allen: Okay, so everything else is real?

Andreas Müller: Yes.

Justin Allen: Everything's real and unreal?

Andreas Müller: Exactly. Everything is real and unreal including that you might assume that there is a "you."

Justin Allen: But that's still something that happens; that illusion then of assuming that I'm a "me"?

Andreas Müller: That's what apparently happens.

Justin Allen: Right. But just like feelings apparently happen. So, feelings apparently happen, thoughts apparently happen, walls apparently happen. And then you can't say the "me" apparently happens, you have to say the illusion of the "me" apparently happens?

Andreas Müller: Exactly. But you sitting in a room, for example, stating, "Yeah, but I am a real person," is what apparently happens.

Justin Allen: Yeah.

Andreas Müller: Not because there's a "me" inside of you. That's why I would say, "the illusion of 'me.'" It's not that "you" state that you are "someone" because there is a "me" inside you which is real and unreal. No, there is no "me" inside you, but what apparently happens is that you state that you are "someone," which is how you feel or what you assume to be real. It's not logical in that sense, but you saying, "But I am a person," is what apparently happens. And it's as whole as feelings and thoughts and chairs.

Justin Allen: It's as equal a happening as thoughts?

Andreas Müller: Absolutely. Totally.

Justin Allen: So, that's what I said. And then I think Tony followed me, meaning we understood each other. Well, I wasn't sure if we were following each other or if I was getting what he was saying and neither if he was getting what I was saying (laughing). But this is where it kind of gets tricky. So, for the "me," feelings apparently happen, thoughts apparently happen, walls apparently happen, and the illusion of the "me" is apparently happening more or less the whole time?

Andreas Müller: At least, that's maybe what happens for most people; that they more or less continuously think they are someone. But no one really knows, because whenever there is the impression, the sense of the "me," the illusion of the "me," it feels like as if "I" had always been there.

Justin Allen: The tricky part is when the "me" collapses or disappears or merges back into wholeness or whatever – and this is where it got confusing with my question to Tony –, the illusion of the "me" never happens again?

Andreas Müller: Yes.

Justin Allen: But that's the only thing that apparently doesn't happen anymore, because thoughts and feelings still happen to the "no me." They're not happening to the "me", but they still happen?

Andreas Müller: Yeah.

Justin Allen: It's weird to me ... I mean, why wouldn't the "me" or the sense of the "me" still happen, even to the "no me"?

Andreas Müller: Because in the story, exactly this would be liberation. In a way, one could say when there is the illusion of "me,"

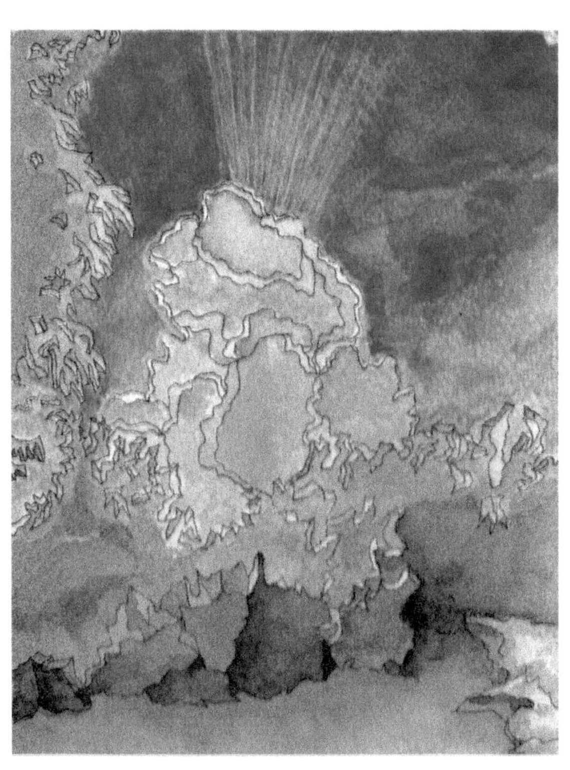

exactly what you just said is what happens all the time. There is the illusion of "me" for "no one."

Justin Allen: That's still the freedom of the "no me"; that it would also be possible to have the illusion of the "me" still happening?

Andreas Müller: You can't really do that, because in liberation, the interesting thing is that there is no illusion of "me" in that sense.

Justin Allen: Yeah, but then that to me means that that's not a happening, meaning that the "me" is apparently not ever happening. That it has to somehow be qualified differently because thoughts do happen.

Andreas Müller: Apparently.

Justin Allen: Yeah, thoughts apparently happen, feelings apparently happen, walls apparently happen, but the illusion of the "me," why does that apparently happen? That seems like it should be phrased or described in a different way. Because if it's something that apparently happens, then it should in a sense be able to constantly apparently happen, even after the liberation of the "me"?

Andreas Müller: Yeah, but the dilemma is that now you turn it already into something which happens, as if there were a real illusion.

Justin Allen: Okay, so the only ...

Andreas Müller: I know what you mean now, but it's just ...

Justin Allen: The distinction is that the "me" is the only illusion? Because thoughts and feelings aren't an illusion?

Andreas Müller: So to speak, yeah. One could say so.

Justin Allen: But it's only because the "me" is an illusion? It's the only artificial thing basically?

Andreas Müller: One could say so, yeah. And it's almost impossible to call it a thing in the first place.

Justin Allen: Because it's artificial?

Andreas Müller: Exactly. Yes, one could say so.

Justin Allen: It is like being an actor in a way. If I play the character of Romeo, I'm not and never will be Romeo, and Romeo doesn't even exist.

Andreas Müller: Yes, one could say so.

Justin Allen: So, while I'm playing the role of Romeo, feelings are still happening, thoughts are still happening, so acting is still happening. The only thing that's not really happening is "me" or Romeo (laughing)?

Andreas Müller: The only thing that never really happens is Romeo (laughing). Yeah, one could say so. It's quite a good picture (laughing). Never, not at all, not for a single second is there a Romeo. No matter how strongly you even believe you are Romeo. Never is Romeo happening (laughing).

Justin Allen: And one thing that could happen to somebody that plays the character of Romeo is that at some point they discover that they are not Romeo? So, before I put on the costume of Romeo, before I read the play and before I start to learn about the history of Romeo and what the character of Romeo was like, I'm just me. In this analogy, let's just say that I'm "not me," I'm just whatever. And thoughts and feelings and objects all around me are still happening. But they're not happening to anybody yet, because there hasn't been anybody kind of superimposed on to whatever this "whatever" is yet. And then I read about Romeo and put on a costume and then play the role of Romeo. And in doing this, the thoughts and feelings that were happening to "me" or whatever was happening before (blindly and without a point) are now happening to "me as Romeo" in this context of me playing the character Romeo. And then I think that those feelings and thoughts and objects are happening to this character Romeo. Right?

Andreas Müller: Yeah.

Justin Allen: So before, when I wasn't an actual "me" or an entity, there were still thoughts and feelings, but they weren't happening to anybody yet, because an I or a "me" hadn't yet been created. And then with the creation of a "me," whatever is apparently happening I assume to be happening to this entity because I've now assumed the Romeo position or the Romeo point of view position?

Andreas Müller: Yeah.

Justin Allen: And then, if at some point I'm not Romeo anymore, thoughts and feelings would still go on happening. But they wouldn't be happening to the Romeo?

Andreas Müller: Yeah, exactly. That's the story of before birth, during life and after death.

Justin Allen: And that's what happens every morning in a sense; that when you wake up, somehow you assume the "me," and then everything's happening to "that" all over?

Andreas Müller: Yes, but you can take that analogy for the whole life, from the three year old with a "me" appearing to the eighty year old dying. You can also use this analogy for one day and for a single moment where out of nothingness apparently self-consciousness, self-awareness arises. "Oh, I'm here." In one moment I experience everything as separate happening to "me" and as being real, and in the next moment that's not there anymore, there's just whatever there is for "no one." All of this is what apparently happens for "no one."

Justin Allen: Because there is ...

Andreas Müller: No one. So, even the presence of "me" only is what apparently happens, but there is never really someone that gets born, and there never really is "someone" behind that who is blinded by that illusion or who could awake from that. That's what I mean: You saying, "Yeah, but I am someone," – I don't know if you do do that – it just is what might apparently happen. Nothing gets born in that, nothing is imprisoned in that. It's not even an illusion with a negative connotation; it's just a description, an apparent description, of what seems to be happening.

Justin Allen: The same way as you would describe life and situations after playing Romeo?

Andreas Müller: Yeah.

Justin Allen: You would describe it like, "Andreas Müller put on the costume and transformed into Romeo"?

Andreas Müller: Not even that really. It's not that there's something really transforming or being transformed into Romeo (laughing).

Justin Allen: That would only be like this in the analogy of a theater play I mean. In this case, your true self is Andreas Müller. And then you'd be separating away from your true self to something else, to the role of Romeo. You've created something else, and now you're separate from what you previously were.

Andreas Müller: Yes, but as you just said, also in the analogy I never really become something else. Because I would just remain Andreas Müller thinking that he has become something else. It would still be me (laughing).

Justin Allen: And even in this case, you have to say that Andreas Müller doesn't exist in the way that we think. In that analogy, you can't help but think that Andreas Müller's already non-existent.

Andreas Müller: Exactly. That's why this analogy doesn't work. It just is that Andreas Müller in that sense would be wholeness or what apparently happens, which never becomes something else when it comes to the illusion of "me." That would be the picture of Andreas Müller transforming into the role of Romeo: It's like wholeness becoming the "me," but it never really becomes it, in the sense of something else. In becoming separate nothing really becomes separate.

Justin Allen: This reminds me of something that I've read or heard from Rupert Spira, but I don't know if he got it from Ramana Maharshi or somebody else. Anyway, he uses this analogy of King Lear. So, he starts off more or less by saying that an actor, let's call him John Smith, takes on the role of King Lear. So, he's John Smith, and then he puts on the costume and goes out to perform King Lear in the play of the same name. And he's so enraptured by it and takes on this identity so strongly that after the play, he forgets that he's John Smith.

Andreas Müller: Yes, I mean that ...

Justin Allen: And then he is devastated and depressed because of all the misfortune that happened to him, and then maybe a friend who watched the play comes backstage and congratulates him, but he's too depressed and overwhelmed and can't appreciate the praise. Instead, he's describing how his life is a mess. And so, the friend goes, "Yeah, but what's wrong? You're not King Lear, you're John Smith." But he's totally forgotten John Smith, he doesn't even know anything about John Smith, so he's stuck as King Lear. And then you can make that analogy in the sense that it's such a prison in a way, like a futile trap, because he thinks he's King Lear. And he thinks he has this depression and all these bad things have happened to him. So, he's going to try to resolve his life, for example, he sees a psychiatrist, but they are addressing him and his history as King Lear, although none of that happened in the first place. So, he could spend ten or twenty years trying to unravel and improve this character that doesn't even exist in the first place.

Andreas Müller: Yes.

Justin Allen: And I always found that this is something one can comprehend. I don't know exactly how Rupert Spira intended that to be interpreted or understood.

Andreas Müller: I can tell you what I think (laughing). Namely that this whole description is used for an awareness situation.

Justin Allen: Yeah. I know how he's using it for the awareness situation, but I'd say you can use it for this situation that we are addressing as well.

Andreas Müller: Yes and no, because it's not someone finding the true identity "behind" the role. It's not someone unraveling something. It's just apparently the death of the sense of being someone.

Justin Allen: Right. But it's a good description in a way of what apparently is happening to the "me."

Andreas Müller: Yes.

Justin Allen: Because during her or his whole life, the "me" is trying to understand and kind of correct and work on itself, either trying to get ...

Andreas Müller: Totally, yes.

Justin Allen: The futility of it is that it doesn't exist in the first place. And that's why that's the big joke or the big shock ...

Andreas Müller: Yes. Totally, of course. It's working on a problem that doesn't exist. It's its own separation. It's life, and it's separation.

Justin Allen: And it's the same way as you can see clearly that there's nothing you can do about it. Because anything that you're trying to do as King Lear to solve your problem is just perpetuating the problem?

Andreas Müller: Yeah, totally.

Justin Allen: And then you could see that if you were the friend or somehow you were the liberated or the enlightened one, there's also nothing that you could do to try to jolt this person out of the conviction that they're King Lear or Romeo or a "me," a somebody?

Andreas Müller: Yeah. I mean, the only chance in a way you would get in that personalized picture is the assumption that there is another real identity behind the role to whom you could speak and who could wake up from the role.

Justin Allen: Yeah, that's the awareness teaching.

Andreas Müller: That would be the awareness teaching, exactly.

Justin Allen: And this would be addressing the "thing" behind, your true self, which is the awareness?

Andreas Müller: Exactly. But there's not even a real communication possible. Of course, what comes out is that you are not King Lear, Romeo or a "me." But it's not saying this to "someone," in order to awaken someone, because being "someone" in a way already is Romeo. It's not just a mistaken identity, which can be replaced by the right identity. Identity itself is the illusion. But as I said, for "no one," so it's not even a real illusion. It's not even something that should go away. You can't make Romeo go away, only if he died physically in the play, of course.

Justin Allen: Well, it is a real illusion in the sense that every illusion is a real illusion. But every real illusion is also fake because it's not real.

Andreas Müller: Yeah, I know what you mean.

Justin Allen: But now back to the beginning where I was saying how thoughts apparently happen, feelings apparently happen, walls apparently happen. And then we said the illusion of the "me" doesn't apparently happen, because it's an illusion. So, it's not even happening in a sense. But then awareness does happen, or is awareness also the "me"?

Andreas Müller: What apparently happens is the function of awareness. But when there is "no one," there is nothing aware of that. There is no meta-level, as we said in our last talk. Or every appearance of a meta-level is also just what's happening, but on the same level.

Justin Allen: Yeah, but there still has to be an awareness thing happening?

Andreas Müller: Apparently. But it is not different than having an arm or there being a computer. It's just that I'm apparently aware compared to a stone or compared to the table. But it's neither "who I really am" nor is there an experience of being aware. It just is what apparently happens.

Justin Allen: That has to be the kind of dropping away. Because of all the things that are apparently happening, the one that the "me" grabs on to first would be awareness; it would be thinking that it's the awareness. Whenever this separation occurs, that's kind of the mechanics of it.

Andreas Müller: Yes, either way, "me" is self-awareness. It's the experience of there being something which is awareness or present.

Justin Allen: But I mean that can in a way change for the "me" experience, like we talked about in our last conversation. Often it's the case that it thinks it's its thoughts first. So, the experience of life is, "I'm my thoughts and my feelings and my sensations."

Andreas Müller: Yes.

Justin Allen: And then it might come to the conclusion, "Ah, no, I'm not those things," because in order to be those things at all, it has to be something that's aware of those things. So, then it might conclude, "I'm awareness."

Andreas Müller: Of course. Yeah.

Justin Allen: But it never concludes ... I mean, in general, nobody's going around feeling as if they were their hands or their fingers or their toes. They feel more like they're their body (as a whole) and their located maybe in their head. You know what I mean?

Andreas Müller: Yeah, all right.

Justin Allen: And generally, nobody's saying, "I'm also the bird outside. I'm also my automobile in my driveway."

Andreas Müller: Well, some people actually seem to feel like that. They feel one with everything.

Justin Allen: I'm just saying the majority of people don't think that they're also something else, in the sense of other people or animals or objects. They draw the line outside of the body.

Andreas Müller: Yeah.

Justin Allen: And some people draw the line where they might say they're not their body, but they are their thoughts and feelings or something less physical, let's say. So, the "me" from its own experience is concluding these things, but always still from the perspective that first and foremost it's this awareness, the consciousness?

Andreas Müller: Yes, of course.

Justin Allen: And then it starts saying, "Okay, I'm this awareness first and foremost, and secondly, I'm my thoughts and feelings and sensations, and thirdly, I'm my body and then my family and whatever. So, all of that kind of goes out from that?

Andreas Müller: Yes.

Justin Allen: But somehow that's the illusion; the same way that everybody can clearly see how it's an illusion to think that you're your thoughts and feelings?

Andreas Müller: Yes.

Justin Allen: So, you can kind of grasp that. And then that can feel like an awakening moment where you go, "Oh, I'm not my thoughts and feelings."

Andreas Müller: Yes.

Justin Allen: And then, if there were a moment, which can't happen either, but if there were a moment where you realize, "Oh, I'm not 'me,'" or, "I'm not awareness." If that could happen, that would be a similar experience to realizing that you're not your thoughts and feelings and sensations?

Andreas Müller: Yes. If it were like that, it would be similar (laughing). But that's the thing. There is no real "me," and there is no real illusion. And there isn't something which is an illusion, and there isn't something which is real. There isn't anything waking up, there isn't anything asleep in being "me"; it just is what apparently happens, and that's the dilemma. In the personal picture, exactly there is already something to discriminate: something which is real, something which is not real, something which is bad, something which is better. And all of that stuff, this whole setup, doesn't work, so to speak, with liberation at all.

Justin Allen: But what happens in liberation then? Nothing actually? I think we have to come up with a better word than "liberation." But for now, let's say when there's liberation, then awareness still apparently happens, and thoughts still apparently happen, and everything still apparently happens. But that's something that a "me" could still kind of understand because when the "me" is liberated from not being its thoughts and feelings and sensations, it can feel like a liberation.

Andreas Müller: Yes. But it's never really liberated from that.

Justin Allen: I know. But I mean it in the sense of compared to before where it thought that it's only the thoughts. It is a limitation when you think that you're only your thoughts and feelings and sensations. And if you realize you're not, that is or can be a liberating feeling.

Andreas Müller: Kind of, yeah.

Justin Allen: But even when you're then "liberated," all your thoughts and feelings and sensations still happen. They don't stop happening.

Andreas Müller: Apparently, yes.

Justin Allen: And you still function. It's not like when you're liberated from your thoughts and feelings and sensations that all of a sudden you don't have thoughts, feelings and sensations that dictate what you do in life anymore? So, similarly to how you and Tony Parsons try to describe liberation; that everything still happens?

Andreas Müller: Kind of, yeah. But other than in your example, there is no one there anymore who thinks that they observe that.

Justin Allen: But that's the dilemma. That's a hard thing for everybody to grasp because you think from the "me" perspective that when there's no "me," then there's nothing ... Like you wouldn't even eat and work and might not do anything.

Andreas Müller: Oh, yes. Because the "me" takes ownership of those things before they happen.

Justin Allen: Right.

Andreas Müller: That's what I mean. "Me" can't comprehend what it is, what it's actually doing, so to speak, and what it's not doing at all. And suddenly it turns out that it never did anything. It didn't even do itself, so to speak. It didn't even do the illusion to be "me." All of a sudden you don't find the "me" behind anything. It's impossible to squeeze the "me" in somewhere. Because it's not there. It was never there. But yes, of course, "me" thinks that so many things would be different "after liberation" because it falsely takes ownership of them.

Justin Allen: Right. But even without the ownership, everything still happens just like it did before (laughing)?

Andreas Müller: Yeah, of course. I mean, this is the most miraculous thing about this message: that it's constantly saying, "It's 'this' already." Absolutely. One hundred percent. No movement, no step in or towards anything. Nothing that is closer to perfection than how it actually is, timelessly, instantly. It's constantly saying yes, so to speak. It's constantly pointing towards itself, which is the same thing. It's constantly pointing towards what happens now, so to speak, for "no one," so timelessly. It is exactly how it is, with no discrimination between thoughts and awareness and between "me" and "not me." And with no discrimination like, "That's closer to the truth, and this is a little bit caught up in the illusion," and all that stuff. All that is the illusion (laughing). It completely eradicates all those illusionary assumptions or however you want to call them. There is no step to take in there, there's no step towards what's better. There's no step towards less illusion. There's no step towards anything in us sitting here talking to each other (laughing). Sorry, I had to admit that.

Justin Allen: Just like Romeo doesn't exist?

Andreas Müller: Yes. And it never will exist. And it's never more or less Romeo or anything. And there was no way of being more Romeo and becoming less Romeo. There never was Romeo, he never existed.

Justin Allen: Isn't that a good way to put it? That's a good picture.

Andreas Müller: More or less, because it's generally a very personalized picture of someone who thinks that he's Romeo and could somehow un-think/do that. But yeah, the lovely part of the picture is that it really points out that Romeo never existed, no matter how much you believe it, no matter how much you think it, no matter how much you feel Romeo – he just never existed. That's the good part about the picture. But it doesn't really say anything (laughing).

Justin Allen: I wonder if that is similar to helping the disillusionment of romantic love. Like when people divorce or go through some super hard breakup; at some point they might conclude that it wasn't even real.

Andreas Müller: Yes, but that's the thing. There's just someone concluding it.

Justin Allen: Right. It's not like liberation, but it's its own kind of realizing that there actually wasn't something there that they had thought was there before.

Andreas Müller: Well, what's believed about that is very individual. Because people can think it was there, but it ended. And some people, let's say, after it happened five times, think they don't believe in it anymore. But I think the "person" would still conclude that, in some way or the other, it was something that happened, whatever it was.

Justin Allen: I like that Romeo never happened.

Andreas Müller: Yeah, it's beautiful. I know (laughing). The whole drama didn't happen. It's not only Romeo in that sense, but all that seemed to have come out of Romeo. The whole story, the whole drama, all what Romeo stands for and what he believed to have gone through and all the connections that come out of this Romeo story. There never was a Romeo in the first place (laughing). It is all completely based on all the thinking around the work; the whole attempt to make Romeo's life work and the suffering of Romeo and all that stuff was based on someone who never existed (laughing). Can you then even call it suffering? Did someone really suffer? That's the dilemma with the actor picture because now you can say, "Yeah, but the actor who played Romeo suffered." You see, that's the problem with a personalized picture.

Justin Allen: Yeah, but even that analogy works in a way because if "I" as Justin Allen play the character Romeo, I also physically will induce an increased heart rate. If I have to fake crying on stage, I'm going to ...

Andreas Müller: Yeah, of course.

Justin Allen: I'm going to put my physical body through stress.

Andreas Müller: Yeah, of course. That's what happens. That's what apparently happens. And one could say, of course, that those thoughts and feelings drop together with the illusion to be someone, apparently.

Justin Allen: It's only for that moment, it's only for that one hour that I'm playing the character, but then afterwards, when I let go of the character, at least in that sense, I'm not carrying around his story with me anymore.

Andreas Müller: No, exactly.

Justin Allen: So, it's really liberating for "me" as Justin Allen playing the character of Romeo that I can play it and then ...

Andreas Müller: It's totally liberating. But in the end for "no one," because there is no real character Justin Allen either.

That's where the picture doesn't fit anymore.

Justin Allen: Yeah, except if we say Justin Allen is the "no me."

Andreas Müller: Wholeness or whatever.

Justin Allen: Justin Allen is the "no me," which then plays the "me" character of Romeo. But that's something that doesn't happen. That's the other thing that we've said here: that when the illusion disintegrates, it doesn't come back?

Andreas Müller: Yes. Before that, there would be awakening, so to speak. But these are all very superficial concepts anyway. There being "me," there being awakening, there being the total end of "me." It's stories.

Justin Allen: Well, it's been a little more than an hour.

Andreas Müller: Yeah, I'm sorry.

Justin Allen: All right.

Andreas Müller: All right.

Justin Allen: Have a good day.

Andreas Müller: Yeah, you too.

Justin Allen: Ciao.

Andreas Müller: Thank you. See you.

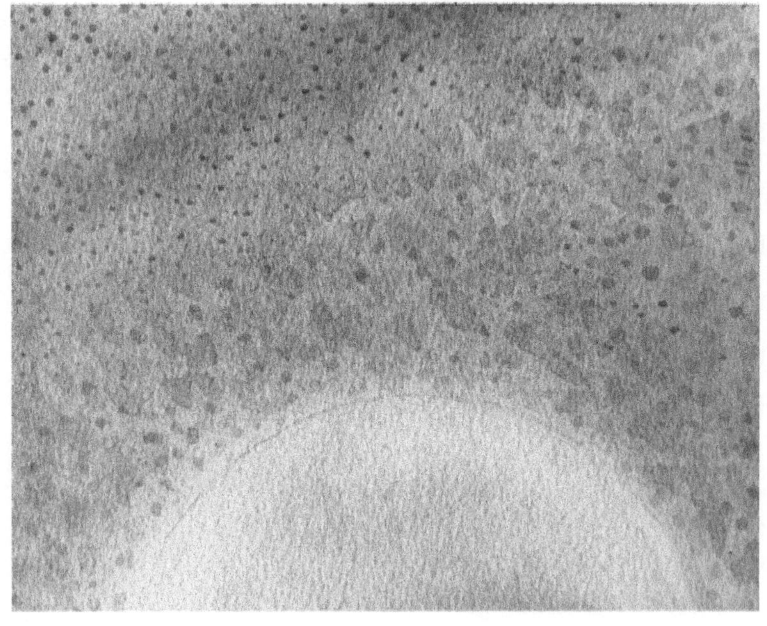

December 12, 2019 Talk 07

BLINDLY AWAKE

Justin Allen: (He is wearing ear protection because he is in a woodshop.) It looks like I can't hear you, but I can (laughing).

Andreas Müller: Okay, all right.

Justin Allen: It's to block out the table saws (laughing).

Andreas Müller: Sorry for yesterday, but it wasn't possible.

Justin Allen: Yeah, no problem. I just randomly ended up in a wood shop today, and my ears need protection (laughing).

Andreas Müller: All right (laughing).

Justin Allen: So, what I found interesting from the last time we talked was the statement that Romeo never existed.

Andreas Müller: Yeah, I liked that, too.

Justin Allen: So, I have been ruminating about it over the past week and was wondering if there are other examples or other ways to talk about it or to put that sentence into another frame of reference within this topic.

Andreas Müller: I don't know. It depends on the picture, but it's basically just saying that Romeo never existed, which just means there is no "me."

Justin Allen: Right. But it seems almost tangible when you put it that way; when using an actor as an example.

Andreas Müller: Yeah.

Justin Allen: When you say, "the 'me,'" then that seems more difficult to grasp.

Andreas Müller: Yeah, it's impossible to grasp (laughing). But what the seeker grasps about the actor in the Romeo picture also is not what is meant, so to speak. Because it's still grasping something which can't really be grasped. That's the dilemma with all the pictures and the teachings; that they are graspable. They seem to grasp a circumstance, which in that sense doesn't exist in the first place. So, I understand the seeker wants something to grasp, which seems like a step towards wholeness: "At least I can grasp that concept." Yes, that's all right, but it's not an approach, it's not coming closer, it's just "me" grasping something else. In that sense, it doesn't really matter.

Justin Allen: I guess that's what I find interesting though; that what the seeker has to do is to keep on seeking.

Andreas Müller: Exactly.

Justin Allen: And it's the same in a way as if you lost your keys: You're going to go around the whole house, and you're going to ask everybody in the house where the keys are, and you're going to keep on doing it day after day. But at some point, you're going to have looked everywhere possible, and that's when you finally give up and get a new set of keys or a new house or a new car or still keep looking futilely (laughing).

Andreas Müller: Yes (laughing).

Justin Allen: So, that's what I think is important – if there's anything important to do, in a way. I think it could be important to try to turn over every stone where the key ... No?

Andreas Müller: No, no. Not at all. Because that's the thing; that's the interesting thing that even in your picture with the house and the keys, it sounds like there is something over after having looked everywhere for five days and having realized that you will not find it. But in that metaphor, the story actually just goes on by buying another key, house or car. It's not really an end; it's just going on in a different way. So, the seeking or the being someone or the having a circumstance in that sense hasn't really stopped. Which means that the seeker will go on seeking; they will never come to a point where they're not seeking anymore "because of ..."

Justin Allen: Right, not "because of ..." You can't say because of anything, except that it could happen that through the apparent searching of "everywhere" for the keys ...

Andreas Müller: Exactly. And in the end, there is no such thing as "having looked in all the corners."

Justin Allen: Right, that I understand.

Andreas Müller: Exactly. It can be a bit like that, but if you take the seeker, so to speak, it always lives in time. Every moment, there is a new moment to seek in. In that sense, the seeker is never really done in the sense that they have experienced everything. In that sense, liberation is just the falling away of the seeking setup for no reason. Not because I give up, not because I've seen it all, not because I understand that I will not find it, and so I can stop seeking. It's just the end of it, like death, so to speak. It can happen in the middle of life, with thousands of unresolved issues that haven't even been looked at.

Justin Allen: Like everything though, just like getting fired from your job (laughing).

Andreas Müller: Yeah, in the end, like everything. Exactly.

Justin Allen: Or your best friend dies, or your partner leaves you.

Andreas Müller: Yeah, exactly. It's rather like dropping out without having completed the path. Like for example, you don't usually get a diploma after not having studied. But that's the general picture of the spiritual path: developing, developing, developing until you finally reach somewhere.

Justin Allen: But also because there's nothing, there's never a "because of," also because there is not a thing there to be changed ultimately.

Andreas Müller: Yes.

Justin Allen: Right, ultimately it's because there's just nothing there to disappear, there's nothing there to vanish, there's nothing to be liberated from.

Andreas Müller: Exactly, yes. There is no real happening in time and space.

Justin Allen: Then that goes back to the sentence that there never was a Romeo, so there can't be a "before a Romeo" or an "after a Romeo."

Andreas Müller: Exactly, yes.

Justin Allen: We probably talked about this in different ways already, definitely the last time: So, if the "me" hears about the death of the "me" or that there is no "me," then it automatically wants to insert something like a replacement?

Andreas Müller: Yes, yes.

Justin Allen: I do that, too, even in the past talks: The "me" can't avoid it in a way, somehow it must find some replacement.

Andreas Müller: Yeah, yeah.

Justin Allen: But there is no replacement?

Andreas Müller: No, there isn't.

Justin Allen: There's also nothing there to be replaced in the first place?

Andreas Müller: No.

Justin Allen: But the thing that the mind can't get, and it's impossible to get, is that how without the "me," using you as an example (laughing) or Tony Parsons, feelings are still happening and thoughts are still happening.

Andreas Müller: Yeah.

Justin Allen: But it still makes me think that awareness has to be happening for you in order for there to be something to ...

Not in the sense that you are awareness, but awareness has to be happening in order for it to be aware of the thoughts that are still happening?

Andreas Müller: Yes, one could say so.

Justin Allen: Okay. So, that's the other thing that I was trying to get at: Just by logic, if awareness is happening, awareness is also a "me" in a sense?

Andreas Müller: Actually, one could say these are two things: There is the function of awareness, which seems to be happening, and compared to a stone or a table I seem to be aware. But there is no experience of being aware, whereas the "me" would live in the awareness of being aware or of being something which is aware. But in that sense, when there is "no one," awareness is as blindly itself as everything else. It's like an arm or feelings or thoughts.

Justin Allen: But you still wouldn't call that a "me"?

Andreas Müller: No, not at all. It's just a function, which is empty and meaningless. "Me" being aware of what I'm aware of, a sound or whatever, is what apparently happens, and it's utterly meaningless.

Justin Allen: Yeah, but wouldn't it also be aware of the sense of a "me"? The sense of a "me" would also be something that happens?

Andreas Müller: Apparently, yes.

Justin Allen: But for you also?

Andreas Müller: No, because there is no sense of a "me."

Justin Allen: So, that's what I'm saying; the general population has a sense of being awareness or of being aware?

Andreas Müller: Of being something, which is there and aware, yeah.

Justin Allen: But it's really that they have a sense that they are awareness at the foundation?

Andreas Müller: Yes, yes. One could say they have the impression that they are something in here which is aware of itself and connects to the outside world. In that sense, it uses the function of awareness.

Justin Allen: But for you then, there's just awareness happening in the same way that thoughts are happening and feelings are happening?

Andreas Müller: So to speak, yes. It just is what apparently happens, but "no one" knows it. There is no additional experience of, "Oh, I'm aware."

Justin Allen: But that's what I can't get: Just like you'll have a thought or a feeling happening that says "anger" or "sadness" or something, why wouldn't there also potentially be something like, "Ah, there's a 'me' here."

Andreas Müller: Oh, I mean in a way that happens all the time, but only when there is a "me" here (laughing). People tell it over and over again when they experience themselves as someone. But there is "no one," because there is "no one." Saying that there is "no one" is as much an honest report as someone else saying, "But I feel like someone."

Justin Allen: No, I get that the majority of the population has that happening to them, but what I'm saying is when the apparent "me" apparently vanishes, within that frame of the apparent liberation, why wouldn't there still occur a happening of a "me"?

Andreas Müller: Because that is liberation; that the happening of "me" doesn't occur anymore.

Justin Allen: Right, but in full liberation, there should be so much freedom that this also could happen. You know what I mean? Not that there's something there that could do any of this, but why wouldn't it still occur that a "me" would apparently happen "again"?

Andreas Müller: Well, this is the point where it becomes illogical because in liberation, it turns out that it was never really happening. In that sense, it's the melting together of presence and absence. It's way more illogical and way more weird that one can imagine. In a way, one could say that all the personal stuff, or all that seemed to be personal, turns out to be totally impersonal. That's true. But in the story, it's just the end of the experience to be someone, which is illogical. And in the end, we talk about apparent liberation because we talk about apparent bondage and about apparent separation and apparent wholeness.

Wholeness (laughing), and now it gets really theoretical, doesn't care at all about "me" or "no me." That is liberation. It is totally free to be "me," to be "no me," to be whatever. Nothing cares at all. Or you could just say, when apparent liberation happens, which is already within the story, it's just the death of the sense of "I am." But it's difficult here to not give it more reality than it has because yes, what is, is absolutely free to be "me," "no me" or whatever. But that's the funny thing, when there is "no one," even to be Andreas isn't experienced as such.

Justin Allen: It's not experienced as such?

Andreas Müller: I mean it in the sense that I'm only Andreas, but yes, Andreas is absolutely personally happening. My thoughts, what I want, my feelings, all the things that "me" would see as personal; of course, those things still happen, but they turn out to be not personal at all. In that sense, the person is as much happening as everything else. But strangely, what isn't happening anymore is the experience of only being that.

Justin Allen: Okay, that's what I think is the distinction or the point that I wanted to try to ...

Andreas Müller: Because that's the interesting thing, which also can't be explained. I can't explain it, because it's not logical. But in liberation, it really turns out that there never was a person behind anything. This is when those ideas or those points of presence and absence basically somehow melt together into something unknowable. That's why the picture of presence, "me," and its falling away is very superficial. It doesn't really get to the point. And there is no point, of course.

Justin Allen: But then there's still "me" happening in a sense?

Andreas Müller: Yes, of course. Andreas is happening; what "me" thought is "me," namely the person and the conditioning, is what apparently happens. And in that sense, even the function of awareness is what apparently happens.

Justin Allen: Right. That's a pretty good answer to give to people, isn't it?

Andreas Müller: Yeah.

Justin Allen: Because that's one of the most confusing ...

Andreas Müller: They don't understand it anyway, but yes. Actually, yesterday evening in a talk someone said it's like being in deep sleep, but being aware.

Justin Allen: Which is what's happening to you or what's happening to the majority?

Andreas Müller: It's when there is "no one." It's like while being awake, while everything happens, not being there experiencing it.

Justin Allen: Right, yeah.

Andreas Müller: That which is can't be imagined. It doesn't have to be imagined, by the way.

Justin Allen: I don't know if you talk about this, but Tony Parsons talks about glimpses and pre-stages, in a way, to liberation.

Andreas Müller: Sometimes I do, yes. It's not really stages though.

Justin Allen: But some kind of shifting?

Andreas Müller: Yeah. I had glimpses for many years.

Justin Allen: What would be an example of a glimpse?

Andreas Müller: It can be anything. For example, when I had my first glimpse, I only understood five years later that it was a glimpse. Because there was basically nothing happening, and in the next moment, so to speak, I was there again. It felt a bit like waking up, but all I knew was that I wasn't asleep before. It was something like, "Ah, I'm here." It wasn't special at all, I didn't store that as something amazing or great. It didn't fit into any box, and I actually forgot about it. But that was when for me, a me-ing and being phase started.

Justin Allen: But when you said, "Ah, I'm me," that was you coming out of the "no me"?

Andreas Müller: So to speak, yes. Exactly.

Justin Allen: So you came out of it, and then you're the "me," and then you're telling the story about what just happened?

Andreas Müller: Yeah, but there was no story about before. As I said, somehow I knew that I wasn't sleeping, but that there was nothing nevertheless.

Justin Allen: Right, but as you returned to the "me," then you have to tell a story at that point?

Andreas Müller: Well, as I said, it was so unimportant that I forgot about it quite quickly. This moment didn't play a big role in my life, and also at that point, it didn't play a big role, because there was nothing.

Justin Allen: Right, but I mean, while it was happening, you couldn't have addressed it really, because you weren't there in the ...

Andreas Müller: Exactly. Nothing to be addressed meanwhile and nothing to play a big role afterwards. Just nothing really.

Justin Allen: Let's just say it occurred for five minutes, so five minutes before, you were you, then for five minutes, you weren't you, and then you became you again. And in that switch from "no you" to "you," there was a recognition, but this was happening to the "me"?

Andreas Müller: "Me" is the recognition, exactly.

Justin Allen: So, the "me" acknowledging that something just happened is the story then?

Andreas Müller: Exactly. All it could process looking back is something must have happened.

Justin Allen: Right. So, you're only saying now that five years later or whatever, after your liberation, you can look back at it in a sense and be like, "Ah, that's what was happening."

Andreas Müller: No, no, it was actually within my story. Five years later, I was talking with someone about awakening and stuff like that, and I remembered that situation. That's when I understood, "Whoa, actually there was no one." And looking back, it fit my experience because the me-ing and being started after that thing. But at that time, I wouldn't have had words for all of that. Neither for the glimpse or the awakening nor for the me-ing and being that started. Because I went into a spiritual game after that, and this was about seeing and not seeing "the truth." It was a completely different story in a way compared to what was actually going on. And that something that was actually going on was a story in the first place. Then I had another glimpse where, so to speak, there was "no one," but everything just went on.

Justin Allen: And you still went on as you?

Andreas Müller: Yes, so to speak, exactly. But if you would have asked me how it really was within the glimpse, I would have lacked words as much as in the first glimpse, so to speak. But these aren't really stages; it just is what apparently happens. Many people have glimpses

Justin Allen: I would think everybody has glimpses (laughing).

Andreas Müller: Yeah, yeah. Then let's say many also recognize them as such, apparently.

Justin Allen: But then also, there are probably people with whom the glimpses happen more frequently, maybe even once a day for a while.

Andreas Müller: Maybe, yeah. Everything is possible, and nothing matters. Glimpses are not needed; they are just part of the story like everything else.

Justin Allen: They're just what happened, but I'm just curious if there's some kind of consensus on the average.

Andreas Müller: Not really, no. There isn't really an average. In a way, it's all very normal and ordinary, you can't really make rules.

Justin Allen: Going back to the Romeo example we talked about last time: The problem with that analogy is that there's the actor John Smith or Justin Allen or whoever, playing the character of Romeo. So, you can understand that Romeo doesn't exist, but then you still think that John Smith or Justin Allen exists.

Andreas Müller: Exactly. That's the big disadvantage of that picture.

Justin Allen: But I've been walking around since our last talk really just going, "Fuck. Justin doesn't exist."

Andreas Müller: Yeah (laughing).

Justin Allen: I'm not really afraid of that, I can imagine I might have been afraid of that some time ago, but then it's like the whole thing doesn't exist. It feels like my parents as my parents don't exist, my brother as my brother doesn't exist, my girlfriends, all my relationships, my job; they all don't exist.

Andreas Müller: Yeah (laughing).

Justin Allen: All my thoughts and my feelings and times that I've cried and times that I've been happy, all the drama. So, I can't say anything's happening other than it's just like, "Fuck, none of this ... It's all a big dream, it's all just what's happening or happened." And it seems like it's all happening to an entity, to a concentrated point, which I call "me," but then I go, "But that's also just a happening, just like a thought is a happening or a wall is a happening."

Andreas Müller: Yes.

Justin Allen: But then I might have a thought like, "Ah yeah, but I could still get cancer, maybe if I smoke cigarettes, so I shouldn't smoke to avoid getting cancer."

Andreas Müller: Yeah, so there's still someone there.

Justin Allen: So, it feels like there's still someone there controlling, but then I go, "But isn't that just what happens also?" That seems to happen: If you smoke cigarettes, then you might get cancer. But it still feels like I can control my life, I still have to go and make decisions.

Andreas Müller: Yes, because, apparently in the story, there's still someone there.

Justin Allen: But even when there is "no one" there, decisions are still being made, apparently?

Andreas Müller: Yes, apparently. Exactly.

Justin Allen: Right, so that's when I start going on in my thought process, when I start thinking about ...

Andreas Müller: That was just the sentence that I had on my lips: There is still apparently something that's processing.

Justin Allen: That's what I mean, that whole thing, that's the dream also. The decisions and the feeling that you have to make a decision and the consequences that come from that decision is all just still within that story or within that dream or whatever you want to call it?

Andreas Müller: Yeah, yes.

Justin Allen: So, there's the sense that it's happening, and at the center of it all is just the biggest element of the dream: the seemingly "you" that all of this is happening to?

Andreas Müller: Yes.

Justin Allen: Then even without that sense of "you" though, it is still there anyways. It doesn't go away.

Andreas Müller: One could say so, yes. However, this is useless information then. But yes, the utterly big surprise is that when the "me" dies, so to speak, nothing really changes (laughing). For the "me," of course, the assumption is, "Oh, when I die, that's the biggest change ever."

Justin Allen: That sentence, too, I know what you mean by it, but I just want to point it out: It's a big surprise, but it's not a surprise for someone?

Andreas Müller: Yeah. It's an apparent surprise (laughing).

Justin Allen: But it's still okay to say that even without the "me," it still goes on as though there still were a "me," in a sense, right?

Andreas Müller: In a sense, yes, absolutely.

Justin Allen: Because the apparent "me" is just like an apparent thought or an apparent feeling or an apparent wall. It's just something that does happen?

Andreas Müller: Apparently. The illusion of "me," yes.

Justin Allen: And only to humans as far as we know?

Andreas Müller: One could say so, yeah.

Justin Allen: Animals might have thoughts or instincts or feelings.

Andreas Müller: Oh, they do have, at least that's what scientists say now. Actually, scientists don't understand the difference between humans and animals anymore.

Justin Allen: But wouldn't it be possible to still have feelings and thoughts happening? Maybe it's not possible without awareness.

Andreas Müller: Oh, but they also say that animals have consciousness or that consciousness and awareness in that sense are the same thing. I would say they're the function of consciousness, like humans, but scientists are really struggling with that, because twenty, thirty years ago, they weren't sure if animals had thoughts and feelings. So, they thought that thoughts and feelings have everything to do with consciousness in the sense of being a "me," of having self-consciousness. Now they found out that animals also have thoughts and feelings, but that humans don't have self-awareness (laughing). They have absolutely no clue anymore about what's different, except the size of the brain. I've read that, I don't know the details.

Justin Allen: But maybe they still don't have the happening of a "me"?

Andreas Müller: Yes, exactly. At least, that's the assumption, and I would follow that assumption that a dog is not additionally experiencing itself as, "I'm a dog."

Justin Allen: Or as, "I'm a happy dog."

Andreas Müller: Exactly. "I'm an unhappy dog," or, "I'm a happy dog." There's just being a dog.

Justin Allen: Right, because from the human perspective, it does seem like one dog is happier and the other one's more melancholic or something. But you never really think that the dog feels that way, and that's why they're so attractive to us (laughing).

Andreas Müller: Yes, but some people would even personalize a dog, like some spiritual people personalize everything and assume a soul in everything. But that's another thing. So, me too, I would say that no one really assumes there to be a "dog-me" in the dog.

Justin Allen: But that's what I think could be the comparison in a way; that liberation might be like being an animal, when things are happening, but to "no one."

Andreas Müller: Yes, it's like being a dog as a human (laughing).

Justin Allen: I just mean even if we take the assumption that dogs don't say, "I am Koko, the dog," they still function. They're still going around eating and looking at things and smelling.

Andreas Müller: Having feelings.

Justin Allen: Yeah, having apparent bad days and apparent good days.

Andreas Müller: Yes.

Justin Allen: Apparent anxiety and apparent release from the anxiety.

Andreas Müller: Yes.

Justin Allen: But it doesn't seem like they are. Even though when a dog's stressed because you leave the house, and they pant for a little while, it doesn't seem like it's that stressful for them, at least not the same stress that a human has.

Andreas Müller: Yes, one could say it's exactly because their stress is not connected to the idea of, "Am I a happy dog or not?"

Justin Allen: Right. And if there's not a sense of something being there, there also wouldn't be a sense of changing the situation.

Andreas Müller: In that sense, yes, one could say so.

Justin Allen: Because that's like the human dilemma really; it's not necessarily that you're depressed or unhappy or anxious, it's that you think you can change it.

Andreas Müller: Yes, the assumption is that you are someone who can or is theoretically able to consciously do life, which means to us to consciously do feelings and happiness and all that stuff.

Justin Allen: And that it's (life) happening to you.

Andreas Müller: Yes, that's the first thing. First, you have to become conscious, or basically apparently conscious, about what's going on. "Oh, I'm really sad, but I've read that I could be happy also." Or maybe, "Oh, I'm sad; this means that I'm an unhappy person." It starts with being "me," being really conscious of something else as the only reality. There is me, and there is sadness. As the only reality, I am something which is aware of something else.

Justin Allen: So then, using you, let's say that you're the minority of the population, as far as talking about liberation.

Andreas Müller: Yeah, one shouldn't really print that (laughing).

Justin Allen: Well, how else, we have to do it some way (laughing).

Andreas Müller: No, I said that in order for it to get printed, but it shouldn't be (laughing).

Justin Allen: Is there a better way to try because it's not possible to really talk about this without making a distinction between you and I, for example?

Andreas Müller: I understand, yeah. I'm sorry. It's not really possible, and it's a fake distinction.

Justin Allen: But in the fake distinction, I represent the majority and you represent the minority?

Andreas Müller: Yes.

Justin Allen: And so for you, a feeling of sadness might apparently happen?

Andreas Müller: Well, yes, of course.

Justin Allen: Whatever. Let's say a tragedy, an apparent tragedy happens in your life.

Andreas Müller: Yes, or sometimes I get sad by watching the news.

Justin Allen: So, when that happens to the majority though, they would be processing it and internalizing it and maybe thinking of ways to make it go away, or they might turn off the TV so that they can avoid feeling the sadness. But you might do all those things also?

Andreas Müller: Yes and no. Those things might happen, but really not because there is someone doing it "in order to ..." It's not out of the assumption that I'm someone who has to consciously do life in order to gain something from that.

Justin Allen: But even that setup could happen to "you," couldn't it?

Andreas Müller: Not really, no, because that setup is the "me." I know what could happen is apparently that I turn off the TV because I don't want to see that anymore or whatever. But it would just be what apparently happens; it wouldn't be because of the assumption that there is a personal gain in any of that.

Justin Allen: So, let's say the distinction is that you and I ...

Andreas Müller: There is "no one."

Justin Allen: There is no you and I, but in our fake scenario, there's "me" representing the majority and you, Andreas, representing the minority, and we're watching TV and something sad comes on. For me, I would want to change it so that I could experience less unhappiness.

Andreas Müller: Yes.

Justin Allen: I would turn it off so that I don't have to be sad.

Andreas Müller: Yeah, because sad means that you are on the wrong path, compared to your actual goal, which is happiness.

Justin Allen: So, I would be looking at turning it off as a goal to avoid feeling unhappy or to be happier?

Andreas Müller: Yes, and this seems to have value in itself.

Justin Allen: It seems to increase my quality of life.

Andreas Müller: So to speak, yes.

Justin Allen: And it makes me feel like I'm here in life, active and doing things and making the best choices for me.

Andreas Müller: Yes.

Justin Allen: As something that's constantly being worked on in some way?

Andreas Müller: Exactly. But it starts with you already being there, just confirming that you are.

Justin Allen: And then you would turn it off also, except that it wouldn't be because you don't want to be sad anymore?

Andreas Müller: It would just be what apparently happens, yes. But there would be nothing which wants to do a certain thing in order to have a real outcome. It would just be what apparently happens for nothing, and it would be whole and alive and okay and free to be like that at the same time.

Justin Allen: Right, but because it would be a functioning, there would be certain functions going on. It's still somewhat mechanical, but not that you're controlling the mechanisms?

Andreas Müller: Oh no, of course not.

Justin Allen: But it would still be mechanical in the sense that ...

Andreas Müller: Apparently.

Justin Allen: Apparently mechanical, because you watch something sad, which triggers a thought or a feeling of apparent sadness, which then triggers a response, which would be, "Turn it off."

Andreas Müller: Or it could be that I go on watching it or whatever. Of course.

Justin Allen: In that sense, it's really no different, because also for "me" it's a mechanical process in a way. It's like, "Ah, I'm sad." And either the decision is to avoid being sad by turning it off or to be aware of being sad, let yourself be sad and keep watching it, not trying to avoid things. It's also just what's apparently happening.

Andreas Müller: Yes (laughing). Exactly. That's why it's an apparent difference, not a real one. It doesn't even matter. Neither of those is better or worse, and in neither of those does someone have an advantage and someone else a disadvantage. No, both just are completely what apparently happens, for "no one" in the end.

Justin Allen: That's what keeps on puzzling me, especially over the past five weeks of talking to you. It's just that there's no fucking difference.

Andreas Müller: Yes.

Justin Allen: And that's the big difference (laughing).

Andreas Müller: Yes, exactly. The assumption of a difference is the difference. But there's no real difference.

Justin Allen: Right.

Andreas Müller: But the hope for a difference, of course, is so much ingrained into the person's experience because the experience is that it can't be this, so it must be different. Whatever fulfillment is, whatever enlightenment is, whatever liberation is, whatever that is which I seek, it must be different. But there is nothing different; it's exactly this (laughing).

Justin Allen: How do you say that sentence again? The big difference is that there is no difference (laughing)?

Andreas Müller: The assumption of there being a difference is the only difference. It is what makes the apparent difference.

Justin Allen: Right.

Andreas Müller: Or the "me" which thinks, "I'm different," makes the difference. "Assumption" is a bit superficial actually, because it sounds as if you could not assume it. But the "me," where the assumption arises from, so to speak, is the only thing which separates itself, which says, "I'm different from everything else. I'm 'me,' I'm different."

Justin Allen: In that sense, you could also say that the life of somebody that's in prison isn't really any better or worse than your free, out-of-prison lifestyle?

Andreas Müller: So to speak, yes.

Justin Allen: Or the life of somebody that experienced twenty or forty years of some absurd tragedies from when they were a child, or maybe diseases or addictions or whatever?

Andreas Müller: Yes.

Justin Allen: You can't say their life is worse or better?

Andreas Müller: Yes, not really. I'm not trying to make it sound good; it's painful, and it still is what it is. But yes, you can't really say it's better or worse. Basically because there isn't really someone alive.

Justin Allen: Because I have these things that my mom told me when

I grew up that got stuck in my head, and one of them is, "Life's not fair."

Andreas Müller: Yes.

Justin Allen: I always thought that you could say that, but you could also say that life's completely fair. Because tragedy that happens to people has nothing to do with them. You can even see that without going into this topic of non-duality, it's automatically like that: If you're born in a certain part of the world, your life is going to be relatively less safe than in another part of the world. There's nothing that a person can do about it, but they still have the same potential in a sense; they're just living life like you are. There's not this hierarchy in a way.

Andreas Müller: Not at all. Yes, exactly. One could say there is no fairness in circumstances, but the fairness is that no circumstance is real. That's the fairness (laughing), that nothing matters. That everything is empty.

Justin Allen: Then if you bring that back to being someone in the audience watching a play, like Romeo and Juliet, you think some people have a better life than others, and then you might say, "Oh, it's so tragic what happened to Romeo and Juliet." They killed themselves, but the brothers and sisters still went on living, so you might say, "Oh, even though they weren't the main actors of the play, at least they're alive and get to go on living their lives, and they didn't die this tragic way of killing themselves." But then at the end you go, "Ah, but it's all just a play anyway, none of them are there."

Andreas Müller: Yeah.

Justin Allen: So in that sense, none of them had it better or worse?

Andreas Müller: Totally, yeah.

Justin Allen: So, if you think about it in the context of the world, everybody's just playing a role, this is all just a big play or a big dream?

Andreas Müller: Yes, everyone is already being played, with "no one" really in there. "No one" really is in a better or in a worse position.

Justin Allen: I don't know if it makes sense to talk about a personal thing, but you have a son.

Andreas Müller: Yes.

Justin Allen: And I would just assume from our conversations that maybe you wouldn't want to put your son into a public school or into the conventional school system.

Andreas Müller: Yes. Actually, that's what we are doing, to not do that (laughing).

Justin Allen: So, if I were going to judge you or analyze you from the perspective of the majority, assuming also that you're the majority, I would think that you're doing it so that your son doesn't grow up the same way that all of us grew up, under the same kind of conditioning.

Andreas Müller: Well, in my story, but that's just my story, it doesn't mean anything. In my story, it's actually coming from my partner (laughing). This whole issue probably wouldn't have entered my life, because my time in school wasn't so bad actually. I would have probably gone for a normal school, but now, since I've got to know the whole system, I'm totally happy that it is like that, and I enjoy him going to this school and stuff. But in my story, it wouldn't have come out of my thoughts or feelings.

Justin Allen: So, even if it wasn't your choice, you're still doing it from your story in a way?

Andreas Müller: Yeah, which is what apparently happens. That I am as I am because of A, B and C (laughing). How else should it appear?

Justin Allen: In some way, you've been pre-programmed from your past of twenty to forty years?

Andreas Müller: Of course. At least, it seems like we're all more or less conditioned by our past.

Justin Allen: Are your next twenty or forty years going to be somewhat calculable?

Andreas Müller: Apparently, no. Not really.

Justin Allen: They're going to be somewhat predictable, don't you think so (laughing)?

Andreas Müller: No, I don't think so. In a way, I know what you mean, but it's not really predictable. But not for you either.

Justin Allen: Well, it seems like it would be super unlikely for you to ... I don't know.

Andreas Müller: To naturally regain hair (laughing)?

Justin Allen: Or become a billionaire (laughing).

Andreas Müller: Well.

Justin Allen: That's not in the cards for you?

Andreas Müller: Yes, I don't see that coming either, just like I don't see that I start growing again. That seems to be predictable, but it's not knowable.

Justin Allen: No. But based on your foundation, for example that you're born in Germany, live here and are around forty years old now, you're going to follow a certain pattern in a sense, of the typical German because of your upbringing and your background?

Andreas Müller: Oh, yes, totally. That's what apparently happens.

Justin Allen: Same way as if somebody grew up in an uneducated environment and they've reached forty years old and haven't really done some kind of major ambitious step to get themselves way out of that world, then they're probably going to follow that particular pattern of life circumstances?

Andreas Müller: Yeah. One could say, what else? Because obviously, that's what apparently happens.

Justin Allen: Right, and everybody in that sense should be equal. That's the equality of liberation or of non-duality; that it's available to anybody. I mean, it's not available to anybody, because nobody's there, but it's available regardless of circumstances and regardless of ...

Andreas Müller: Oh, yeah, totally. And it's one hundred percent equal and available for everybody in the sense that everybody is it already.

Justin Allen: That's what to me seems fair. And if it weren't available though, then that would be unfair.

Andreas Müller: One could say so, yes. And actually, we apparently pointed out that the fairness is that there is no difference in the first place. Not even in a way that it's theoretically available for everyone, which is kind of true, but still one could say, "But it's unfair that only some people die before they die physically and most of us not." But no, the fairness is completely that there is no difference. That it doesn't matter, that nothing really matters. There is no real separation, and there is no real unification or liberation in the sense of two opposites. That's the fairness, of course. It levels everything out.

Justin Allen: Right, and because it takes away the duality, it automatically takes away good or bad and right or wrong and fortune or misfortune?

Andreas Müller: Yes.

Justin Allen: But still it seems like it's the more well-to-do people that are into spirituality or non-duality and are pursuing all of this as though it were something to pursue.

Andreas Müller: Was that a question? If it was a question, I didn't get it.

Justin Allen: It's not really a question, but it's pointing out that the people that seem to be interested in this tend to be wealthier people.

Andreas Müller: I don't know. I guess considering the German circumstances, I'm coming from kind of a wealthy background, but I never followed that. So, compared to many other parts of the world, I'm wealthy, but compared to the region where I live, I'm not wealthy at all. I'm a bit of an exception (laughing).

Justin Allen: Right, but I'm just saying that going to a spiritual retreat, for example, costs money. It seems to be happening more in the Western world. And even here, the people that are attending a week-long silent retreat or something like that, where you pay between 1000 and 2000 euros for a week of listening to somebody or just being silent together, are relatively wealthy.

Andreas Müller: Yeah, but that's just spirituality and the Western stuff, that has not really something to do with that message.

Justin Allen: Yeah, but it also just seems like the people that tend to be interested in this have enough income and leisure time to entertain these thoughts.

Andreas Müller: Yeah, I don't know.

Justin Allen: I don't know, there might not be any point in talking about this.

Andreas Müller: Yeah, no, because it's not really like that. I, for example, wasn't starving, because, of course, in Germany, you don't really starve. But having enough money was always a big issue for me, basically because I didn't care much about money, so I often didn't have much and was wondering how I would pay my rent next month et cetera. So, it was something that indeed kept me busy, and I know quite a few people for whom it was or is similar. I just wouldn't make a rule out of that. It doesn't mean anything; it's just what apparently happens. It could be happening in poverty and in wealth equally. It seems that when the interest is there, it finds a way to be acted out, no matter the circumstances.

Justin Allen: One other question that is a little bit off topic: To put it into a contextual framework, how would you classify someone who would be asking me, "What are you doing?"

And I would go, "Well, one of the things is I'm having talks with this guy, Andreas Müller, about non-duality." And they would ask, "Oh, what is that? Is it philosophy or spirituality or psychology?" I wonder how I would try to answer this. First of all, I don't like to call it non-duality, because I don't even know what the fuck that is myself.

Andreas Müller: I hate that term (laughing).

Justin Allen: And I don't want to call it spirituality either, because I don't consider myself a spiritual person, and I also don't want to be categorized as that. Also, it's definitely not philosophy, and I'm not really a fan of philosophy as how I've come to understand it. Then it's not psychology either, so I want to call it science actually (laughing).

Andreas Müller: No.

Justin Allen: Out of the available options, it's the best one because ...

Andreas Müller: No.

Justin Allen: But isn't science about the nature of reality?

Andreas Müller: No. Well, it is whatever it means for you. But science for me sounds like inquiry.

Justin Allen: See, science to me sounds like questioning and the search for truth, as close as you can get to it.

Andreas Müller: That's what I mean, that's maybe what you think this is about; searching for something.

Justin Allen: No, it is about that there's the dream and then the non-dream, and well, not even that. And science was the "thing" that took away the illusion people had before. So, that was the freedom of science, at least during the Renaissance; it was that idea of getting rid of the beliefs in mythology and religion and the world being flat.

Andreas Müller: I understand where you're coming from, of course.

Justin Allen: Science is something else now with different meaning than before, but I feel like originally, at the time at least or at its roots, it was supposed to be the illusion killer.

Andreas Müller: Yeah. But many people would regard spirituality as science as well; as a science in consciousness that is about exploring consciousness, exploring states, looking within, checking out and finding out how everything fits together.

Justin Allen: That's not what I mean by it though.

Andreas Müller: All right, that's fine.

Justin Allen: How would you try to ...

Andreas Müller: Yeah, that's what I mean. I understand science as the attempt to find something, but every finding and also every scientific discovery is just apparent, actually it's just another belief, not really different from the beliefs that were seen as "true" before science came up. Maybe the beliefs aren't as dogmatic and as permanent anymore nowadays, but they are still considered to be true or real. It all operates within the story, within the dream of reality, so to speak. But I'm not like a scientist; I'm as helpless as everyone else to tell the truth, whatever this would be. I just say something for the sake of words, like, "non-duality," or, "Have a look," or sometimes I say it's a combination of philosophy and meditation. But the thing is it's impossible. You can't categorize it, because any categorization would already be a misconception. An apparent misconception, of course, because any categorization would just be what happens. I can't tell anyone anything, really. And that's very different from what scientists attempt to do.

Justin Allen: In the United States, they have these days where you bring your father or your mother into work or where children or teenagers visit the workplaces of their parents, and they talk about what they do (laughing). Maybe something like that exists in Germany as well?

Andreas Müller: Yeah, maybe, but not necessarily (laughing).

Justin Allen: I can imagine you there with fifteen to thirty children, and you start off explaining to them, "So, at your birth (laughing), you start off as unseparateness, and then somehow, in some unknown way, at the age between around one to two you become separate. And from that point on, you're constantly searching for fulfillment (laughing)."

Andreas Müller: You don't really want to tell that to someone, especially not to kids (laughing). But still, maybe some would surprisingly resonate with that, with not being real and nothing being real. It depends on the age.

Justin Allen: Yeah, they probably would handle it better than an adult would (laughing).

Andreas Müller: Yeah, it's possible. Absolutely. They sneak into life with the me-ing and being phase, but they don't necessarily leave life with me-ing and being.

Justin Allen: This week I got stuck on this Romeo thing that we talked about, and then I also kept on coming back to how Tony Parsons was talking about walking on a road, and then all of sudden, the road became everything.

Andreas Müller: Or there was just road.

Justin Allen: Yeah, there was just road. So when I'm going around or sitting in a room sometimes, ... The words are going to fail me, but something happens that makes me question my experience at the moment. Then I think about what it would be like actually to be able to say the sentence ... I'm not doing it as a practice or anything, I'm just ...

Andreas Müller: Yeah, yeah, yeah.

Justin Allen: So I just say, "What would it be like to be able to say that all of a sudden there's just road?" What would have to happen for that sentence to resonate or be said? And then also, when I wake up, it's so clear that I'm there, but that I wasn't there before. Not that it's clear to me that I wasn't there before, because I wasn't there to be clear of it, but it's still so clear that I was nothing, and now I'm something.

Andreas Müller: Yes. But in a way, already as a conclusion out of a process.

Justin Allen: You mean out of a process of thinking and reasoning?

Andreas Müller: Of thinking and observing, yeah.

Justin Allen: Yeah, but that observation is the thing. I am awake, that's the observation.

Andreas Müller: Yes, yes.

Justin Allen: But it's so clear that there was a period of time where there wasn't an observer. At least, that's how I would put it in language.

Andreas Müller: Yes, but it's not clear by only being present. It's only clear by already going into a process of thinking about reality and turning it into a story. But yes, then it's logical.

Justin Allen: But there are – and this could all be bullshit, but it does seem to be happening that I can't use another word, so I have to say "experience" –, so there are moments where I have experiences of things that do seem illogical or un-experienceable.

Andreas Müller: Yeah.

Justin Allen: But I'm also not trying necessarily to make them logical or experienceable.

Andreas Müller: That's true, but actually only because they seem to be so unimportant that you don't need an answer for those specifically (laughing).

Justin Allen: I've generally always considered myself to have a really good memory, and I tend to hold onto things to be able to recall them. I've always placed so much value on that I can recall what we said in a conversation or what happened five minutes ago. I feel like that is falling apart (laughing).

Andreas Müller: That's possible, yeah (laughing). Especially because it was just empty, just words apparently, with no meaning at all (laughing).

Justin Allen: Then I also find that during my whole life, if somebody did what I consider an injustice to me or I didn't get what

I wanted, it would churn around in my mind, "What did I or the other person do wrong, or how can I rectify it?" and then I was judging them, myself and the situation. I always recognized that as such a torturous way to go through life, like holding a grudge or not forgetting or forgiving somebody or not moving on from something. I recognize this tendency to want to hold on.

Andreas Müller: Yeah.

Justin Allen: So within the past, maybe through talking with you, or maybe it's been going on for years, I've been noticing a change. It's not like there's an act of letting go of things, but it feels like just a loss of wanting to put energy into these types of things. But then, I don't want to let go, because it feels like I'm giving up or I'm quitting or something like that.

Andreas Müller: No, no.

Justin Allen: You know what I mean, right?

Andreas Müller: Yeah, absolutely.

Justin Allen: Because this is where I start to feel that it's existential in a way, like if you're letting go of the steering wheel, you're going to crash.

Andreas Müller: Yeah. That's how it feels. "If I'm not doing life, it will crash. And it hasn't crashed so far, because I was doing it."

Justin Allen: But then you put that into the context and start to – again the words are wrong, but if you start to feel like you actually don't exist, then really nothing matters. And all that stuff like holding on to things really doesn't matter anymore.

Andreas Müller: Yes.

Justin Allen: It seems that it's hard to let that happen.

Andreas Müller: Yes, one could say so. I know what you mean. If there were someone who could decide, it would be the weirdest thing. To not keep some sort of backup (laughing), some sort of control, just someone who's still at least observing (laughing), to just in case be able to regain the steering wheel.

Justin Allen: Yeah. At the recent Tony Parsons talk in Munich, people would ask some questions, and then he'd say something where at some point the person would go, "Oh, my god, so it's just hopeless." And then he would say, "Yeah, it's hopeless." And the person might reply, "Oh, but that's such a relief, isn't it?" And then Tony would say, "Yeah, it's such a relief. You don't need to care. You don't need to worry so much."

Andreas Müller: That's possible, yeah.

Justin Allen: Without qualifying it, however, I'm thinking, "All these people are just thinking, 'Oh, what a great message. Actually, my whole life doesn't matter, and everything that I've done doesn't matter, and that's so great. I'm relieved of everything.'" Which is true in one sense, but it's not true in how the person's interpreting it.

Andreas Müller: True.

Justin Allen: But sometimes I got the sense that Tony's okay with letting them "have" that satisfaction, so to speak.

Andreas Müller: Of course, of course.

Justin Allen: Yeah?

Andreas Müller: Yes. What else? Nothing else is expected. "Me" will misunderstand, no matter if I talk for one and a half hours straight through or if I only say three sentences; "me" will come up with its own interpretation of what this is about and what this means for "me." Of course. Only as long as someone survives it, there will be an understanding of what was being said. An apparent one, an illusion of understanding, of course. This can't be prevented, it's just inevitable, and it's not even wrong. In a way, that's what's happening all the time when there is the illusion of being a "person," running around with some ideas and understanding about what seems to be going on. This message doesn't try to prevent that from happening. Not at all. It just is what apparently happens. It will just be like that, and nothing will change that. Except the change is what apparently happens, but nothing can bring that change about.

Justin Allen: My friend went up to talk to Tony Parsons personally when he was sitting down and was asking him about living in the countryside or something like that. Because he's having one of these moments where he's trying to figure out the best thing for his life, and he was hoping for an answer. I think Tony just said something like, "Oh, I know people who lived in the country, and if you want to live like that, you have to know what you're doing." So, he just gave totally normal advice (laughing), but then he also said something like, "You don't have to worry, it's all just a dream (laughing). It's all just a dream, it doesn't matter what you do or what happens, it's all a dream." So, my friend told me this story, and I suspected he might be processing it in the way of, "It doesn't matter what I do." But when Tony's saying it, he's meaning it literally, like this is a fucking dream (laughing). "You're" not happening.

Andreas Müller: One could say so, yeah.

Justin Allen: Right?

Andreas Müller: Yeah (laughing).

Justin Allen: He's not meaning it in a way that the majority of us would interpret it, like it's a free-for-all, it's all fine, it doesn't matter. Choose A, choose B, whatever. Or maybe yes, he also means it like that. But at the same time, he is saying, "You can't decide if it's A or B."

Andreas Müller: Yes. It's not really given as an answer to bring about an experience of relaxation like, "Don't be scared, it doesn't matter." No, as you said, it literally doesn't matter, because there is "no one," because there is no A or B, because there just is what apparently happens. So yes, either way, it doesn't matter (laughing).

Justin Allen: So, that just triggered something for me right now. When I start to feel like I'm not "me" – and within this sentence, I can already hear the mistakes –, then in the experience of trying to explain that, it does feel like I am, or "me" is, like an arm or the wall or the floor. I'm as much how I've always thought of myself to be, I'm as much "me" as I would be a table or a chair or an object in space (nods of agreement by Andreas). And then, that's when I have the sense that I disappear, that I'm not there. But then, and this is like the thing that blocks me, I immediately say, "But then, what is that that's there?" You know what I mean? It's so hard to not place some-thing that is still somehow conscious or consciousness.

Andreas Müller: Yeah, this is inevitable. I don't say that it should be possible; it's not possible. For that which starts the inquiring in the first place, there's no other possibility than ending up with itself again. No way, it's hopeless.

Justin Allen: I think that's a good word (hopeless) to end on (laughing).

Andreas Müller: Yes, I'm fine with that (laughing).

Justin Allen: Then have a good rest of your day.

Andreas Müller: Yeah, you too. Thanks.

Justin Allen: Ciao.

Andreas Müller: Ciao.

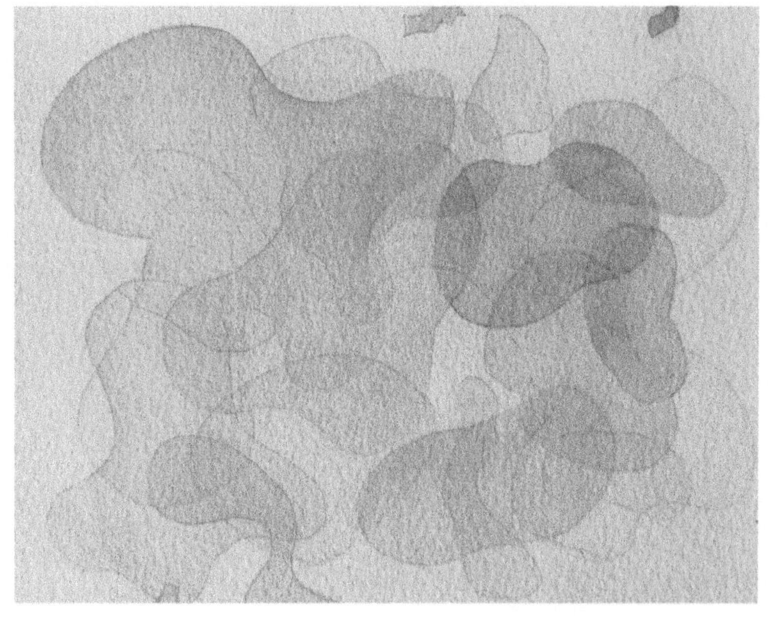

December 18, 2019 Talk 08

EXPERIENCE IS I AM

Andreas Müller: Hi. How are you?

Justin Allen: I'm good.

Andreas Müller: Good.

Justin Allen: How are you?

Andreas Müller: I'm good, too, thank you.

Justin Allen: What if I said that I wasn't good (laughing)?

Andreas Müller: Well, that would have been okay, too (laughing).

Justin Allen: So, to start off, I thought I'd read something from Tony Parsons.

Andreas Müller: All right (laughing).

Justin Allen: In one of his essays, The Dream of Separation, he wrote, "The dilemma for the dream seeker is that the feeling of separation drives the seeking for resolution, which further fuels the sense of separation." We've kind of talked about that in various ways, but not in the way that this implies that seeking increases the separation.

Whereas for me, I've always understood in a way that there's not really a hierarchy in a sense; that you can't really make your situation in the dream worse or better. But as far as how I read and interpret Tony's statement, it's definitely implying that somebody who, for example, is going to a guru, working for the porsche or house, or going to a Zen monastery or is constantly inquiring and meditating, is worse off than the guy or the woman that's just working a normal job and having a normal life and not doing any of this spiritual or obvious fulfillment seeking stuff.

Andreas Müller: Yeah, not really. Because I would say that the people who "just live a normal life" are as much seeking as people in spirituality.

Justin Allen: Right, that's what I've gotten from talking with you. But from what I've heard from Tony Parsons, he might not mean it that way. But it's definitely being interpreted that way: that the seeker, the religious or spiritual person or the person going to a therapist or better house seeking, is essentially worse off because they're doing this extra effort. Because they still have a job and are still dealing with other life situations, and on top of that they're spiritually seeking.

Andreas Müller: I mean, you know, it's in the story, because there are no people, no "me's." But yes, one could see it exactly like that; that the spiritual search is like an extra job. But like with every other job, it can be fun also, and then you wouldn't see it as being worse off, you would rather see it as enriching. Or what also seems to be happening is that in spirituality, the seeking energy often is much more focused than in so-called normal life where it's about getting your life done, so you have to juggle with several construction sites, so to speak: the job, the relationships with your partner, your parents et cetera, the money situation. But in "hardcore spirituality," one could say it's all about just being or becoming enlightened. Nothing else matters but that. So in the story, or in the experience of the seeker, this has a huge potential for frustration, and often it seems to be much more a dance between bliss and desperation, between two extremes, than for people who have, so to speak, their focus spread. But it's not that in one thing or the other, there is someone who is more or less separate.

Justin Allen: All right. But it ...

Andreas Müller: So, essentially it doesn't matter.

Justin Allen: Okay. But do you agree though that it would be easy to interpret it this way?

Andreas Müller: I don't know if it's easy to see it like that. But yes, I know that there are people interpreting it like that (laughing).

Justin Allen: But I suppose though that you've had to have experienced this in your life before. When maybe you're having a conversation with somebody, and you ask them about the meaning of life or some existential, deep, more philosophical questions. Then the person might sense that you're kind of searching for the answer to life, and they might say, "Oh, these questions ... You're too intelligent." Or, "You're thinking about this all too much." Or, "People that are really happy are the ones that don't ever think about or question this kind of stuff." And then the cliché sentence is, "Ignorance is bliss."

Andreas Müller: Yes.

Justin Allen: It does seem that way. For example, a woman working at a punch press machine who just goes into work, punches her card in and then presses a button all day. Then she goes home, cooks dinner, watches TV, talks with her family and goes to sleep. In this routine, maybe there are some little grievances about the job, about not having enough money, about wishing for a better relationship. But there's not this deeper question like, "Am I living my life the right way?"

Andreas Müller: Well, I know what you mean. One could say so. For some people it may be like that. But I think that for most people, it only is like that as long as it seems to be working.

Justin Allen: Right. But that might be working for twenty years or longer (laughing).

Andreas Müller: But same in spirituality for many people.

Justin Allen: Yeah, that's true.

Andreas Müller: Yeah, exactly. I wouldn't make a real distinction between so-called normal life and spirituality, which, for me, is just another part of life in which people seek fulfillment. So, the distinction is already not quite true, because in normal life, it's also about fulfillment, and there can also be a lot of these questions going on, in a rather material sense, of course: "Is this the right partner?" "Is it the right job?" "Is this the life that I really want to live?" At least, when there is the possibility to make a change. Or if there's not much space for change, there is still living in stories about ...

I just thought about India, for example, which generally is a very poor country. But still, or just because of that, people adore those shiny, happy Bollywood movies. The same happened in Germany after the war: People were very poor but still somehow referred to those sentimental films in a regional setting. You know, these movies that played in the countryside or in the mountains where there were no real problems and everyone was happy. There was also a reference to something holy or to a picture of perfection.

Justin Allen: Yeah, like *The Sound of Music*.

Andreas Müller: Yes. But yeah, in hardcore spirituality people can be really desperate. When I was seeking, I had a phase, so to speak, where I checked almost every moment, "Am I enlightened or not?" And the result was, "Not enlightened yet." It was all about feeling happy, about feeling really good, and becoming "enlightened" was what promised me that.

Justin Allen: Every moment was like, "Here I am still."

Andreas Müller: So to speak. And this caused intense suffering, apparently.

Justin Allen: Right, but that's what I think is implied by this: that intense suffering is apparently greater, or relatively greater, for such spiritual seekers than for the person that's not checking in on themselves every second.

Andreas Müller: Yes.

Justin Allen: That seems to happen more to the intense spiritual seekers than to the ones who are not engaging in existential questions or conscious searching. As you said, everybody has multiple construction sites in life that they're trying to manage. So, a "normal" person might be constantly questioning their marriage or something like that. They might be intensely focused on that, the same way that a "spiritual" person might be focused on their consciousness. But it seems that these spiritual seekers tend to have marriage problems, job problems and "How do I live?" problems also. Then they add the whole spiritual realm, which makes it seemingly worse for them.

Andreas Müller: I know. But for me it wasn't really like that. Yes, I had these problems as well, but spirituality just took over.

Justin Allen: Okay.

Andreas Müller: I know where you're coming from. I just wouldn't make the distinction too big. Because basically when there is seeking, there is ...

Justin Allen: So it's basically, when there is seeking, then that fuels the sense of separation?

Andreas Müller: Exactly. And opposed to what the "me" thinks, which always has the impression that seeking is good and leads to a real result, it's exactly the seeking drive which seems to fuel separation, apparently.

Justin Allen: Right. And it doesn't matter if you're seeking one percent or ninety-nine percent?

Andreas Müller: Yes, exactly.

Justin Allen: In a sense.

Andreas Müller: In this sense.

Justin Allen: It is apparently worse for the person. The person that's seeking with ninety-nine percent of their energy seems to suffer more than the person that's only seeking with one percent of their energy.

Andreas Müller: Yes, exactly, so to speak; if you want to make that picture up (laughing). Because the frustration of not getting it is much bigger when you put a lot more energy in the search.

Justin Allen: Right. Because the ninety-nine percent energetic seeking doesn't have a ninety-nine percent better chance of "reaching liberation" than the one percent energetic seeker?

Andreas Müller: So to speak (laughing).

Justin Allen: And the one percent doesn't have a better chance either?

Andreas Müller: Yes, exactly.

Justin Allen: Although then what this sentence seems to imply is that the one percent energetic seeker isn't fueling the sense of separation as much as the ninety-nine percent seeker?

Andreas Müller: Yes, and that would have been my next sentence: I immediately have to doubt the picture of the ninety-nine percent and the one percent.

Justin Allen: Because you don't believe there's a one percent, really?

Andreas Müller: Yes, exactly. Because I think in most people, you just don't really see it that strongly. Because life seems to work out, also in spirituality. There are many people who just go through life, which is totally fine. So just at the beginning, seeking is totally fine. It just is what it is. But you have many people, also in spirituality, who go through life taking a seminar here, a course there, a therapy session here or five years of therapy there. After that, they do ten years of continuous Hellinger sessions or become a trainer or therapist themselves.

Also in that field, so to speak, you have all kinds of people with all kinds of variations. But also in "normal life";

as long as it seems to work out, most people are just basically fine. Also, the "me" is fine, as long as the path seems to work and the goal seems to be reachable, so to speak. As long as the job more or less functions and the relationship more or less functions. Or even if it doesn't function, you just get a new one. As long as life functions and it all seems like, "Yeah, it's all good for something. It's all leading towards something," even the seeker is more or less happy.

But what happens if you lose your job, your partner and all that stuff? Same in spirituality. Or if you get a depression in "normal life," because it's obvious that it doesn't actually lead anywhere? That there is all this struggle going on for nothing? So, also the person in so-called normal life can easily get into an existential crisis. Which then isn't very different from a spiritual crisis, so to speak.

Justin Allen: Right, except that the spiritual crisis seems to be self-induced in a way.

Andreas Müller: Yeah.

Justin Allen: I'm just saying, that's a problem: the viewpoint from the "normal" person when they might have a conversation with a spiritual seeker or with somebody that's constantly self-analyzing or questioning life. Their advice to them is, "Don't question life. Stop doing that. That's what's causing your meltdown or your depression." They almost aggressively avoid life questions. Even in that example that you gave some time ago where two women came into your talk and were like, "Whoa. Let's get out of here." There's something operating in them that knows, "This might bring me into an existential crisis. This might make me start to question life."

Andreas Müller: Yeah. Well, question existence.

Justin Allen: Yeah. But isn't that somehow an act of wisdom or intelligence? Because I feel like there's some kind of understanding that listening to you or going into these questions does fuel separation. They might already recognize that they're separated. They already might recognize that there's some "lack" in their life. But they might also recognize that by trying to solve this problem, the problem will be increased.

Andreas Müller: I didn't have the impression with them.

Justin Allen: I'm not meaning those two ladies necessarily.

Andreas Müller: Yeah, okay.

Justin Allen: But people in general.

Andreas Müller: I don't know. But is it more intelligent to understand? I mean, there are some people who seem to understand the futility of spiritual seeking but still have their games going on. In relationships, for example, one partner says all the time to their "spiritual" partner, "Why do you care about all these weird questions? Why do you seek at all? What are you seeking for? What is this enlightenment stuff? It's just dreams." But one minute later, they're just going back to their story about what brings fulfillment, what a good life is and what needs to be done for that: how you should live, and how you should behave et cetera, not noticing that they just created the same story in the material world, so to speak. In that sense, it isn't really that kind of intelligence that you were speaking of.

Because, of course, what happens within the "me" world or in time, so to speak, or in so-called religious values? "Your path doesn't lead anywhere, but my path is the right one." There are the materialistic people who say of the spiritual people, "It's all bullshit," while the spiritual people say the same about the materialistic people. The punk would say, "It's bullshit to go for money and career," and the money-and-career type says, "Well, don't be a punk." So, that's happening all the time, and that's not really intelligent in that way.

Justin Allen: Okay, and probably ...

Andreas Müller: It depends on how you see it.

Justin Allen: Right. And your and Tony Parsons's audience tend to probably be people that are on the spiritual path. Or had been.

Andreas Müller: Had been, yeah.

Justin Allen: So, that's why probably this message, the verbal message, is addressing that specific audience in a way.

Andreas Müller: But see, that's what I'm already doubting because actually, it's not even really addressing someone. But it refers to the seeking setup itself, which doesn't need the spiritual field. That's what I mean. It applies also to so-called normal life.

Justin Allen: Right, it applies to normal life. But Tony Parsons is not really focusing all his energy on talking about your job. It's always more in general about meditation or self-inquiry that he's commenting on.

Andreas Müller: All right. Yeah, it may be possible.

Justin Allen: If it was an audience of Wall Street bankers ...

Andreas Müller: No, you can't do that. Because if there is a Wall Street banker sitting in the talk, it would one hundred percent apply to his dream world as well.

Justin Allen: Right. But I mean, if the whole audience was Wall Street bankers, then you might not be so much talking about going to gurus and meditation retreats. Because maybe for the Wall Street bankers, their focus has always just been on career, while the spiritual seeker is all into how they're meditating for ten hours a week.

Andreas Müller: Yeah. I understand.

Justin Allen: All the energy of the bankers is devoted to their career or to increasing their salary or whatever.

Andreas Müller: Yeah. But the message itself wouldn't change.

Justin Allen: Right. But the wording would change.

Andreas Müller: Not too much, but I know what you mean. With the stories and stuff.

Justin Allen: Right. Because I mean, it just always seems to be really addressing the dilemma of this niche type of person, this spiritual seeking type person. Even the language: There's a certain terminology that you only seem to get if you've been a spiritual seeker for ten or twenty years. It would be very foreign to somebody that just walked in on one of your or Tony Parsons's talks off the street.

Andreas Müller: Oh, but I know those cases as well.

Justin Allen: Right. But still, only talking about the dream state, the hypnotic dream and the dream seeker – just the word "seeker": If I just pulled somebody off the street and start talking about that stuff ...

Andreas Müller: But that doesn't work. The thing is that the picture you're painting is that this message speaks to people.

Justin Allen: No, I'm not trying to say that it's the people.

Andreas Müller: But my impression is that it's rather an answering of the questions that are coming. Really, I know it's not just exceptions. There's quite a bunch of people who don't really have a spiritual history. In a funny way, they catch up quite quickly about seeking, seeking energy and those so-called spiritual sentences. But if it comes to the guru stuff and "the real thing" and what is seen as spiritual, they have to say, "Well, I don't know all these people. Who is Mooji? For five years, I've been listening to Tony, and he's always talking about this teacher. I have no clue who that is." So, they're not familiar with the spiritual language, but somehow quite quickly they catch up with this setup or with the seeking setup in general and how it is being described, and they can easily see themselves and their life in that: with studying and pursuing a career and a successful job, for example. That exists, and I know too many people like that to call them exceptions. But yes, it's not the majority.

Justin Allen: Even with the example of the two women that came to your talk and then wanted to get out of there as quickly as possible: A spiritual person might also come into your talk and be like, "Oh, no, I don't want to hear this." Right?

Andreas Müller: The two women were kind of spiritual, but not deeply spiritual, so to speak; more like a mixture between spiritual and esoteric. They were sweet. I mean, we were talking about it. Something in them, which is a story though, immediately recognized what this is about. They were just honestly saying, "Oh, sorry. We don't want to go there."

Justin Allen: Right, because they don't ...

Andreas Müller: "It's too much or too intense. Because it's about us and death, really. We don't want to end life. We are not here to die, basically." Which is totally fine. There's not a problem in that. But it was clear that they didn't want that.

Justin Allen: Yeah, but they also won't get it (laughing).

Andreas Müller: Of course not (laughing).

Justin Allen: I can remember when I was eighteen or sixteen, I was questioning things, and my friends and family were almost angry at me for pursuing this kind of thing. My father especially would be worried in a sense; his question was always, "Don't you think you might be wasting your time?" He's right, to some degree.

Andreas Müller: Oh, yes, of course (laughing). Well, there is no other possibility. So, it's not really wasting time. But yes, seeking doesn't lead anywhere.

Justin Allen: Right, and I think everybody in a sense recognizes that to some degree. I think some people, like the hardcore believers, can turn it off and somehow be like, "No, it's totally not a waste of time. Everybody has to do this." As for me, I've never gone full on into anything. Because

I still have my doubt, and I'm skeptical. For example, I think I won't ever go to a monastery for any extended period of time. Because I'm thinking, "Well, that just means I'm going to be ten years without A, B, C, D and E," and without any certificate or proof of time spent with some reward.

Andreas Müller: Yeah.

Justin Allen: So, another thing that's going to be hard for me to express, but still I would like to talk about it again, is how in the Tony Parsons talk, he mentioned how he was walking on a road and that it's so stunning and the mind can't imagine what it's like when all of a sudden, there is just road. "You can't express this in words. But it's so stunning. One day you're walking down the road." Then he gets up out of his seat, starts walking forward and is like, "You're walking down the road. Then all of a sudden, the road just becomes road." (laughing) The way that my mind seems to try to grasp and understand that is to try and imagine what he's talking about.

Then I try to combine that maybe with what I've read throughout the years from people that claim to be enlightened and talk about what it's like. There is a little bit of this consensus, even though Tony Parsons might mean it differently. But it always kind of comes down to this experience (or non-experience) of everything all of a sudden being one thing or everything being connected. There's no separation anymore. This can also happen when you're on drugs apparently.

So for me, the simplest way that I start to imagine it is that if you weren't separated, by definition you'd be everything. Not that there's an experiencer to experience something at this point ...

Andreas Müller: Exactly, yeah.

Justin Allen: That's what I mean. Without the experiencer, distinctions don't exist anymore, so this would suggest no separation.

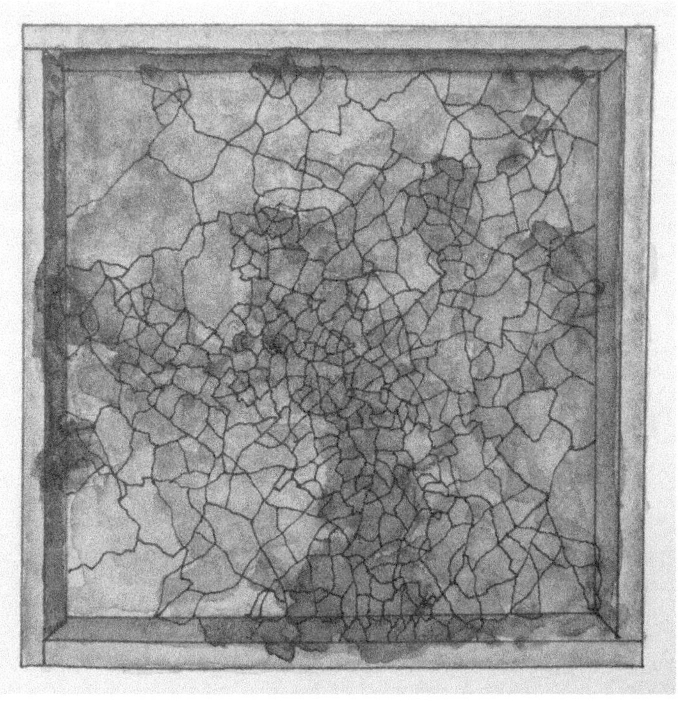

Andreas Müller: Exactly, yeah. Because the only thing that separates itself from everything is the seeker. Nothing else has the experience to be separate. Not even the body. The body and the thoughts and the feelings don't have the experience to be something separate. The only thing that experiences separation is self-consciousness, so to speak. It says, "I am me and not everything else."

The dilemma or just the thing with many spiritual experiences is that the person seems to be able to have a so-called oneness experience where they can experience that everything is one and nothing is separate. But it's still an experience. This is where I would make a distinction between what Tony says and what you say about taking drugs, for example, or what many spiritual people may refer to as being enlightened.

But yes. When the "me" dies, so to speak, the only thing that experiences separation, distinction and living in a divided reality disappears. The "me," this thing which is the first separate part and for which everything therefore is only and really separate parts, dies.

Justin Allen: You've mentioned this before, but I want to try to talk about it in more detail. You just said it already: that the only thing that we know of in the world or in the universe that separates itself out from un-separateness is the "me."

Andreas Müller: Yes, by just experiencing, "I am." Not even thinking, "I am," no; it's its natural experience.

Justin Allen: One example that a "me" can kind of relate to, where there's not this "me" happening in a way, is the body. So, the "me" experiences its body, but in a sense, it doesn't. Right? You feel like your whole body is your whole body. You don't really feel like you're your hand or your foot, as if your body were separated into parts. You don't really feel like your foot is more you than your hand is you. The experience of the human is just that the body is one whole thing, right? I am aware that we also tend to divide the body into parts like brain, stomach, bones, veins, organs et cetera, but in general we also experience our body as "body," as us, as one thing?

Andreas Müller: Yeah.

Justin Allen: You don't really know what your body's doing. You kind of accept that you're not really in control of it to a certain extent. Right now you and I are sitting here, and blood's moving around in our bodies. Cells are dying and being reborn and whatever else is just happening. You're not doing anything about it. So, that's something where the body isn't separating itself out from the world or from its own volume.

And that's something that you could kind of relate to as oneness. I know it's not necessarily helpful (laughing). But it is an example of experiencing oneness through apparent body parts. Because at least scientifically, you can break this entity, this oneness, so to say, down into all the body parts.

Andreas Müller: Yeah. But seen by the "person," the body is just something; something else or another part which is made out of small parts.

Justin Allen: Right. But they still think that they're their body. Or at least they're contained in it.

Andreas Müller: Exactly. It's actually rather that they are contained in it. Yes, many people think they are their body and their thoughts and all that stuff. While in spirituality you say you can't be your body, because you're aware of it. So yeah, the basic experience is that the body is actually already something that you have.

Justin Allen: Yeah, but it's also ...

Andreas Müller: Also actually in Christianity they say that the body is just some thing, but what you actually are and what lives in the body is the soul, the living essence or something like that. And it's the same from a more materialistic background. The basic idea is that the body is a gift or a temple or just a vehicle or a machine where you live in for a while.

Justin Allen: I don't know if I want to go this route, but that also has to be the case with transgender people that don't identify with being born a male or female. They're thinking, "I'm not a male/female." But then they look at their body which has every indication that they are a male or a female. So, that transgender phenomenon also feeds to this belief that you're not your body.

Andreas Müller: Yes. One could say so, or the "person" would experience it like that: that how I feel doesn't fit with how I look like. So yeah, the function isn't right.

Justin Allen: But still, everybody more or less accepts that within the body, there's not really separation happening?

Andreas Müller: Yes and no. Because everybody accepts separation, also in the body. Because it's seen like a clock made out of a lot of small parts which just seem to work together perfectly.

Justin Allen: Right. But somehow you recognize or accept that the body is not creating the separation?

Andreas Müller: Oh, yes. Yeah.

Justin Allen: It's the same like with a dog, what we talked about last time. A human looks at a dog and thinks in a way that the dog is kind of this unseparated, perfect life form. Like, "The dog doesn't have my problem." Somehow there's a recognition that it's like that because the dog doesn't have self-consciousness or maybe not even thoughts and feelings, how it was assumed previously. So because a dog doesn't have these presumed human attributes, they are seen by us as such beautiful, happy creatures.

Andreas Müller: Yeah.

Justin Allen: So, I'm just saying that there is some kind of recognition or understanding that there are examples of unseparateness in the world and maybe even a sense that it is only the "me" creating the apparent separateness.

Andreas Müller: Yeah. I know what you mean in a way. But the "person" would still see another condition, namely a dog who is a dog; a something which isn't separate. Anyway, I actually don't think that many people think that through in the sense how you just presented it. Seen by the "person," the "person" will just remain another part, another something which has a certain condition or multiple conditions.

Justin Allen: The reason I'm trying to do this with these examples is to build up to something that maybe is apparently happening to me. Or maybe some glimpses that I'm having. So when I hear this example of Tony Parsons and "the road" becoming "just road," I start to relate that to how I've really always separated, like, "My thoughts are my thoughts," which implies duality because I am there as something separate that can experience and be aware of my thoughts and my feelings; they're happening to me. So already, there's a separation.

Then I look at my hand, and I'm like, "Here's my hand." Then I can do things with my hand: move it away from me and closer to me. I don't think I've ever felt like I've had a soul, but let's just pretend that I felt like that: Then it would be my soul; something that I still have. Or I look at an object that's separate from me, and it's clear that it's not me and it's over there. But I start to recognize that the only thing that's creating all that is the sense of "me."

Andreas Müller: Yes.

Justin Allen: Then within that sense of "me," another recognition takes place, backwards. The sense of "me" is recognizing itself and the separation that it is apparently causing, and it even seems to recognize that it is nothing, an apparent illusion. But still, the sense of "me" is going on recognizing: a thought or a feeling or my hand. So even in that description, the sense of "me" has no more value than my hand or my thought or my feeling. It is equally occurring as a thought, feeling, hand or the objects outside of my body that I'm aware of, like a wall or a table or a tree.

So, that starts to feel like just an intellectual understanding. Still, it does kind of break things down a bit. It does automatically kind of eliminate the "me" because it's in a sense denying the "me," isn't it?

Andreas Müller: Denying would be too strong because it means that there is something that can be denied and someone who could deny something. In the end, it's denying something that isn't there in the first place. But yeah, it just can become what is seen ... I mean, that's the story. This can't be explained. Because now one has to take these process-related words, but it isn't a process in the end. But yes, the "no me" can become obvious, but obvious to no one. Apparently. And it goes together with a breakdown of it, apparently, which is timeless. You know, it's not a rule, and it's not a process. But what can happen is the questioning, like what you said. Until now it was so clear that there is something in here, looking outside. Looking at things. That it just was like that. Or when it turns out that the thing which looks at things isn't real in the first place.

Justin Allen: That's what I mean.

Andreas Müller: Yeah, exactly.

Justin Allen: So when that possible "dropping" of the "me" happens, that's what I feel like has ... I can't say when, but I feel like even maybe this has happened before. But for sure, before I didn't know what the hell was happening. I wouldn't have even been able to point it out like a red flower in a field of white. But if the "me" isn't real and there's some acknowledgement of that, but in this sense from "no one" really acknowledging it, "just acknowledgement," not from a point of view that acknowledges it, then that's how I can relate a bit to that experience of "the road" becoming just "road."

Andreas Müller: Yeah. I mean, you still relate to a picture of it. You can't really relate to that. But yes and no. I know what you mean. I know that it can "feel" as if you could relate to that (laughing). I'm sorry (laughing). But yeah.

Justin Allen: But that's what I'm saying, too: that I don't know; right now I'm trying to explain this intellectually.

Andreas Müller: No, you're trying to somehow bring the experience of there "just being a road" into your experience. How that would apply to something experienceable. That's my impression. It's not just intellectual; you want it to be a little bit closer.

Justin Allen: Well, that, but also that it does seem to be happening occasionally. Where, let's say, I'm questioning things or I'm just going to break it down into a process that probably isn't the actual process of what's going on. But the process that seems to be going on is that maybe I'm thinking about something that Tony Parsons or you said or about our conversations. Or maybe I'm thinking about ten or twenty years ago. This is all happening at once.

Then maybe I'm trying to think about what the "me" is. Is it there, is it happening? You can't find it anywhere. Then it's all just happening, the sense of "me" is occurring in the same way that my thoughts and my feelings are occurring, the same way as the senses, the objects, the apparent separation, the possible oneness. Then I can go, "Oh, I'm aware of my thoughts and feelings." But I can also go, "Ah, but I'm also aware that I'm aware," making awareness and the sense of "me" nothing different, special or distinct from a thought or a passing cloud or a noise.

This awareness is in a sense just occurring the same way that a thought or a feeling or my hand is occurring – or a cloud or a raindrop. So what seems to happen in a way is that – and I'm not saying it's through inquiry or meditation – it (this) all of a sudden feels a little bit like bullshit. But it feels like then the "me" isn't there, and then there are no longer thought, feeling, chair, wall.

Then it's just ... I don't know how you would define it at that point, other than saying then it's everything or nothing.

Andreas Müller: Yeah, exactly.

Justin Allen: Then later on, if there's anything I can do, it's to say if there's no "me," if the "me" that I've been, that has been my point of perspective my whole life, which has created this world – because it is a world that's created by the sense of "me" –, then there's a whole other world created without the "me."

Andreas Müller: Yes, the illusion of a world. Yeah, exactly.

Justin Allen: Right. The illusion of the world is only created by this dream of the "me" or this sense of "me-ness."

Andreas Müller: So to speak, yeah.

Justin Allen: So without it then, there's no world anymore, just as there was no world previously when there was a "me"?

Andreas Müller: Yes.

Justin Allen: Then it just seems so stupid in a way. Because there's not a difference in a sense.

Andreas Müller: Yes, exactly. Because it's not even that our so-called real world has really been created. Nothing has been created in the apparent creation of the illusion of a world. That's why there is no real difference at all in the end. Because the whole world "me" lives in, including its own existence, actually never really happened. It's not that there was this real happening, and then it's really over. In the end, yeah, that's how it feels; that nothing really changed.

Justin Allen: Then nothing really happens either, because together with the vanishing of that one-point perspective of a "me," anything measurable, like time, for example, is taken away as well. Right?

Andreas Müller: Yeah.

Justin Allen: So without time then, there can't be a beginning for you, and there can't be an end for you. Because there's nothing, there's not a point that began or a point that can end.

Andreas Müller: Yes, and there is not a point of presence now here.

Justin Allen: So then in that sense, intellectually speaking, that creates the meaninglessness of searching and life in general ... Because only with the "me," there's meaning. There has to be meaning. Meaning seems to happen automatically out of the sense of self or "me"?

Andreas Müller: Yes, and this is what, in the story, we could call an artificial reality, whereas without the "me," it's a natural reality. It's already meaningless. It's not opposing a state of meaningful to a state of meaningless. The whole idea of meaning is only part of the dream of the "me" that is experienced as something "real." Only in this world, so to say, is there real meaning.

Justin Allen: Then that's why whatever's happening is just happening, and whatever is just is. Because, I don't know ... Because there can't be more or less of anything. Then when things happen like war or some catastrophe or something good, it's just the same as a thought or a feeling. It's just happening out of nothing.

Andreas Müller: Or is actually nothing.

Justin Allen: Yeah.

Andreas Müller: Yes. Including the own body, so to speak. Which all just is what apparently happens.

Justin Allen: Right. Then whatever movement happens is also just what apparently happens. So here, I'm moving my hand (waving his hand back and forth). Before, I'm convinced that I'm doing this, right? And now, there's an apparent location that I'm still doing it. But without the sense of "me," the hand would still move but not because of a someone or for a someone – it would just be happening in the same way that other things just seem to happen without explanation or meaning?

Andreas Müller: Yes! Exactly. It's just blindly what it is.

Justin Allen: Right, blindly. The same way as when you look out your window and see birds flying around doing weird flight things. They're just doing it, or it's just happening, for no reason. Of course, we also have explanations for that as we try to find explanations for everything. But let's just pretend there's not the explanation and we are okay without needing or finding an explanation, and you just look out and see a bird do a weird flight maneuver.

The same way with cloud formations or rivers flowing. They're just that way for no reason, always slightly differently. It's not like a machine that's perfect. Even a machine can't ever be perfect. So, you just accept those things happening for no reason, also from the normal point of view. You can accept that a dog might not have a "me," and your body doesn't actually have a "me." It's the same for the "me" and for the "no me"; that it just happens for no reason.

Andreas Müller: Yeah, just that the "me" can't really accept that.

Justin Allen: Right.

Andreas Müller: I mean, the "me" can accept the concept. But it is just not its experience. "Me's" experience will never be to not be "me." That's the thing. But yeah, it can go through all those thoughts and somehow like the concept. Your point was different though, but yeah.

Justin Allen: "Me" can question. I'm not saying there's a way. But by questioning itself in a sense and by using examples that it has already accepted or confirmed in life, there seems to be something happening. I'm not saying that the questioning or inquiry turns into the end of the "me." But I don't know; there's something about that apparent happening of questioning, especially about the road example Tony Parsons talked about. That maybe it triggered something.

Andreas Müller: Which is lovely.

Justin Allen: Well, I don't know if it made me do anything. But that was something where in that moment when that was said ...

Andreas Müller: BOOM! Oh, yeah. Because in a way, I mean that's now a bit in the story, but that's the fascinating thing in a way. That's the unknowable thing. How is that? No one knows. It's impossible to know that. It's impossible to experience that. But that's the question. How is it when there's "just road"? When there's just sitting in front of a screen and talking? When there's just this? How is this actually, for "no one"? It's whole and complete and kind of fascinating. At the same time, utterly and completely unknowable (laughing).

Justin Allen: I'm sitting and looking at the screen and you. Then I'm looking at my knee. Then I can see a chair from my peripheral vision, and I ...

Andreas Müller: Yeah, don't even go there (laughing).

Justin Allen: Where do you think I was going to go (laughing)?

Andreas Müller: Some observing stuff going on (laughing).

Justin Allen: No, well maybe. I was going to say that without the "me," I can't ... It's like the distinctions fall away. Even though they're there at the same time.

Andreas Müller: Exactly, yes. This in the end would still be a difference compared to this oneness experience we talked about. Where everything is only one ...

Justin Allen: Right, one would be ...

Andreas Müller: Exactly. That's the amazing thing. Separation falls away, and it still remains as it is. It's not that the reality turns into something else and you see something new like a new realm or something like that. It's not the replacement of the experience of separation by an experience of oneness. That's why these words like "real" and "unreal" come out. It is as it is, by not being real and not really happening in time and space. Not having real meaning and all that stuff. In a funny way, it remains exactly how it already is or was (laughing).

Justin Allen: Having this oneness experience where I'm one with or merge into everything, that's the opposite in a way of what I think is the message from you and Tony Parsons. If a so-called enlightened person or a person on drugs were to say, "I became one with everything," that's more of an intense version of separation.

Andreas Müller: Exactly. Well, it's not the opposite. It's just another personal experience.

Justin Allen: Yeah, but it's an extreme experience because the person before wasn't feeling that way. Now they're in this state, some new state where they're one with everything. So they really feel, "Oh, my. I'm god. I'm oneness. I'm everything." But still feeling like a super-version of "meness" is happening.

Andreas Müller: Yeah, but usually this doesn't stay. Usually there is just one or maybe a couple of oneness experiences. Then a concept and a teaching and a working around that come into play. They start breathing into the heart to feel this love again or something like that. They start telling themselves stories and turning it into a conviction and all that stuff. "Actually, I'm god. Actually, all is one. Everything is beautiful." But my impression is not really that people stay in that permanently. For most people it just comes and goes. I don't expect, for example, a spiritual teacher, who claims to have reached enlightenment or to be consciousness or one with everything, to always be in that state. Probably or maybe they have seen it and then developed a whole teaching around it.

Justin Allen: Adyashanti does talk about this, too. I'm not that familiar with him, I just went to one of his retreats, but I have a friend who's been going to him for fifteen years or something like that. He also talks about how there's fake enlightenment in a sense. Or where somebody feels like they've become enlightened or one with everything, but they haven't really.

Andreas Müller: Yes, there's a lot of that stuff around because people turn all kinds of experiences into enlightenment. But of course, it depends on how you define enlightenment or if you mean it in the sense of liberation. It's all just words and stories, but what I speak about when I refer to liberation just is not an experience. Period. But that's the funny thing with those teachings in a way; that they all think and promise that it is or leads to liberation, so to speak.

That's maybe why there's also a little bit more fun in talking about that. Because the claim is different. It's a bit like when there is a burglar. It's kind of okay. But if, for example, a policeman is a burglar, it's a bit like, "Oh, wow. That's funny." It's the same with spirituality. Everybody's seeking happiness, and all kinds of teachers promise fulfillment in whatever. But the comedy is that hardcore spirituality exactly promises liberation from this stuff but is perpetuating it at the same time (laughing).

Justin Allen: That's also what you and Tony talk about, I guess: how it's so simple. Or that the stunning thing is how nothing changes actually.

Andreas Müller: That's the stunning thing. That's the simplicity. That what we talk "about" already is the case. It's not simple in terms of doing it.

Justin Allen: Yeah, well, that's ...

Andreas Müller: That's how the seeker might understand it. That it's easy and simple to do. That's what a lot of teachings are about. "It's just about recognizing yourself. It's so easy. You just have to step out of the thoughts. After a little bit of training it's easy. It's not much to do." But that's not how it's meant. For the seeker, it's not easy at all; it's impossible to do. But the simplicity is that there is no seeker, and that there is nothing to realize. There is not a single step to take. That's the simplicity and the stunningness of it.

Well, apparently stunning because the stunningness already is a contrast to what the seeker thinks. So it's not really stunning in a way, because it's quite ordinary at the same time. And that's the simplicity of it. That it's exactly how it is.

Justin Allen: Well, it's just so simple. This might be a bad example, but it's kind of similar when your seven hours of sleep are almost coming to an end and you wake up from a dream. There's still a little momentum of the dream. So, whatever was happening in the dream, you might not be sure if that happened or not. Then you go, "Oh, it was a dream." That's kind of stunning in a way. Because whatever was happening ... Let's say you were being chased by a lion. You were totally afraid, and your heart rate might have increased. I don't even know if your heart rate is up when you're dreaming or not, but I think so. So then you wake up and kind of feel like you're still running. Or you're worried that the lion's still around. But then there's kind of this quick change that happens where you go, "Oh, no. I'm in my room. I'm not actually out in a field. The lion doesn't really exist."

I'm not saying that that's the same thing. It's not really stunning to change from the dream to the waking state, but in a way it is stunning.

Andreas Müller: Yeah, yeah, yeah, I understand. Yeah.

Justin Allen: Because in reality, if you were running from a lion in your waking state, and then somehow you got transported to your bedroom, you'd be like, "What the fuck just happened?" That would totally fuck you up for life (laughing).

Andreas Müller: Yeah (laughing). Though you are safe, you would be fucked up for life (laughing).

Justin Allen: But that's the thing. That's what's so simple in a way. It's really just that sense; that's what's so dumb or obvious. That it's just this apparent difference of the sense of "me" and no sense of "me." It's not like a complicated method which leads to a transformation or manifestation.

Andreas Müller: Not at all, yes.

Justin Allen: It's not a complicated machinery or an engine that you have to find out and fix.

Andreas Müller: Not a single thing, exactly. There is no "me." There are so many traditions trying to find out how the "me" and the psychology and thoughts and feelings work, and they want to find a way through that jungle. But that's absolutely futile. In the end it comes down to "me" or "no me." At the very end (laughing), which sounds like a process when we talk about the end, it turns out that even that difference is not a question.

So, that's right where we started off the conversation. The seeker thinks that this whole seeking process has some kind of value. Whatever it's about; if it's analyzing the "person," dividing thoughts and feelings or trying to avoid these thoughts – this whole investigation, also what the "me" is and how it functions, is futile. It's not wrong, of course. Because when it happens, it is what happens, but it's totally futile. There is no outcome of it. There is no use of that at all.

Justin Allen: Right. But it's futile all the time, for "no one" still?

Andreas Müller: Absolutely. Yes, totally. In that sense it's not really futile and not really wasting time. Because it just is what apparently happens. It's not that there is "someone" who could live a non-seeking life and be better off, so to speak.

Justin Allen: That's what I "get." Not that I can "get" anything. But that's what I "get" from it being futile but also not really being futile. It's not really like you're wasting your time, and it's not really like all those years of suffering happened either.

Andreas Müller: Yes, exactly.

Justin Allen: So, there's not actually any suffering, and there's not actually any opposite like non-suffering or pleasure or happiness.

Andreas Müller: There is no better way.

Justin Allen: Yeah, there's no better or worse way. There's no "way" even.

Andreas Müller: Yes. Yeah.

Justin Allen: There is just "what is." Whatever's happening is just what's happening, even if it could switch, even if all of a sudden, you're in your bedroom after just having been chased by a lion in a field. If right now all of a sudden the world changed, and instead of you seeing this screen (referring to the video chat computer screen), you would be seeing something else, or this wall behind me all of a sudden became red, it wouldn't matter?

Andreas Müller: Yeah, totally. It would just be what apparently happens for "no one," yes.

Justin Allen: Or if we all of a sudden turned into dinosaurs (laughing).

Andreas Müller: Yeah (laughing). Why not (laughing)?

Justin Allen: That would be a catastrophe for the "me."

Andreas Müller: That would be very traumatizing, yeah.

Justin Allen: What was that famous book, *The Metamorphosis*? I think it's by Kafka. Where the guy wakes up, and he's an ant or a fly or something like that.

Andreas Müller: I haven't read it, I'm sorry.

Justin Allen: But you know what I'm talking about, don't you (laughing)?

Andreas Müller: Yeah, I've heard it (laughing).

Justin Allen: I don't think I've read it either. But it's one of those books that we were supposed to have read. It's the same as when you wake up and you think that you have cancer or something like that.

Andreas Müller: Well, again, the actual problem, so to speak, is just waking up in the first place (laughing).

Justin Allen: Yeah, but I mean, if you're awake, and then you discover that as a "me" you have cancer, it's terrible.

Andreas Müller: Yes, of course. But a "me" experiences a changing world all the time, so to speak. Whether it's a potential threat or not.

Justin Allen: But a "no me" doesn't experience a changing world?

Andreas Müller: Yes, exactly. But it's also not experiencing a world which remains the same or is the same all the time. There's just no experience.

Justin Allen: Yeah. And that's where the "no me" can say it's just everything?

Andreas Müller: So to speak, yes. Which is not a claim or a statement, but yes. Exactly.

Justin Allen: It would just be the reality?

Andreas Müller: It would just be the reality, and apparently there can be a "report" about that reality. Which would just again be the reality (laughing).

Justin Allen: So, if scientists or whoever figured out an immunization or a pill you can take that somehow removes self-consciousness, that would essentially be a way of liberating everybody?

Andreas Müller: So to speak. In the story where you assume that there is something like self-consciousness in the first place, yeah.

Justin Allen: So just to go back to those two ladies that came into your talk and then left. Imagine that somebody did create this immunization and offered it to them as an option. They would describe it like, "Yeah, if you take it, you lose self-consciousness." Then the two women would maybe say, "Well, what do you mean by self-consciousness?" Then you answer, "Everybody has a sense of 'me.' That 'I'm' here and 'I'm' doing life and 'I' make decisions."

Andreas Müller: Well, if you sell it with a promise to the "person," people will take it. If they realize ...

Justin Allen: I actually think they won't.

Andreas Müller: If they realize that it's actually about the death of the "me," they won't take it.

Justin Allen: That's what I'm trying to say. If you say that life is still going to happen exactly as it's happening, but you're not going to be there to experience it, nobody would take the immunization or pill.

Andreas Müller: Exactly. Oh, yeah.

Justin Allen: As soon as you say the sentence, "But you won't be there to experience it" ...

Andreas Müller: The "me" doesn't want to die. "Me" doesn't want to hear that message. Those two ladies, they just recognized the threat. They were very relaxed saying it to me, "We don't want that. That's too dangerous." They even used the word "dangerous."

Justin Allen: Yeah. My grandma was the same way, and my parents to some extent and myself as well. People will basically say, "Stop talking" (laughing).

Andreas Müller: Yeah.

Justin Allen: But what I wanted to say with that is that Hollywood movies and books and spiritual teachers and religious people and therapists and whatever – everybody's kind of tapped into this in a way. There are messages in Hollywood that are somehow on the borderline to this idea of "not being there." You see it in things like, "Just be yourself." Or even in, It's *A Wonderful Life*. I don't know if you're familiar with that movie. Or, do you know Scrooge?

Andreas Müller: No. I'm sorry.

Justin Allen: Well, these are movies where people are discontent with their life. Then a ghost or holy spirit comes, for example, around Christmas time (laughing). The holy spirit shows them different perspectives of their life. Then all of a sudden they become clear, they lose the searching element. They're like, "Ah, okay. My life is great the way that it is." Now they're not seeking, and they're happy.

Andreas Müller: Yeah, but it's often being replaced by new values and finding out "who you really are" or that life is a beautiful gift, not a misery.

Justin Allen: Right. But I'm just saying that it's kind of going in that direction. The lyrics of famous songs also tap into this a little bit. At least, they explore the question that life may not be or does not need to be what we think it is.

Andreas Müller: Yeah.

Justin Allen: Even the interest to take drugs, MDMA or ecstasy, for example. I'm not exactly sure, I've never done it. But people lose themselves in those drugs. Or at least they lose their familiar self.

Andreas Müller: Yeah, exactly.

Justin Allen: And people do extreme things that put their life at risk, like skydiving or free climbing.

Andreas Müller: Yes, yeah.

Justin Allen: So, there is this desire to kill or lose yourself in a way.

Andreas Müller: Yes and no. Basically ...

Justin Allen: But you still want to be there for it in the end.

Andreas Müller: Exactly, yes.

Justin Allen: To have that experience. Right. But I'm just saying everybody seems to have that. People are even trying to make money out of that.

Andreas Müller: Yes. In a way one could say it's oddly attractive. But when it comes to the point of, "Now it would cost my life," then it's better to survive.

Justin Allen: Yeah. It's similar to this other kind of cliché thing that Hollywood's tapped into. Where the overly ambitious Wall Street banker, the overly ambitious doctor, the overly ambitious activist or the person giving charity invests so much time and energy in their pursuit that at some point it starts to become life-threatening. Then they start to get a depression, their marriage starts to fall apart, or something starts to break down because of this concentrated pursuit, so they start to get worried and question their commitment. Another example is the case where someone declares, "I want to make ten million euros by the time I'm forty." And when they're getting close to that point, they realize it's at the cost maybe of their health, so they go, "Oh, my god, what good are these ten million euros going to do for me if I'm not there to enjoy it?" You know what I mean?

Andreas Müller: Yeah.

Justin Allen: It's that point of wanting to be there to enjoy it. It's the same with this. It's that you like the promise of the "no me" because things like suffering disappear, let's say. Everybody would like to have a life with no suffering, but they want to be there to enjoy it as a "me." Okay. That's why you can't sell this message (laughing).

Andreas Müller: Absolutely, yes. Not that there would be someone to sell it to. I mean that's the other thing because it's not a personal message right from the start. Because it doesn't recognize a "me." But yeah, it's impossible to sell it. Honestly. So, it's always weird when people start selling it, and it must be something else then, so to speak.

Justin Allen: But you're even going one step further. Because you're saying it's impossible to sell it, because there's "no one" there to sell it to?

Andreas Müller: Absolutely, yes.

Justin Allen: Even if there were someone to sell it to, that "one" wouldn't want this ever. Because that „one“ wants to still be there.

Andreas Müller: Exactly, yes. That's why it's rather an answering than an imposing on someone. It doesn't impose itself at all. It can't. Because there is no message, really. There is "no one" who needs it or who could hear it. There's "no one" who could give it. Even if there would be, there wouldn't be "one" wanting it (laughing).

Justin Allen: How do you talk to people? I assume that your son isn't liberated (laughing).

Andreas Müller: Oh, talking just happens. It all just is what apparently happens. I don't talk to people in that sense. Never, really. It's not that at one point I switch over and say, "Oh, they think they are someone. Now I have to talk to them." No.

Justin Allen: But that still is also happening?

Andreas Müller: Yeah, but not coming from an awareness or a consciousness of "because people believe they are someone I have to talk differently." No. There are no people, and there just is what apparently happens.

Justin Allen: But since liberation, how do people deal with you? Or in your dealings with people, have you noticed a change?

Andreas Müller: Not really. Well, I don't want anything from anyone, energetically. There's no game going on.

Justin Allen: But just for the sake of this conversation, let's talk of pre-liberation and post-liberation. Did you recognize anything? A change in interacting with your mom and dad or with some dear friend, for example?

Andreas Müller: I seem to be in a funny way more relaxed. But in another funny way, I seem to be more relaxed in being myself, Andreas (laughing), which can also include being not relaxed at all.

Justin Allen: But also, you're doing this as a profession, which is kind of a weird profession. So then, do your parents think you're fucking crazy?

Andreas Müller: I mean, I don't know (laughing). I usually don't go there too much in our conversations. Probably they kind of think I'm crazy (laughing). But on the other hand, they are happy that I'm making a bit of money, enough money at least (laughing). So, they don't know how to take it, because it's good and bad for them at the same time (laughing).

Justin Allen: Well, but you could also be seen as bad if you gave spiritual talks. Let's just say I was going around giving spiritual talks about how people need to improve their lives, wake up to love or something like that. My dad would probably be like, "You're full of shit. What are you doing, going around like a preacher telling people what they should do?"

Andreas Müller: No. In that sense it's acceptable. They just can't, they just don't ... It doesn't fit in my story of seeking and all that stuff.

Justin Allen: You don't find yourself explaining what you're doing all the time?

Andreas Müller: No, not at all. I don't have anything to share or to tell. It's not an issue for me in that sense.

Justin Allen: But how do you say what you're doing if somebody asks you? For example, when you go to a parent–teacher conference and then the teacher of your son says, "So, what is your occupation, Andreas?"

Andreas Müller: Oh, I say, "I'm doing seminars" (laughing).

Justin Allen: Nobody asks you, "On what?" (laughing)

Andreas Müller: Well, sometimes. It depends, you know? I say whatever comes out. I don't have something prepared. Maybe I say that it's something about freedom. Most people think it's something like, "Live your life," or something like that. Whatever. It also depends on who's there. So, sometimes I'm just like, "Yeah, you know. It's about freedom of 'me,' and stuff like that."

Justin Allen: Yeah. They're just, "Oh, one of those guys."

Andreas Müller: Yeah, exactly.

Justin Allen: Don't you in a way dislike being categorized into the pool of spiritual teachers and "Oh, one of those guys"?

Andreas Müller: I don't care. It doesn't hurt me personally. Of course, I can understand how people do that. But I don't have to convince anyone that it's not like that. Because everyone who is into that message sooner or later will come to the point, so to speak. Everyone, I don't care. You know?

Justin Allen: That's interesting to me. All right, well it's been one hour and thirty minutes.

Andreas Müller: Yeah. I should ...

Justin Allen: Get back to it. Okay. Then if I don't see you, have a good Christmas.

Andreas Müller: Yeah, thank you very much. You too, have a nice Christmas.

Justin Allen: Bye-bye.

Andreas Müller: Bye. Bye.

January 21, 2020 Talk 09

MY IMAGINARY FRIEND IS ME

Andreas Müller: Good morning.

Justin Allen: Morning.

Andreas Müller: Long time no see (laughing).

Justin Allen: So, how have you been? (laughing)

Andreas Müller: Yeah. Very good. Nice holidays, Christmas and all that stuff. And last weekend, I had my first journey this year, to Amsterdam.

Justin Allen: Oh, okay.

Andreas Müller: Yeah.

Justin Allen: So, you gave an Amsterdam talk?

Andreas Müller: Yeah, exactly.

Justin Allen: Well, there was no (laughing) ... Because it was in Amsterdam, that didn't change anything, right?

Andreas Müller: No, it didn't (laughing). Not for me at least. Maybe for some participants, but ...

Justin Allen: Because you go to different places, do you feel there are differences in where you give talks?

Andreas Müller: Well, yes and no. I mean, of course, it's somehow different, but in a way, the issue is the same. In that sense it's surprisingly the same everywhere.

Justin Allen: But there's not really a difference between the people you meet in New York City and the people you meet in Hamburg, for example?

Andreas Müller: Not really. I mean, what to say? In New York, they are Americans, and in a way you notice that. But I have the impression that the talks are quite the same actually. It maybe differs a bit more in the conversations during the break.

Justin Allen: Yeah. Okay.

Andreas Müller: And also not really. How have you been?

Justin Allen: Yeah, I've been all right. I went to Tenerife, and that was nice, weather-wise. And I like small towns actually. I'm from a small town (laughing), and I like to go back to small towns and be in that slower environment.

So, I was thinking over the past week what to talk about today. And I was thinking maybe I would prepare something, but then I didn't necessarily want to do that, because I feel it's better to just let come up whatever comes up.

Andreas Müller: Yeah. That's cool.

Justin Allen: And so, I was thinking about trying to give these talks a structure. But so far I haven't really done that.

Andreas Müller: Yeah.

Justin Allen: And then sometimes I think about trying to make it more personal. I guess our talks haven't really been like that, at least not from my perspective.

Andreas Müller: All right.

Justin Allen: You know what I mean? I mean "personal" in the sense that I could say, "Oh, I'm having this dilemma or this problem trying to decide on." Right?

Andreas Müller: Yeah.

Justin Allen: So, I don't know how you would define that. That seems like a typical thing in this setup of talking to a teacher or a guru. Not that you're the teacher or guru, but you know what I mean? People usually ask, "What is love?" or, "I'm having a hard time." And I think the thing is they always want to know how you do it. And we've talked about that, about how the experience is for you to not have the "me"? How do you solve the life problems?

Andreas Müller: By not being there (laughing)? Yeah, yeah. I understand.

Justin Allen: But it always comes up empty when I think, "Oh, I could ask him this," and it makes me feel like I would rather be doing it for the audience.

Andreas Müller: Exactly, exactly. Though already, in a way, it would become some "doing," and that's how it feels for me, too. And in the end I would say the thing is that that's not really the issue.

Justin Allen: Right.

Andreas Müller: I mean the personal stuff. Not in order to make it wrong not wanting to have it, but it's just not an issue. And in a way, I'm not the right person to talk to about that, so to speak.

Justin Allen: Right.

Andreas Müller: Except in a way, one could say in the story, it comes to just a personal friendship.

Justin Allen: Right.

Andreas Müller: But again, this wouldn't have, in that sense, anything to do with so-called non-duality or the issue we talked about.

Justin Allen: Right.

Andreas Müller: Because referring to that or regarding that, it completely and utterly doesn't matter how you are and how you solve problems, and I'm completely not an example of how to do life, because I am no one, so to speak. That's why I can totally go there. However, whenever you start thinking about that or asking me something personal, it didn't really have energy, which is the same thing often in the talks. I mean, there are hardly ever those kinds of personal questions, and my impression is not because it's not allowed or seen as wrong. It's just so obvious that it actually doesn't have any meaning.

Justin Allen: Yeah, I think that's probably one case, but I also think because you're normally giving a talk to fifteen people or more, people might be uncomfortable to talk about their personal issues in front of the others, and they also don't necessarily feel a friendship with you. But that's what I'm saying; because you and I have talked so many times now that we've developed a different relationship and because it's one-on-one, in some sense I could go, "Hey! Andreas, I'm having this problem trying to figure out what to do with A and B. What do you think?"

But I'm just saying that if I were to ask you that, I think I'd be doing it more for the theoretical audience and the theoretical experiment that we're doing to test the waters of that conversation. You know what I mean?

Andreas Müller: Yeah.

Justin Allen: Or what I'm saying is that it wouldn't feel authentic. It would just feel like I'm doing it in order to test out another way of seeing how you would react to those kinds of questions.

Andreas Müller: It would be for an idea about what we are doing, about the project, about the audience. Yeah, yeah. No. That's not ...

Justin Allen: Exactly. So, the other thing that just came to mind and that I'm curious about is that we've had eight talks so far and we've both reviewed them in text format. And then you responded to me after one talk saying that sometimes after you reread it, you would see how I meant a question or a statement and that you didn't understand or interpret it right at the time and ...

Andreas Müller: Oh, maybe I just went into another aspect. I mean, often in one question there are actually already several aspects contained, and I just went for one in my answer.

Justin Allen: Okay. That's what you meant.

Andreas Müller: Yeah. I guess it was rather like that.

Justin Allen: Okay. Yeah. And then you lost the other aspects because you went off on that tangent and the brain can't remember and go back to ...

Andreas Müller: Exactly. And then out of that a completely other stream went on. But my impression also is that we covered that aspect at a later point in time or in another talk. So, if you see the eight talks as a whole, it should be fine.

Justin Allen: Yeah. That's the value of the multiple talks (laughing).

Andreas Müller: Exactly. Yes.

Justin Allen: But then you have to go through all eight of them to get the bits and pieces.

Andreas Müller: Well, yeah. You have to read the book, so to speak (laughing).

Justin Allen: So, anyways, the thing with this kind of introduction today, the thing that's been on my mind where I feel like the ... I don't know the right word.

Andreas Müller: I don't know if that's where you want to go to, but I think we don't have to turn it into an issue that has to be continued for the sake of the issue. Like thinking about a structure or about personal things in order to continue the talks or to add another dimension to them. That would feel a bit like coming out of an idea or having an intention or maybe go on speaking where actually everything had already been said.

Justin Allen: Right.

Andreas Müller: Actually, it feels quite round to me. We would say it like that in German; maybe you don't say it in English. I mean that it feels complete.

Justin Allen: Yeah, I was saying the only reason why I would hesitate to want to try to talk about the thing that's coming up is that I feel like we've probably talked about it already. So, it might just be repetitive.

Andreas Müller: Oh, yeah. That doesn't matter. If it comes up, it comes up. It's okay if it's the same.

Justin Allen: But I do think the drive that I have to push it is different. So, what we're talking about is the "me" and the "me" not being there?

Andreas Müller: Exactly. Which already is a contradiction.

Justin Allen: Right.

Andreas Müller: But yes.

Justin Allen: That's what I'm really interested in, but it's just talking about the "me" in an almost technical way. I don't know if it'll be boring. But I think it's okay.

Andreas Müller: That's fine. Yeah.

Justin Allen: So, it's just that there is no "me." That's the illusion. The illusion is "me"?

Andreas Müller: So to speak. That there is a "me" is the illusion.

Justin Allen: Right, right. So, I wanted to ask, and this is giving you as much freedom also to expand, not keeping it simple, what is the definition of a "me"?

Andreas Müller: Well, that's already the problem. In the end there is no real definition of the "me," just because there is no "me."

Justin Allen: Right.

Andreas Müller: So, it's a story. It's not a truth. That was my first thought when you said you wanted to approach it rather technically, so to speak, because since it's all stories, you can't really do that.

Justin Allen: Yeah. But that's already what I want. That's how I felt. To start off by pretending that there is a "me," so we could talk about it. But if you're trying to define the "me," you can't really, because we're saying that it's an illusion?

Andreas Müller: It's already talking about something which doesn't have any substance ...

Justin Allen: Right.

Andreas Müller: And which, technically, is utterly illogical (laughing). "Technically" is already gone at that point (laughing).

Justin Allen: Right.

Andreas Müller: So to speak. It's stories.

Justin Allen: But that would be what the "me" is. That's what I think it is. Then you could give it the quality of being illogical. You could give it the quality of not being technical or not being something that will ...

Andreas Müller: The whole narrative is illogical.

Justin Allen: But it's also illogical in the sense that it's not ... It's like a unicorn. If we accept that a unicorn doesn't exist, we can draw the unicorn, and we can talk about the unicorn, but the unicorn doesn't exist, period.

Andreas Müller: Yeah. Yeah.

Justin Allen: And that's the same with the "me." We can talk about the "me," we can address people as being "me's," we can have our own "me," but it still doesn't exist.

Andreas Müller: So, that's pretty ... Yeah.

Justin Allen: So then, the definition of the "me," in a way, would be that it is the unicorn or the boogie man or ...

Andreas Müller: Yes. Now we could come to the definition of "me." The thing is that if there is the illusion of "me," so to speak, it just feels utterly real. And now we come to the point of how it feels within the illusion, and then there can be all kinds of definitions.

Justin Allen: Yeah.

Andreas Müller: Namely that it seems to be experienced as a sense of presence, as self-awareness, as something which seems to be now here. And most people would fight for that sense of presence, or the sense of presence would fight for itself and say, "I am here."

Justin Allen: Yeah. With total conviction.

Andreas Müller: That's with total conviction coming from an experience. The conviction seems to come from a self-experience.

Justin Allen: Right. And what comes to my mind now is a child that has some kind of traumatization or something that they're not processing or dealing with well, and then there's that scenario where they develop an imaginary friend. Or maybe it's not coming out of a trauma, but just happens for no reason to some children.

Andreas Müller: Yeah.

Justin Allen: And, I mean, I never had an imaginary friend as far as I can remember. But the way that it's portrayed in a book or a movie is that the imaginary friend is created just like the other "real" characters. Especially in the movie format, it works well because you can visually create this imaginary friend. And then you see the child talking to them as if they were there, and not only "as if," because visually we're seeing the child and the ghost or the monster or another person. And then the mother, the father or a psychiatrist comes in and also addresses the imaginary friend as if they existed because there's no other way of relating to the child. It would be kind of bad if you flat out said, "It's imaginary. It doesn't exist. You're crazy." So, they have to go along with the game of this imaginary friend a little bit, although it doesn't exist. But, to the child, it feels like it really is there.

Andreas Müller: Yeah.

Justin Allen: And so, that's another way maybe of talking about the "me": that, at least from your standpoint or your conviction, the "me" doesn't exist. And then, for the majority of us, we feel that the "me" exists.

Andreas Müller: Yes?

Justin Allen: Yeah, so that's just the same with the child with the imaginary friend. It's impossible in a sense to convince the child that the imaginary friend doesn't exist.

Andreas Müller: Yes and no. I mean, it is like that, but it's a very personalized picture, and in that picture there could always be the possibility, at least theoretically, that the child is convinced that there is no imaginary friend or that they at one point understand that it was an illusion or something by ...

Justin Allen: Right. I mean, I'm not using that as a way to say it's a similar experience to where, all of a sudden, the "me" disappears for me but I'm there to realize that the "me" disappeared.

Andreas Müller: Yeah. All right.

Justin Allen: I'm just saying that one thing that every human can experience in a sense is ... Let's take this example: If you're convinced that you have a disease and go to the doctor and they say, "You have cancer," then you're convinced that you have cancer and start to go, "Oh, my God! My doctor says I only have one year to live," and you talk about how terrible that is. And then you go visit another doctor a month later, and they run tests and prove that you don't have cancer. Then that illusion goes away. It was an illusion because it wasn't actually true that you had cancer.

Andreas Müller: Yeah, yeah, yeah.

Justin Allen: But you went about life for a month convinced that you had cancer and that you're going to die in a year, and then the new tests all confirmed that there was a mistake and you don't have it.

Andreas Müller: Yeah.

Justin Allen: So, the illusion is gone.

Andreas Müller: For you it was exactly the same experience as if you really had cancer. For that month, so to speak, you really had cancer in a way (laughing). Not really, but in your story (laughing) everything went as if you had: how you felt, how you acted, what you thought, what your problems were, what you thought about the feelings that came up around that. Exactly. Yeah.

Justin Allen: Yeah. So, that's the "me" in a sense. The "me" is something that doesn't actually exist according to your message. It's not there, but to the majority, it feels like it is there.

Andreas Müller: Exactly.

Justin Allen: And with the "me," life plays out in different ways or intensities. Similar to if you took five people and told them, "You have cancer," each of them would be going to deal with that seeming fact differently. Some might cry and be devastated, and some might be, "Oh, well, it happens." Same with the "me." As soon as you experience the "me," you're stuck with that as if it were a fact, and then you deal with that fact in your individual way. There are the people that are more neurotic and the people that are less neurotic and everything in between.

Andreas Müller: Yes. One could say so. Absolutely.

Justin Allen: But still the definition of the "me" is that there is no "me." That's, in a sense, the definition of the "me": that it's a story. It's an illusion.

Andreas Müller: Which already is a story, too, because in the end there just is no such thing.

Justin Allen: Right.

Andreas Müller: In that sense, it's not even an illusion and all that stuff.

Justin Allen: Yeah. It can't even be that. Somehow it has to be less than even an illusion (laughing).

Andreas Müller: Yes, exactly.

Justin Allen: Yeah. Well, then you have to say, "It's an illusion, but it's not an illusion. It's ..."

Andreas Müller: Well, it depends on how you interpret the word "illusion," because the "me" would replace it by, "Ah! There is no 'me.' I get that, but there is a real illusion I can or have to see through." That's in a way just replacing words and still kind of searching for something like truth or clarity.

Justin Allen: Correct. But there's not even a real illusion?

Andreas Müller: Exactly. It's an illusion that there's a "me." There is no "me." It's impossible to describe that, because it's not there. But yeah. What apparently happens is seven or eight billion people running around stating, "I am someone," by coming from an experience.

Justin Allen: And even that's weird ...

Andreas Müller: It's seemingly an experience.

Justin Allen: Yeah. That's a weird sentence to me because it's also not really experienced.

Andreas Müller: Yes, exactly. And this is the illogical part.

Justin Allen: Yeah. Well, it's not even really illogical, but it seems illogical.

Andreas Müller: Well, it's illogical because the experience feels so real. Actually it's not only illogical coming from a conceptual point. It's illogical coming from an experiential point.

Justin Allen: Right. But even that experiential point is also not really happening?

Andreas Müller: Yes, exactly. That's the illogical thing about it.

Justin Allen: Well, yeah. I mean, it's illogical in the sense that if you have the "me" and it seems like you're having experiences, then you can't ... It's illogical for you to hear that that doesn't happen. But for you (Andreas), I don't think it's illogical.

Andreas Müller: Well, it's also illogical but, of course, there is not the need that the concept is logical, so to speak. For me, the concept is illogical, too.

Justin Allen: It could be that on paper it's illogical.

Andreas Müller: Exactly. That's what I mean. That I can go there, too. But, yes, it's not illogical in the sense that there is a need to bring it together or to find an answer or to come out with the truth. It's just what apparently happens. People experience themselves as someone, but without that, there just is no one.

Justin Allen: But also, I mean, this might be starting to get too philosophical or abstract, but logic is also illogical in a way. Logic is something created by the "me" in a sense.

Andreas Müller: Well, logic is what apparently happens, but it's not real. Yes.

Justin Allen: But, I mean, scientifically, when we watch nature or nature shows on TV or read books, we're trying to find logic to why it is like that, but there's not really an explanation. I feel if you really talk to top scientists, they would have to confirm that as well.

Andreas Müller: Oh, absolutely. Yes.

Justin Allen: At least if they were being really accurate in a way, they'd have to confirm that they can't really figure out why something does something.

Andreas Müller: Absolutely. And they confirm that. In the end, at least as far as I know, the top scientists all have to confirm that they have no clue at all about almost all the issues.

Justin Allen: Right. Even in math, and this always baffles my mind, it's confirmed that two plus two doesn't always equal four, you know (laughing)?

Andreas Müller: All right (laughing).

Justin Allen: I don't know what that sentence means (laughing), but they've said, "Two plus two can sometimes equal five." I don't know the explanation, but I've heard this repeatedly, and it's really troubling.

Andreas Müller: Yeah.

Justin Allen: And there's also no real proof in scientific experiments. Even if they do a test where they pour hot water on their hand, they confirm that they burn their hand by testing it one hundred times, but maybe out of that one hundred times there's some time that it doesn't burn. Or at least there's always the chance that it doesn't. Right? So, even that removes logic in a way, even when you look at it logically. The logic shows its own illogicality.

Andreas Müller: Yes.

Justin Allen: Logic doesn't seem to be a cool ...

Andreas Müller: But, as you said, you're already kind of using logic.

Justin Allen: Yeah.

Andreas Müller: But, yes, even by thinking it through, you logically can come to the conclusion that it's actually illogical.

Justin Allen: Yeah. And the same with religion. All religions kind of have logic.

Andreas Müller: Oh, totally.

Justin Allen: Yeah. They always have an answer to things, but at some point it's always kind of like, "Well, that's God's will," or, "That's the miracle." They use these words to explain the unexplainable things.

Andreas Müller: Exactly. And it seems logical, not only on a conceptual level, but also on an emotional level. It seems logical because it reflects the "person's" experience.

Justin Allen: Yeah.

Andreas Müller: Because in many religions or in spirituality today, it's not only about giving answers on a conceptual level in the sense of, "Just believe it, it's the truth," like it may have been in former, less educated times. They also want you to feel it, to experience it. It's supposed to become your true experience. Love and wholeness and all that stuff. But yes, the logic in all of those teachings is that they reflect the "person's" experience, so the "person" can say, "Oh, yeah, I can feel that. I'm there to understand that." But as you said, at one point it just comes out. If you think it through, if you start doubting, so to speak, you "recognize" that it's still in the "person." It comes to the point of, "Hey, it's actually all made up."

Justin Allen: Right, right. And that's the dilemma; that in the scenario you just described, you come to the point that it's all made up, but you don't end there. Now you need something that does make sense to replace ...

Andreas Müller: Exactly. And the problem, so to speak, is that this conclusion is still happening within the same personal setup.

Justin Allen: Yeah. And that's the nature of this "me-ness," that's what it seems like to me: always wanting to have some kind of meaning or purpose or logic or explanation.

Andreas Müller: Yeah. The need for an answer, the need for something.

Justin Allen: Right. And that's the searching mechanism, in a way, manifesting itself how it does.

Andreas Müller: How it does, yes. And the problem, so to speak, is that even becoming aware of that is within the same setup. So, the next question would automatically be – but not because there is someone consciously in control of the seeking process –, "Oh, so how do I end that? How do I come out of that?" Almost naturally there is the next question or the next need for an answer. "Oh, now I became aware of that. What are we going to do with that?"

Justin Allen: To walk through how it happens is how I go searching for the meaning of life in some way. So, let's say you start off, and you're kind of told that the meaning of life is to ... I mean, it's changing all the time, but let's say it's to have a family and get a good job and not just any job; it's better if you get a job that you love to do. Right?

Andreas Müller: Well, mostly it's what your environment thinks you love or should love.

Justin Allen: And you might be like, "Well, I don't believe in that, because I see my parents did that, and they don't seem to be happy. So, I'm not going to make their mistake (laughing)." And then you go, "So, what else is there? Maybe I can just pursue my career and be the best in my career." But then you say, "Ah, yeah, but then there's this guy I heard in an interview who only pursued his career but is also taking anti-depression medicine. So, that probably doesn't work either." Then maybe you turn to religion, or maybe you already abandoned that, so you might pick spirituality or Zen Buddhism or something like that. And then maybe you're stuck in that for ten or twenty years.

Andreas Müller: You are stuck in that believing that you are on a good path (laughing). Yes.

Justin Allen: And then at some point when you realize that that's just another "mistake," you're kind of like, "Oh, well, fuck, I'm still here, and A doesn't work, and B doesn't work, and C doesn't work." But then it's always, "So, what does work?"

And then you might go, "Well, nothing works, I'm convinced of that now, so I'm just going to give up." And that's your new belief in a way. And you can really get confirmed and feel good for a while in that belief, like, "It doesn't matter. I don't have to try so hard." And so, that's the definition of the "me" in a sense?

Andreas Müller: Yes. And just one sentence; you just said it already, but just to say it again: It will turn out in the end, or it won't turn out, that nothing works or nothing matters. But in the end, this "insight" doesn't work either, of course.

Justin Allen: Right. But even if you really realize that it doesn't work and nothing's going to work, that doesn't do anything either?

Andreas Müller: Exactly. Because "really realizing" already is part of the dream. So, there is never a real realizing of anything.

Justin Allen: So, that's the definition of the "me," we could say. This quite chaotic definition from the last five or ten minutes of our talk (laughing), even though it's not definable, because it doesn't actually exist in a sense?

Andreas Müller: Yes.

Justin Allen: So then, what is the "no me"? Then you're in the exact same boat, in the exact same problem. The "no me" also is not definable or describable, because in order to do so there would have to be something there to define it or describe it.

Andreas Müller: Yes.

Justin Allen: And so, the "me" actually doesn't exist, but the "no me," which is what you think would be the opposite, of course doesn't exist either. Even by definition: It's a "no me," so it's not there.

Andreas Müller: Yes. But it also doesn't exist as another state opposed to being "me."

Justin Allen: Right.

Andreas Müller: Yeah.

Justin Allen: It's not like its absence. That's what's weird because the "me" doesn't exist anyways, so it's the same thing. Being a "me" is basically the same as being a "no me."

Andreas Müller: Yes, yes. Absolutely.

Justin Allen: So, you can't ... Let's say me coming from the one-point perspective or the "me" perspective, I can talk about all this stuff, and it feels like there's meaning to it. But for you, it has to be that you're constantly recognizing how impossible it is to talk about it because you're addressing things that don't exist. But for me, when I say it, I sense that it exists. I feel like it's real, like it has meaning to me. It's the same as, for example, if I talk about my family, it's different than if I talk about some family in China where I don't have any skin in the game.

Andreas Müller: Yeah.

Justin Allen: So, for the people that come to your talks and want to figure all this out it's unbelievably important. They're trying to solve the problem of life (laughing).

Andreas Müller: Yeah, that can be (laughing). Yeah, absolutely.

Justin Allen: And for you as "no one," the absence of the "me" is like nothing's there. You can't even talk about it.

Andreas Müller: Exactly. Yes. I don't even recognize the issue, or the issue isn't even recognized as such. Yeah. That's the freedom in the end. Not that there is someone who knows the answer. Not that there is someone who has reached somewhere, but yes, the whole issue is part of an illusion.

Justin Allen: Well, let's just talk about the "no me" then. Or we can't, but we just talked or didn't talk about the "me," so we can also not talk about the "no me" for a while. So, the "no me" is just what is, in exactly the same way basically as the "me." It just is what is?

Andreas Müller: Oh, yes. The illusion of "me." Yes, absolutely. That's the thing in this setup, like you just said: What seems to be happening is that "you," superficially said, think you are someone, and I don't, but in a very funny way, both just is what apparently happens, and the difference is totally illusionary. But by there being no real difference, it still remains as it is, apparently, which means you are assuming you are someone and I don't, so to speak.

Justin Allen: Yeah.

Andreas Müller: Yep.

Justin Allen: And then I think you saying, "And I don't," is complicated because you're not experiencing it. You're not experiencing it one way or the other. There's no ...

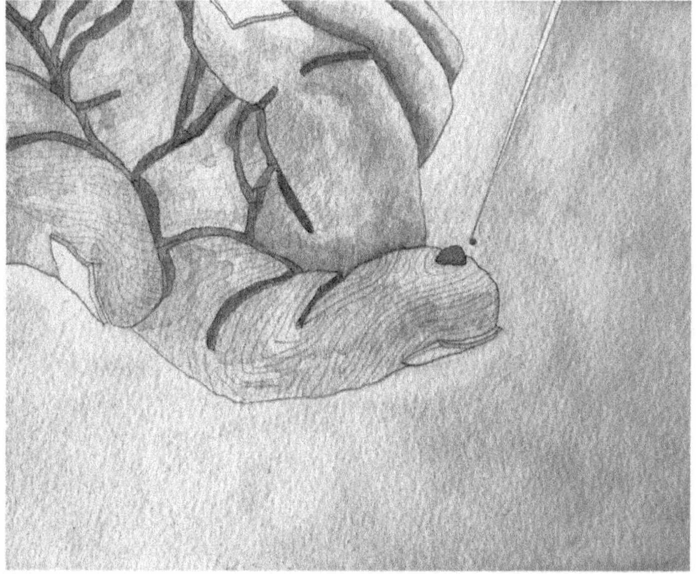

Andreas Müller: Yeah, it was equally superficially said.

Justin Allen: But also when you say there is no "me," kind of the best way that you're trying to define it or describe it is to say that there's no one there experiencing anything.

Andreas Müller: Yes. But this is not coming from an experience.

Justin Allen: Right (laughing).

Andreas Müller: And that's the other thing. I'm not trying to describe it; it's just the words that come out here.

Justin Allen: Yeah. Right.

Andreas Müller: And I'm not trying to find the best words or the right words to describe anything coming from an experience with an intention to do so. It's just the apparent functioning of this.

Justin Allen: It is just like if you cut your arm right now, blood is going to come out.

Andreas Müller: Exactly. Yes. That's a good example.

Justin Allen: But for me, my words are coming out because I'm kind of actively searching and trying to find the right words and to express them in the right way and to get somewhere.

Andreas Müller: That would be the experience of the "person." Yes.

Justin Allen: And words are coming out of my mouth, and words are coming out of your mouth, but for you, there's not a "you" that's making the words come out. It's just what's happening. But for me, even though it's also just what's happening, it doesn't seem that way. It seems like it's ...

Andreas Müller: Yes, in a way, even that it seems like that is the blood flowing out of the arm. But yes, it feels like there's an attempt behind it and an intention, which is already seeking; it's the hope to come to a point by expressing oneself in the right way or understanding something right.

Justin Allen: So then, if there is an apparent "me" here, like myself, my face, my body, and then all of a sudden or through a process or whatever, the "me" isn't there anymore, I'm still going to go on doing life but without the feeling that I'm doing it?

Andreas Müller: Yeah. One could say so. Yes.

Justin Allen: But then there's still somehow a recognition that there was a change in a way?

Andreas Müller: No. No. Not at all, actually.

Justin Allen: Okay.

Andreas Müller: That's the thing: There seems to be a recognition when we talk about it, but there is nothing here which lives in a recognition of, "Oh, yeah, I remember it was very different five years ago." Not really. No, it just vanished. Recognizing, as a true reality, vanished.

Justin Allen: So then, is there any way of talking about that somehow? Because that's where my interest is from my own "personal experience." I've been thinking about how, of course, to some degree people "experience" talking about the happening of "no me." We kind of talked about it in one of the talks where we were calling it glimpses. But I feel that puts too much significance on these glimpses, and then you're like, "Oh, I had a glimpse. Was that a glimpse?" You know what I mean?

Andreas Müller: Yeah. I mean, just seeing it from the personal perspective, it's kind of logical to regard it as that. But yes, they don't have any meaning at all, but within the personal experience they can also have a strong impact.

Justin Allen: Yeah. I mean even that is not necessarily true, because ultimately there's no impact period, because there's nothing to impact?

Andreas Müller: True. Absolutely. And yes, it can be anything. For some people it seems to have a strong impact on their life, on their "person." On their apparently personal life after the glimpse. But yeah, it can also be nothing special.

Justin Allen: Yeah, but then that's the "me" putting a significance onto it?

Andreas Müller: Absolutely. Yes. But it never has a real significance, of course.

Justin Allen: Right. So, I could have a glimpse, and what happens in this is that somehow the "me" collapses or temporarily isn't there, right? And then the "me" comes back, and you go, "Oh, my God, I wasn't there. That's so crazy. How can that be? How could I have gone through the last five minutes, and I'm still alive without the 'me'? That's amazing." And that person could turn it into a big deal, whereas somebody else might disappear for five minutes, and they don't recognize anything. They don't even acknowledge it. It's just nothing. And maybe if they were analyzing it, they can be like, "I feel really relaxed." But they might just take that as a daily thing: Sometimes they're relaxed and sometimes not.

Andreas Müller: Yeah.

Justin Allen: But so when it happens that the "me" is permanently gone, there's no difference?

Andreas Müller: Exactly. Yeah. I mean, that's the thing in the whole glimpse story. It's pretty much based on the experience of the story of presence, absence, presence, absence. But in liberation, it rather seems that, just as we said before, there actually is no difference anymore between so-called presence and so-called absence.

Justin Allen: Well, there's no presence or absence for you?

Andreas Müller: Exactly, yes.

Justin Allen: There aren't moments, for example in talking to me right now – which seems from the audience's perspective like there's a you and you're talking to me –, where you're thinking of the right things to say? That's not really happening?

Andreas Müller: Yes, exactly.

Justin Allen: If I went and ...

Andreas Müller: And same when I see you, so to speak. It's not that I see a presence, an illusory presence, not at all. It just is what apparently happens. You. What you say, how you are. And even if you say, "Yeah, but I feel present." Okay. That's what apparently happens. But there's nothing which recognizes any additional presence in you, so to speak.

Justin Allen: Yeah. And when I address you, then you answer me and what I said, so to me it seems like you can only do that because there's a controller in your brain or there's something navigating through the world. And here's me, and I'm able to recognize, "Ah, he's talking to me. So, I'm programmed that I have to talk back to him."

Andreas Müller: Yes. That's the same as an experience center. An individual. Yeah.

Justin Allen: That's missing for you? It's also missing for me because it just doesn't exist, but it seems like it's there for me?

Andreas Müller: Yes.

Justin Allen: So if that were to vanish for me permanently, so to speak, there also wouldn't be a recognition like, "Oh, I just disappeared," or, "I know this conversation couldn't happen," because then there's no experience of having a conversation? Because when the "me" drops, it's not an experience of the "me" dropping?

Andreas Müller: Yes, exactly. Yes, yes, yes.

Justin Allen: That's what, for me, is illogical. That's something where you ... I mean, we said this probably in every single talk, but I keep on thinking, "Ah, when the 'me' drops, then it's going to be like an aha moment or like, 'Oh, my God, my whole life ...'"

Andreas Müller: Yeah. Maybe in the story this moment exists. And maybe there is an "aha." And maybe there is an event. But liberation still wouldn't be that event. Liberation would still be the melting away of the experience to be someone.

Justin Allen: Yeah, but that "aha" is still the "me"?

Andreas Müller: It is what apparently happens.

Justin Allen: Yeah. But I'm just saying that ...

Andreas Müller: I'm just saying that in death or in dying, there can be an "aha." Maybe not even a processing but just, "ah," or the feeling that it's so natural. And there can also be something more intense like, "Oh, my God."

Justin Allen: Same with if I got told I have cancer and I'm living with this fact or assumption for a month and then it gets confirmed that I don't have it, it might provoke very different reactions. Some people might be like, "Oh, my God, awesome, let's go out and celebrate and have a good time," and somebody else might just go on, take it totally stoically and just be like, "Oh."

Andreas Müller: Exactly. Yes, yes.

Justin Allen: But then after that, life just goes on, and there's not ... In this scenario with the wrong cancer diagnosis, somebody might come to a conclusion and be like, "Well, I'm going to live every moment now to the fullest because you never know when you're going to die." That's not happening anymore?

Andreas Müller: Yes, exactly. And as I said, liberation, so to speak, is not the event of that which seems to be happening. It would be just the end of that coming and going and being present with all the stuff. But there can be an event, there can be no event, there can be a big, "Oh, my God, there is 'no one.'" But it doesn't have to. That doesn't matter. That wouldn't be liberation, so to speak. It's not that moment where ...

Justin Allen: It's not that moment, but it's also not one day after that moment or two days after that moment. What it is, is just that it's kind of flat-lined, and you're ...

Andreas Müller: But without having these periods of flat-lined. Just flat-lined without having an opposite. Yeah, as you just said.

Justin Allen: Supposedly enlightened people have also talked about how there's a ... Let's use "liberation," for lack of a better word. There's a liberation event where the person's liberated, and then that's it. They're never going back to whatever the situation was before. But then there's the kind of liberation that is taking place in stages, so there's still the "me" around. Like, let's say, the "me" is ten percent or twenty percent there, and then it's slowly fading away. Right? So, there's maybe the one example where there's a sharp cut from night to day, but there's also the process of dawn between night and day where it's happening over time that the "me" is slowly dying.

Andreas Müller: Yeah. But in the end, I would say, it is still a cut. It's a total story, but liberation is just the end. Another metaphor would be a car crash versus a fading out in a hospital for ten years with some disease or something. It's a complete story though, because there is no experience of an end. At one point it's just over. That one point is kind of sharp, seen from a story perspective.

Justin Allen: Yeah, that's what I always have a problem with, I guess.

Andreas Müller: Oh, of course. Because it's not happening. It's so much not like that.

Justin Allen: And if you say it the way that you're saying it, then it seems like there has to be something still there to recognize. That's my problem with what you just said, that's the thing that I can't ... It might be a problem of logic and reason, but it seems like if the "me" dropped off with the sharp cut, then life would just go on completely without recognition because they would see that there wasn't even a "before." It wouldn't be like you were stuck as a "me." Then all the realization would be in a sense that there's no difference.

Andreas Müller: Yeah, yeah, yeah, yeah, yeah. But wait. Of course, there can be an apparent recognition.

Justin Allen: But that would still be in the story then. That would still be in the "me"?

Andreas Müller: No, recognition can be what apparently happens. But the recognition of a difference wouldn't be real; it would be an apparent recognition, and there wouldn't be someone who has that recognition who then goes on with another story about themselves.

Justin Allen: Okay, that's clearer then. So, let me try to paraphrase it in my own words, and you confirm or deny it (laughing).

Let's say that the "me" collapses. There still can be, or it is even likely that there would be, the recognition of the "me" dropping and of now not being a "me" because compared to before, the "me" is not happening to "me" anymore?

Andreas Müller: So to speak. But it doesn't turn into a constant state of being "no me." But of course, there can also be a recognition like, "Oh, there is no 'me' anymore," which sounds utterly weird and can't be comprehended from a "me" perspective because it still sounds very personal.

Justin Allen: Yeah.

Andreas Müller: But liberation also wouldn't be that apparent constant recognition, like sitting there and saying, "Oh, there is no 'me' anymore," or, "Oh, there is 'no one.'" Liberation still would be just the end of the separate energy.

Justin Allen: Right. Then in liberation, the "me," would still be there going on as ... Well, it wouldn't be the "me" in the old way of it being something that's there, but recognitions could still be happening and ...

Andreas Müller: The thoughts and the functioning; all that goes on. For example, the brain can apparently bring out information like, "I'm hungry, I'm tired, I'm this or that." And also stuff like, "There is no one." Recognition goes on.

Justin Allen: So, there really isn't a "me," and a "no me." That's what I'm trying to say.

Andreas Müller: Yes.

Justin Allen: So in a sense, even when the "me" dies or disappears, it's not any different?

Andreas Müller: Exactly. Yes.

Justin Allen: Because it wasn't there in the first place?

Andreas Müller: Yes.

Justin Allen: And even if it had been there in the first place, it's not being replaced by something else?

Andreas Müller: Yes. Yes. So, many apparent things, like thinking, functioning, being human, stayed or stay there but only have been falsely addressed by something in the sense of, "Oh, this is personal."

Justin Allen: Yeah.

Andreas Müller: Same with recognition in a way. Recognizing is what apparently happens; we're using the experience to recognize. "Me" never really recognizes anything. It lives in the experience of recognizing. So, one could say the experiencing of recognizing drops, the experience of recognizing being real and recognizing something that is also real, has meaning to "me" and is happening to "me." That experience of recognizing just drops, but recognition or noticing or being aware is just a function that goes on.

Justin Allen: To every single person. Let's just say that there's a distinction between "me" and "no me," and the "me" recognition is happening to "me," and "no me" recognition is happening, period. To no one, like nothing. There's no extension, so to say.

Andreas Müller: Yeah. Every recognition and everything else that happens is full and complete and right in its way, but it's empty and meaningless and ...

Justin Allen: It's only empty and meaningless in the sense that conventionally we think meaning needs a "me" or an experience or ...

Andreas Müller: Yes.

Justin Allen: For us in that state of illusion or whatever, everything seems to be meaningless without that experience of the "me"?

Andreas Müller: Yes.

Justin Allen: So then, as a "me," I might love my job because it makes me feel good and valuable and worthy or whatever else. There are certain qualities about it. Then as a "no me," I might also love my job, but for no reason.

Andreas Müller: It would just be what apparently happens. Yes. When there is someone, this someone would need a story for itself about what seems to go on to please itself.

Justin Allen: Right. So with the "no me," it doesn't need a story, and there doesn't need to be any kind of justification or conviction or ...

Andreas Müller: Yes, exactly. It would just be additional, but it's not needed. It's completely not needed. Yeah.

Justin Allen: Then when seeming bad things or seeming good things are happening to a "no me" person, they're not taken as such in a sense?

Andreas Müller: Yes. Absolutely. One could say so.

Justin Allen: Although the recognition could still be there, for instance, that this is a bad thing?

Andreas Müller: Yes, exactly. The information could still appear, and it also could feel bad or good. Well, I would say more or less bad or good because a lot of these feelings come from the story about it. So, then the potential for something to be really good or really bad is less, but it still could feel good or bad in a sense.

Justin Allen: It would feel good or bad, but that feeling would just be a function, just a recognition that something feels good or bad?

Andreas Müller: An apparent recognition.

Justin Allen: Yeah. When there isn't a "person," then if there were a good feeling ... Let's say you sell a million books, in some sense it'd be recognized that this is generally a sign of success, and maybe that feels good, but it wouldn't feel good in the sense of, "Ah, I'm making it to the top."

Andreas Müller: Exactly, yes, yes, yes.

Justin Allen: Although even that thought could still happen?

Andreas Müller: Yes.

Justin Allen: Right? But you'd be recognizing the thought happening in the same way that you recognize that you have a tingling sensation in your leg?

Andreas Müller: Yes.

Justin Allen: It's just happening?

Andreas Müller: Yes. This is not separate. It's just what apparently happens. It would be whole and complete. It's apparent functioning. Functioning in that sense sounds a bit dry because, of course, it's utterly alive itself. But yes, exactly, it would be how you described it.

Justin Allen: Yeah. Well, functioning sounds dry to the "me," I think. I don't think it necessarily is dry. I mean, it's the same as there's nothing boring about your body functions. There's nothing dry about the blood going through your body and all the complexities of it. There's nothing really dry. Even you just putting your hand to your face; there are so many complicated things to make you have done that. But to the "me," it's dry.

Andreas Müller: Yeah, exactly, it's not dry. It may only sound dry. Functioning, no meaning, empty; these words seem dry or cold or dead to the "me" or the intellectual. But it's also not an intellectualization, it's just happening; our feelings are just functioning.

Justin Allen: Yeah, right.

Andreas Müller: That's not how it's meant, in a dry sense, but basically it is like that. It's just what apparently happens. Apparent functioning, recognizing, thinking, feeling.

Justin Allen: Yeah. Do you know Jerry Seinfeld, the comedian?

Andreas Müller: Not much, but yeah, I have a picture of it.

Justin Allen: I don't know if this comes from his standup routine or maybe from a book or an interview. He is talking about how you're standing in a room and a dog goes running by. Then you go, "Hey Fido." Then the dog stops whatever it was doing and comes over to you.

Andreas Müller: Mm-hmm (affirmative).

Justin Allen: Then it probably will never go back to doing whatever it was doing a moment before (laughing). So, the interesting question is what was actually making Fido go run that way?

Andreas Müller: It remains unanswered in the end.

Justin Allen: Right. Then because you called out Fido and he came to you, you've changed its course of action in a sense, and you would attribute that to you.

Andreas Müller: Yeah, maybe. But in a funny way, the dog already changed your actions by being there and calling your attention.

Justin Allen: Right. That's kind of what I'm thinking; we just accept in a way that an animal is going about life without there being something doing it. We're constantly convinced that we're doing it and that we have to do it. That seems to be one of the reasons why we suffer as humans: because of the pressure that we put on ourselves to do it and to do it "right."

Andreas Müller: Yeah. Absolutely.

Justin Allen: But still everybody has to kind of recognize that they have zero control in their life or that they're not really doing anything.

Andreas Müller: What do you mean with, "Everybody has to recognize"?

Justin Allen: I mean that, for example, when I'm going to say, "I'm going to put my hand to my forehead," now I just put my hand to my forehead. So, I feel like I did that and controlled my action. But even where did that thought come from to put my hand on my forehead? I didn't choose that thought. That just happened.

Andreas Müller: Yeah. But in a funny way, you already imply control.

Justin Allen: Right. But I mean still rationally somehow I understand that I don't have control. Of course, I think I do, but I recognize that I really don't.

Andreas Müller: Yes. But that actual experience may give you the assumption of control.

Justin Allen: Right.

Andreas Müller: It seems as if you were able to at least think that through (laughing).

Justin Allen: Yeah.

Andreas Müller: Just as the experience of the "person." But yeah.

Justin Allen: I have to say that sense of control is the thing that has given me the most stress in my life.

Andreas Müller: Oh, yeah. Of course. It's hell.

Justin Allen: There are so many other things in life which I'm just doing without being there, kind of, without controlling it constantly. Those are the moments to which I would attribute less pain or less suffering. You logically conclude, "Ah, life's better when you let go of control," and that's where the sentence or the advice, "Just let go," comes in. It has become so popular now because it's confirmed in everybody's life in a way that when they let go of controlling, things seem to be better.

Andreas Müller: Yeah.

Justin Allen: But if the "me" isn't there, the thought, "Put your hand to your forehead," would still come up?

Andreas Müller: Yeah. One could say so. I mean, not necessarily, because not every action is embedded into an apparent process of thinking a thought first and then following the impulse. But yep, it would be possible that such a thought still arises.

Justin Allen: But I recognize that when I'm doing it now, I'm thinking that I'm doing it, and I'm trying to prove a point to you, but still, if there were "no me," I might be doing it also to prove a point to you?

Andreas Müller: Kind of. Yes and no. Not really. But it in the story, yes, it might be what apparently happens. But there wouldn't be an experience of that there is a real point that you could come to. All of it would be ...

Justin Allen: Yeah. It would be pointless.

Andreas Müller: Yes.

Justin Allen: For no one. Whereas now I'm doing it because I feel like there's a lot of meaning embedded and ...

Andreas Müller: So to speak. That now you've really come to a point, a real one, which has a value.

Justin Allen: But also you're putting your hand to your forehead, and you're coming up with arguments and examples to prove things to me, even though it's just happening like that. You're not doing it as though you had to, as though it were necessary or as though there were some huge personal motivation to do it?

Andreas Müller: Yeah, one could say so.

Justin Allen: Then if it was, let's say, some kind of a process of the "me "gradually approaching its death. The death is like an end, but still ...

Andreas Müller: Exactly. The process of dying in the end is still life. The process of dying is still being alive, so to speak.

Justin Allen: Right.

Andreas Müller: That's another life.

Justin Allen: So, when you are born, you start off breathing, normal heavy breaths, and when you kind of get sick, let's say, in this analogy, then your breath starts to get less and less and worse and worse, and then eventually there's no more breath, and then you're dead.

Andreas Müller: So to speak. The breath in the picture could be seen as the seeking energy, as the drive to seek for fulfillment or a way out or whatever.

Justin Allen: Yeah. Then also there are the people that just suddenly don't breathe anymore, like in a sudden death from a heart attack, for example.

Andreas Müller: So to speak. Yes.

Justin Allen: But in the longer process of the breaths getting slower and weaker, I feel that doesn't necessarily mean that there is seeking energy. Couldn't a slower death be happening to somebody that's not really aggressively seeking?

Andreas Müller: Oh, yes, but whenever there is someone, there is some seeking energy.

Justin Allen: Right. By one of the definitions of the "me," there's automatically the seeking.

Andreas Müller: But it can be pleasant, or it can be unpleasant. It can be smooth or painful, it can be anything. When I faded out for two years, which I can only say when I look back ...

Justin Allen: You can only say that you faded out for two years looking back from the perspective of a "no me"?

Andreas Müller: From the apparent perspective of a "no me," exactly. Because within that, it was another life experience, which to "me" in my story, just felt as if life got easier and easier.

Justin Allen: That's what I'm kind of interested in: During that two year phase where life was getting easier, it was getting easier for you in the sense that you were kind of recognizing that you care less about things?

Andreas Müller: Exactly. So to speak. It ...

Justin Allen: Why didn't that trouble you in a way? For example, let's say all of a sudden, a father wakes up in the morning, and his child does something bad at school, and then his boss tells him that he might be losing his job. He's got to pay bills, and he's got to take care of his family, and then he's dealing with his child misbehaving, and in all of that trouble he doesn't really care. But it's not that he doesn't really care in the sense of, "Oh, I don't care anymore. This is bullshit." It's rather that he genuinely, for whatever reason, doesn't have this caring energy anymore. And then I think he could be worried and think, "Oh, what's wrong with me? Why don't I care like I used to?"

Andreas Müller: Yeah, but that's what I mean. It can be different from each story to another. But no, I think for me it was pleasant because it was just less and less burdening "happening." I was coming from a story where a lot of issues just seem to have been burdening me. As you just said, when you feel there is control, you are suffering. But I was just apparently suffering from this meaning and that I could do things et cetera. So for me, it was basically the losing of the meaning of the spiritual stuff which became so unpleasant and such a prison for me.

Justin Allen: Yeah. Then do you ever feel that in your story you had to put yourself through that spiritual suffering in order to die?

Andreas Müller: No. Actually not. It just was what happened in my story. It was not needed. Nothing is needed; the "me" drops or not, and nothing can really bring that about.

Justin Allen: Yeah. That makes me want to think though, if you had to have put yourself through that suffering, then whatever would have made you ...

Andreas Müller: You can't do that, it's too theoretical. The suffering was just part of my path in a way, because for quite a while I thought that when I suffer enough, that means that I'm in a deep process and progressing quickly. It was quite interesting at one point in my story when I noticed, even as a "person," that, well, I just don't have to suffer (laughing). Because I always thought that suffering had a lot of value.

Justin Allen: This is something that I remember I wanted to bring up, and it's probably leading us on a different tangent in a way. But when I start to talk about this more and more, I tend to hear people say, "Oh, this is nihilism."

Andreas Müller: Yeah.

Justin Allen: So, you can get that a lot. No?

Andreas Müller: Yeah. Not really, because I think it's just people who are very distant to it who put it into that category.

Justin Allen: Yeah.

Andreas Müller: I think in the talks or when we talk about it, it doesn't really feel nihilistic.

Justin Allen: Right.

Andreas Müller: But if you just remain on a conceptual level: When people think it's nihilism and think that this is seen, it's trying to give an answer.

Justin Allen: Yeah. Because if they hear it's hopeless, then (laughing) ...

Andreas Müller: Exactly. Yeah. You can't do anything. It's hopeless, but it has nothing to do with nihilism. And in the talks, it seems to be recognized that it's not that at all.

Justin Allen: Yeah. I don't think so either.

I can't help but go down this path in my mind right now to when I was in middle school. I remember I felt all the pressure to put gel in my hair and style it a certain way and wear the clothes that were popular at that time - skidz pants with a bottom roll. If I was friends with the cool kids, then I couldn't be friends with the non-cool kids. So, I remember I did that. I fell into that for maybe half a year or a year.

I don't know what it was, I don't know if it's necessarily that I came to some conclusion or that I was behind it in some way, but I literally gave it all up. Just like, "Fuck this. I can't do this." Somehow I was telling myself a story, "I'm just going to give this up. I'm not going to care about doing my hair and wearing the cool clothes and being friends with specific people, I'm just going to do what I want."

Andreas Müller: Mm-hmm (affirmative).

Justin Allen: So, I replaced one thing with another, but it felt really good to let go of all that.

Andreas Müller: Yeah.

Justin Allen: Also, later on in my life I kind of recognized that I felt good or pretty content. These words aren't explaining it well, so hopefully you get the vibe or the feeling. I wasn't really driven or going somewhere necessarily either. But then I felt like I have to go somewhere.

Andreas Müller: All right.

Justin Allen: I felt like, "Ah, this isn't enough. Maybe I'm missing out on something by just being content and happy with how things are." And then I started seeking. Not that I wasn't seeking before, but I kind of felt like, "Oh, I might be missing out on something." So, I put myself out into the world to kind of push myself in a sense to get somewhere. That got me in some kind of a pursuit for sure; in various pursuits of trying to do this and that and this and that. Even though I knew that it really wasn't going to

make me happy, I still had to do it. Now I'm looking back at it, and I'm going, "Man, why did I have to do all that? Why couldn't I just have stayed back?" I know that's all part of the story, but at the same time it feels like ...

Andreas Müller: Yeah. "Why couldn't I just have stayed content?"

Justin Allen: Yeah. Or imagine that you spent ten years in a monastery, convinced that that was going to make you enlightened, let's say. Right?

Andreas Müller: Yeah. That exists.

Justin Allen: Yeah, I know. Then after having realized that this isn't going to make you enlightened, you would kind of feel that you wasted ten years of your life and think, "I probably would have been better off if I didn't spend ten years in the monastery." Or you might say, "I had to spend those ten years of suffering in the monastery 'in order to ...'" So, you don't feel that with yourself? That you had to go through a certain phase? Or that you asked yourself something like, "Why did I have to do this or that? Why couldn't I just ...?"

Andreas Müller: Actually not. No, no, no. It's almost like looking back on having had a normal good life with all the ingredients, but I know that thought from being a "person," so to speak.

Justin Allen: Yeah.

Andreas Müller: Yes, of course.

Justin Allen: This is a personal question, I guess, but I feel like asking you about having a child. Because it's something we would consider a major life decision. Was this something that, even in the "me" story, just happened? Or was it something that was kind of wanted? You know what I mean?

Andreas Müller: Yeah. "Wanted" is maybe too much (laughing) with that story; there was just no reason to say no to it. So, it was somehow like, "Yes, I would," because there was just no "no" coming up in a way. Maybe there was some in the story. The story would be that it somehow had to be. But having kids wasn't a conscious wish for me, because most of my life I thought this wouldn't happen anyway.

Justin Allen: Yeah. That's why I wanted to ask because I would've put you in the category of somebody that probably would have tried to avoid getting married and having kids and …

Andreas Müller: It was not even really out of avoidance, maybe psychologically, but not coming from a concept that it will take away my freedom or something like that. It was just that I didn't see that happening (laughing); I couldn't imagine that at all. A little bit maybe, but not really, because I was struggling with money and not having a real job, and I spent big parts of my life in my twenties in this spiritual thing. I think I could tell many stories about it, but I think one aspect or reason or example was to find healing and salvation in spirituality from a lot of psychological stuff that was going on. That's just where my focus was, not on family and children.

Justin Allen: Yeah, right. But then you having a child now, would you say it's just what happened?

Andreas Müller: Yes, which sounds a bit sad, but in the end, yes (laughing).

Justin Allen: You mean it sounds sad in the sense that I'm going to judge you, like, "Oh, you're not supposed to have a child just because it happens. You're supposed to want one?"

Andreas Müller: No, I was just kind of looking through the eyes of my child (laughing).

Justin Allen: Yeah. When he overhears you saying (laughing) …

Andreas Müller: When he reads this in twenty years or something. No, it's fine. Exactly, it just was what apparently happened. In a conventional sense you would say it had to be like that or there was no other possibility or there was no "no" coming up. I was also looking forward to it when it happened, and to the adventure. I was quite normal, I guess.

Justin Allen: So, when you were looking forward to it happening, you still have to put it in a different context, like you were looking forward to it happening in the sense that you recognized that feeling of looking forward to it happening?

Andreas Müller: And the adventure and joy, yes.

Justin Allen: But a "me" person would say the same thing. I also was excited about having a child, playing sports and doing whatever with them. But we, as "me" people, want it to be different for you. You know what I mean?

Andreas Müller: Exactly. Oh, yes. Absolutely. The "person" thinks or even hopes that I'm having another experience.

Justin Allen: Yeah.

Andreas Müller: Which is the basic idea of the "person" or of fulfillment or enlightenment or liberation: to finally have another experience.

Justin Allen: But you're not?

Andreas Müller: Nope. Exactly. One hundred percent, I'm not having another experience. Yes, that's brilliant (laughing). But as I said, the "person" almost longs for that. Of course, everyone who's claiming, "Oh, yes, I do have another experience," is like, "Wow, finally. That's what I want, that's what I longed for, that's what I work for, that's what I'm aware of for; to find this one experience which finally makes a difference." Yes, that's not here.

Justin Allen: Should we end it there (laughing)?

Andreas Müller: I would be good to go on, but I think right now ...

Justin Allen: I guess, before we end, something that feels like I want to bring up is I've recognized, generally in my life, that I seem to have an inclination to avoid things, because I don't want it to jeopardize my freedom or I don't think this is right or good. However, that's always put a lot of pressure on me because then I have to live my life a certain way with the consequences. But when the consequences happen, I don't want them and wished it would be different. You really recognize that it's coming from such a strong identification with you as somebody doing life and going ...

Andreas Müller: Assuming to know life.

Justin Allen: Yeah, or trying to know as much as possible to make sure that you always make the best decision for you and that it's going to give you some reward.

Andreas Müller: Yeah.

Justin Allen: But there's also the recognition that when that entity or that feeling or that sense (me-sense) isn't there or not strongly there, it's much more relaxing. But like with the example of the father with all kinds of problems I gave earlier, there's also been a backlash of feeling like, "Why don't I care as much as usually?" and being worried about that and asking yourself if there's something wrong with you.

Andreas Müller: Yes, that can happen. The caring also gave, of course, a sense of safety. "I'm safe because I do care." Of course, when the caring becomes less or when there are holes in the caring or even when it drops away completely for a while, afterwards it can be very scary because you think that all the things that you usually don't want or didn't want to happen didn't happen because you controlled them. So yeah, it can be both; relaxing and nice but also scary. You don't even know what you do (laughing). So, it's not only about not knowing what the others do (laughing) and the world out there, it's also suddenly, "Oh, dear. What will I do if I'm not in control? I might do all the silly things or exactly what I actually didn't want, and then I have to face the consequences."

Justin Allen: So, you recognize that also; the fear of not being "you" or of letting go of the "me" or of the "me" disappearing?

Andreas Müller: For the "me," it is scary, yeah. It can feel like giving up one's own path.

Justin Allen: Just to give an actual example: Did you ever have a fear like if you keep on dying, you die completely? I mean, of course, the fear of death is there, right?

Andreas Müller: Well, I think the basic fear is if I keep on dying, I'm losing being on the right path. This being on the right path towards what I'm looking for is so important for "me." There's so much value and meaning in that because, of course, I will only arrive at enlightenment or my happiness when I keep seeking for it, when I stay on the path, when I'm consciously controlling, when I'm trying to get it. Actually, the goals or what you are afraid of or what you want don't matter, but suddenly not caring anymore for the "me" seems to eradicate the possibility to ever arrive there. That's utterly scary. Or it can feel that from now on, I suffer for the rest of my life, for example. That's also a fear. The "person" thinks, "Oh, I don't suffer now, because I'm in control," but the fear is, of course ...

Justin Allen: To lose that control. Or the opposite: that they feel like they suffer because they're trying to control so much, so then they're trying to control how much they control.

Andreas Müller: Exactly. It's still the sense of being in control. The person lives in that, no matter what it believes to become aware of or recognize. But if that vanishes, if the energy goes out of there, it's unknowing, and you don't know what happens. This might include the theoretical possibility in the "person's" story of, "Oh, my God, maybe I will suffer from now on forever."

Justin Allen: The way that you're earning money right now is by giving these talks, and there is a career path in that in a way, right?

Andreas Müller: Yeah, it looks like it. So far.

Justin Allen: But you don't have the fear a "me" would have about running a business; that it might not be successful or that at some point people will stop paying you or needing your services?

Andreas Müller: No. In the story, one could say I'm facing that possibility, of course.

Justin Allen: Yeah, you're facing it, but also you have to plan your year in such a way to make sure that you're making enough money. So, you have to be putting effort in a way into ...

Andreas Müller: I don't really ...

Justin Allen: I'm just trying to talk about your job; even if you weren't doing this but working in an office or something like that.

Andreas Müller: Yeah, but it happens quite naturally. I never really had a big focus on money and being safe and that stuff, but yeah, of course, it could theoretically be an issue. I'm still not pushing it or anything, I never pushed it. There seems to be interest, and then I go for it.

Justin Allen: Yeah. Then, let's say that all of a sudden, you became interested in architecture for some reason.

Andreas Müller: You would recognize it if I started speaking a lot about architecture in the talks (laughing). Yeah, it might change again. Of course.

Justin Allen: If there were a change in interest happening, that could be a dilemma for a "me" person. Let's say they've invested fifteen or twenty years of their life into profession A, and then it happens to them that the interest in profession A has gone and there's an interest in profession B. They might have a tremendous anxiety about this new interest and might not want to let themselves like it and pursue it because it would mean they'd have to give up profession A and all that's been invested in it. They would have the dilemma of giving one up for the other, or they might have the dilemma of trying to repress and deny this new interest that has come up in them. So, that would be the two situations of the "me." The "me" wouldn't fall into accepting the new desires.

Andreas Müller: Or something in between.

Justin Allen: Or something in between, yeah. But for a "no me" person, it's the same thing, no?

Andreas Müller: So to speak, but it wouldn't be a "real" dilemma. It would be a real dilemma for the "person" that lives in the dilemma of the illusion that, "I have to solve it, and I have to find an answer. I should accept the new desire. I should go for that." That wouldn't be there for the "no me," but yes, it would be an apparent dilemma, which is just life, basically. "Oh, I'm doing this job now, and this is what I need money for, but suddenly, it's not fun anymore, and actually I want to do something else," is just life happening. There is no answer to that. There is no right or wrong answer. Either a complete job change happens or a compromise, or you stay in your old job, or the money issue vanishes because you win the lottery or something like that. Whatever happens. And yes, there will probably be correspondent thoughts and impulses that, in the story, seem to lead to doing A, B, C or D.

Justin Allen: Yeah, except that the "me" feels like there is an answer and something to work out, and that's its burden. That's what I'm trying to get at. So, for you it would be the same? You might stay in job A because you have the security and it's working?

Andreas Müller: In the end, not even "because of." Staying or leaving would be what apparently happens, yeah, but I don't ...

Justin Allen: The "because of's" are also just what apparently happens?

Andreas Müller: Exactly. They are not experienced as such. The "person" would live in the experience of this huge burden. "I have to stay in this job that I don't like anymore because of ..." You know?

Justin Allen: Yeah.

Andreas Müller: Well, that's life in a way. What to do (laughing)?

Justin Allen: What I'm getting at is that you're not out of that mess other than how it would be dealt with. If all of a sudden you started to develop a new interest, you would still have the exact same dilemma of, "Should I continue doing my talks, or should I do something else?"

Andreas Müller: Oh, yeah, absolutely. Apparently, Andreas would react to it as Andreas would react to it. But as I said, it wouldn't be a real dilemma.

Justin Allen: Because you've been doing this for ten years, right?

Andreas Müller: Yeah. There was no job ever that I did that long. It's eight years now, I think. No, nine years.

Justin Allen: Yeah, so nine years, and then when you first started, you weren't as successful as you are now. Generally, when you do a business, you get more successful the longer you stay in it. If you kept on changing your business every two years, you probably wouldn't be successful. That's part of having a business; sticking with it for a while, right?

Andreas Müller: All right. I don't know, but yeah, I guess so.

Justin Allen: Well, it seems like it, at least in many cases.

Andreas Müller: I never started it as a business, and in a way I still don't really regard it as a business, to be honest. So, I'm a bit alien to the business story.

Justin Allen: Yeah, well, I'm just calling it a business.

Andreas Müller: Let's just say it turned into an occupation.

Justin Allen: Anyway, it sounds like money and your time have become a little bit more critical since you have a family. But it still can happen to you that you could get into the dilemma that you lose interest in this or that it becomes ...

Andreas Müller: Or that people stay away.

Justin Allen: Then you have to figure out something else to do?

Andreas Müller: Oh, yeah, of course.

Justin Allen: Then you'd be in the same dilemma as everybody else?

Andreas Müller: Of course, apparently.

Justin Allen: Okay. Let's say you do have a new interest, and it's architecture. The reasoning or a thought that would come up might say, "You should stick with what you're doing because it's working and you've already invested nine years into this and probably it's going to get better."

Andreas Müller: No. Well, yes, of course, theoretically, this may come up, but this just wouldn't really be Andreas.

Justin Allen: What do you mean by that? I understand more that there's no Andreas, but I understand also that you don't ...

Andreas Müller: It's not what matches my conditioning. That's not how I seem to function.

Justin Allen: Okay.

Andreas Müller: Not because there is a "person" Andreas, but there is a functioning of Andreas.

Justin Allen: You mean from day one? That from one years old there's a conditioning ...

Andreas Müller: From the age of a young child, not from day one.

Justin Allen: Yeah, so for example, it wouldn't be Andreas, because you're not an overthinker, necessarily?

Andreas Müller: Well, I'm thinking about it, but not in terms of a career and for myself and all that stuff. Not yet. Maybe in ten years, who knows?

Justin Allen: Yep. You're just acknowledging that because of your personality type, certain thoughts probably aren't going to arise in your ...

Andreas Müller: Or wouldn't take over until so far. I don't know. I've no idea, of course. I just can't really imagine the thought that I invested so much.

Justin Allen: No, maybe you're interpreting it wrong; I just mean you've put nine years into this, right?

Andreas Müller: Yeah, that's what I mean.

Justin Allen: And comparing where you are right now with your first year, you could maybe see a projection of a possibility of continued success in a way. Whereas on day one, you couldn't really have had any idea other than ...

Andreas Müller: Oh, absolutely. Yes.

Justin Allen: So now, if in your first year you would have had an interest in doing architecture, it would have been a pretty easy decision to be like, "Well, I've only done this for one year, so I can easily change to another occupation."

Andreas Müller: I understand. Yeah.

Justin Allen: But now, after nine years, you would have a dilemma in the sense that you already have a potential career. You could switch it now to architecture, but you'd have to start from zero, and this would be a dilemma to most people.

Andreas Müller: Yes. It would be an apparent dilemma. Oh, yeah.

Justin Allen: That's what I'm saying. For you, as a "no me," it would also be an apparent dilemma where you might have conflicting thoughts?

Andreas Müller: Oh, yeah, of course ... Or, I don't know, I have no idea (laughing).

Justin Allen: Yeah, or not. You would maybe have conflicting thoughts, I would maybe have conflicting thoughts, but there'd be an increased anxiety or increased burden for a "me" because of the big significance this decision has.

Andreas Müller: Yeah, so to speak. It's not necessarily that when there is "no one," there is less fear, but one could say when there is someone, there is usually more fear.

Justin Allen: Yeah, and there's always a sense that it's you deciding and that it's you that's going to be affected by it. But for you it's not like that?

Andreas Müller: Which is a contradiction to say it like that; to say for "me" it's not like that. But yes, so to speak. The only thing that has a real conflict with anything is the "person." So, having a dilemma about going left or right isn't really a dilemma. It's just what apparently happens. It's life happening, which is fine. The actual dilemma, so to speak, is the illusion that I need to find or could know the right path. That's the actual dilemma; going left or right is just an apparent dilemma. It can still be what it is, but it actually is not a real problem. It happens all the time, in a way.

Justin Allen: Yeah. What seems to be happening to me is I've always tried to really analyze dilemmas from every angle that I can to figure out what to do. But I've also been recognizing that that's such a painful way to live life, in a way.

Andreas Müller: Oh, yeah.

Justin Allen: Then, also recognizing that I don't really have control, but also recognizing that I can't let go. It's so alien to me, in a way, to be like, "You're not doing anything," you know what I mean? If I start to feel like I don't care or that life's fine ... Even the sentence, "Life's fine how it is" ... That sits so (laughing), at least traditionally or conventionally, that doesn't sit well with me.

Andreas Müller: Mm-hmm (affirmative). All right.

Justin Allen: You know what I mean?

Andreas Müller: Yeah. I think I get an impression. I wouldn't go that far either, of course, and use those sentences like, "Life is fine," in the sense of ignoring the bad stuff or something like that.

Justin Allen: Right, I don't mean it like that. I just mean that ...

Andreas Müller: Yeah, the possibility of it just being whole and complete and right.

Justin Allen: Traditionally, I can't accept that everything is okay how it is and that my life, how it is, is fine and me, how I am, is okay. Even if that brought me happiness to just be okay with that, there's a huge part of me that doesn't want to allow that, although it's so obvious that life would be easier and better like that. It's the same with how you were saying you felt like you have to suffer to get something.

So, if I find myself in a situation where, let's say, everything's working and seems to be okay, I would immediately not want to accept that (laughing). I would immediately want to problematize it. Do you know what I mean?

Andreas Müller: Yeah. The answer is that you are not really enjoying it, because in some way there is some ... That's now pretty deep in the story, I'm sorry. But there is, in that sense, some wisdom about it; that somehow you know that you can't count on that. The wise "person" would answer that with, "Yeah, just enjoy it. It's going well right now, don't think about it," but of course, you can't count on things going well, even though the "person" would love to do so.

Justin Allen: Yeah, but if the "me" is dropping away, let's say, and it's slowly dying ... Even in physical death; when you're close to death, there's probably some huge relief.

Andreas Müller: Oh, yes, absolutely.

Justin Allen: So, what I'm saying is that ... Let's just pretend that the "me" is slowly dying and even though there's still elements of huge fear and worry, I'm starting to get a little taste of how relaxing and easy-going it might be. Let's just pretend that that's the transformation or the change that could be happening. As things get easier, I recognize this huge part of me that doesn't believe ... It's like you're so convinced that you have to struggle and there has to be pain.

Andreas Müller: "Life is hard." Yeah.

Justin Allen: Yeah. If life is too easy and everything's going too well, then it means that ... It's the same with the search. You only feel like you're really searching when you have conflict and struggle. Without that, you feel like, "Oh, I need to get busy here. Nothing really is happening."

Andreas Müller: Yeah.

Justin Allen: Okay, should we end it here?

Andreas Müller: Yeah. I'm getting hungry now.

Justin Allen: I'm hungry, too.

Andreas Müller: All right, have a good day.

Justin Allen: Yeah, you too.

January 30, 2020 Talk 10

"THANK YOU FOR YOUR SILLINESS"

Justin Allen: We are recording now.

Andreas Müller: Okay. All right. Good.

Justin Allen: How are you?

Andreas Müller: I'm fine. Slept enough. And you, how are you?

Justin Allen: I'm good, too. So, this is our tenth talk, I think.

Andreas Müller: Yeah.

Justin Allen: And what I thought would be interesting is (laughing) if you've seen any changes in our talks, so to speak? From the first talk to now, have you noticed anything worth pointing out?

Andreas Müller: Yeah. Well, I don't know if it's worth pointing out, but there are observations, apparent observations (laughing). I mean (laughing), yeah, do you want to hear them?

Justin Allen: Sure.

Andreas Müller: Yeah. Well, I think what I'm going to say is not very deep in a way, but what I noticed is that we started off kind of general, which is fine. We talked about the other speakers or teachers, about Ramana, for example, and it was like comparing the teachings to this message. And I have the impression that over the talks, it has gotten much more to the point, so to speak, about what this message is saying and not really caring so much about it as if it were another teaching which one could choose.

You know what I mean?

Justin Allen: Yeah.

Andreas Müller: That's my observation.

Justin Allen: Do you think you can talk about this topic or about the "no me" point or the "no one's there" point? Do you think you can talk about it "deeply"?

Andreas Müller: You can't talk about it deeply.

Justin Allen: Well, then my question is: Can you talk about it at all? Because your observation in a way was that we started off in a kind of broader, generalized and maybe more superficial sense, and then over time it started to get a little bit more to the point. But my impression is when you get more to the point, you can't talk about it so much anymore.

Andreas Müller: Oh, yes, of course. Absolutely.

Justin Allen: You know what I mean? To a general audience, it might seem like we were having a deep conversation in the beginning, and as it goes on, it gets less deep. Even though from your point of view, in a way it might be getting deeper because it's more to the point. But then, in a sense, the nature of this is that as you go on, there's less material to try to grab onto, you know?

Andreas Müller: Oh, yes, totally (laughing). One could say so.

Justin Allen: So, in a way it feels like the opposite of the general idea of a deep conversation where you tend to think there's a lot to talk about, and you keep on talking about more things and grabbing onto more concepts.

Andreas Müller: So to speak. Yes, absolutely. But yes, it turns out, but not because it's deeper or important, that there honestly just is no real issue. Nothing is deep, and nothing can be found.

Justin Allen: So it's not deep (laughing)?

Andreas Müller: Yes, exactly. Nothing is deep, so to speak. I mean, some people may turn it around and say, "Yeah, that's the actual depth of this topic," or something like that.

Justin Allen: Well, I think people in general would feel like our conversation is deeper the more personal it gets.

Andreas Müller: Yeah, that's possible.

Justin Allen: And if the topic or the point is that there's no "me" and no one really there and this is it, you can't say much more, unless you try to relate it in some ways to all the strings and lines coming out from the made-up point of view.

Andreas Müller: Yeah. And in a way that's not really deep either. It just is like that. The "person" might regard it as deep information or deep conversation because it thinks that it can get something out of that. But it's not really like that, so an expression like "deep" or "to the point" is just in the story.

Justin Allen: Yeah. But another way you could somehow look at something being deep is that it comes from you swimming in the ocean or digging down into the ground. And then the deeper you get, the less there is in a way. Like when you start off digging at the top, there's grass and plants and everything, and as you get in, it's just earth, and then at some point maybe you hit mere clay, and that's it. So, in a conversation like ours you start off maybe by talking about a bunch of things, and then at some point you get to the thing, which isn't a thing. There's nothing there, there's no one, or that's it. And then when you hit that, it's not actually really deep. In a sense, it's extremely simple or extremely basic or ...

Andreas Müller: Exactly. Yep, yep, yep. Absolutely; that's a picture that would work. That's what we are doing, and we're not coming to a result in the end. In the end, it's just that after having dug all through, there's just nothing left.

Justin Allen: Yeah, yeah. And that's the no-point?

Andreas Müller: Yes, exactly. It's not even that we hit ground, it's that the whole digging world (laughing), the whole seeking world, turned out to be nonexistent in the first place.

Justin Allen: It's kind of like when I'm looking through the talks, I feel like maybe I try to come up with another way of digging another hole. So, that's kind of what I feel like we've done: Every time we talk, you start off digging a hole at area A, and you get down and realize there's no point from that spot where we started digging, and then you might say, "Okay, then I'm going to try digging from this B area over there." And in some way that just felt like something that I had to do; to start from another point.

So then, us talking about spiritual teachers was a way of starting off by questioning what they're saying and by exploring if it is just another belief. Is what they're offering or teaching just beliefs, and what do they mean by it? And then, what's your take or your perspective? Then that seemed to be a kind of strategy: to try to come up with some potential illusory point of view and break it apart a couple of times (laughing). Then you're either fishing for some new area to go about it or you try to just talk about the point. And that's what I find difficult: that once you get to the point, there's no point (laughing).

Andreas Müller: Yes, there is nothing to say really, which, again, in a way is not a point that you could come to.

Justin Allen: Right. Yeah, yeah.

Andreas Müller: The "person" can't take it as another point and then say, "Oh, you can't talk about it, so let's talk about something else as an answer to that point or no-point." But yes, there is no message. There is no point. That's the point, kind of. See, you can't go there. There's just nothing really to say.

Justin Allen: And that's as deep as it can get?

Andreas Müller: Yes, exactly. Because looking at it already takes place within the story, so to speak.

Justin Allen: Yeah.

Andreas Müller: Yeah, yeah, totally. Absolutely.

Justin Allen: So, with that said (laughing) ...

Andreas Müller: See? There is no conclusion from that. There is no point coming from that.

Justin Allen: But with that said, then I think I've come up with another way (laughing), and why not try it out? So, forgive me if this is a bad example; maybe we can change it as we go along. But as far as starting off, I was just thinking about how we're doing these talks as Justin Allen and Andreas Müller, and maybe we publish a book or make a podcast or something like this. And then I was thinking we could go back to the example where I'm coming from a "me" perspective and you're coming from a "no me" perspective to somehow create a distinction. And then, in a typical scenario of two "me" perspective people that might want to publish a book, you could imagine that there might be a conflict of how the names of the two people get printed on the book cover, for example. Because each person could think that they're a "me" and might have some kind of egoic desire to be recognized. So, one person might want their name to be first or in bigger print and the other person's name to be in smaller print.

Andreas Müller: Okay (laughing). Are you trying to tell me something (laughing)?

Justin Allen: So, if we used such a case, such a personal situation between us (laughing), and accepted that I'm the "me" perspective (laughing) and very egoic and competitive and want my name to be first and in bold print (laughing) and your name to be misspelled (laughing) and in smaller print (laughing). And then typically, we would think that you should accept that (laughing) because you're a "no me," so you're not really there and don't care (laughing).

So, I was just curious if we analyze that in a way, the way that I would talk about it based on our previous talks would be that for a "me" perspective it might be important where and how their name gets situated, whereas for a "no me" perspective, one would assume that it wouldn't be that important, because there's no real intention or motivation. But at the same time, thoughts and feelings might happen to the "no me" perspective that also are somehow indicating that there's some importance of where their name gets placed. So, how could we talk about that, because they're both dealing with the exact same dilemma?

Andreas Müller: Yes. I mean you can't really point out a difference in the behavior, because the difference between "me" and "no me" is illusionary in the first place. But of course, when there is someone, there is the dream that I am someone and that I have to consciously act and that my action is of value: My actions need to make sure that I get what I deserve and that my wish becomes fulfilled in the future, which, in some way or the other, adds something to my unfulfillment.

So, there would just be the assumption of there being a "person" in there who lives in this added artificial reality; that's all. And when there is "no one," so to speak, it could also be an issue where or how the name gets printed, but it just wouldn't be connected to the idea that there is someone who gains or loses anything from however it goes, including, for example, one's own reaction to it, namely to care (laughing) and not to not care because there is "no one" or because there is enlightenment or liberation. There would just be a reaction, and it would be wild and free, so to speak. And it could also be like, "No, I'm sorry, I thought I'm the main person here because you interviewed me, so I want to have my name bigger."

Justin Allen: So, outwardly, a third person viewing it might not recognize any difference between the two people kind of being in conflict of where their names get placed?

Andreas Müller: So to speak, yes, it could be. I mean, what's being said is that there just is no "person" behind the "person" behind the personality.

Justin Allen: But from a third person's perspective, there might be an expectation that you would kind of submit and say, "I don't care where my name goes," whereas they would expect me to really care about where my name goes. And then if they see that you care where your name goes, they would be like, "Hey, what's going on Andreas? I thought you are liberated from the 'me,' so why should you care about such egoic stuff like where your name gets placed?"

Andreas Müller: Yeah, that would be the assumption because they would assume a real difference.

Justin Allen: And because if you did "care" about your name and where it gets placed, the only difference is that there's no one really there that cares, even though caring might be expressed?

Andreas Müller: Exactly. One could say there is no one that cares about caring, for example; that cares about how I behave. Andreas might seem to care, but there is no one behind that, so to speak.

Justin Allen: So, you're expressing care and concern potentially equally as I would be expressing it, but I would be doing it believing that it's "me" doing it somehow or ...

Andreas Müller: And the "person" would, in some way or the other, need a story for itself that says that it's right or necessary to do it like this or that it's wrong and if I would be enlightened, I wouldn't care so much or whatever. Yeah.

Justin Allen: So, that would be one other thing to add to the distinction or definition: that the "me" would always have a story and the "no me" doesn't?

Andreas Müller: Or let's say for the "me," it's not just a story; it's a potential truth that it tells itself, and it tries to believe in the story to make it worthwhile, for example, to make it okay that I care. I have to tell "myself" an additional story.

Justin Allen: And that doesn't happen to the "no me"?

Andreas Müller: One could say so, yes. When there is "no one," there isn't the need to tell a story or justify one's own behavior. There's just no need for anything. Although all kinds of things can happen in the same way, and egoic thoughts may come as well.

Justin Allen: Yeah, that's what's difficult to accept or understand ... So, let's say I care about where my name gets placed, but I start to feel a little bit of shame that I care so much. So, in order to justify that, I start going, "Well, I should care," and I start to come up with arguments for why I should care. But you might also say out loud, "No, I want my name to be here," but you wouldn't feel ashamed about that?

Andreas Müller: Yes. Probably, yeah.

Justin Allen: But it could also happen that a thought comes in that says, "No, you fight for your name to get put there." So then, we'd be equal in a sense still?

Andreas Müller: Well, that's the thing. It's all equal. But in the end it's about if it's for someone or not, apparently.

Justin Allen: So, that's a distinction that you can't make: You can't come up with a way to really diagrammatically express that, can you?

Andreas Müller: Exactly. I can't, because it's a distinction that's not real. That's the whole point. It's not saying there is a "me," which is really different from "no me." There is no real distinction, and we could say, no matter how deep we dig (laughing), we won't ever find a distinction that can be named and pointed out.

Justin Allen: So, I think if there's value to any of this (laughing), that's a valuable thing to point out. Even though we can just talk about this, somehow beat it like in the expression of beating a dead horse. Because I think if we use the scenario where I feel ashamed that I want so badly for my name to be first, everybody can relate to that because they also felt ashamed sometime and tried to come up with an argument to justify it. And that just kind of lends itself to more shame in a way. And then you start to identify with yourself more and more and kind of really feel like there's the "me" there.

But that can happen to you or to a "no me" as well, except the kind of feeling and it being real wouldn't be there in a sense? You still might have the thought that you should fight to have your name printed bigger or equally big? That you shouldn't just concede and let your name be printed smaller? And you might have all the arguments that your brain's able to come up with to justify this wish, but it wouldn't be felt as so important?

Andreas Müller: Yes, and there would be no need to indulge in that story, but this doesn't have to do anything with what happens or not. I mean, in a way the "me" can get really crazy in that whole apparent situation like, "I want it, I shouldn't want it, I feel bad," and then it goes from A to B to C, and suddenly you are back with your whole life dilemma of, "Damn, I'm always holding back," or whatever (laughing). Either way, one could say when there is "no one," there is no one indulging in that stuff, or there's nobody left who would have that tendency or that need to follow that road, so to speak.

Justin Allen: Although outwardly it might seem like you're indulging?

Andreas Müller: Yes, yes. Kind of.

Justin Allen: Can you think of any example of an experience of indulging in something from, let's say, before you were liberated? You have to have had thousands of such experiences as well.

Andreas Müller: Absolutely. I mean, the whole personal existence in a way is indulging into the personal existence (laughing).

Justin Allen: Right, but even then, not everything that they're doing throughout a day is an indulgence. For example, there are people that don't have a problem deciding on what to order from the menu, but ten minutes later they're trying to buy a pair of shoes and are like, "I can never decide what shoe I should get because of ..." whatever. So, they start indulging only in that situation and are not constantly indulging in everything. It's generally some kind of trigger that ...

Andreas Müller: Yeah. One could say so.

Justin Allen: So, do they have experiences of being liberated from the "me" in those scenarios where they're not really indulging in the "me"?

Andreas Müller: Well, no, because that's what I mean. In the story, one could make a distinction between "me" indulging into an issue and just "me" being busy with something else, but in all of these situations, that would be kind of an indulgement in being "me."

Justin Allen: Okay, so you're just saying that ...

Andreas Müller: You know, "me" can be very concentrated on buying shoes, for example. Then it doesn't seem like I'm indulging into a problematic story about myself or into a conflict, instead I'm just concentrated on doing my stuff, but it would still be within the experience to be "me." Of course, "me" can have the experience of indulging and getting lost in problems versus not thinking about things too much. I mean, that's what a lot of spirituality is about; to not think too much, to not follow bad thoughts or associate more and more problems to your thoughts and go deeply into them.

Justin Allen: But doesn't it just happen sometimes that the "person," also without indulging or without trying, just kind of organically isn't really there and isn't really giving a shit?

Andreas Müller: Oh, yeah, of course. Absolutely.

Justin Allen: But isn't that a situation in a sense where at least they're temporarily liberated from the "me"?

Andreas Müller:	Well, one just doesn't know if there is a "me" or not. There is no real answer to that, because when there is "no one," no one knows anyway. And when there apparently is someone, it could be anything. It could be having a flow experience but just not thinking about it. I mean, the "me" isn't there in the first place, but to be "me" doesn't only mean to have bad experiences. Within the apparent "me" cosmos, it goes from bliss to desperation.
Justin Allen:	But I'm talking about the moments when there's no bliss and no desperation, no intense feeling, let's say, and I think everybody experiences that at times. Not necessarily that they're there to experience it, but in the story of a day, a "person" is kind of aware that they're there and that they're actively doing something that's making them blissful or desperate. But there might also be some times in the day where they're just not doing something; something's going on, but they're not really participating in it. So, aren't they temporarily not there then?
Andreas Müller:	Oh, yeah, of course. That's quite possible. Totally.
Justin Allen:	So then, people are "experiencing" potentially daily "no me" moments?
Andreas Müller:	Totally. Oh, yes, of course.
Justin Allen:	So, but the way that you're talking about liberation somehow is when that's permanent?
Andreas Müller:	So to speak, yes.
Justin Allen:	That's the thing that I can't (laughing) ... Because I just always think nothing can be permanent. For me, it still has to be totally potential that you could re-indulge in life (in the "me" and the personal story) at some point.
Andreas Müller:	Yes. I mean, in the end what we talk about right now is all in the story. So, there's nothing really permanent.
Justin Allen:	Yeah. So then, you'd have to kind of concede to say that theoretically, tomorrow you could wake up, and the "me" could be there again, in a sense?

Andreas Müller: That would be logic. Yes, logic would say that I should say that, but that wouldn't be liberation then (laughing). I'm sorry. It's not logical, but yes, theoretically I would need to say this. But then I would also admit that there is a "me" waking up in the first place or that there is the possibility that a "me" wakes up in the morning or not. But the surprise in liberation, so to speak, is not that there is a "me" or that there was a "me" which now is no more. In a way, the death of the "me" is the turning out that it was never there and that nothing leaves, which is just totally illogical. And this means that there isn't anyone indulging or re-indulging or not indulging. It's always just what happens.

Justin Allen: Yeah. But there's nothing there, and there never was. And it's the same as if a "person" went through a day, and, let's just pretend, for forty percent of the day, they're not really there and not really participating, but there's no one there to recognize that as such. So, they're only kind of familiar with the sixty percent of the day when they feel like they're there. And the other forty percent get totally disregarded as being nothing, basically ...

Andreas Müller: Yeah, same as deep sleep or death. It's actually not even regarded as something (laughing). It doesn't ...

Justin Allen: And that's what I'm saying: It's regarded as not existent; it's just ignored in a sense, like not seen, not felt, not touched. It's just nothing.

Andreas Müller: It's nothing. Yeah, absolutely.

Justin Allen: But from what you're saying that is in a sense the true reality?

Andreas Müller: Yes and no, because one could say when recognizing and the "me" thing happens, the sixty percent as an opposed state to the forty percent, it's also the true reality, but in the end, it's as unrecognized as when there is "no one." But then there is an apparent recognition about an apparent life. I wouldn't say that there is a real difference between those two, but "me" would make an apparent difference.

Justin Allen: Right. And the sixty percent of the time, the "me" would be saying that this happened and this didn't happen or …

Andreas Müller: Exactly. So, the outcome of the sixty percent is the illusion of a difference, namely that all there is, are those sixty percent moments, and that's all that matters and has value. But in the end I wouldn't be able to make that distinction, because all of that would just be what apparently happens and all of that is blind. All of that is what it is, and all of that is blindly itself. And that blindness, one could say, is the natural reality, but it can also be an apparent recognition of an apparent life. And it can also be an apparent recognition of an apparent life taken for real and as the only thing that is, which would be the "person's" experience.

Justin Allen: That would be the "person's" experience, and then your "experience" would be an apparent recognition that in the past, there was a sense of there being a "me," which turned out to not be a "me"?

Andreas Müller: Yes and no. Not as a state of recognition that I am in. However, such a recognition can arise and can be expressed, like in the talk we are having.

Justin Allen: But in one of our previous talks, you also talked about how there were some moments where you recognized that there was no "me" before you were liberated.

Andreas Müller: Yes, yes. Yeah.

Justin Allen: And that's what I'm kind of getting at: Would that have been an example of the forty percent?

Andreas Müller: Yes, but in the recognition I was already there again in a way. There was already an assumed person again.

Justin Allen: Recognizing that there was this moment of forty percent?

Andreas Müller: Yes, exactly, which was rather a conclusion from, "I'm here now." And there was no one there before, but I didn't know how or what that was. But it was kind of clear in a way.

Justin Allen: But then in that scenario you're talking about the forty percent from the perspective of the sixty percent?

Andreas Müller: Yeah.

Justin Allen: So, that's what I mean. I'm not trying to put any importance on this, I guess I'm just talking about it technically, but people are going through their lives, daily and literally not being there or not having a "me"?

Andreas Müller: Yeah. Not having a self-experience. Oh, yeah, of course.

Justin Allen: But without any kind of recognition? And then what you were saying in some of the previous talks is that the glimpses in a sense are when something somehow starts to recognize that those forty percent are happening?

Andreas Müller: One could say so, yeah.

Justin Allen: It's a distinction that's not real, but at the same time, by the "me," it's experienced as a real distinction, like how you were able to say, "I wasn't there."

Andreas Müller: Which still doesn't turn it into a real distinction, but yes, it seems to be for the "me"; the experience of presence makes the distinction. Yeah.

Justin Allen: And do you think it happens that the "me" drops out, and they don't recognize it as such? So, life is still totally going on as a "no me." And then what would happen when someday there is some kind of recognition where they go, "Oh, that's it. This is just life going on without 'me' here."

Andreas Müller: I mean, it's absolutely possible that it's apparently recognized as that, and the same thing happened here in a way. It's not even recognized as something special or as something that has happened to "me." It's more like as I said, "Oh, that's actually quite all right everything or something." It's not being turned back towards oneself having become anything or gotten anything or having turned into something enlightened or someone liberated or any of that. It would just be the apparent recognition that there is "no one." Maybe that's not even recognized as such, but it's just that there's no problem that you know ...

Justin Allen: Yeah, like it's just life.

Andreas Müller: Exactly, and it's not even a processed information of there being no separate person. Saying that there is "no one" is also theoretical again, especially for someone who hasn't lived at all in those spiritual stories about ego and there being a "person" or no "person" and about enlightenment or liberation. I mean, today there's probably hardly anyone who hasn't heard those words somewhere along the way, because it's even in the magazines and newspapers, but it doesn't have anything to do with all that stuff and all that processing and checking like, "Have you reached no me?" and, "I became liberated."

No, it can just be like you said, a total ordinary, "Oh, boo, there's no point in anything at all," or, "Nothing really matters," but not even as a processing in the brain and giving value to all those insights and thoughts. No, it just fucking is like that. And it would be just ordinary, how it actually already is for everyone (said excitedly).

Justin Allen: Right, but this is my question: Let's say that it "happens" to me. And then because I have been educated and I studied philosophy and I've read books from Ramana Maharshi and I've gone to a therapist and I'm familiar with psychology and whatever, I go, "Ah, that's just it. This is just life." But when I put it into the context of all my knowledge, I've already taken myself out of it again, like I've ...

Andreas Müller: Yeah. But then it wouldn't have been liberation, so to speak. Because then you can't really put yourself back into all that blah, blah, blah of all those concepts, at least not seriously.

Justin Allen: Yeah. For me, if I was going to try to contribute to those kinds of examples, I can say that there have been moments when I felt like there was "no one" there, and then I definitely couldn't talk about what that was really like. And I can also talk about moments where my life went generally well and I didn't really care and I wasn't lost in my thoughts and blah, blah, blah. But then I know that I was kind of actively still there somehow.

Andreas Müller: Yes, in a way, that's exactly what I meant.

Justin Allen: But I also recognize those moments when I wasn't really there. And then that moment when I came back in a sense, that which was coming back or just that "coming back" was terrified, or maybe not terrified, but somehow like, "What the fuck was that!?" Or like looking back at that was kind of like, "How can that be? Something's wrong in a sense." I guess it recognizes that as something undesirable or scary or dangerous.

Andreas Müller: Undesirable, dangerous, terrifying ...

Justin Allen: It's like going near the road as a kid. Your parents tell you, "Don't go near the road, don't go near the road." And as you go near the road, you start to feel more and more uncomfortable. And if you go and stand on the road, you feel like, "Oh, my God, I'm breaking the rules." As a child, you feel that you're going against what you're supposed to be doing and it's really uncomfortable.

Andreas Müller: Yes. Well, I think it's a little bit more because I think going against can also be fun for a child, but I think the situation is you're going against what you're supposed to do, and it's becoming really fucking dangerous to have done that.

Justin Allen: Like the child itself is aware that it's dangerous?

Andreas Müller: Exactly. It's like standing on the road and the lorry passing by in that moment. It's like, "Oh, I shouldn't have done that, but damn, it was fucking dangerous right now."

Justin Allen: Right, your whole instinct and your whole physical reaction and whatever you have as your resources in a sense totally go against that. Or at least it seems that they go against that previous "no me" moment or experience. And it's like a logical reaction.

Andreas Müller: Yes. Oh, yeah. Yeah. That can happen.

Justin Allen: And another example is that you're trained to think that you should take care of your parents and that you should love them more than everybody else in a sense and you should be loyal to them and whatever, right? And if there's a "no me," then there's not really the story going on anymore saying that I'm supposed to do this. If all those things start to disappear, that can be a huge conflict in a way where you think, "This isn't good. What kind of person am I if I don't care about my parents?"

Andreas Müller: Oh, yeah, of course. That's the danger the "me" faces, and of course, that's also dangerous and scary in absence. There are no should's, there are no rules. So, it's not only that the stories disappear that you didn't like. It's also about somehow losing your values and about what you think is important.

Justin Allen: And same in your mind. Then you think, "What if everybody were like this? That would also mean, for example, that my dad doesn't necessarily have to take care of me." Or it makes you feel like, "Oh, my God, then everybody can just do what they want; there's nothing holding anybody to any kind of ethics or whatever." Would you say that that's preventative to liberation?

Andreas Müller: No, no. It's just the "me" living in its story and facing the possibility of death, so to speak, or facing the apparent possibility that nothing of that is real and that nothing is personal and that "care" or "caring" is only in the story. I mean, it's a dream that people do take care of their kids or their parents because they live in this story of morality and have to do that or the other way around. Taking care simply happens or not.

Justin Allen: But when I've come to these kinds of precipices or cliffs, I really want to step back. Same as when a child gets close to the road and wants to move three meters back away from the road to feel safe again. It doesn't want to go forward. So, in a sense, isn't that you're actively preventing yourself from liberation?

Andreas Müller: No, because it's all in the story. I mean, in the picture it's like that, of course. But it would already assume someone who consciously does oneself and their decisions.

Justin Allen: So if we use this example again: The child's walking towards the road, and it starts to feel uncomfortable because in its head, it's thinking, "Dad told me not to get close to the road." And with every step that the child takes closer to the road, he's going against what his dad's taught him, and then he's seeing cars whiz by him. So, in front of him, he's seeing the potential for death or danger. And then as he steps back and kind of listens to his father's warning and to his body, because his body is also probably getting tenser as it gets closer, it starts to feel more relaxed again and maybe starts to breath slower, and the heart rate goes down, and it recognizes all that, and it thinks that it's doing it, and it's listening to its father's advice and using its own intelligence to go, "Oh, that probably is a good idea not to get so close to the road."

And as the child advances, it also thinks that it's consciously advancing and deciding to not defy the father and is going to wait before he steps on the road. And of course, he's going to wait until a car passes, and he's not going to stand there for five minutes before he moves away. But in your scenario, you would say that the child still isn't really there doing any of this ...

Andreas Müller: Yes, exactly. Not even the illusion to be conscious and thinking, "I do this and that" is done by the child.

Justin Allen: And that's also why liberation is the same as non-liberation in the sense that it's just as wild and free to be liberated or non-liberated?

Andreas Müller: So to speak, yes. It's just what apparently happens, and it's wild and free, and there is neither real imprisonment nor real liberation.

Justin Allen: And because there's no real control and no real free will and no actual "you" deciding anything, that's why if apparent liberation happens to a person, it's a total accident in a sense?

Andreas Müller: Yeah, absolutely, one could say so. It's not intended, but you could say the same about the illusion of "me." It's an accident, everything is an accident again.

Justin Allen: Yeah. And if you lose your job, it's an accident. And if you get married, it's an accident.

Andreas Müller: The earth is an accident. Trees are an accident. Climate change is accidental, which is all in the story now. We operate here in existence in manifestation, which is already a story. But yes, exactly.

Justin Allen: I don't want to use this word, but it just came to my mind, so I have to: There is a "fate" then in a sense? If you're going to be liberated or not, it's either going to happen or not? It's kind of like "in the cards" for you or not?

Andreas Müller: Yes, one could say so, and I understand how you come to that conclusion. But you know, again, that's within manifestation and time and the real happening and so on. It's already within the story.

Justin Allen: I mean I could just imagine people hearing this and then projecting that idea of fate onto it also.

Andreas Müller: Oh, yeah, totally. As it being predestined.

Justin Allen: Yeah, I mean that's bullshit, but because it's already set up in a way, you're either going to get liberated or not, and it's going to happen when you're twenty-seven or fifty-two or eighty-six or never.

Andreas Müller: Well, in a way it happens definitely. It will happen for everyone in the end (laughing), but yes, I know what you mean. And there is an end apparently. Yeah, yeah, yeah. You can't do it. There is no "you" who can do it. There is already no "you" who does anything. Everything is what it is. So if you put that in time, you end up with fate. "Everything is predestined."

Justin Allen: You're also saying that the "no me" has nothing to do with circumstances, right?

Andreas Müller: Yes.

Justin Allen: Like liberation has nothing to do with circumstances, but the "me" would naturally conclude that the circumstances have everything to do or could have a lot to do with this?

Andreas Müller: Yes, of course, absolutely. Just like the "me" thinks that liberation is an event and real; so it kind of automatically embeds it into certain surroundings that fit in its picture.

Justin Allen: And that's why people are convinced that the kind of circumstance of meditating or going to a retreat will potentially induce or increase the chances of becoming liberated?

Andreas Müller: Yes. But one could even say it more in general. Seen by the "me," seeking is the best circumstance to find, and liberation is finding something. So, the best thing that I can do, the best circumstance that I can be in, is the seeking setup.

Justin Allen: Right. But at some point it even gets concluded that the searching is part of the problem in a sense. And at least the idea or the concept of meditation, even though it's also another searching, is that during these thirty minutes in a day you're not searching and just trying to do nothing in a sense.

Andreas Müller: Yeah, just be present.

Justin Allen: And same with the retreat. Most of us live in a situation where we have a job and maybe a family, and maybe you live in a city where it's all hectic, and nowadays you're on your phone a lot, so you're constantly being stimulated. And then going away for a week to a small village or a monastery type setting where you don't use your phone and maybe don't even talk to people, the idea might be that that increases your chances of becoming liberated. So, you totally think that it's circumstantial.

Andreas Müller: "I only have to choose the right conditions, and it is because of them and of "me," that I will get liberated." Of course, totally.

Justin Allen: I mean, nobody's convinced that the best scenario for them to become liberated is getting into an argument with their wife in public or something like that (laughing).

Andreas Müller: Oh, yeah, which sounds actually like a very good ... (laughing). Yeah.

Justin Allen: But what you're saying is the chances of getting liberated are as equal and as impossible in this scenario of meditating or being in a retreat as they are in getting into an intense argument with your partner or in brushing your teeth or in standing at the supermarket check-out?

Andreas Müller: Oh, yeah, of course.

Justin Allen: And that's where everybody in general would think, "Bullshit." There's no way my chances of getting enlightened are increased while I'm spitting from my mouth arguing with my ...

Andreas Müller: Exactly (laughing). Oh, yeah. But of course, it's already coming from a picture that liberation or enlightenment has anything to do with someone becoming happy or relaxed or silent. So, it's already coming from a very misconceived assumption. Apparent death can happen at any time under any circumstance. It doesn't ask anything. It doesn't ask you to be relaxed. It doesn't ask you to have reached anything before or gained or understood or to be in a certain condition. It doesn't have anything to do with you in the first place; not with how you are, where you are, what you think, how you behave and all that stuff. It just doesn't care about that at all.

Justin Allen: (Laughing in a pause) I mean, you can really see, even just intellectually or conceptually, or well, I don't even know if it's true that it's intellectual or conceptual, but you can totally see that if there's someone there (apparently), then you're blocked. You know what I mean? If there's something there, then there's something there and that's ...

Andreas Müller: Yes. That's the apparent dilemma of the "me": to only be able to be "me." And to only operate within the realms of "me" and in the story of "me" and the assumptions of "me."

Justin Allen: It's so fucked up to think that you're not there, you know (laughing)? Because that's not ...

Andreas Müller: Well, seen by the "me," that's just another idea, another concept, and it doesn't make it better. It doesn't help at all (laughing).

Justin Allen: But it's also that you know it somehow. I don't know, it's hard to explain, but you know that you're not there (laughing).

Andreas Müller: It's in the air meanwhile. Yeah. That it's not real.

Justin Allen: But I don't even mean conceptually or intellectually. Somehow you know that you've touched that a couple of times, and I really think it's like that feeling when you ... It's because I grew up kind of in the country, and we had this high speed road, and for whatever reason I'm stuck on that example of getting close to the road; so that's why it feels like you're there. It feels like you're in control of your liberation in a way. And it feels like there's something you can do or not do.

Andreas Müller: Like you could take the step. Yeah.

Justin Allen: Yeah. And it feels like you're not taking this step because of the fear of the unknown and ...

Andreas Müller: And all that stuff, yeah.

Justin Allen: It feels like it's more intelligent to not take that step because you're like, "Well, at least I'm kind of familiar with this life of sometimes being good and sometimes bad and ..."

Andreas Müller: Yeah. You're back into a known reality, which is "I'm saved."

Justin Allen: "I don't want to lose my relationship with my parents and my friends or my girlfriend or ..."

Andreas Müller: Exactly, the things that "I have." Yeah.

Justin Allen: And then if you do say, "I'm open to the idea of dying, and I'm open to staying alive," that's still the same thing.

Andreas Müller: Yes. So to speak.

Justin Allen: And whether you do take the step onto the road or back away, it has nothing to do with you.

Andreas Müller: Oh, yeah, exactly. Totally (laughing). Because basically there is no you, because behind or within all of that, there never is a real separate instance with choice. There is "no one" really standing at the road being able to ask themselves whether to step forward or not. And the whole situation of there being a road and a step to take in a way is already imagined by this apparent "me."

Justin Allen: And that's kind of like the extreme shitty feeling that people who follow these spiritual teachers probably tend to have at some point. I mean, they also probably feel really good sometimes because they feel like they're moving towards the road, but then they feel really shitty when they're not taking that last step because they recognize that they're not actually liberated and then blame themselves that they're too afraid.

Andreas Müller: Exactly. Just like they already "blamed" themselves for the success of having come near the road. Well, they were rather proud of having done that and very happy, and then the last step, so to speak, doesn't happen, and now it's their fault again. Yeah.

Justin Allen: Yeah. Or they perpetually will keep on trying to take that step and keep on having to revisit that terrifying feeling over and over again, like, "Oh, I'm going to do it today. Oh, shit, I can't, I just can't." And then the teacher's all the time saying, "Just take the step," which is keeping the torture going (laughing).

Andreas Müller: Yeah, exactly. "Just do it, it's nothing" (laughing).

Justin Allen: It's like your friend trying to convince you to jump off the bridge into the water, and because you're reluctant, your friend's going, "Just do it. It's fine. Watch me, I'll do it." Then he jumps in first, and it seems fine. And then if you gave up, if you conclude, "Oh, this is fucking bullshit"; when you let go of all that spirituality stuff or your job, car, house or previous life, you could feel pretty good for a while probably, also because you felt like you figured something out and left something behind. And then because you believe in that, you would have let go of all that pressure that you've been putting on yourself, and you might convince yourself that you're liberated now or ...

Andreas Müller: Yeah, for example; this can happen.

Justin Allen: And so you or Tony Parsons will say that it might happen that some people, through these talks and through talking with one another, are open to liberation, open to the death of "me," and that those people might hear or resonate with the message.

Andreas Müller: Those people are open to the possibility that there is "no me" in the first place.

Justin Allen: But those people actually don't need to hear that message or be in the circumstance of the meetings?

Andreas Müller: Yes, absolutely. Yeah.

Justin Allen: But at the same time, if it's all kind of accidental and that's like the thing that they need to hear ...

Andreas Müller: Exactly, that's what apparently happens then. Although you can't really squeeze need in that, because nothing needs to be in a certain way. But if it is what apparently happens that people come to the talk and hear the message, that's what apparently happens.

Justin Allen: And that could be the same with a guy that becomes liberated apparently because he walks into the woods and hears a bird chirping. And he goes, "Oh, my God."

Andreas Müller: Yes. And it could be ...

Justin Allen: And if the bird could talk, it might say, "Some people are open to my whistles." (laughing)

Andreas Müller: Yeah, exactly, exactly. Or the man that shouts at his wife in utter rage, and at that moment there is "no one" screaming, and he would fall down on his knees before her and say, "Thank you for your silliness." (laughing) Yes, but it's never really "because of ..."

Justin Allen: It's never really "because of ..." but at the same time it sort of is.

Andreas Müller: I know. Yes, exactly. Yeah.

Justin Allen: Because it couldn't have been any other way, just because that's the way that it happened?

Andreas Müller: Exactly. Because it just ...

Justin Allen: It just is what it is, and there's ...

Andreas Müller: Yes, totally. That's why some people sometimes ask me, "If you wouldn't have seen Tony and if you wouldn't have done this and that, would it have happened as well?" And that's totally theoretical because that's just how it happened. That's just how it was.

Justin Allen: That's the same shit as when people fall in love and get married to the person they think is the only one for them in the world. But before they met them, they became paralyzed, so now in their story, they go, "Yeah, if I wouldn't have gotten paralyzed, I would've never met my wife, and we wouldn't be happily married now."

Andreas Müller: Yeah.

Justin Allen: So, you don't ever think, "Oh, I wish I would've met Tony ten years earlier"? (laughing)

Andreas Müller: No, no, no. I had a great life. It was all fun. No, honestly, never. Nothing was lost. Nothing was missed. And nothing happened now, and I didn't gain anything through apparent liberation. So, nope, I never thought that.

Justin Allen: But before you were liberated and first started listening to Tony, you had spent ten years following a guru, so you might have thought, "Oh, my God, I wasted ten years with this fucking guru."

Andreas Müller: Yeah. But I hardly looked back in anger or something like that. Of course, I thought several times that the seeking was wasted, but it never really was. It was whole and complete also. And I'm probably much too young to regret it in the sense of wasted time. Maybe also because in the story that I was telling myself, I was kind of a successful seeker. So no, it wasn't a bad time really.

Justin Allen: Should we call it?

Andreas Müller: Yeah, that's fine.

Justin Allen: All right, well, then you're here in Berlin on February 15th, no?

Andreas Müller: Yes, exactly.

Justin Allen: Then have a good day.

Andreas Müller: Yeah, you too. Thank you.

Justin Allen: Ciao.

Andreas Müller: Ciao.

February 5, 2020 Talk 11

THERE'S NO ONE IN THIS ROOM

Justin Allen: All right.

Andreas Müller: All right. So, today I would have to leave pretty much at ten.

Justin Allen: All right. No problem. I wrote down some notes ...

Andreas Müller: Yeah.

Justin Allen: Just as it came to me ten minutes ago (laughing).

Andreas Müller: All right. A long-term preparation (laughing).

Justin Allen: Yeah, I realize that I can forget things within five minutes (laughing).

Andreas Müller: Yeah (laughing).

Justin Allen: One thing that I wanted to go into a little bit more was the sentence, "There's no one."

Andreas Müller: Yes.

Justin Allen: We've talked about this, how there's no actual "me," right? The "me" isn't there, but the reason why somebody thinks that they're a "me" is because they think they are experiencing, "I'm here. I'm me"?

Andreas Müller: Yeah.

Justin Allen: Maybe it's the same thing, but I just wanted to maybe define it better. Is it the experience that's the illusion, and from that illusionary experience, the "me" can then be talked about? Or is it more accurate to say the "me" is the illusion, and then the experience comes secondarily?

Andreas Müller: Yeah, that's true. But you can't really say one is first. It seems to simply go together.

Justin Allen: Right, okay.

Andreas Müller: One could say, in that sense, that the "me" is not necessarily "the story about me." The story seems to come out of the experience to be something which is present, but in a way it just seems to go together.

Justin Allen: So then, the famous quote, "I think, therefore I am," is touching on that experience, basically?

Andreas Müller: Yeah.

Justin Allen: It might get updated now. Today's spiritual teachers might say ...

Andreas Müller: "I'm aware."

Justin Allen: "I'm aware, so I am," or something like that. "Because I'm aware, I am."

Andreas Müller: Yeah, exactly.

Justin Allen: That's exactly what that's touching upon; that undeniable experience basically, to the majority of people, that they're there as "something"?

Andreas Müller: Yep. It's really a funny thing because this is absolutely not logical, but people experience themselves as someone, and many people would fight about that, like, "Yes but I am someone," or, "But here is something which I am." I can't explain it either, but it just isn't real.

It's not just that there is an experience to be something which is not real or which has another quality than being real; no, there is nothing at all which has any substance. There is no center at all, and in the end, it's totally unexplainable why seven billion people run around claiming that they are someone. It's not logical, and I can't explain why it is like this; that it feels so utterly real for everyone. I can't even say that it's wrong. However, there is no one. Sorry. And this is as unexplainable as people saying, "I am someone." Funnily, both is just what arises. Life is free to appear as both.

Justin Allen: Yeah, that's what I wanted to say: It's equally illogical and unexplainable to say that actually there is "no one" there.

Andreas Müller: Oh, yeah totally, of course. It's also not a statement or a truth in a way that could be known.

Justin Allen: Right, because just as you're claiming or giving the message that "no one" is there, as if it were a belief or an experience, then somebody playing the devil's advocate would have to say, "Yeah but that has to work in reverse for you also"; that saying, "I'm not there, there's 'no one.' None of this is actually happening," is just as shocking and unexplainable or potentially illusory as someone claiming that they are there.

Andreas Müller: Yes, but it's in a way being admitted that it's not another experience or belief or mindset or reality that tries to be the opposite of the personal reality. In a way, the message admits that freely, and there is nothing that has to defend the message, so to speak, while the "person" would apparently have to defend its reality.

Justin Allen: Right.

Andreas Müller: I don't have to defend being "no one." It's not something that has any value or importance for anyone. I don't need to know that I'm "no one" or if anybody else recognizes that I'm "no one." There's no need in there, while the "person," in some way or another, needs to be recognized. It needs to recognize itself, and of course, it needs to be recognized by others as a confirmation of itself. But there is no confirmation of being "no one." This can't be confirmed in the sense of an additional proof or reassurance of something like a state that has been reached (laughing).

Justin Allen: Maybe this won't be a proper analogy, but when I was a teenager, I would get into arguments every once in a while with another friend who was religious or at least was being raised to be religious. This had to happen to a lot of people, I think, in my generation, where you'd say, "How can this religion be real, how can God be real, have you ever seen God?" You'd come up with all the arguments, although it's just you being in disbelief and your friend repeating whatever he heard in a sermon or whatever his parents told him. However, both sides can get really argumentative.

Andreas Müller: Yep.

Justin Allen: And you feel like you have to convince the other one (laughing) that religion is an illusion, and the other one probably feels the same way towards you.

Andreas Müller: Yep.

Justin Allen: In this case, what you're saying though is that somebody that's a "me" is like the person that believes in God but also like the person that doesn't believe in God?

Andreas Müller: Yep, yep. It automatically has to take sides.

Justin Allen: And when there's no belief anymore, which is the case for you or Tony Parsons, then there's no need to convince or confirm or argue, because there's no point of view anymore; that's what's fallen away, in a sense?

Andreas Müller: Yes, exactly, absolutely. Especially, this so-called topic, which isn't a topic, so to speak, it's just not a belief or a concept. It's just everything, that's its nature, so it's also having concepts and beliefs. But yes, this message is not coming from a standpoint; it's not on a mission trying to convince other people or to confirm itself. All of that isn't needed, because it's not a message, it's not a way of seeing reality, it's not a belief, it's not a concept, it's not another religion and all of that stuff. So, there almost is nothing to defend. That's why you also can't really go into discussions with people. It's not about imposing or suggesting one's own truth on/to others.

Justin Allen: Yeah.

Andreas Müller: Not at all.

Justin Allen: There's nothing to defend, because there's no position and, again, no perspective or no point of view?

Andreas Müller: Yes, exactly.

Justin Allen: There's no reference point or no center that something can come out from?

Andreas Müller: Yes.

Justin Allen: And the experience of the "me" is exactly this sense or feeling or understanding or knowledge – whatever descriptive words you can come up with to explain it – that you feel like you are there as something and as a point of view?

Andreas Müller: Yes, exactly; with a certain truth, with a certain reality, with a certain belief.

Justin Allen: Sometimes it makes me wonder if even that experience, just the nature of that experience, has to defend its position, in a way.

Andreas Müller: Oh, yeah, absolutely (said excitedly). Yeah, yeah. One could say this feeling of defense is the "me."

Justin Allen: It's the same as if you were standing in an open field and the wind were blowing against you: As a human physical body you have to brace yourself and stand in a position against the wind, so it doesn't blow you over.

Andreas Müller: Well, yeah, that's what I mean. Of course, one could say so.

Justin Allen: Or else, the wind blows you over, but you're there, as a physical body, experiencing it happening, so you either have to resist it or go with it, but it's still that you're there with and as something. And it's the same if you're somehow experiencing yourself as something: You have to either argue for or against something. You have to either accept or believe or embrace something or resist it.

Andreas Müller: Yeah, and in the picture, it is to not be blown away.

Justin Allen: Yeah.

Andreas Müller: So that wholeness doesn't just eradicate you, so to speak. That would be the picture, or that's the personal experience: I have to constantly confirm myself by doing something, by believing in my story or by defending the story if it's attacked by others. In the end, it's because of the fear of dying.

Justin Allen: Yeah, because something is there in the first place?

Andreas Müller: Of course, of course, in that setup ... That's the dilemma for the "me": that whatever it does or believes or tries to prevent, it's already there to do so (laughing). Whatever it thinks about, no matter how slight the movement or the seeking energy is, it's already there (laughing).

Justin Allen: Yeah, and that's the thing because that's the nature of it, in a way. It has to because it is thought of or sensed to be there.

Andreas Müller: Oh, yes, absolutely.

Justin Allen: Automatically, the experience, the perceived and ultimately illusionary "experience," forces itself into resisting or ...

Andreas Müller: As you said, that's its nature, yeah. It's not that I think it should be otherwise.

Justin Allen: Yeah.

Andreas Müller: That's the dilemma. One could say when there is the illusion of the "me," apparently, these seem to be the consequences. Experiencing oneself as someone equals this whole bunch of apparent consequences like living in belief, defense, self-confirmation and all that stuff. Yep, it's natural.

Justin Allen: Great.

Andreas Müller: At least to some degree. In the story, the degree could vary from one to another, but it would just basically be the same setup. Apparently.

Justin Allen: Why do you say "apparently" in that instance?

Andreas Müller: Because there just is no real "me." Because it's an illusion, and that's the illogical part about it; because the self-experience is not something that really happens.

Justin Allen: Okay.

Andreas Müller: It's kind of an artificial or dreamt reality that has no real actuality at all. But it seems to be what's going on; people believe themselves to be someone, including all the consequences. But those apparent consequences are also only assumed for or by that assumed center (laughing).

Justin Allen: Yeah.

Andreas Müller: Well (laughing).

Justin Allen: When somebody moves their hand or speaks, that's real. The hand movement is real, and the speaking is real, it's just that the sense that I'm doing it is the dream or the illusion?

Andreas Müller: One could say so, yeah.

Justin Allen: And the experience that I moved my hand is also the illusion?

Andreas Müller: Well, the assumption that there is an I who consciously moved a real hand is an illusion. In the end, if the hand is real or not is not knowable, and there is nothing that really knows the presence of a hand, but yes, one could say so.

Justin Allen: Yeah, to keep it simple, without ...

Andreas Müller: Yeah, exactly. To keep it simple, sitting in a room, moving the hand; that's it. The only dream would be that there is something separate from it that is only experiencing or only watching or witnessing it.

Justin Allen: Right. Trying to keep it as simple as possible: I'm in a room right now, and there are walls around me and a floor and objects, and I am a body, or there is a body. That's real. Those things are real, the physical world is real. And us talking is real also. But in this sense that we're talking about, to kind of minimize things, the only thing in this room right now that's not real is my sense of me being here?

Andreas Müller: Yes.

Justin Allen: And then to make it more complicated, you could say, "But actually that there are objects in a room and walls and space and a physical body, that's unknowable also. You can't know if that's real or not real."

Andreas Müller: Yes, but it's not really to make it complicated.

Justin Allen: No, but it's complicated for our understanding – "me" understanding. The majority ...

Andreas Müller: Exactly, it would again be the part the "me" can't experience.

Justin Allen: Yeah. This is the thing that I think is complicated in a way; that you, as a "no me," don't experience anything.

Andreas Müller: So to speak, yes.

Justin Allen: But at the same time, it's kind of like you experience ...

Andreas Müller: Yes, the dilemma is in the story. That's the problem because those are all stories. Of course, I could say, "Apparently, the body experiences ..." That's what apparently happens, but no one knows that. Same with the question whether the room and the body et cetera are real or not. That's also already a story which is just what apparently happens.

Justin Allen: Yeah.

Andreas Müller: It's just not another experience in an awareness sense, so all these descriptions like, "Yeah, there is seeing but no one who sees," or, "Yes, there is a room but no one in the room," are all right, and yes, it's to keep it simple, in a way. But it's also still something that can be comprehended to some extent, at least conceptually.

In the end, the utter conviction, the utter statement, "Yes, there is a room," can only be made by the "me." The brain or the body may put out this information, "I'm sitting in a room," or, "There's a room," but it's really utterly empty. It's empty information that only seems to become real by someone experiencing it.

Justin Allen: Yeah.

Andreas Müller: So for me, regarding this message, it's kind of important – well, not really important, but yes, to keep it simple it's kind of useful to point out that the only illusion is the "me." Nothing else is an illusion in that sense.

Justin Allen: Right, but then, to move away from it being simple, because there's no "me," it also means, in a sense, that there's no reality to objects and to the walls and to the floor?

Andreas Müller: Exactly, yes. Which of course, isn't really important.

Justin Allen: But it's important coming from the perspective of the "me." Because the "me" tries to conceptually think about this.

Andreas Müller: Exactly, so to speak, yeah.

Justin Allen: Because the "me" also is convinced that they're in a room with four walls and a floor and a ceiling and objects in the space. The "me" is convinced that that's a reality.

Andreas Müller: Exactly, yes.

Justin Allen: The "me" can also understand how the outside world might be an illusion.

Andreas Müller: How this might be not only real, yes.

Justin Allen: A "me" perspective can understand how everything that we are seeing and touching and feeling could also just be some kind of visual manifestation of something.

Andreas Müller: Now it gets a bit tricky because the "me" would assume this to be something else, something separate from itself.

Justin Allen: Yeah, I'm not saying this is important. I'm just saying that every "me" in a way can kind of say that this could all just be an illusion; that they could be in a film or something.

Andreas Müller: Yes, exactly. Absolutely.

Justin Allen: What the "me" can't do, and we've said this over and over again, is that it still can't take itself out of any picture.

Andreas Müller: Yes, exactly. Totally.

Justin Allen: Even if it ends up in this being just a dream or an illusion, there being no reality to the physical world that we thought of as being real, then there is still the "me" there to become at some point aware that this is all just an illusion, which would be another finding, another belief.

Andreas Müller: Exactly, exactly, yes. That's actually what I meant, yep. So, in that sense, I wouldn't say that everything is an illusion.

Justin Allen: Yep.

Andreas Müller: Yeah. In that sense, nothing is an illusion.

Justin Allen: Right.

Andreas Müller: Everything is what it is, even the illusion to be "me" and also this message pointing to this apparent recognition.

Justin Allen: Right, and that's also why you can say everything is what it is, which is whole and full and complete, just because it can't be any other way (laughing)?

Andreas Müller: Yes, exactly.

Justin Allen: It can't be minus, and it can't be plus?

Andreas Müller: Exactly.

Justin Allen: Also, this makes me think of when I was in my twenties: I was drinking with two of my friends, and we were having some kind of philosophical discussion about something, and I remember saying that whatever's going to happen in any situation is the only thing that could happen, you know (laughing)?

Andreas Müller: Yeah.

Justin Allen: It's the only thing that could happen, and then a friend might argue and say, "No, if you would have pressed this button, then something else would have happened." And I go, "I know, but then that would just be what was going to happen."

Andreas Müller: Yeah (laughing).

Justin Allen: And I remember at the time, I was thinking I understand the dilemma of how you think there's so many scenarios that can or could happen; so with everything that you do, there's an infinite amount of possibilities of what could trigger the next thing or what could happen as a result – but also not.

Andreas Müller: Yes (said with enthusiastic emphasis).

Justin Allen: There are not infinite possibilities, there's just whatever there is, and that's the only thing that could have happened. And also in the future, five minutes from now, I'm going to do something, and that something is just what's going to happen.

Andreas Müller: Yeah, and in a way it's both at the same time. There's the openness and the freeness that anything could happen, potentially, theoretically, but in actuality there's just one thing that apparently happens, and no one chooses that. Life is totally free to appear as whatever and totally bound to appear as how it appears.

Justin Allen: I remember back then also being shocked a little bit because I was like, "Wow, that is ..." Somehow there is this feeling like, "That's true," or, "That's right," but I also didn't want it to be true and right.

Andreas Müller: Mm-hmm (affirmative). Oh, yeah, the dream of the "person" is very much based on the idea that there are several possibilities and that I have choice and that I have the possibility to do that instead of something else.

Justin Allen: Exactly, and you feel a little bit afraid for yourself, but you also feel afraid because of other people, of what they could do. Because usually you blame everybody.

Andreas Müller: Oh, yeah. The assumption that you could blame yourself or anyone else, that it could be different, that I or they could have done differently. That there were other possibilities.

Justin Allen: The whole judging of somebody ... You want your friend to not hurt you, and you believe that they have control of what's going on.

Andreas Müller: And that theoretically, or seen by the "me," is quite practical. It looks as if there would have been a practical, real possibility for a different behavior or reaction or outcome. Yeah.

Justin Allen: I just brought that up because it just popped in. It's not necessarily relevant. When you really get to that, when you get to this simple thing ... I don't even know if it's simple, but it feels simple right now; that it's just the experience that I am, that I am here, that I am something, and if you just take that feeling and look ...

Andreas Müller: Which is not even really a feeling. It's not there, but yeah, sorry.

Justin Allen: But that's the best way you can talk about it, right? It's a feeling or a sense; it's some kind of strong ... But it's true what you're saying; it's not really a sense or a feeling or an emotion that you're there, and it's also not really a

thought. Compared to thoughts and sensations, it's just not there, it's nothing.

Andreas Müller: Yeah (laughing).

Justin Allen: But somehow it seems like it's all of those, all together. Even when I ask people, "What are you?" or, "Who are you?" they like to go, "Well, I'm my brain," or, "I'm my thoughts, I'm my emotions, I'm my body, I'm everything, I'm all this all at once." So, you kind of don't look at it. In general throughout life, you just accept that you're there, without any proof.

Andreas Müller: Yeah (laughing), it is like that, yeah.

Justin Allen: But if you start to try to prove it, then the proof is like, "I feel like I'm here, and if I touch my face, I feel it, I sense it," you know?

Andreas Müller: Yes, but still it is based on assumptions.

Justin Allen: Right, but even those assumptions reiterate that you're there.

Andreas Müller: Yeah, yeah.

Justin Allen: There are those assumptions where you're going, "Am I really ..." and then you're questioning yourself in the sense of, "Am I there?" So, you are having a conversation with yourself, which makes you feel like you're there. "Who's asking the question, and who's listening to it?" That inquiry is confirming "me" again.

Andreas Müller: Yes, absolutely. It's already confirmed, yes.

Justin Allen: So, you are just constantly confirming yourself. There's no way out, because every way out, even if you're trying to not get out, is kind of holding you locked in. Just someone asking you, "Who's there?" or, "What are you?" just you having this question and being aware of the question, is confirming that experience of you.

Andreas Müller: Yeah, yeah.

Justin Allen: What I'm saying is that when you look at it and break it down, like we just did in a way, even going, "Am I my thoughts, am I my feelings, am I blah blah blah? What is there? I can't touch it, I can't feel it, I can't actually sense it, I can't actually think it," at some point feels empty for me, like there actually isn't anything there. Then you go, "How can it be that there's not an experience?"

Andreas Müller: Mm-hmm (affirmative).

Justin Allen: And that's what I start to try to imagine, in a way. That's essentially what you and Tony Parsons are claiming, so to speak: that it's actually the experience which drops away.

Andreas Müller: Yes, one could say so, yeah.

Justin Allen: I don't even think you have to say, "the experience of a 'me.'" It's just ...

Andreas Müller: Well, it's the same, but yep.

Justin Allen: It's the same, but I think language-wise ... I don't know, maybe it's just ...

Andreas Müller: Tony sometimes says, "The seeking energy."

Justin Allen: Yeah.

Andreas Müller: One doesn't really have to personalize it, as a story and by using the word "me," but it's experienced as something which goes on here now, as a centered experience, and it's the seeking dynamic, the seeking energy, the experiencing dynamic, the separate energy.

Justin Allen: But it's really that you don't experience it? I'm thinking of flow experiences now and of Michael Jordan because he's the example that people use a lot when they talk about flow. So, when Michael Jordan was in the zone or in the flow and was playing a perfect game of basketball, the argument was that he was not really experiencing what was happening.

Andreas Müller: Yeah, no one really knows, but I think many people mistake a flow experience with being "no one."

Justin Allen: Yeah, I am not necessarily saying that he was "no one" temporarily or that he got liberated in the basketball game. I mean it more as an argument that they're talking about it as an experience in a way, but it might not be. Do you know what I mean?

Andreas Müller: Yeah.

Justin Allen: It might be that when you are in this state of flow while playing or doing some action, you are doing it all, but without you being there to experience it.

Andreas Müller: Yes.

Justin Allen: I'm just saying that everybody can kind of relate to moments in their life when they might have been so involved in something that they weren't there.

Andreas Müller: Yeah, or they can somehow apparently relate to not being there.

Justin Allen: Yeah. But if you were Michael Jordan playing this perfect basketball game and you weren't there, and then later on you came back, you would talk about that experience of not being there, now from the perspective of a "me." Even though you weren't there for that game, you'd put yourself in there afterwards.

Andreas Müller: Yes, to some degree, absolutely. At least you would try to do that.

Justin Allen: Yes.

Andreas Müller: Yeah, yeah, yeah.

Justin Allen: That's what I was thinking about. Like last time we were talking about that maybe forty percent of the day you're actually not there and sixty percent you're there, so you're calculating only sixty percent of your day as if you existed in it.

Andreas Müller: Yeah.

Justin Allen: And then you might be putting yourself into that forty percent, like Michael Jordan would do when talking about a flow experience.

Andreas Müller: Well, yeah, in the story, it could even just be one percent. Maybe the "person" is just there one percent of the time. Maybe that's what you can remember during the day or from your life. I mean, how many minutes do you actually remember from your life? It's probably not much what you remember from your last forty or thirty years.

Justin Allen: I have to take notes from five minutes ago to remember. (laughing)

Andreas Müller: Yeah, exactly. But the actual experience is that whenever I'm there, it feels as if I were there the whole day, as if I were there the whole week, as if I had lived for my whole life, so to speak.

Justin Allen: Right.

Andreas Müller: But that feeling doesn't actually say anything.

Justin Allen: Yeah, that's what I mean: The "me" also is constantly projecting itself or placing itself in made-up time or in ...

Andreas Müller: Yeah, it is the placement in made-up time. It makes up the placement.

Justin Allen: Because even in sleep, you don't know what the hell ... When you fall asleep for seven hours, you don't know what happened really.

Andreas Müller: Of course not, yep.

Justin Allen: Even when you know ... When you're like, "Oh, I had a dream," you don't know how long that dream lasted, you probably don't know at what point in the night that dream happened. You can't place it anywhere anyway, other than making up a story. And then there are times when you weren't dreaming, but when you wake, you say, "I was sleeping and dreaming." So, even every morning when you wake up, you place yourself into something that you don't even know if you were really there.

Andreas Müller: Oh, absolutely, yes. That's what I mean; the whole placing, the whole processing, only happens or is only taken seriously when there is someone. It's all being made up, or it all just arises, in the morning, as a story about what happened in this apparent nighttime.

Justin Allen: You even do that with yourself. I place myself in this body that I have.

Andreas Müller: Exactly.

Justin Allen: I might not be ... (laughing)

Andreas Müller: It's the same thing.

Justin Allen: Yep.

Andreas Müller: Suddenly, when there is self-awareness, it seems to be that I'm something which is now here. That's the placement. And in a way the "person" seems to move between those two aspects; the moment and continuity. That's also why there are those two basic spiritual teachings nowadays, one of which says, "All there is, is this moment," and the other says, "You are infinite." Which is both the "person's" experience: "I am now here, and I must have been here all the time."

Justin Allen: Yeah, forever.

Andreas Müller: The normal person would say, "Yeah, at least since I live, I was there all the time. I'm a continuum." And in all spiritual traditions, they even say that there is something like a soul that goes on living; that goes beyond this one life, which is also relating to or coming from the "person's" experience.

Justin Allen: "I'm here, even when I'm not here." (laughing)

Andreas Müller: Exactly, and all the rest is just assuming. It's not even assuming, because it so naturally thinks that it's something that lives. It doesn't care about deep sleep, and it doesn't care about all those moments, which are the majority, where there is nothing recorded, where it doesn't know what happened, which it can't remember anymore. It's so fragile (laughing). It's so nothing (laughing), it's so much nothing already.

But once there seems to be self-awareness, you have the whole package again, with all the consequences. "I'm now here, I lived my whole life, there is a real life, there are those problems, there is the world, and the world functions like that," and, "But, but, but ..." All the reality is back, but it's utterly fragile.

Justin Allen: Yeah, and I think everybody senses that also.

Andreas Müller: That's possible, yeah.

Justin Allen: I feel like I've sensed it, and I feel like that was my searching energy, some kind of an awareness or an understanding that the sense of "me" and everybody else and my beliefs and what I think what's right and wrong et cetera; that it's all so fragile, and I didn't want it to be. There's a part of me that goes, "It can't be like this. It can't be that this might not be real or that all my thoughts have no meaning or ... (laughing) I have to be here." That sense of fragileness; that makes you want to be robust or to make something stable or to find something out that's real or permanent or ...

Andreas Müller: Yep.

Justin Allen: Because you can't accept ... (laughing) There's no way the "me" can accept that it might not be there?

Andreas Müller: Yeah, yep, yeah.

Justin Allen: Even that sentence ... The "me" or the "I am" comes from that experience of "I am"?

Andreas Müller: Well, it's not really coming from that. That's what it apparently is.

Justin Allen: Yeah, but I mean the "I am" is already a story, and it comes from some assumed or some illusioned experience of something before it's even a "me."

Andreas Müller: Yes, but I would say that this is the "me."

Justin Allen: All right. But I'm trying to say that the "me" comes from the origins of the "me." It's the same as when you're born?

Andreas Müller: Yeah.

Justin Allen: Essentially, you come from nothing, but as soon as you're an embryo or come out of the womb, you're something; you're physically something in the sense that a human is then there or appears to be there.

Andreas Müller: Yeah, all right.

Justin Allen: And it's like the "me" also comes from nothing?

Andreas Müller: Yes.

Justin Allen: Maybe I'm just putting too much significance on that, but the experience is the thing that gives birth to the "me"?

Andreas Müller: Yes, but I would say you can't really do that, because experiencing is the birth of the "me."

Justin Allen: Yeah.

Andreas Müller: I can't separate experiencing and "me," that's what I mean.

Justin Allen: Yeah.

Andreas Müller: I think we talked about it already, but it's a bit like waking up in the morning and becoming self-aware: Suddenly I'm something which is separate from nothing. I'm something which has risen out of nothing. Suddenly I'm something which is now here and came from something. This is the "I am," and in the subtlest form. Oh, dear, it's such a story. There is no process of "I am," but there is a centered experience of being here now.

Justin Allen: And that's not actually true that there is an experience of, "I am here now"? There's only the illusion of this experience?

Andreas Müller: Exactly, and that's what this message is saying; that this birth never happened.

Justin Allen: Right.

Andreas Müller: That even if it feels like that, nothing really arose from nothing. Yeah (laughing). But why it feels like that for people is unexplainable and not logical. There isn't a reason for that; you can't bring that back into a story to make it logical or to find a deeper cause for that or something like that.

Justin Allen: No. That's what Tony means when he's saying that somewhere between the age of one and two, the experience and the "me" or the experience of the "me" happens.

Andreas Müller: When it starts, yep.

Justin Allen: He's not claiming that scientifically, like it happens between the age of one and two because then such and such happens in the brain. I don't know. He's just saying it as a diagram.

Andreas Müller: Yeah, that's what apparently happens, at the age of one, two, three. I met a woman whose story is that she only became self-aware when she was seven.

Justin Allen: Yeah. I also feel like it happened to me later in life (laughing).

Andreas Müller: Oh, yeah, it's possible.

Justin Allen: For me, it happened when I was sixteen (laughing).

Andreas Müller: No, that was just the end of the innocence of being a child and entering the fucking adult world (laughing).

Justin Allen: That was when I wanted a girlfriend.

Andreas Müller: Yeah, exactly.

Justin Allen: Or that was when girls caused me insecurities. Then I really felt like, "Oh, my God, I'm here, I hope girls notice me."

Andreas Müller: Yeah. But becoming a child almost already means having lost the innocence of being "no one."

Justin Allen: Yeah.

Andreas Müller: But for many people the childlikeness is still too close to absence. For most people it's like me-ing and being at the beginning of life, then mostly me-ing and then maybe less me-ing at the end of life.

Justin Allen: I'm watching this nature show, and they showed this tree frog or green frog. It's one of the frogs that can live in the most northerly part of the world. In winter time, it shuts down at certain temperatures. So overnight, it freezes and gets a coat of ice over its outer skin, and then the heart stops.

Andreas Müller: All right (laughing).

Justin Allen: So from an outside perspective, for all intents and purposes it's dead (laughing), until the morning, it starts to warm up, and when it gets warm enough, the ice on its skin melts away, and then the heart starts to beat again, and the frog comes back to life, you know?

Andreas Müller: That's amazing (laughing).

Justin Allen: But also for humans it's kind of like that. If we put an EKG on us, we see that our heart doesn't stop beating at nighttime. But let's say the "me" is like a machine or like a heartbeat. It's part, or it can be a part, of being a human, in a way. It also has to pump, and its pumping is the constant confirmation that it's there, experiencing. At least it keeps the story going; in that sense it's as essential to self-hood as the heartbeat is for the body. And the only time that it stops, or at least the guaranteed time that it seems to stop, is when you are in deep sleep.

Andreas Müller: Yeah, all right.

Justin Allen: And that for us, from a "me" perspective, is a death, right?

Andreas Müller: Yes.

Justin Allen: In this frog's case, we would assume outwardly, as humans looking at it, that it doesn't have self-consciousness and it doesn't have a "me" or an identity.

Andreas Müller: Yeah.

Justin Allen: But it's alive. We would all accept that it's alive, and the confirmation that it's alive is that its heart's beating.

Andreas Müller: Yeah.

Justin Allen: So for us, looking at the frog, when its heart stops beating in winter, it's not there anymore. It's dead.

Andreas Müller: It's supposed to be dead, yeah.

Justin Allen: Then that's the same as us. We kind of have two lives: this physical life, which is our heart beating and blood moving and breathing in air. But then we also have this other life or this other aspect, which is the "me," the psychological sense or whatever. That's why we always refer to ourselves as our mind and body.

Andreas Müller: Yeah, or as spirits or some ... Yep.

Justin Allen: So, we have all this work that we are doing; trying to keep our heart beating, but also trying to keep our sense of self or our identity going on.

Andreas Müller: Yeah, we think we have to do both. That's what the "me" experience is like. It experiences itself as a second reality. Usually "me" sees itself as the first reality, but actually it's an extra. Everything is there somehow, separate from "me," and I'm additionally there. That would be the dual reality or the assumption of there being dual realities. The world or what happens, and spiritual people would say also the body, happens to something like awareness; to a foreign kind of entity or to something which is aware of everything else.

Justin Allen: But it's also so obvious that the "me" isn't there.

Andreas Müller: Yeah. Many people probably wouldn't be able to say that (laughing), because they think so much that they are someone who is there. But yep, it is quite obvious. It's not real, of course.

Justin Allen: Yeah, if you just look, you're totally not there. You are not there, and any of the resources that you have at your physical disposal ...

Andreas Müller: Yeah, nothing actually proves your existence. You can't find a self behind anything or in anything.

Justin Allen: Yeah, at least intellectually you can't. I guess spiritually you can because in spiritual thinking, you're free to do whatever, but, I don't know. Physically you can't see it, you can't touch it, you can't smell it.

That's what all these spiritual or religious or philosophical teachers from the past, like Jesus Christ and The Buddha and Lao Tzu; I don't know if they're all the same, but there's generally this question, "Look and see what's there, are you there?" If we assume that they also were liberated from the "me," that's probably how that sentence or that question arises.

Andreas Müller: Yeah. It seems that in a way the question can arise naturally or be a method or be turned into a method or a spiritual something. But yeah, in the end it's just, "Look ..." I can't say that really, because it's become so methodical meanwhile, especially when the word "who" is used, like in, "Who's asking this question?" But yeah, "What is there, is there actually someone? What are you speaking of? Have a look, check it out." Not as a method, so, "Check it out," in that sense is already too much, I would say.

Justin Allen: Right, it probably got turned into that, but maybe the origin of Socrates going, "Question everything," or the energy behind that might have been generally that. He might have been absent of a "me" and looking at everybody around him as apparent selves, while they thought that they were there, and then he was going, "Are you really there?"

Andreas Müller: Exactly. "What are you speaking of? Are you there? Come on. Is there someone? Check it out. Don't ask me, don't ask anyone. Don't even ask yourself. Don't seek. Who the fuck is there? What are you talking about?" Yeah.

Justin Allen: That's what children ask too, in a way. I'm not familiar with what happens at what age, and I don't even know what they do when they are two or three years old, but at some point they ask tons of questions that parents can't answer.

Andreas Müller: Yeah (laughing).

Justin Allen: (Laughing) All right, well, it's ten.

Andreas Müller: Yeah, I should go.

Justin Allen: All right then.

Andreas Müller: All right.

Justin Allen: Ciao.

Andreas Müller: Bye. Ciao.

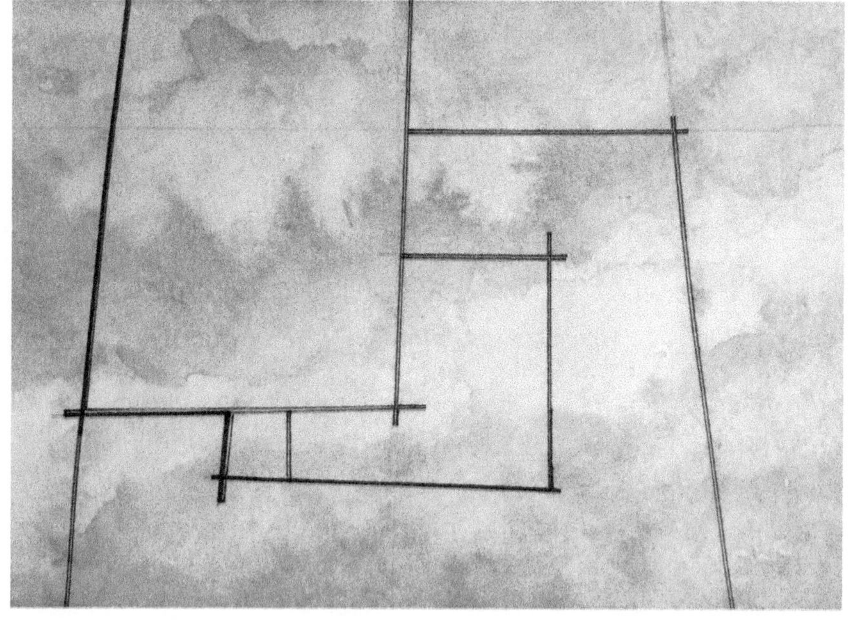

March 4, 2020 Talk 12

THE NO BANG THEORY

Justin Allen: So, from our last talk, one of the things that have stuck with me is that we were talking about the "me" and how it's kind of like a belief and illogical to explain. And that it's illogical that it's not there and also illogical that it feels like it is there.

Andreas Müller: Yeah, yeah.

Justin Allen: So, it's illogical for you, Andreas Müller, and also for Tony Parsons, for example. And it's also illogical for me and the other seven billion of us that think that we're there. So, it's illogical on both sides; on the side of the "me" and on the side of the "no me," so to speak?

Andreas Müller: Yes, one could say so.

Justin Allen: And then somehow through that discussion, for lack of a better way, I kept on saying, "Yeah, it's just like this feeling that we're there or that I'm there." And then you said something like, "Yeah, it's not even or not really a feeling." And I find I can't ... Because when I try to think about "me" or the sense of "me," the best word for it is a feeling of "me." Right?

Andreas Müller: Yeah, one could say so.

Justin Allen: When it comes down to it, because you can't explain it, we end up having to say it's a feeling because we accept feelings as something that we can't explain.

Andreas Müller: Exactly. Yes. It's like a sense of presence, an energetic feeling, a sense of being there.

Justin Allen: So, even that just brings up another question for me: That sense of presence or that feeling of being here automatically assumes a duality?

Andreas Müller: Yes.

Justin Allen: That's kind of a ... Not a contradiction, but that's one of the unexplainable points. How can I feel present and here without already being here? You know what I mean (laughing)?

Andreas Müller: Exactly. Yeah, that's the unsolvable dilemma. Or if you said that as a question, it would be the question which never finds an answer.

Justin Allen: Yeah, right.

Andreas Müller: Yeah.

Justin Allen: And that's the question that can only exist in a way with already being there and then having the ...

Andreas Müller: Exactly.

Justin Allen: So, the feeling kind of already happened to you for the question to arise, even though last time I think you were also saying that you can't really separate those two.

Andreas Müller: Yes, exactly. Presence and seeking go together. You can't have the question without someone asking it, so to speak.

Justin Allen: Yeah.

Andreas Müller: Exactly. And on the other hand, what seems to be the case is that you can't have someone without having some kind of question, seeking or processing going on.

Justin Allen: Yeah.

Andreas Müller: It's one thing, so to speak.

Justin Allen: So, that one thing that kind of just instantly happens – not that anybody knows that it instantly happens, but let's say that it just kind of instantly happens or emerges – is at the same time its presence and the feeling or sense of presence?

Andreas Müller: Yes. I mean, that's the interesting thing; that in the end the sense of presence is the presence or the apparent presence.

Justin Allen: Right.

Andreas Müller: So, nothing becomes really present in that.

Justin Allen: And also, that would be duality in a way. But the way that I just said it – that it is happening at the same time – makes it almost non-dual because it's the whole thing. The presence and the sense of presence simultaneously exist, so they're not even separated in time. It's not that presence happens first, and then the sense of presence comes; those two things are one, they're together?

Andreas Müller: Oh, yeah, exactly. Yes. Yes. Yes. But what do you mean by presence right now?

Justin Allen: I just mean the sense of presence (laughing).

Andreas Müller: Yeah, exactly. I mean ...

Justin Allen: What I mean is this sense of presence can only happen – using language at least, or logic – to something that is present?

Andreas Müller: That's already there, that apparently came before. Exactly.

Justin Allen: So, it's duality, but at the same time it's not duality, because one can't exist without the other in a sense?

Andreas Müller: Yeah, but wait a moment. That's a story already; that there is a sense of presence which is separate from what happens.

Justin Allen: Correct. I'm just saying that when we use words, we kind of automatically have to make a concession, so it can't help but sound dual or story-like. Because in order for there to be a sense of presence, there has to be something like presence "before."

Andreas Müller: All right. But that's a picture coming from logic. That's a God picture.

Justin Allen: Yeah.

Andreas Müller: Because I'm there, something must have created me. Or there must be something where I came from or where I was born from.

Justin Allen: And what you're saying ...

Andreas Müller: Is that those two don't exist.

Justin Allen: Right. But what you're saying is that it's not the case that there's something that exists and then that something gets this sense of presence? It's that this energetic presence is the illusion? It is the thing that you falsely think that you are?

Andreas Müller: Yes. I'm not sure though if I got it. It just is what apparently happens. People assuming themselves to be someone is what apparently happens.

Justin Allen: So, back to the beginning to where we were saying that this thing that just kind of happens immediately or out of nowhere all at once is instantly a sense of presence. And then that sense of presence says, "Ah, this sense of presence, it can only exist if something is present to sense that I'm here." Then it tells the story and kind of creates a "pure being" that all of a sudden gets imbued or embedded with this sensing ability. And that creates a duality in the story?

Andreas Müller: Yeah, I think I know what you mean. And yes, one could say so. But in a way, the sense of presence already creates an experienced duality which isn't necessarily processed in the story. Because the moment I say, "I am someone, I am me," there is automatically the experience that I'm not everything else.

Justin Allen: Exactly.

Andreas Müller: Yeah.

Justin Allen: But it's not even using the word "me"; it's just saying that I feel something, whatever.

Andreas Müller: Exactly, that's what I mean. It's not processed in the story, which is why it was a bit superficial when I said, "I'm me." It's just an experienced sense of presence of this.

Justin Allen: Right. So when I wake up in the morning and all of a sudden I feel lethargic or energetic or good or like I didn't sleep well, it automatically translates, without even logic or without anything, that something's there to receive these feelings or this input?

Andreas Müller: Yes. One could say so, but on the other hand, there is already something there to do so.

Justin Allen: Right. That thing though is just the sense of being there or ...

Andreas Müller: Yeah.

Justin Allen: And from that sense that you're there, in the story you can say, "Ah, I must be here, something must be here that is getting these things, these "happenings" happening to 'it,' and that's separating it."

Andreas Müller: Yes.

Justin Allen: And then that sense of being someone is also already an energetic separation?

Andreas Müller: That's how it's experienced. Exactly.

Justin Allen: In our last talk, I kept on saying, "Yeah, it's like this feeling that I'm here, but it's not really a feeling, maybe it's a belief." And you said, "It's not even a feeling. It's not even a belief. It's all just assumptions."

Andreas Müller: Yeah.

Justin Allen: And now that we just talked (laughing), it doesn't seem important anymore. I was interested in how you consciously or intentionally use the word "assumption." Is there something more significant about using this word than "belief" or "feeling"?

Andreas Müller: No, it was just when we were trying to pinpoint the "me," I said in the end that all the "me" is or could be are mere assumptions. "Is it a feeling? Is it a thought? Is it a sense of presence?"

Justin Allen: Yeah.

Andreas Müller: Because in the end, there is no "me." So, even assumptions (laughing) don't really apply to it, because it sounds as if there were at least something, but we don't know what it is. And the thing is it just does not exist; there is no something in the first place.

Justin Allen: Yeah.

Andreas Müller: Not even as a feeling in the end.

Justin Allen: And not even as an assumption?

Andreas Müller: Exactly, yes. In trying to figure out what the "me" is, we only end up with having assumptions or questions that have no answer. That's how it sounded to me when we were talking. And we already talked about that in another talk: that it is actually impossible to grasp and define the "me."

Justin Allen: Yeah. You were just saying more or less that it's not really a logical thing that you can explain.

Andreas Müller: It's not an "it."

Justin Allen: Right. You can go through the list of all the things that you kind of traditionally or conventionally think that it is, but in the end you have to call all those things or strategies assumptions, just because you're talking in the story.

Andreas Müller: One could say so, yeah. And in the end even those assumptions about what the "me" is only come from the "me" (laughing), so to speak. "What am I?" Who "else" would want to know this, if not the "me"?

Justin Allen: Those are just storylines or chapters or ...

Andreas Müller: Right.

Justin Allen: But when you're talking about the "me" from the "me" perspective, you do have to say, "I assume that I'm here because I feel things and I'm able to push another object. And an object is able to push me and I can feel it. And I have a sense of not being here and of being here. So, I assume that I'm here."

Andreas Müller: Yes.

Justin Allen: Or another sentence can be, "I feel like I'm here because one minute ago I was sad and two minutes later I'm happy, so there's a change that I was aware of, that I took notice of." Or I can say, "I'm logically here because if I go to sleep, I wake up again every morning."

Andreas Müller: Yeah. Or something even much simpler without a real reason for it, like some people would say, "Yeah, I'm here. How can you deny that? I'm here. I feel it. I'm here, damn it." (laughing)

Justin Allen: Yeah. They just have to say, "I'm here. I feel it." Or they have ...

Andreas Müller: Yeah, exactly.

Justin Allen: Like, "You hear me say, 'I'm here.'"

Andreas Müller: Yeah, you're right.

Justin Allen: And then what you're saying is that's not true (laughing)?

Andreas Müller: Well, yes and no. I would say, "Yeah, of course." I don't say anything as an answer to claim that that's not true. But what this message is saying in a way is that there is no one present, that there is no one. There is just what's apparently happening. So, of course, you saying,

"I am here," is what apparently happens. So, it's both. It's not really saying that it's a lie or not true in that sense, because that's totally how it is. But yes, it's not real in a sense that there really is something present. But it's not turning the other one wrong either. You know what I mean?

Justin Allen: Yeah. I mean that when you're "born" in the sense of your sense of self, all of a sudden you sense you're there.

Andreas Müller: That would be the story.

Justin Allen: Yeah. But then that is kind of automatically whole. It feels like I could argue logically that that would still be wholeness because if before there was no sense of self, there was still ... Let's say there's nothing, and out of the nothing, all of a sudden there's a sense of self, which also is still a nothing in the sense that you still can't touch it or grab it or do anything with it. And also, nothing can't be anything else; it just stays nothing.

Andreas Müller: Yeah.

Justin Allen: So, it comes from this source that isn't necessarily a source; it's a source of nothing.

Andreas Müller: Yeah, yeah.

Justin Allen: But because it comes from it, it's still whole, you know? It's still ...

Andreas Müller: Totally. It isn't. It remains nothing, so to speak. It doesn't really come out of nothing or become something.

Justin Allen: Right. If we take nature as an analogy, you can make the claim that a tree exists as a tree, and it's just the trunk and the roots and the branches and the leaves. But in a way it's not just that, because it's also part of its surroundings. It's coming out of the earth, and it is dependent on having water and air, and every single thing actually makes it exist. But we're kind of trained or we tend to see it as separate; we can only see it as one little individual tree.

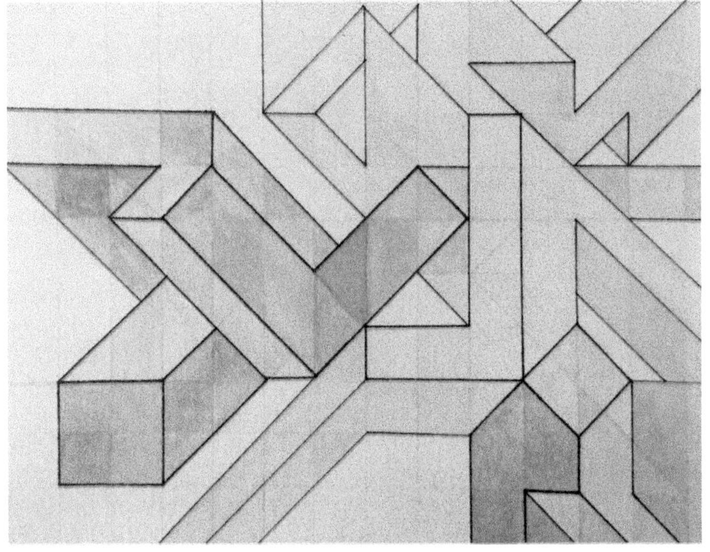

Andreas Müller: Yeah.

Justin Allen: It's kind of like in the old spiritual ways. Spiritual people (earlier people) or the old shamans or maybe pre-modern man, at least how we romantically look at them, seemed to have seen the world as one whole thing.

Andreas Müller: Yeah.

Justin Allen: And we, definitely as Westerners, see everything as separate, and we separate everything out more and more.

Andreas Müller: Yeah.

Justin Allen: But it's all still coming from nothing or ...

Andreas Müller: It is nothing. It all is nothing or no-thing. Yes.

Justin Allen: So, it never actually separates out from the nothing, which is an actual nothing, not a something-nothing. It just somehow creates an illusion of separating out of the source of nothing?

Andreas Müller: Exactly. It's an illusionary experience of, "I'm now here," of separation.

Justin Allen: Yeah.

Andreas Müller: That's why "it" can't be explained, because even the illusion of separation isn't real; it isn't anything that becomes actually an illusion of separation or a separate reality, like, "Oh, an illusion of separation is now really here." No, never.

Justin Allen: Yeah.

Andreas Müller: That's the thing.

Justin Allen: It's an apparent experience.

Andreas Müller: Exactly. It's not even a real experience. That's the illogical part. "What does that actually mean (laughing)? What is it actually like? What is an illusionary experience? An illusionary illusion of separation? What the fuck?" (laughing)

But yeah, that's what it is. It feels separate, but it never becomes separate. It's never even becoming an "it."

Justin Allen: Yeah, it is still "nothing" masquerading as an apparent something. Or it's nothing apparently. I think you'd say "apparently" before anything, so it's "nothing" apparently masquerading as a something?

Andreas Müller: Yes. That's why I say, "no-thing." It's the combination of those two, of nothing and something. But it's not only the "me," the illusion of "me"; it's also the body, the computer, the trees. Everything is nothing and something.

Justin Allen: Yeah.

Andreas Müller: Yeah. And including the apparent people walking around saying, "But I am someone."

Justin Allen: I don't know if it is something though.

Andreas Müller: No, it isn't.

Justin Allen: So, it's really literally just nothing. Why say, "nothing and something"? I think you could say, "nothing and apparently something."

Andreas Müller: Yep. All right. But in the end nothing would be seen as another something.

Justin Allen: Would it? Why is nothing a something? At least if it was truly nothing, then it would just be nothing. And even though we can say, "Yeah, but there's still objects and apparently things happening," that's all an assumption.

Andreas Müller: Yeah, exactly. It's already coming from an observing standpoint.

Justin Allen: You can say it seems like there's an apparent nothing and something happening, but ultimately you can't really say if there's something ...

Andreas Müller: Or nothing.

Justin Allen: Or nothing. Right, you can't say there is a something or a nothing.

Andreas Müller: Yes, exactly. There is no statement possible at all.

Justin Allen: And talking in this way, then the only birth or the only death that ever happens is happening to this apparent something which isn't anything (laughing)?

Andreas Müller: Yes, yes, exactly.

Justin Allen: But the only birth that could happen, in a sense, is the illusion?

Andreas Müller: Yes. Exactly (laughing). The experience to be alive is the only illusion. "Me" is the illusion. Life is an illusion. It's not real. Yes.

Justin Allen: And that is a miracle. Like that literally ... (laughing)

Andreas Müller: Yes. One could say so. But of course, to call it a miracle you already have to process the idea of it all. But yes, seeing it like that it is a fucking miracle (laughing).

Justin Allen: Now I feel like I sense how difficult it is to talk about this.

Andreas Müller: Yeah.

Justin Allen: At the same time, it does seem like you truly can't talk about it.

Andreas Müller: Oh, truly, of course not. In a funny way, this message is very honest. It's not making up those sentences in order to be mystical or to create some "wow" or some wonder. No, you can't talk about it. You can't talk about what is. I don't know. I don't know "it" and all that stuff. Yes. It's impossible.

Justin Allen: But at the same time, let's say in coming around to this "understanding," it seems like there's some kind of recognition that starts to grasp what's not possible to grasp. You know what I mean?

Andreas Müller: At least apparently one could say so.

Justin Allen: Yeah.

Andreas Müller: Because there is nothing to understand and no one gaining anything from it. But yes, I know what you mean.

Justin Allen: It still kind of starts to feel like you figured something out. Again, not that there's a "you" that kind of figured it out, but at the same time it seems like there is an apparent process going on, kind of a coming around to this realization, for lack of a better word.

Andreas Müller: Okay. You mean that's what's happening over there with you (pointing to the screen, to refer to Justin on the other side of the screen), so to speak?

Justin Allen: Yeah.

Andreas Müller: Yeah. Oh, yeah.

Justin Allen: So, it still seems like when I heard you from our last talk, I couldn't help myself from still having this kind of doubt. It was, for lack of a better way of putting it, somehow seeping in; like it was a clear, "Ah, this is so true." But then there was doubt like, "What if it's just another belief? "Or what if something just happened to Andreas and Tony Parsons, through all their searching and trying to figure all this stuff out for so many years, so that they now go, 'Ah, no one's there.' And what they've done is they've come up with the best argument that's flawless. You can't poke holes in it, because you can just keep on going forever with, 'There is no one.'" (laughing)

Andreas Müller: So, at least you come to the conclusion that they are really brilliant (laughing).

Justin Allen: They've come up with an indefensible argument by saying, "Yeah, but nobody's there. This is all just apparently happening. These are apparent words coming out of my apparent mouth, so I'm apparently talking." It just looks like you are a clever lawyer who came up with the most perfect contract where nobody can sue you.

Andreas Müller: Yeah.

Justin Allen: There's that element of still wanting to play the devil's advocate in a way and kind of say, "But it's still just another belief. You just believe that you're not there, and you can't defend that. You can't prove if it is real or just your belief; you are not able to prove if you are there or not."

Andreas Müller: No, I can't. I mean, one could say the dilemma for the "person" is that the only way how they can process this whole message is to see it like another belief. But it's neither a belief nor really a message, so there is nothing really to accept or reject or argue about, at least from my side.

Justin Allen: Yeah.

Andreas Müller: All the "person" can do is what they do with any other spoken words: to believe it or not.

Justin Allen: Right.

Andreas Müller: Of course. I totally understand in that sense.

Justin Allen: So, what I'm saying is that a part of what's going on over here, for me, is that I'm kind of "figuring things out," but there's also a "recognition" that as I go along with that, I more and more feel like this would imply that I'm (the "me") disappearing at the same time.

Andreas Müller: All right. Yep.

Justin Allen: Or in the sense of the sense of "me": Then what you say starts to make sense in a different way than if I compare myself to talk one or to a year or two years ago.

Andreas Müller: Yeah.

Justin Allen: So, there's this "recognition" that, let's say, the meaning or interpretation that the sentence, "I think, therefore I am," might have had for me when I was twenty and thirty and forty has changed. And I would generally think that while several years have gone by, I've changed, and that's why my opinions and my beliefs and my feelings have changed, but now through talking with you and maybe especially through our last talk, I can start to feel like that whole chronology of things happening and changing also is part of this setup.

Andreas Müller: Yeah (laughing).

Justin Allen: Then you're just left with, for lack of a better word, a feeling (laughing); a feeling that none of this happened. None of this was real, and none of this is true, and this whole feeling that you're there isn't a feeling. It's just not there. It's not real. And then I think, "But is this even going on for me anymore?" Normally, I would say, "Yeah, but who is the one that's figuring this out? Or who is the one that this is real or not real?" That kind of self-questioning, for lack of a better way of explaining it, isn't there or is weaker.

Andreas Müller: Yep.

Justin Allen: Before the huge dilemma or the huge problem I was thinking, "Yeah, but I'm there to know this, or I'm there to feel it." And if that feeling isn't really real, if it's lost its strength, then you can't talk about it.

Andreas Müller: Oh, absolutely. Yeah. Yeah.

Justin Allen: I listened to Adyashanti recently.

Andreas Müller: Yeah.

Justin Allen: I haven't listened to him for some time. And I just thought, "Oh, I want to see what this guy is saying now." And it's so similar in a way to what you or Tony Parsons say. But he's always still inserting an experiencer. You can see that he is trying so hard to say the same thing that no one's there – or maybe he is not trying hard, but still he is inserting consciousness or something that's there to experience that no-experience. And that's the critical distinction to what we're talking about here; that there's literally no experiencer or only an apparent experiencer and only an apparent experience.

Andreas Müller: Yes. Which in the story has a whole different flavor than assuming an experiencer because out of that assumption a whole teaching arises.

Justin Allen: Yeah. And the whole illusion of life for seven billion different people.

Andreas Müller: The illusion of life. Yeah. With a path and goals and moving forward in time and space and with right and wrong and actions and responsibility and stuff. Which isn't wrong and also, it's totally common, but as you say, regarding what we are talking about here, it just doesn't exist. It's not real (laughing).

Justin Allen: It's not wrong or right. And there's nothing you can do or not do about it.

Andreas Müller: Yeah.

Justin Allen: I watched this show on Netflix, "One Strange Rock."

Andreas Müller: I haven't even heard about it.

Justin Allen: It's more or less talking about planet earth, which is the one strange rock. It's making the argument, through astronauts and science and through our current and updated understanding of the planet, why we need to stop polluting. And in general, if you read Carl Sagan or Michio Kaku or these kind of more modern scientists, which try to talk about life and humans and our understanding, it still always starts with the Big Bang Theory. And that Big Bang theory, as far as I understand it, is still something like a miracle. They say that it's miraculous that out of nothing, somehow all this got created.

Andreas Müller: Yeah.

Justin Allen: And that's the same picture that we just painted in a sense?

Andreas Müller: Absolutely.

Justin Allen: It's that the apparent sense of self just happens or doesn't happen, like probably it doesn't happen to some people?

Andreas Müller: Yeah.

Justin Allen: And if it doesn't happen, they would not know it ... (laughing)

Andreas Müller: Yeah, exactly. They might know it if everyone else around them was saying they are a "me." And kept on referring to the "me" and fighting for the "me." Then there might be an apparent recognition like, "Oh, dear, what are they talking about?" (laughing)

Justin Allen: Instantly they might say, "What's wrong with me?" And then they discover they're there.

Andreas Müller: But yes, the picture of the Big Bang is just an utterly personalized picture. It's exactly mirroring the "person's" experience.

Justin Allen: You're right.

Andreas Müller: "The moment I was born, the world or the life of the world started. And time and space and development and moving on and change and evolution started." And seen by the "person," the personal life is also kind of an evolution. At least that's the hope (laughing); that there's an evolution during my whole life towards the actual or the best. And the Big Bang theory is just projecting the "person's" experience on the universe, so to speak, or on what the "person" regards as the universe or as existence or as a separate real reality.

Justin Allen: Right. But when scientists are using the instruments of technology and whatever resources are available, they start to come to the conclusion that there's nothing and then somehow there's something. They still think that the something is real and tangible.

Andreas Müller: Yeah.

Justin Allen: But some scientists might say differently and dare to question the whole basis of their assumptions and their observer standpoint. They kind of come to this through a series of gaining knowledge and reasoning, but in the

end, they might come to the conclusion or to the same apparent conclusion that we are having, "Holy shit. There's just nothing, and there's always been nothing, and it just seems like there's something."

Andreas Müller: Yes.

Justin Allen: And the same happens to the spiritual seeker. They kind of go through a similar process as a scientist. When they started off they were, for example, brought up on Christianity, so they believed in that, and then they started to question God just like a scientist might do.

Andreas Müller: Yes.

Justin Allen: They come to the conclusion, "Oh, this hasn't been real; this is all a big lie or a big show." And then they maybe fall into some other belief and into another one, but at some point, they might start to think, "Oh, my God! What if it's just that I'm not really here, I don't exist, this doesn't exist, none of this exists?"

Andreas Müller: Yeah.

Justin Allen: And the same could happen to the kind of non-scientific and non-spiritual person that chases having a job and a family and the good life or whatever, and after a while they also come to the conclusion that there's nothing.

Andreas Müller: Yeah. Yeah.

Justin Allen: I'm just saying that ... Not that it's really a process, but in all of these different examples you start to reach this sense that you're not there.

Andreas Müller: Yeah, but wait. I don't know if you meant that, but what you just said are two things for me: coming to the conclusion that there actually is nothing, be it from the scientific, spiritual or so-called normal angle, is not coming to "no me."

Justin Allen: Right. They probably want to know "me."

Andreas Müller: They want to come to a conclusion, like from an observer standpoint.

Justin Allen: And they're actually being "no me"? They're not really observing, because they can't take themselves out of their observation?

Andreas Müller: Exactly.

Justin Allen: So, not that it's possible or not that anybody knows if there is a coming close phase to the death of the "me" or not, but let's just pretend that the illusion of the "me" starts to fade away and that it does happen that there's "no me." Then the former scientist, the former spiritual person and the former normal person would, in case they talk about it at all, probably each talk about it differently because of their apparent past life of being a scientist, a spiritual person or an average person. Not that that's relevant, but ...

Andreas Müller: Yes and no; maybe it would differ only in details. Because in all three setups, it's just "me" inquiring into a separate reality, no matter what it looks like. So yes, afterwards, in liberation, so to speak, when they speak about their story, of course, some words would be different, but the apparent outcome would always be the same.

Justin Allen: Yeah, the outcome would be the same, but it's the same with how sometimes you refer back to the story of your life, also when not talking about this subject but just in a conventional sense.

Andreas Müller: Yeah.

Justin Allen: They would also have to do that. So, the story of the scientist's life would be different than the story of the person that was embedded in different religions and spirituality. And then ...

Andreas Müller: I understand, but it would really only be in details. So, I would tell about how I went to my guru and how I was happy after having had a new insight in reality, and I was dancing of joy because of that. The scientist might say exactly the same: "One day I came into my laboratory, and when I was looking through the microscope, I saw another piece of how it really is, and I was dancing in my laboratory out of joy."

Justin Allen: Yeah.

Andreas Müller: And the other guy would say, "Well, the moment when my castle was finished, I was happily dancing." That's what I mean.

Justin Allen: Right.

Andreas Müller: The stories wouldn't be so different, because the "person" or the seeking setup or the value system and all that stuff would still be quite similar.

Justin Allen: Right. I'm just trying to say how it's still the same in the sense that you're liberated now.

Andreas Müller: That there is no one there anymore.

Justin Allen: Right. But it's still different in the sense that you don't really erase your apparent former life.

Andreas Müller: Oh, yeah, of course not.

Justin Allen: Because in a way one might think ... I could see somebody playing the devil's advocate and saying, "Ah. So when you're liberated, it means that all of a sudden you all become identical, like indifferent and non-attached?"

Andreas Müller: No, no, not at all.

Justin Allen: I think that's a really hard thing for the "me" to "understand" in entertaining these pictures and talking about this. Because they think that when there's a "no me," it erases everything and you ...

Andreas Müller: Yes, you're right.

Justin Allen: And I think what's key to this message, to the way that you or we've been talking about this, is that you're just going back to the sentence that the "me" never existed in the first place. So when the death of the "me" happens to a scientist or a religious or spiritual person or a normal average Joe person, it's that they were never really scientists or spiritual persons or average persons?

Andreas Müller: Exactly, exactly.

Justin Allen: And that's ...

Andreas Müller: Exactly. So, that picture would actually show the arrogance, or the apparent arrogance, of the "me" that says, "I was or am there, and I'm the creator of all those things. I'm the creator of being a scientist, I'm the creator of being a spiritual person, I'm the creator of living a normal life."

Justin Allen: Right.

Andreas Müller: And when I'm not there, all that drops or whatever. But you're right, it never was there. It never did those things. There never was someone doing those things, creating those things. But in a way the "me" would assume it, so the step from "me" to "no me" sounds like the biggest step of all because "me," my life and my presence is all I know and all I have. So if that's not happening, it must be really, really different. And as you said, all the things that I was identified with, of course, had to be erased, so the human must appear in a special or weird way, holy or empty or something like that. Seen by the "me," that's logical.

Justin Allen: And then that's why when there is "no one," you can't really talk about it or about what it's really like. But, and this is a sentence that's going to be "contaminated," it's still "like" an experience?

Andreas Müller: No.

Justin Allen: But the way that you would talk about it would sound like an experience to the "me"?

Andreas Müller: Yes, for the "person," for the experiencer, it would sound like another experience.

Justin Allen: Right, but that's also the only way you can talk about it (laughing). That's the huge dilemma I see for a "no me"; that you can't help but still talk about it as if you were a "person" and as if you were there.

Andreas Müller: No, not really. That's what the "person" would hear and assume, but I don't speak as if I were a "person." "Me" speaking is what apparently happens.

Justin Allen: Right. But to the outside world it's always going to seem that way. You appear as Andreas talking about something.

Andreas Müller: Absolutely, totally. Yes.

Justin Allen: Yeah, that's what I mean. That's another or maybe still the same dilemma.

Andreas Müller: It's not really a dilemma, because I don't want to bring something else across.

Justin Allen: No, not for you, but for the potential seven billion or the actual people that listen to you.

Andreas Müller: Yeah. Okay. I thought you thought I'm in a dilemma.

Justin Allen: No. They go and sit there and listen to you, and you're talking about the "no me" or about how the "me" doesn't exist and never existed and how it's just this energy, and they're looking at "you" (laughing). They're seeing a separate person talking about their own experience. You know what I mean?

Andreas Müller: Yeah. Absolutely. It's wonderfully absurd. I mean, that's the "me's" dilemma: to only be able to be "me" (laughing).

Justin Allen: Yeah. And only be able to see other "me's."

Andreas Müller: That's its apparent dilemma; to experience everything only through the filter of its own presence, so to speak. It's all a story.

Justin Allen: It can't not do that until it happens that ...

Andreas Müller: That there is "no one."

Justin Allen: Yeah.

Andreas Müller: Yeah. Because of course, the attempt to not do it, seen by the "person" who just did the attempt to have another experience, is wondrous (laughing).

Justin Allen: A "me" would still have to say, "How can he see it as being wondrous if he's not there?"

Andreas Müller: Yeah, I don't, of course. But, I mean, that's again the illogical part of it all. "How can he say that? How can he say that when there is 'no one'?"

Justin Allen: Exactly.

Andreas Müller: That's the question the "me" has all the time. It believes itself to be separate. It looks out in the world and asks, "How can this be? What the fuck is the answer to all or some of this?"

Justin Allen: Yeah.

Andreas Müller: "What is the answer to there being trees and clouds and stars and people and animals and thoughts and feelings and problems, and how can that all be?" It's exactly the same question.

Justin Allen: Right. And that just doesn't matter anymore when there's "no me"?

Andreas Müller: Of course not, because there is no question, because there is "no one" separate, because there is no separate reality. There is nothing existing which can be questioned.

Justin Allen: Exactly. And that's what I mean: You can try to talk about that as a "no me," but at the same time you can't do it, because that's just what is happening for you?

Andreas Müller: Yes, yeah, absolutely.

Justin Allen: And that switch from being a "me" to a "no me" is such a subtle ... It's like a magic trick in a way. It's like when somebody performs a magic trick and you're amazed at it, and then they actually show you the trick, the non-magic part about it, which is just a slight of hand or a fabricated clever illusion. And then you get it, and nobody could ever perform that magic trick on you again.

Andreas Müller: Yeah.

Justin Allen: The difference between before and after, between you being amazed by the magic and the trick being revealed, is not a big difference.

Andreas Müller: Yeah, one could say so.

Justin Allen: And you'd never be able to explain that very well either. You just ...

Andreas Müller: You just saw it in a way.

Justin Allen: And it's dead to you. The magic is dead, at least in that trick, and it'll never come back.

Andreas Müller: Yeah. At least the magic of the illusion is gone. But that which "remains," so to speak, is still totally or even all the more magical in a way.

Justin Allen: All right, I got to go.

Andreas Müller: I know.

Justin Allen: Have a good day.

Andreas Müller: Cool. You too. Nice to see you.

Justin Allen: Nice to see you, too.

Andreas Müller: Bye.

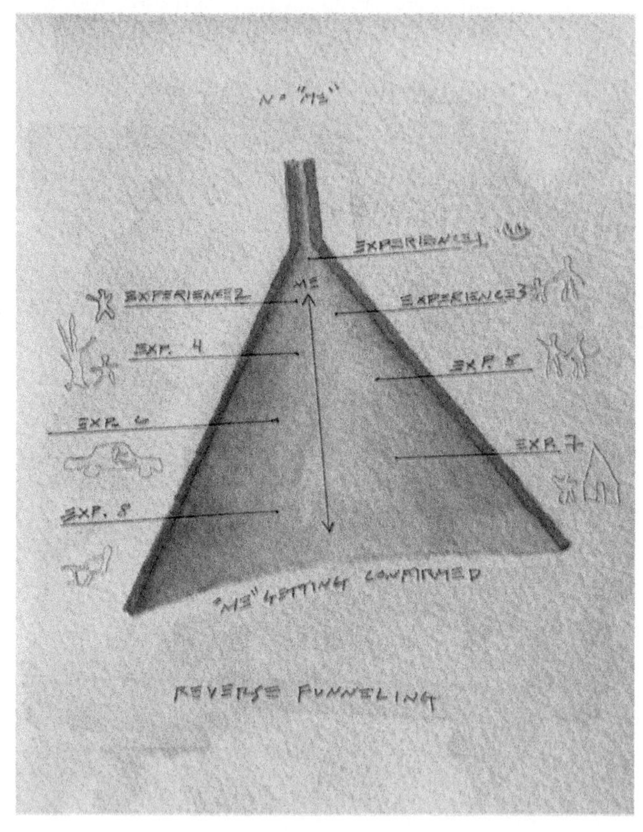
NO "ME"
EXPERIENCE 1
"ME"
EXPERIENCE 2
EXPERIENCE 3
EXP. 4
EXP. 5
EXP. 6
EXP. 7
EXP. 8
"ME" GETTING CONFIRMED
REVERSE FUNNELING

March 13, 2020 Talk 13

REVERSE FUNNELING

Justin Allen: All right.

Andreas Müller: Yes.

Justin Allen: So you, too, have talk 12 in front of you (we are reviewing the previous Talk in written/transcribed form)?

Andreas Müller: Yeah.

Justin Allen: I went through it and highlighted the paragraphs that I wanted to revisit.

Andreas Müller: Yeah, all right. I haven't read it yet.

Justin Allen: Okay. Well, on the first page, I say, "So, it's illogical for you, Andreas Müller, and also for Tony Parsons, for example. And it's also illogical for me and the other seven billion of us that think that we're there. So, it's illogical on both sides; on the side of the 'me' and on the side of the 'no me,' so to speak?" So, that's saying how from a "me" perspective, it's illogical listening to you or Tony Parsons or hearing that I don't exist, for example? And also from your perspective, it's illogical that I think that I exist (laughing)? But it's also illogical that there's no one there?

Andreas Müller: Yeah, exactly. And in a way, seen by the "me," it's illogical, but there is the assumption that theoretically it is logical or that actually it should be logical or that there is some deeper logic behind it. That's why there is God and all those concepts, but in the end, when there is "no one," one could say it becomes obvious that logic itself doesn't really apply to how it is. There isn't really a "how it is."

Justin Allen: Okay. So, there's no logic for anybody?

Andreas Müller: Exactly. Logic itself would only refer to a real reality where real things interact, where things really are a certain way. Then something could theoretically be understood and concluded by means of logic.

Justin Allen: Right. So then, a bit later you say, "Yeah, but wait a moment. That's a story already; that there's a sense of presence which is separate from what happens." Here we were talking about the "me" being an illusion and what that is. And the best way that we've been able to address it is to say it's a feeling or a sense of being there or a sense of presence. And then the dilemma is that any time you're addressing or thinking or feeling something, it already implies that there's something there to do so?

Andreas Müller: So to speak, yes.

Justin Allen: But they're the same thing? You can't really separate the sense of presence out?

Andreas Müller: Exactly, yes. But it's not the feeling proving that there is a "me"; it's in a way whenever there is "me" feeling something, "me" is already there. Just to be clear, it's never the outside that proves that there is "me" in that sense. But yeah, that's what's being said; that there is no one separate. You can't separate anything out.

Justin Allen: Right. But when you say that there being a sense of presence is a story already, that's just commenting on how as soon as there's someone there, there's a story also?

Andreas Müller: Yes, but the thing is that it's a story which is being seen as real, like a truth. It's actually the same with logic. We started talking about the sense of presence, about what the "me" is and that it's illusory, but the dilemma is, even when you say that, somehow "me" would still hear that there is a sense of presence (laughing) which has certain qualities like being illusory, for example. And this would mean that there's a real way of seeing through the illusion and instead see "the truth" or something like that, and that's what the spiritually seeking "me" wants. But in the end, it means that the seemingly felt sense of presence does not exist, at least not as something really separate.

Justin Allen: And that there is this separate sense is also already automatically a story?

Andreas Müller: Exactly.

Justin Allen: And that story's unavoidable as soon as there's the illusory "me"? This sense of presence is the story also?

Andreas Müller: Yes, one could say so. But it's a story that's being regarded as real, as statements about a real reality.

Justin Allen: Because the "me" can't really make this distinction in a way. It has to have the story, and it has to have itself being there and that it is feeling things, which is what's verifying that it's there?

Andreas Müller: Yes.

Justin Allen: But it can't really understand that the "thereness" is also already the story, which, however, is not real?

Andreas Müller: Yes, exactly.

Justin Allen: But still that's the main assumption; that's just a given, a fact: that I must be here, or at least that "something" is here and now, which generally is referred to as "me" or "I," but it could also be considered spirit, soul, God et cetera?

Andreas Müller: Exactly, exactly.

Justin Allen: Of all the things in the world, the one fact or the one truth that you (the person or individual) can say is, "Something's there." Whether you call it "I" or "me," there's something that's there, and because of that, all of these things, thoughts and feelings happen to that "thing" that's there, but the "thing" that's there isn't actually there?

Andreas Müller: Exactly. That's the dilemma; that the sense of presence can't be questioned anymore on an experience or observation level. Everything else can be questioned, and of course, intellectually or conceptually, "me" can question itself, too. But not as an experience. It can't un-experience itself, so to speak. That's why it assumes itself as given already, all the time, so to speak.

Justin Allen: So, that's what you mean when you say, "That's a story already; that there is a sense of presence"? You're just saying that that's a story because we're kind of giving meaning and actuality to this "thing" that actually isn't there?

Andreas Müller: Yeah, exactly. Because as I said, "me" would immediately turn it into, "Yeah, all right, but there is something." It will end up with this one given thing, even if it's just a residual. "See? There is something." However, it's an illusion. It's an illusory illusion. It's an illusory sense, just an impression of presence. But "me" processes it still as a reality, as something that's undeniably there, so to speak (laughing).

Justin Allen: Yeah. And that's the story?

Andreas Müller: Yes, exactly (laughing).

Justin Allen: Okay. So then, a bit further down, I say, "Right. But what you're saying is that it's ..." I just wanted to repeat this one because I think both of us didn't get it (laughing).

Andreas Müller: All right. I think that happens again and again (laughing).

Justin Allen: I go, "Right. But what you're saying is that it's not the case that there's something that exists and then that something gets this sense of presence? It's that this energetic presence is the illusion? It is the thing that you falsely think that you are?" That's kind of what we just said, right?

Andreas Müller: Exactly. There isn't "something," which suddenly has the illusion to be "me." I think that's the question or the statement that you make. It's not that the sense of presence really comes out of something "else."

Justin Allen: Right. So, it looks like we were saying the same thing?

Andreas Müller: Yeah.

Justin Allen: So, that's just saying that there is that "me" which we all seem to agree on. I mean, the seven billion of us all say, "Yeah, there's 'me.'" And then all kinds of things happen to that?

Andreas Müller: No, I wouldn't say so. Now I can't follow anymore (laughing).

Justin Allen: I'm saying that the assumption that seven billion people seem to have is that first there's "some thing," like a source, and you call that a "me" or an "I" or a soul or a spirit or whatever. And because that "thing" is there, attached to that is a sense of presence or the sense of feelings, thoughts and things happening to that "thing"?

Andreas Müller: Yeah. Well, that's automatic, exactly. And the sense of presence is the "me." That's why everybody's saying or unconsciously assuming that there is "me"; because, "I feel it, I'm 'me,' that's how I experience." And automatically all the thoughts, feelings or actions are only being experienced. Automatically there's a separation between an experiencer and the experienced, between subject and object.

Justin Allen: Right. But what the seven billion of us might say is that the sense of "me" isn't an illusion, but all the things that might be happening to that could be illusory.

Andreas Müller: Yeah, that's how the "person" could process it, and that's what many spiritual teachings say, by the way.

Justin Allen: Yeah. And also religion in a way.

Andreas Müller: Yeah, exactly. "I'm real, and everything else is not real, coming and going, not something you can depend on." That's an awareness teaching, basically.

Justin Allen: And what you're saying though is that this very first thing that we all or most people think of as the foundation of reality is the illusion?

Andreas Müller: Yes, exactly. Or let's say the illusion is that it's a real foundation.

Justin Allen: So then, a bit further down from that, I say, "So, back to the beginning to where we were saying that this thing that just kind of happens immediately or out of nowhere all at once is instantly a sense of presence. And then that sense of presence says, 'Ah, this sense of presence, it can only exist if something is present to sense that I'm here.' Then it tells the story and kind of creates a 'pure being' that all of a sudden gets imbued or embedded with this sensing ability. And that creates a duality in the story?" And then you answer, "Yeah, I think I know what you mean. And yes, one could say so. But in a way, the sense of presence already creates an experienced duality which isn't necessarily processed in the story. Because the moment I say, 'I am someone, I am me,' there is automatically the experience that I'm not everything else."

Andreas Müller: Yes. Actually you were saying it quite right in your paragraph. I mean, I was saying yes also in my answer (laughing). What I might have wanted to point out or what I might add now is that there doesn't have to be a story all the time. There are those silent experiences where actually the mind isn't active or where there is no processing going on for a while, so to speak. So, it's not necessarily that when there is a "person," the story's running.

Justin Allen: The silent mind, by definition in a way, wouldn't have a story at that moment of silence?

Andreas Müller: Exactly. "Me" lives in attention and focus. And in those moments, one could say that the attention doesn't go outside but rests at or as itself. Those are just possible experiences which are still personal. It's just a detail, but I somehow wanted to add it.

And you described it in that paragraph: There isn't really a "first" and an "after" in the illusion of "me"; it's simultaneous, it all goes together. There is a self-experience or one's own presence which seems to prove its own existence, but it's not really a conscious, logical process that is seen by the "me." All of that usually is unspoken, and that's why I also mean it's mostly not doubted. As you said, when there is someone, it's already there. "I'm already there." And that's why you can't really turn how "me" invents itself into a linear process.

Justin Allen: Right. I don't know if this example works, but it made me think that if you accept that a human baby doesn't really become self-conscious until one or two years old, then before, things are still happening to the baby. But the baby's not aware of it as a "person." And then as soon as the baby is somehow embedded or imbued with this self-consciousness, all those things are now happening for the experience of the baby; they're actually now happening to a "me."

Andreas Müller: Exactly.

Justin Allen: That's the same in a way like when we go to sleep; we're still lying in bed, but nothing happens to "you" anymore. So when you lie in bed, you feel the mattress and the sheets and you're aware of your thoughts and stuff, and then at some point: nothing.

Andreas Müller: Yes.

Justin Allen: And then again when you wake up: something.

Andreas Müller: Yes, exactly.

Justin Allen: But just like the baby, you didn't really physically change? So when the baby is one or two years old and it has this self-consciousness, the body's experiencing in the same way, but on top there is now a "me"?

Andreas Müller: Exactly. Which seems to experience experiencing, which seems to experience the body, a living body with feelings and thoughts et cetera.

Justin Allen: And that's that simultaneous thing; that as soon as you wake up in the morning, it's immediately recognized that you're there, and ...

Andreas Müller: The experience of waking up is the recognition to be there.

Justin Allen: Right. And then all of the other recognitions confirm that?

Andreas Müller: Seem to confirm that, yeah.

Justin Allen: Right, they just seem to confirm that (laughing). So then, a bit later, I say, "Right. So when I wake up in the morning and all of a sudden I feel lethargic or energetic or good or like I didn't sleep well, it automatically translates, without even logic or without anything, that something's there to have to receive these feelings or this input?"

Andreas Müller: Yeah. I'm just reading my answer, and that's the thing: Because it's not really that those things confirm that there is a "me"; it was just "me" experiencing them, which kind of confirms that there is a "me." But not having slept well or waking up and feeling good or lethargic or like not wanting to do anything is what apparently happens. It's still the baby functioning. That doesn't prove the "me" itself, so to speak. It's again "me" proving itself by only experiencing, but it's not the feeling itself. That's wholeness. Just like with the baby: The eyes open, and there is feeling good (or whatever). But of course, the observer or the experiencer experiences and confirms itself by experiencing sleep. It's basically saying, "Oh, I can experience the sleep, so sleep is separate. And because I can experience it, I must be there." But as I said, all of that is basically unconscious or unspoken, which is all right. Not that someone has to or could really become conscious about that, not at all, but ...

Justin Allen: So you answer, "One could say so, but on the other hand, there's already something there to do so."

Andreas Müller: Exactly. When there is an experience of, "I didn't sleep well," or, "I feel good," then of course, there is already someone there to do so.

Justin Allen: Which is again the illusion?

Andreas Müller: Exactly, yes.

Justin Allen: So, that's like the sharp point of the needle. That's the real deal that you're talking about?

Andreas Müller: Exactly. There is no one (laughing). Absolutely. Yeah.

Justin Allen: But it's really difficult, or it seems really difficult, at least for most people and myself included, to kind of hone in on this concept or no-point perspective. Like with a funnel, so you start off broadly or widely.

Andreas Müller: Yeah, all right.

Justin Allen: Then you get narrower and narrower and narrower until you come to the point. And it's the same as if you asked somebody who they are or if they are here: They start off with the point and might go backyards, "Yeah, I'm here, obviously." And then they can spread out with all kinds of ways to prove that they're here. And then when you come back reversing to try to come to that initial assumption, "I'm here," you have to go through all those layers, or at least it seems like it. It's like using a funnel in reverse, I think.

Andreas Müller: Yeah, I understand.

Justin Allen: So, it's the same as how you miss the point when you say, after waking up in the morning, that you feel like you had a good or a bad night's sleep. You're already kind of skipping over the first assumption?

Andreas Müller: Oh, yeah, absolutely.

Justin Allen: I'm already saying, "I feel good." And it confirms that I'm there, but it's only in the feeling that I feel like I'm there?

Andreas Müller: Yeah, exactly.

Justin Allen: And you skip over questioning if you are really there?

Andreas Müller: Yes. But that would only be the "me" again questioning itself.

Justin Allen: Yeah. I'm just saying even that is difficult for the "me," to actually question itself, to actually question if the "me" or presence is there in the first place to even start questioning anything.

Andreas Müller: Yes.

Justin Allen: Because normally it'll question its feelings and all the spreading or reverse funneling that comes out from itself (from the point), but it won't question that fundamental assumption – it can't actually question that point it seems.

Andreas Müller: Yeah. It can't really, in a way.

Justin Allen: Right. Because every time you try to do that, it just seems ridiculous because ...

Andreas Müller: On the one hand it seems ridiculous, but on the other hand the dilemma is, and that's also somehow felt, that it needs "you" to do that in the first place.

Justin Allen: Yeah. But also it can't even fathom and it can't even begin to comprehend itself not being there as it's struggling to figure out if it's there or not, because it automatically needs that "thing" there to try to struggle or to figure something out.

Andreas Müller: Exactly, exactly, yes (laughing).

Justin Allen: So, then I say, "And from that sense that you're there, in the story you can say, 'Ah, I must be here, something must be here that is getting these things, these 'happenings' 'happening' to 'it,' and that's separating it."

Andreas Müller: Yes.

Justin Allen: So, it's kind of what we just talked about. It's not even a sense of "me" or a sense of being or a sense of happiness or a sense of depression or ... I don't know – it's just sense?

Andreas Müller: Yes. That's what I mean with a sense of presence, it's just sense. It's just ...

Justin Allen: Reducing it to just something or just sense?

Andreas Müller: Yeah. Some awareness, but that all sounds like a story because it's not really processed yet. It's just a sense of existence, just a sense that there is something. But it's blind, it's not conscious.

Justin Allen: So then, the last part I highlighted is where you go on to say that that's how it's experienced; that the sense of being someone is also an energetic separation.

Andreas Müller: Yes. Automatically.

Justin Allen: Right. So before that, let's say that this sense never happened. And that's how you would say it. It apparently happens, right?

Andreas Müller: In the end it never really happens, yes. Only apparently.

Justin Allen: That's what you say to somebody that says, "I feel bad because of X, Y, Z"; you go, "Yeah, that's what apparently happens." And that's the same with that foundation of everything that's happening to you and that seems to be just first: That sense that seems to be there is also just what apparently seems to happen?

Andreas Müller: Yes.

Justin Allen: So if that sense never apparently happened ...

Andreas Müller: Actually, one could say the illusion of that sense is what apparently happens.

Justin Allen: Okay. And if that illusion of sensing never apparently happened, then there would never be a "person"?

Andreas Müller: Exactly, yes.

Justin Allen: But that wouldn't necessarily mean that there wouldn't be things being experienced ... Well, it would mean that things wouldn't be experienced (by a "me"), which is why I was trying to put it into the picture of the baby as an example of pre-self-consciousness.

Andreas Müller: Yes, there would just be an adult baby. There would be a baby with an adult functioning: brain size, brain functioning with certain patterns, apparent logic functioning, feelings happening – all of that stuff, exactly. There would just be an apparent adult body functioning, probably more or less conditioned, probably more or less influenced by what happened in the past and in childhood. I don't know. Something like that, yeah.

Justin Allen: Kind of the way that we imagined that it must be like for trees or for animals, so for creatures that we don't give self-consciousness to?

Andreas Müller: Yeah. As I say, there is also the function of consciousness. I mean, it would still be human. It wouldn't become dull or superhuman or whatever.

Justin Allen: Right. But I mean, the way that humans imagine what life is like for a tree or an animal is that generally we make ourselves distinct from them because we say we have self-awareness and they don't.

Andreas Müller: Exactly. At least up to now, because as far as I know, neuroscience is just destroying this picture. That's why we have been seen or rather seen ourselves as the crown of evolution; because we have a self-experience.

Justin Allen: But from our perspective all trees are different, and if a tree grows up in area A, it's going to be different than if it grows up in area B. And it has certain characteristics because of its genes, where it came from and where it actually is right now.

here because it implies a "me" or a "feeler" that is there to feel, but I do not mean it that way) like everything's all connected, or not that it's connected, but that there's no …

Andreas Müller: Separation (laughing). Yeah. It may sound very clumsy, just like I sound in my own ears (laughing). They wouldn't really understand what they should describe. It's not even that there's a certain "it" which can't be described. In the end there isn't even an "it" in the first place which can be described.

Justin Allen: Right. I think I'd just keep on having to come back to the sentence that there's nothing.

Andreas Müller: Exactly, yeah. So, all those questions like, "How is it for you, and how do you perceive the world?" and all of that stuff; you can't really answer them, because the first thing that's being addressed, the "you," is in a way already not there?

Justin Allen: Right. So if somebody asks, "How is it for you?" you get lost because you can't find yourself?

Andreas Müller: Exactly, yes. And you said it as a story, I know, but you don't really get lost; you are lost already (laughing).

Justin Allen: Well, you can't get lost, because you're not there in the first place, but in order to talk about it, that would be the best way to … You would go to look for yourself for an answer, but there'd be nothing that you could acknowledge as actually … You wouldn't be able to acknowledge a point of view that could give a proper, satisfying answer?

Andreas Müller: Yes, exactly. Maybe you didn't mean it like that, but it's not because there is something which has a look first to see if there is someone or not; it's just by already there being no one.

Justin Allen: So, then it would be like you're just floating around (laughing).

Andreas Müller: Yes. Exactly.

Andreas Müller: Yeah. How much rain there is, what the ground is like et cetera. Absolutely, yeah.

Justin Allen: Then if you as a human hammer a nail into a tree, it reacts to that nail. But we never assume that it's thinking, "Why are you putting this nail in me?"

Andreas Müller: Not really, exactly. I mean, some spiritual people do so because they assume everything to be self-conscious (laughing).

Justin Allen: But then as a human, we also feel like we're more separate from the world than the actual world. We kind of accept that nature is one thing working together in a way, but that we aren't totally part of that.

Andreas Müller: Yeah, kind of. If you look closely, there are many set concepts about a separate reality there, too. But yes, I know what you mean.

Justin Allen: Yeah. But I mean without water and without the sun nothing lives, and somehow we see ourselves as different, maybe also because of technology or something, but just the fact that we've seemingly found ways around nature to keep on surviving ... But if there was a human that existed without this sense happening that makes them feel like they're a "person," then they could never go around the world feeling like they're separate from anything. Even though they might be going around the world and reacting and communicating with things as if they were separate, it wouldn't be experienced ever that they were really separate?

Andreas Müller: Yes, exactly, of course.

Justin Allen: So, it would all just feel like one (but for no one) ... If they could feel and talk about it (laughing), they would feel like there's just nothing ...

Andreas Müller: They wouldn't be able to explain it as much as I'm not able to explain it (laughing).

Justin Allen: Right. Because it would just feel (feel is the wrong word

Justin Allen: Floating around aimlessly.

Andreas Müller: Yes. Like a leaf in the wind (laughing). That's freedom. It looks very ordinary, and it looks how it looks. But that's in a way the natural reality; floating like a leaf in the wind (laughing). Already everything is like that, kind of. Every feeling, every thought, every joy, every depression, every movement – everything. A computer, trees, cars, clouds. It's all a bit like leaves in the wind.

Justin Allen: So if you took a fork as an inanimate object, there's no difference between you and a fork?

Andreas Müller: Yes. I'm like a talking fork (laughing).

Justin Allen: That makes me think of what they say; that when you become enlightened or something, you merge with everything. It's just because of my knowledge – not that it's an extensive knowledge (laughing) – of spirituality and religion and Buddhism and all this stuff, or of the Tao Te Ching or Lao Tzu. That's what they're referring to, possibly.

Andreas Müller: Possibly, yeah. Or yes, probably.

Justin Allen: And then when the normal "me" reads in one of those books, "He went and sat under a tree, and then he realized that he was the tree," or something like that, they think, "Oh, what an amazing experience that would be to be one with everything."

Andreas Müller: Yes.

Justin Allen: And they don't take themselves, or their selves, out of that picture?

Andreas Müller: Yes, exactly.

Justin Allen: And then generally when they read or hear a sentence like that from somebody, they think that this person has somehow transcended the normal experience of being a human because of having merged into everything. But they're still there as that human experiencing or imagining what it's like to merge into everything.

Andreas Müller: Yes. Exactly.

Justin Allen: And then what you're saying here is that this merging is all there is already. But when there's this apparent separation, which never really happened, and then that apparent separation dies, all that this really means is that the sensing is gone?

Andreas Müller: Yes.

Justin Allen: And that means that there's no more separation, so you merge into everything, and there's no distinctions anymore, blah, blah, blah, but there's also no one there or left experiencing that (illusory) experiencing?

Andreas Müller: Exactly. Yes.

Justin Allen: And I would think that that's the sad part about the message to a lot of people because they still want to be there.

Andreas Müller: Yes, exactly. That's what all the longing is for, to find personal fulfillment.

Justin Allen: And to be there for it.

Andreas Müller: Yeah, that's what I mean with personal fulfillment: to be there to experience it. Seen by the "person," there are so many dreams and longings and hopes connected to that idea, so indeed, sadness is the right word. For the "me," it's really sad, or it can be really sad, that my deepest dream will never be fulfilled. That's what this message is also saying in a way because there is no one having dreams. It's not that bad (laughing), but seen by the "person," of course, that's actually an impossibility.

Justin Allen: Yeah. And there is also positive energy in that for the "me"; I'm going to call it improbability because the "me" still thinks that it has a chance, so it can be motivated for long periods of time or for the whole life, trying to achieve this goal of non-separation (or fulfillment) but still being there to experience it. So, that could keep it very positive and eager like, "I'm getting closer, I'm getting closer, I'm getting closer."

Andreas Müller: Of course.

Justin Allen: And there can also be extreme desperation when you give up, so to speak.

Andreas Müller: When you give up or fail or ... Yeah.

Justin Allen: Yes, fail is better because you can't really give up, because true giving up in the way that you're talking about it, would be that "no one" is there in the first place, and that's the death of the "me"?

Andreas Müller: Exactly, the giving up, so to speak, is automatic. It can't be brought about by the "me."

Justin Allen: Right. But because you can't do it, that's where the torture and the desperation would come in. Because if you did give up but remained the "me," then it would be you failing and you giving up and you not achieving your goal?

Andreas Müller: Yes. And giving up in that sense would even mean that I betray myself of the possibility of gaining. Because when I keep on searching for something, there is always a chance to arrive and find. But when I give that up and don't look for it or working on it anymore, that again would go against my hopes and dreams. And yeah, that's desperation and depression and hopelessness.

Justin Allen: Yeah. And that desperation and hopelessness is still experienced from the perspective of that initial sense that I'm there?

Andreas Müller: Of course.

Justin Allen: There's no distinction?

Andreas Müller: Yes, yeah.

Justin Allen: So whether that sensing and searching energy is positively searching, like for fulfillment or happiness, or negatively searching, like for its own death, under both options, there's still the false sense or the illusion that you're there doing all of that and hopefully progressing on your path?

Andreas Müller: Yes, absolutely. And I mean, for most people it's both; it's just always moving between those two, back and forth. Because sometimes life works well; sometimes I feel well, and then I go, "Oh, I'm actually on the right path." And then things don't work out, the method doesn't work or just bad feelings happen again, and then suddenly there's depression: "Oh, I don't make it, I can't make it, I'll never reach it." Five minutes or five hours later, something good happens again: "Oh, yeah. Well, who knows, it's not that bad. I'll get it probably." And all of that stuff. Yeah.

Justin Allen: And then if the "me" dies, so to speak, or if it happens that no one's there, then life still just goes on more or less the exact same way?

Andreas Müller: Yes.

Justin Allen: But just absent of that sense that it's happening for or to someone?

Andreas Müller: So to speak. It's an apparent absence because as we said, the presence wasn't real. But yeah, exactly. Just life happening without the assumption that it is happening for something, without the assumption that I need to be there and consciously do life in order to gain personal fulfillment or that there is something like personal fulfillment at all which one has to be aware of and attentive for and all that stuff. Yeah. But that's a surprise. I mean, it's still trees and thoughts and feelings and everything else however it is. And it's also painful, sometimes.

Justin Allen: And so if you took an example, let's say, from a "no one there" perspective, which already is a contradiction, right?

Andreas Müller: Yeah.

Justin Allen: So from an apparent "no one there" perspective, that "no one" would apparently be in the process of making a decision, for example?

Andreas Müller: Yeah.

Justin Allen: It would seem to an outsider that there's someone there contemplating option A or option B?

Andreas Müller: Yeah, kind of. Absolutely.

Justin Allen: And to the "no one there," it would be apparently happening that there's some kind of a conflict or a situation, but it wouldn't actually be happening to anybody?

Andreas Müller: Yes.

Justin Allen: It would be happening apparently, but not to someone?

Andreas Müller: Yes.

Justin Allen: Right, so that's the clearest way of trying to diagram that situation (laughing).

Andreas Müller: Yeah. But of course, when there is "no one," there is "no one" conscious of that apparent situation.

Justin Allen: Although we did say that consciousness is also something that apparently happens, so that's the one thing that I still don't ... You mentioned it today, too, and it caught my attention. But just like how a decision-making process seems to be happening but isn't actually happening to someone, that's similar with consciousness: There would still be consciousness apparently happening, but it would be to no one?

Andreas Müller: Yes, exactly. There would be apparent consciousness about how it is to go left or right.

Justin Allen: There would be an apparent consciousness that there are apparent options?

Andreas Müller: Yes. Or that I'm on a crossing of a path and need to go left or right. But this would just be functioning. It's like seeing, hearing ...

Justin Allen: Like conscious functioning, not conscious ... I don't know. Somehow we ...

Andreas Müller: Yeah. You can't know, because it's not experienced; it's not a real consciousness which is really conscious of real circumstances and real decisions. You can't separate that consciousness out from the functioning of the body, because being conscious of a certain circumstance is just what apparently happens.

Justin Allen: Philosophically that's an interesting topic that just occurred to me. We've talked about it in different ways, but the consciousness that we currently feel like we have is so rich in a way, with this feeling that I'm here. And with meaning and the belief that there's some kind of importance to it all.

Andreas Müller: Oh, yeah. Totally.

Justin Allen: But we also are aware of a body consciousness that we don't give any importance to at all. In a way your body is consciously aware of itself; for example, if it has a viral infection, it fights against it, and that's an awareness, right? It's kind of aware, like, "Ah, there's a virus, and I need to create antibodies," or whatever the body does to fight it. But your brain or your mind, where you think your consciousness is, doesn't do anything to fight the bacteria or the viral infection? There is no self-bodily-consciousness happening that "you" need to be self-conscious of and control.

Andreas Müller: Yes.

Justin Allen: But when you need to make a decision, then you think that you're actively figuring it out and solving it and that there's a right and a wrong or a better and a worse option. But that could also happen without you being there; that seemingly conscious process of making a decision could still ...

Andreas Müller: Yes, kind of. I mean, the dilemma is that when there is someone, it's always somehow burdened or loaded with the assumption that my decision influences my personal fulfillment.

Justin Allen: Yeah. That's what we feel as consciousness. The feeling of consciousness is "me" there doing or choosing. But I'm just saying that even in that state, we acknowledge that there's also in a way a real consciousness going on inside of us that we were not participating in as the "me"?

Andreas Müller: Yeah. One could say so. It seems, at least.

Justin Allen: And we're okay with that.

Andreas Müller: Yes.

Justin Allen: But we would never feel okay with making a decision about where to live or who to marry or what job to take without "me" being there doing it?

Andreas Müller: Yeah, one could say so.

Justin Allen: Or without God doing it for me or without a Tarot card reader just telling me what to do. Because that's what I find so difficult. I mean, everybody could always come to you and be like, "Look. You made decisions in your life, and you're going to make more decisions in the future. And one's going to be better for you, and one's going to be worse for you. And you're there, figuring it out, even though you tell us that you're not there; I can see that you're there figuring that out. And you're going to pick one, which means that you're never going to pick the other option." Because in these situations they can't remove or can't accept that there's not that sense there; that there's not that "me," that being there or that "me-ing."

Andreas Müller: Yeah. In the end, the seeker will always end up with itself. "Me" will again just assume there to be "me."

Justin Allen: And then the only or the best way that you can talk about "you" not being there is to just say that it's a knowing. But it's not really a knowing either; it's rather like a recognition that I'm just not there?

Andreas Müller: Yes. But I can't even say that. It's an innocent report which comes from nowhere, which comes from functioning, from apparent functioning. It's not holy or special or anything; it's very direct and innocent, but not innocent in the holy way or something. No, it's just ... "Oh." And you can add stories to it; that it's coming from an apparent recognition and all that stuff, but it's basically not coming from something separate.

Justin Allen: The best way that you can make an analogy would be to maybe refer to the human feeling of hunger: You can't really describe it, but everybody knows it.

Andreas Müller: Exactly, yeah. It's just apparently reporting what's going on. In the end, it's still an apparent report, also that there is "no one." I mean ...

Justin Allen: Alright. I have a meeting that I have to go to. But, good talk.

Andreas Müller: Yeah. Nice.

March 23, 2020 Talk 14

ENDING AT THE BEGINNING

Justin Allen: All right.

Andreas Müller: All right.

Justin Allen: So, your panic level in terms of Corona is low?

Andreas Müller: Yes. To be honest, it's quite low (laughing).

Justin Allen: You're in a little village though, aren't you?

Andreas Müller: Well, it's close to Stuttgart. There's not really a break between Stuttgart and here, so it's not really a village.

Justin Allen: Okay, well, Stuttgart's like a village.

Andreas Müller: All right, then I'm in a village, of course. Or let's say in a Kiez.

Justin Allen: A neighborhood. A hood.

Andreas Müller: Exactly.

Justin Allen: This morning I listened to a talk you did in Helsinki in 2018.

Andreas Müller: Yes. All right.

Justin Allen: Does it ring a bell?

Andreas Müller: Well, yeah, I remember it.

Justin Allen: You basically gave a five or ten minute introduction, and you ended by saying something like, "We're starting at the end." (laughing)

Andreas Müller: Yeah.

Justin Allen: And I would imagine that the intro you gave is probably similar to all the other talks that you've given. But I'm sure they're all slightly different, too. Anyway, that felt so concisely put. It wrapped up everything that we've been talking about over the past months in a concise five to ten minute message (laughing). Listening to it, I was thinking, "Fuck, we spent thirteen talks to get to that because of me." (laughing) But I'm not criticizing myself or being ashamed or anything. Still, I can't help but see how difficult it really is to just grasp that simple message (conceptually – acknowledging that the "me" can't grasp it). To get back to the narrow end, or to the beginning, of the funnel, so to speak.

Andreas Müller: Yeah.

Justin Allen: And not that you can grasp it the way we're talking about it, but within the "me" kind of understanding (conceptually), there's still a way of getting it or not getting it, like of getting or missing the point.

Andreas Müller: Kind of, but to be honest, not really. I know what you mean because the concept can be kind of understood. But in the end, it's really never understood.

Justin Allen: Right. But even that is something to understand?

Andreas Müller: No, that's the dilemma. Even that can't be understood.

Justin Allen: Right. You can't talk about it without using contradictory words to get to that point of really saying, "You can't get it. There's nothing to get. There's no one there." Because no matter what, if I went back and looked at all the thirteen talks, I would see my struggle. I still keep on inserting the "me" into it. Even as we keep on saying, "There is no me," or speak of "the death of the 'me,'" that can't even happen. There's no death of the "me." There's no liberation, because there's no "me" in the first place.

And even the illusion was still always "something" for me. I was always interpreting that there's some "me," and somehow this has to disappear, and then you're liberated. But that can't even happen, because that doesn't even exist in the first place.

Andreas Müller: Yes (laughing).

Justin Allen: So, that's what I'm saying. When we started these talks, I couldn't help myself from always not being convinced and not being able to be open even to the possibility that there's no "me" in the first place. For me, there always was a "me." There always was a "something." There always had to be "something." And then that something had to collapse or disappear or vanish, or it had to be realized that it's not really there.

And so then, as I was listening to your Helsinki talk, I couldn't help but go, "Holy shit." I've been questioning it in all kinds of different ways, and here it is in five minutes, and it's no different (laughing).

Andreas Müller: Yeah.

Justin Allen: And then I could see how it did seem like some of the people in the audience of that talk maybe kind of got it, but also I saw or heard that some of the people couldn't help but keep on inserting the "me." They just couldn't accept it.

Andreas Müller: I would even say it's inevitable. It can't do anything about it. And then you said just a few minutes ago, "Yeah. But we have to use language and stuff," and then you said, "But to come really, really to the point where you get that nothing can be gotten or that it's impossible to get, the thing is that the 'me' never comes to that." It can understand it in every talk, but also that can never be understood in a way; that it's understood that there is nothing to understand. It's not like an understanding in the sense of, "Now I understood it, and I won't ask a question anymore in my whole life, because it's useless." No. Even that understanding is never real.

You keep on asking, and then you understand again and go, "Yeah, I can't get it at all. It's impossible." But five minutes later, the seeking energy appears again, and you say, "Yeah, but I have another question. Ah, yeah, true. I can't get it yet." But it is still there, this longing for, "I would really, really like to understand," although this just doesn't happen.

Justin Allen: Right. It can't.

Andreas Müller: It can't. It's not a mistake in that sense. It's not wrong.

Justin Allen: Then I found myself as I continued to listen to the Helsinki talk ... I'm going to use the word "critical," although it's not really the right word, but then it was the first time where I kind of thought, "Ah, Andreas, everything he's saying is wrong." (laughing) "As soon as you open your mouth, you're lying." (laughing)

The way that you started off that talk, and every other talk basically, is the same way: "There's this 'me' in this searching energy." But that's not true either, because the "me" never is there in the first place, or the "me" simply is the searching energy. Still, in every one of your talks, in order to even attempt to communicate this message, you have to go along with the assumption that there's a "me" that dies or potentially dies or that the illusion of that "me" potentially disappears. But in reality, if there's a reality, it's not there in the first place, and therefore it can't ever disappear or die. So, the premise on which you start off is already false, so to speak.

Somehow we talked about that in one of these past talks. If there is any kind of a birth or a death, then it would just be this illusion, but the illusion isn't real either. The illusion doesn't actually happen. So then, any kind of birth or death doesn't actually happen either.

Andreas Müller: Yes, exactly.

Justin Allen: So then, it makes every single thing moot. Any kind of talking about it is already a contradiction or an unreality because it automatically can't help but refer to something that actually is nothing?

Andreas Müller: Yes. Seen by the "me," everything, every statement is a potential truth because it assumes truth somewhere. So if statements are not true but mere stories, they must be a lie. But yeah, there is no truth, and there are no lies either.

Justin Allen: Even that way that you just talked about it; anytime you refer to the "me," that's already a mistake in the sense that the "me" actually isn't there anyways.

Andreas Müller: Yes, absolutely. There is no "me."

Justin Allen: But if you didn't talk about the "me" at all, if you didn't address the illusion or the unreality, then you'd literally have nothing to say?

Andreas Müller: Oh, absolutely, but I'm not making concessions here either. It's just what comes out. It's just what apparently happens.

Justin Allen: I'm not saying that you shouldn't do that.

Andreas Müller: It's kind of important because it's making a distinction like, "Yeah, well, in the end you have to make concessions in order to get the event of the talks going or to be able to speak." No, it's not coming from making concessions. It just is what apparently happens as people who come to the talks constantly refer to themselves as "me." So, both is just what apparently happens. But it's not needed. It's not happening in my head like, "Okay, let's assume that there is the illusion of 'me,' and then we can work on it a bit." No, it's just blindly what comes out.

Justin Allen: Right. At least in this particular talk, my interest was to talk about it as technically as you could in a way. But this is not to the point. You simply can't talk about it?

Andreas Müller: No, not at all.

Justin Allen: And that's what I meant by, "There actually is no 'me.'"

Andreas Müller: Yes.

Justin Allen: And there actually never was. Even if you think that there was a "me" or that a "me" somehow came into existence or came into existence as an illusion; that didn't even happen?

Andreas Müller: Yes.

Justin Allen: And even if you assume or go about the assumption that the "me" did exist at some point and for some time and then through some unknown force or some unknown energy or some unknown happening it vanishes, that also never happened?

Andreas Müller: Yes, exactly.

Justin Allen: We've talked about this also, but that's how this sentence comes about then: how there's just wholeness or just this happening. Because there's just no separation ever in reality?

Andreas Müller: Yes.

Justin Allen: Or I don't know if you can say, "In reality."

Andreas Müller: Yeah, exactly.

Justin Allen: And that is totally mind-blowing. But then again not, because it's only mind-blowing to this "me" that doesn't exist anyways (laughing).

Andreas Müller: Yeah. Exactly (laughing).

Justin Allen: I had something else that I wanted to talk about, but I think it's lost ...

I know what it is now. Is it possible for you to go looking for the "me," to go looking for something?

Andreas Müller: No.

Justin Allen: And that's not possible, just because there's "no one" there that could go looking for something?

Andreas Müller: Exactly.

Justin Allen: I don't want to use the word "recognition," because we used it before and already said that it doesn't really work. Maybe there's a better word, but for now I'm going to use it. So, is there some kind of recognition of possibly looking for the "me" or for a point of view and just never being able to find it?

Andreas Müller: Not really, because when I say there is an apparent recognition – as we talked in the beginning, there can be an apparent recognition about something, maybe not about the "me" stuff –, the "person" would immediately again personalize it. So no, it's not possible. There is nothing there in the first place.

Justin Allen: For you then, there's not even at one time in your life some recognizing that there was something that you could go back to?

Andreas Müller: No, exactly. It's blind there.

Justin Allen: But isn't there a recognition of ...

Andreas Müller: I can understand the concept in a way, or the concept is kind of being understood, but it's totally empty. I don't know to what I would go back, what that would be.

Justin Allen: I don't mean it like that. This is already a false sentence based on what we just talked about for the past ten minutes, but before, when, in this story, there was a "me" or the illusionary "me" for you ...

Andreas Müller: Or I thought there was a "me," or something like that.

Justin Allen: Yeah, and then there wasn't. So now there's the "nothing" phase, so to speak. But in the sense of historically speaking you still have memories of when you were a kid, and so you would also have a memory or a trace of how there used to be a "me" for you?

Andreas Müller: Yeah, that's the assumption. But the funny thing is that even when I look back, I have memories and stuff, but I can't squeeze a "me" in there anymore.

Justin Allen: Right. That's what I wanted to talk about. You can't squeeze the "me" in there, and not that you're trying to squeeze it in, but isn't there some kind of a recognition or an understanding that you can't squeeze a "me" in there, because it's just impossible for there to be a "me"?

Andreas Müller: Oh, yeah, one could say so. But that's what I mean. That's an apparent recognition.

Justin Allen: But it's something that apparently happens that ...

Andreas Müller: But this apparent recognition is not recognized as such. It's empty and full. It stands for itself, so to speak. And it's meaningless. And nothing really becomes recognized in that. It's not that there is something really recognized in that, which would make it possible to make a true statement.

Justin Allen: "Shocking" might be too strong of a word, but is it something that's sometimes shocking that this point of reference that used to be there for a large portion of your life and is just not there anymore can't ever be there again? It'd be like somebody took out an organ or some internal body part of yours.

Andreas Müller: Well, in order to be conscious about that, you would need someone to be conscious about that, someone who believes that apparent fact. That's not happening, so to speak, but that's what I mean. I would already need a reference point in order to say, "Oh, how weird it is to have no reference point or contrast to having had a reference point previously." So no, it's not shocking or something like that.

Justin Allen: Still doesn't that happen in some unrecognizable, blind way that there's ... Yeah again, I can't say it without saying "recognition" or without some kind of ...

Andreas Müller: The funny thing is that there actually never is ... Now I'm lacking a word ... There never is judging my states, like how it is now for me and how it used to be. How it is now to be impersonal and how it was to be personal, which doesn't make sense at all. Sometimes there is an apparent recognition if other people assume themselves to be someone. But nothing is really being recognized in that. Same in the talks, for example. One could say it's quite apparent that this doesn't happen here.

And when people approach me coming from their apparent reference point or from their assumption of having a reference point, there can be an apparent recognition like, "Oh, that's not happening here," which is empty though, and no one refers to that as another state, so it's not for myself. That's the thing; when I'm alone, there is no processing of those concepts of what's going on here and how it was ten years ago when I was still a "me" and stuff like that. This doesn't make sense at all for me, so to speak.

Justin Allen: But when that ... Let's call it an event or a moment; when that happened, when there was no longer a "me" for you (laughing), wouldn't that be ... I don't know; it's impossible to talk about, but let's say that the "me" somehow still is lingering on a little bit, and then it is gone.

Andreas Müller: Yeah, one could say so.

Justin Allen: And then there's all of a sudden "no me," but you've been used to it being there; you were so used to there being this point, and now it's no longer there. And it's not like, "What the fuck"; there's just no point anymore. You can't even say the sentence, "I can't find a 'me,'" because it implies that there's somebody looking for the "me."

Andreas Müller: Yeah, but two other things. I know in a way that there is that aspect to it. But on the other hand, the "me" dying is, at the same time, the turning out that there never was a "me." So, it's not really going from one reality into a completely different reality, because there never was anything else than the natural reality. In a way, yes, it's different, but in another way not at all, because there never was anything else than how it is.

Justin Allen: Right, but that's what I mean. Isn't there some kind of a "seeing" that it's all blind and all just empty and there is no point of reference and no one? Isn't there some kind of a "seeing" of just that; that it is so?

Andreas Müller: Yes and no. That's what I mean. One could call it an apparent recognition, but even that apparent recognition is blind because it's equally apparent, equally just what's happening, as everything else.

Justin Allen: Right. That's what I mean; there's still a blind ... I don't know, it's a contradiction, but could we say there's a blind "seeing"? Like there's still seeing, it's the same as you still see things like you see me, not as a "person," but there's still the seeing of me, just like there is the seeing of the computer and the table. So, you're not talking from a personal point of view, but talking is still happening?

Andreas Müller: Yes, exactly.

Justin Allen: Even though you're talking, you're not talking from an "Andreas Müller" point of view, but talking is still happening from Andreas Müller?

Andreas Müller: Yes, talking is what apparently happens, but nothing true is being said.

Justin Allen: While nothing true is coming from something also.

Andreas Müller: Yes, exactly. It's already complete. It's empty, it's meaningless. It doesn't have a message. There is no real conclusion coming from what I say. Same with the apparent recognition. Liberation wouldn't be living in that recognition. It just is what apparently happens, just like millions of other things. And it's empty and meaningless.

Justin Allen: The emptiness and meaninglessness and blindness; this is somehow seen or somehow understood, but not from a point of view? It's like I want to say it's blindly understood, or it's ...

Andreas Müller: It is like that, yeah. I know. However, you can't go there. It's impossible to say or to describe. It's so ordinarily like that. You can't even call it "understood," but I know what you mean. There's no doubt about it; let's say it like that, but it's not being processed.

Justin Allen: Even that, there's a blind understanding that even trying to figure it out or trying to process it is impossible?

Andreas Müller: Yes, but all of that would just be what apparently happens.

Justin Allen: Yeah.

Andreas Müller: Which doesn't mean anything. And I can't say if it's there or not, this apparent recognition.

Justin Allen: Yeah. One time last week I was lying in bed, and I'm going to talk about this like it's an experience (laughing), so the way that I would communicate it is that there was just nothing there all of a sudden, but not even all of a sudden – it just was like that instantly. And any attempt to try to find myself was just dead end. And it wasn't like a realization, and it didn't feel like a discovery or something that had been figured out. It just wasn't possible anymore to (laughing) ... But I knew that before it would have been so obvious that there was a point of view.

It would have always been like, "There I am thinking and figuring something out. I'm working on figuring it out, and for instance, tomorrow I'm going to do this, and if I keep on questioning who I am or if I make this change, then everything will get better." I'm really always referring and feeling like I'm here and doing this all, and then that totally wasn't possible; searching for that point didn't happen. But thoughts were still going on, kind of like how it would have been before, but there just wasn't an anchor, I guess.

Andreas Müller: Yep, yes. But to capture it how it really was, what would you say (laughing)?

Justin Allen: Yeah, you can't say anything.

Andreas Müller: What would you say? How was it actually (laughing)?

Justin Allen: I would say I wasn't there or ... I liked the combination of "blind understanding." But "understanding" might be too strong of a word, so I wonder ...

Andreas Müller: That's what I mean. "Understanding" is saying too much actually.

Justin Allen: And "recognition" is also too much.

Andreas Müller: Yes, exactly.

Justin Allen: Anything that begins with "re-" is too much because there just is no referring to or looking back on something.

Andreas Müller: That's why I say, "Yeah, if you want, you can squeeze an apparent recognition in," but it's actually too much, and the word "understanding" is definitely too much. It's too ... Wait, now I'm looking for the right word ... (he is searching the web for the word)

Justin Allen: "Blind seeing" isn't that bad either, because it's a ...

Andreas Müller: It's too natural, too naturally. Yeah, there isn't even a good translation for what I mean.

Justin Allen: What was it in German?

Andreas Müller: „Selbstverständlich."

Justin Allen: That's „self-understanding – self-obvious," no?

Andreas Müller: No, it's "self-evident." It means that it's so given. It goes without saying.

Justin Allen: Yeah, that's "obvious." That's kind of like saying, "Obviously."

Andreas Müller: Yeah. But all of those words are too strong because they all imply a certain kind of processing. And the ordinariness or the self-evidence comes from not processing it at all. It just is like that. It can't be understood how it can just be like that without someone understanding it. But the "person" doesn't get the "as it is"; the "person" would always refer to this as if it were needed to be seen or recognized or understood.

But exactly that's not happening, but it still just is as it is. You can't squeeze any processing into it. "We" would love to do that, or the "person" would love to do that, but the moment you honestly try, you notice, like you just did, that there's a blind understanding. And again, "understanding" is too much. It doesn't fit. Nothing fits (laughing).

Justin Allen: It's just like blind being or blind seeing or ...

Andreas Müller: Yeah, "blind seeing" is good. A total contradiction in two words (laughing).

Justin Allen: It has to be a paradox.

Andreas Müller: Definitely something that can be understood (laughing). But well, okay, a paradox actually means that you can't understand it. However, that's how the "person" could end up. "It's blind seeing." "Oh, great information (laughing). How the fuck's that going to be? What does that mean (laughing)?" But I can relate to it, totally. And still, apparently it was exactly as it was, however it was. Blindly, unknowably.

Justin Allen: But at the same time, there's a huge difference, sort of?

Andreas Müller: Kind of, yeah. Same with blind seeing. Yes, there was a huge difference, but also not really. Not while there was "no one," so to speak. There wasn't really a difference. Or it doesn't matter.

Justin Allen: Do you ever have friends that want to talk to you about life dilemmas and ask questions like, "Should I move, or should I get married, or ..."?

Andreas Müller: Not really, but if so, more on an opinion-based level than ...

Justin Allen: That's what I mean. I don't mean like in this circle of your oneness talks but in your normal life.

Andreas Müller: Talking about things can happen. Of course.

Justin Allen: But don't you find it impossible to ... Because you'll never give the answer that somebody would want to hear (laughing).

Andreas Müller: Well, I'm just giving the answer that comes out. I mean, I'm not running around and telling everyone that there is "no one."

Justin Allen: No, I know. I'm saying like if I was your brother and came to you and said, "Hey, I'm thinking about quitting my job and living in the woods. Giving up my life and just living off the land." And he was sincere about it, and it would be a huge ... I'm not talking like I know your brother and his situation, but let's pretend that he's married and has a family, and now he wants to throw it all away.

Andreas Müller: Yeah, I would probably react exactly like that. "Well, I don't know."

Justin Allen: That's what I mean. You wouldn't be helpful at all.

Andreas Müller: That's true.

Justin Allen: That type of question either wants somebody to say, "Hey, what!? Are you fucking crazy? Don't do that. You're giving up all that's important." Or they want you to support it fully and be like, "Yeah, you're so cool, go for this adventure."

Andreas Müller: I mean, sometimes if I have an impression about what's most likely to happen, I would say that, or this would come out here as well.

Justin Allen: Well, there wouldn't be a knowing or a clear answer or a clear support for one or the other, except in a way it would be already happening? I just meant it more like you would never, or it would be unlikely that you would ever, give spiritual advice, like how these current spiritual teachers do.

Andreas Müller: That's very true, yeah. Absolutely. I wouldn't really have ideas about the right or wrong way to live.

Justin Allen: Right.

Andreas Müller: For a while I was with a guru, and his mindset was a bit like living a spiritual life is always somehow better than being with a family and visiting your parents and stuff. It was also said that it doesn't matter and there is no difference. Actually I don't know what he meant, but my impression and many other people's impression was that there was a mindset which included an opinion about what would be the better way to live.

Justin Allen: Yeah.

Andreas Müller: And yes, I don't really have that. Maybe I also have some pictures in my head or just preferences, but yeah, there wouldn't be such an idea. I don't know what's right and wrong, so to speak, or there is "no one" who knows that in general, and especially when it comes to a certain situation and to myself or anyone.

Justin Allen: Yeah. Maybe right now I'm trying to just find stuff to talk about (laughing), but it feels like this whole searching energy that I had, and I'm talking more specifically, maybe spiritually, although I never considered myself a spiritual person, so I don't want to be put into that category, but ...

Andreas Müller: Hmm.

Justin Allen: That whole energy to figure it out or become awakened, at least spiritual-wise or philosophical or otherwise; seems lessened or gone.

Andreas Müller: Yeah (laughing).

Justin Allen: And it feels like I was so tricked or duped.

Andreas Müller: All right. Yeah. I understand.

Justin Allen: The same way I can say I feel a little bit tricked job-wise. I picked a profession and thought that it might give me some kind of fulfillment.

Andreas Müller: Yeah.

Justin Allen: You know? I mean, that was something that hit me awhile ago when the reality of it wasn't that fulfilling. So, having the best job wasn't it.

Andreas Müller: Yeah. Same energy.

Justin Allen: Yeah, exactly.

Andreas Müller: Yeah.

Justin Allen: I never was totally convinced, but with the awakening, I really bought into it thinking that's the only way, if there is a way. But at least I was convinced that picking the right partner is not going to be true fulfillment.

Andreas Müller: Yeah.

Justin Allen: Either having a child and a family.

Andreas Müller: Yeah.

Justin Allen: And living in a nice sunny location with good weather also wasn't going to be ultimate fulfillment.

Andreas Müller: Yeah.

Justin Allen: Or even the combination of all those fitting perfectly together in harmony. The right location, a good partner, a happy family and a good job – that's still not going to be totally satisfying.

Andreas Müller: Yup.

Justin Allen: But then abandoning all that and saying, "Fuck it, none of it matters," also wasn't going to be totally fulfilling.

Andreas Müller: Yup.

Justin Allen: But I sort of bought into Lao Tzu, Buddha or J. Krishnamurti or ...

Andreas Müller: Yeah.

Justin Allen: I guess, into these supposedly enlightened guys; that alternative. It seems there's such a small percentage

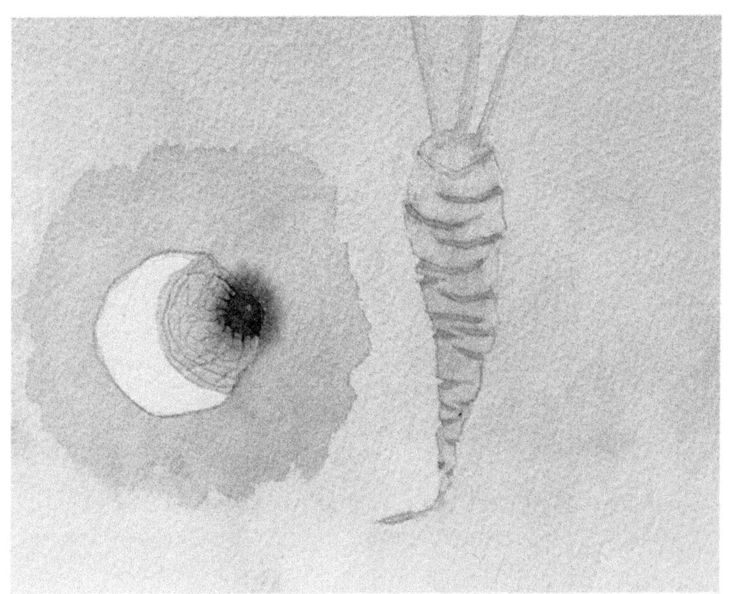

of people really going in that direction, and I was like, "That's the only way. That has to be the only way."

Andreas Müller: Yeah. Yeah (laughing).

Justin Allen: But then I never really wanted to fully go into that way either, because I always interpreted those messages as being so much work at some point. Either work in the sense that you're giving up certain pleasures in life or in the sense that you're giving up pursuing something that you might want to pursue or you're giving up family or you have to meditate for so many years or you have to constantly be focused and aware.

Andreas Müller: Yes. Oh, dear (laughing).

Justin Allen: So, I couldn't even buy into that, but I still thought if I did; if someday I decided, "Fuck it, I put the energy into really getting enlightened," then it would happen.

Andreas Müller: Hmm.

Justin Allen: And so now ... It's not happening to me right now, but there's some threshold phase maybe, where I couldn't let go of that, and I ...

Andreas Müller: Hmm.

Justin Allen: I couldn't let go of that energy. It felt like if that energy goes away, then I'm not going to do anything, and I'm just going to be stuck.

Andreas Müller: Yeah. "If I'm not moving, I'll be stuck."

Justin Allen: Yeah.

Andreas Müller: Yeah. That's the fear. To be stuck (laughing). Stuck in the now (laughing).

Justin Allen: Yeah. That fucking shitty message to be in the moment (laughing). It's such a good sales pitch. But also such horror.

Andreas Müller: Oh, yeah, absolutely. You could do it five minutes a week and still feel good and keep on practicing. You can do it the whole day and still feel good. You definitely have your successes, but you also have your failures. So, it's the perfect carrot that keeps the search going. It's the blueprint for personal teachings. It has all the ingredients. It covers all ages. It covers all intensities.

Justin Allen: Yeah. Like when I was a child. My parents were, I don't know, like working class, and they didn't buy into things in general, so they were always skeptical. And as a child you watch TV, and the commercial comes on, and there's some guarantee or some promise of, "Buy this product, and you're going to be happy," or something.

Andreas Müller: Mm-hmm (affirmative).

Justin Allen: And as a little kid you're like, "Oh, I want to get that cereal." And then my parents went, "That has nothing in it. It's just bullshit."

Andreas Müller: Mm. Yup.

Justin Allen: I don't know, I can't even think of the ones in Germany, but maybe you guys have Fruit Loops, you know, the colored cereal (laughing)?

Andreas Müller: Yeah, I know it. I don't know if it was never big here, but yeah.

Justin Allen: Anyways, you have equivalencies, maybe the Kinder Chocolate thing.

Andreas Müller: Yeah.

Justin Allen: And it's all empty. Same with Coca Cola. It's empty in the sense that it doesn't have any nutrients or vitamins.

Andreas Müller: Mm-hmm (affirmative). Yeah.

Justin Allen: And then there are even deeper promises. There's religion, and that would also be advertised on TV, at least in the US. And then in every community there's the church.

Andreas Müller: Mm-hmm (affirmative).

Justin Allen: My parents were always like, "That's bullshit, too." (laughing) And the only thing that they kind of believed in, if anything, was working hard and being responsible and following the rules, in general. But they were not into making a lot of money. I was born in the Trump era; I mean the time when he was big in business and later also appeared in a reality show. Trump was the hero in a way. He and Arnold Schwarzenegger, you know (laughing)?

Andreas Müller: Yeah. Great (laughing).

Justin Allen: So, those were the role models (laughing), and also, these get-rich-quick schemes were really apparent when I was a child. But my parents were always like, "All that's bullshit. All these ideas of getting rich quickly are all bullshit."

Andreas Müller: Hmm.

Justin Allen: And so you're kind of queued in to society and how it offers all these fulfillments. And you know that they're all empty in general, but you still can't help yourself. It seems you have to buy into one because there's no other option.

Andreas Müller: Yup.

Justin Allen: To narrow it down, either you bought into spirituality or into religion or into the nice car or the nice job or the family life or no life.

Andreas Müller: Or into rebellion.

Justin Allen: Yeah, exactly.

Andreas Müller: Yeah.

Justin Allen: But any way you go, it's still going and seeking, and the going is automatically unfulfilling.

Andreas Müller: Yeah.

Justin Allen: And that's why you feel duped or tricked at some point because you picked one of the paths (or multiple paths), but it didn't really keep the promise. You just don't ever really arrive.

Andreas Müller: Yeah.

Justin Allen: Everybody had to, or let's say, in general, ninety-nine percent of us probably picked something.

Andreas Müller: Yeah. The way which looked most promising to gain something from it.

Justin Allen: Yeah.

Andreas Müller: Yeah.

Justin Allen: And that seeking or dissatisfaction energy is always there, too, because of the "me." Automatically, if the "me" or the illusion of the "me" is being assumed to be there, it has to act on its behalf.

Andreas Müller: That illusion is what apparently happened. It's exactly that your con appeared or separated because to experience oneself as "me" means to live in the illusion that to live like that, in the going and searching, means to be alive.

Justin Allen: All right. And then the conversation with yourself is always, "How do I profit the most? Or what do I get from this?"

Andreas Müller: Yes.

Justin Allen: And so if we talk about the reality of there not being a "me" ever in the first place, and then this blind seeing, for lack of a better way of putting it, then you're basically directionless, even though it's still happening that you're trying to make things better for yourself?

Andreas Müller: Yes. Kind of. It's functioning, it's natural; not for anything, not for anyone, but yeah, absolutely. Even that doesn't have to be consciously done.

Justin Allen: Yeah. Well, it can't be.

Andreas Müller: It can't be. Yup.

Justin Allen: If I were going to try to explain this, then I would say that it takes away the pressure of living your life because before there was pressure, because it always had to be approved, in a way, from this "boss," and it had to be conceived and discussed, and the pros and cons had to be weighed.

Andreas Müller: Yup.

Justin Allen: And then there's no longer the ability to figure things out, in a way? There's no longer the ability to ...

Andreas Müller: The ability and the need.

Justin Allen: Yeah.

Andreas Müller: A "person" would regard it as an ability, but it's also a need for them.

Justin Allen: Yeah.

Andreas Müller: Yeah.

Justin Allen: When that's not possible anymore, then that whole burden or that whole pressure is gone, although decisions will still happen, and outwardly it would look like somebody's making the best decision for themselves?

Andreas Müller: Yes, exactly.

Justin Allen: You feel the freedom, not that you would even experience a feeling of freedom, because freedom always implies something that you're free from, but the freedom would just be in that you can live your life without questioning or second-guessing or regretting it?

Andreas Müller: Without that artificial burden.

Justin Allen: Yeah.

Andreas Müller: Or you were using another word: without that artificial pressure.

Justin Allen: Yeah.

Andreas Müller: Absolutely. Yes. Yes.

Justin Allen: So, I think that's where in a way that spiritual or religious concept of acceptance or God's will would come out, or where that could potentially be applied.

Andreas Müller: Yup.

Justin Allen: Because it seems like there's a predetermined path, in a way, set up for you that you're not involved in at all.

Andreas Müller: Yeah. Exactly.

Justin Allen: But because you think you're involved in it, you might try to stop it or enhance it. It's like those movies where people go back in time to try to change the future, you know (laughing)?

Andreas Müller: Yeah, yeah (laughing).

Justin Allen: And that's what it's like living life; it's like you're constantly trying to change something which can't be changed or which actually changes in its own accord. You're constantly trying to manipulate an outcome which you actually have no control over. You're trying to puppeteer your own self.

Andreas Müller: Yes, absolutely. And it is the artificial pressure that you need to do that.

Justin Allen: Yeah.

Andreas Müller: It's not really hobby-like and joyful, it's a need. The "person" thinks it has to do that to keep life going.

Justin Allen: Right.

Andreas Müller: Otherwise you would be stuck or doomed, or you'd fail, or you'd never get it done or whatever.

Justin Allen: Yeah. And so then, you could just say, "Ah, I can be a father of a child, or I can work here, or I can just let myself live here, or whatever." The dilemmas that were there before, where you constantly had to be involved somehow, vanish, and you'd take yourself out of the driver's seat. It's not that you would take yourself out of the driver's seat, but ...

Andreas Müller: Exactly. There just is no one sitting in the driver's seat.

Justin Allen: Right. And all that seeps, in a way, into spirituality. And I always think that's why spirituality seems so on the right path. It seems like ...

Andreas Müller: Yup.

Justin Allen: But it's really just, in a sense, the cleverest answer to that life dilemma of there being an illusory "me."

Andreas Müller: I didn't understand. What do you mean?

Justin Allen: I just mean that spirituality really gives or seems to give all the answers that somebody that really starts seeking doesn't want. Like they discover that the problem is neither the job nor the wife nor the husband nor the location. It's "me." At some point you say, "I'm the problem," so then you want to escape from yourself.

Andreas Müller: Yeah.

Justin Allen: And then spirituality comes in and tells you that you are not the problem, and somehow they're also saying that you don't exist, at least not as you conventionally thought that you existed. You just exist. They say you're just existence, or they take away the image.

Andreas Müller: Yeah, they dance around the idea that there is "no one" and in a way draw conclusions about what this means.

Justin Allen: Yeah.

Andreas Müller: But then they talk again about how to be that.

Justin Allen: Right.

Andreas Müller: Yeah. So, the "person" has another carrot to chase.

Justin Allen: I also started thinking, from your Helsinki talk, that we can start off saying how it's not a teaching and there's nothing to gain. And all that's true in the sense of there not being a "person" over there. By definition, you can't teach.

Andreas Müller: Mm.

Justin Allen: And then there's also nobody there in your audience. You're not looking at people. And so, there's nothing that they could learn. Right?

Andreas Müller: Oh, totally. Yeah. Absolutely.

Justin Allen: But also, at the same time, it's still a teaching in the same way that I could say, "I'm going to teach you how to cook a chicken or how to bake a cake." And then, after you watched me do it, you know how to bake a cake. I also didn't teach you in the sense that I can really teach you, because I'm also not there to teach, and you're not there to learn.

Andreas Müller: Yeah.

Justin Allen: Still learning happened; now you can bake a cake, and before you couldn't.

Andreas Müller: Okay, all right, yeah.

Justin Allen: Right. In a way your message is not a teaching with the argument that there's nobody there to learn or to teach, but there still is a clear message to somebody that could leave your talk with something new in the same way that somebody that came in to learn how to bake a cake would leave with something new.

Andreas Müller: They could, yeah, kind of (laughing), not really, but yeah.

Justin Allen: How do you see that different than somebody teaching you to bake a cake?

Andreas Müller: Because afterwards I can bake a cake, and after the meeting usually people can't do anything more than before (laughing). Well, I mean what seems to be happening is just the unraveling of the illusion that there is a "person." So, one could say that there seems to be the chance to leave with less compared to before, which would rather be an un-learning than a learning, but that's saying already too much actually.

Justin Allen: Right. I mean, you can also say it's nothing. I can say baking a cake is also nothing.

Andreas Müller: Yeah, I would say so.

Justin Allen: Baking a cake is just that you put flour and some other ingredients in a bowl ...

Andreas Müller: No, that's still saying it's something. I mean that there's not really a difference between baking a cake and not baking a cake.

Justin Allen: I was just thinking about it in the sense that I think it's provocative to say that it's not a teaching for sure. I do think that it's somewhat accurate to call it a teaching or a message. I also think that ...

Andreas Müller: Well, it's both, you know. It's not a teaching, but apparently it does what it does.

Justin Allen: Right, I just had a thought that went, "Is it necessary to say this isn't a teaching?"

Andreas Müller: Well, I know there are some people who would say this is the actual teaching and everything else is just virtuality or fairytales. They wouldn't call any of the speakers not teaching. They would say this is the actual teaching, which is a story though. Of course, there is not the need to say that it's not a teaching; it's a matter of definition in the end. Compared to what I would regard as a teaching, it's absolutely not a teaching.

Justin Allen: Yeah.

Andreas Müller: I'm absolutely not speaking to you in order to create any effect.

Justin Allen: Yeah.

Andreas Müller: And that, within the story, seems to have an effect, which, however, is neither intended nor has it a clear direction nor can it be known or predicted what the effects look like. That's just what apparently happens, just like all kinds of things that aren't teachings or intentions seem to have all kinds of effects in the story. That's all right, but it doesn't mean that it's a teaching, at least according to how I would define it.

Justin Allen: Yeah, I agree. I have a friend who I studied philosophy with, and I was talking to him about our talks and was saying, "Yeah, it's not a teaching." (laughing) And he asked, "So, how is it different?" And I was going, "Well, one way it's different is that all the books that we've read and these kind of spiritual philosophers; they're always teaching a method or a process in a way. But this message doesn't do that."

Andreas Müller: Yeah, they live in a mindset of a goal, of right and wrong, no matter how impersonal it looks and no matter how it-doesn't-matter-like they are; you can see quite quickly that it does take place within a mindset of certain values and an actual kind of right way to live and all that stuff. So, that'd be all teachings.

Justin Allen: Well, my friend couldn't help himself from then also saying, "Yeah, but even that could be a teaching of a non-teaching; like it's a teaching that there is no teaching possible, or it's a teaching ...

Andreas Müller: Exactly.

Justin Allen: That there's no message, and there's nothing to do, but that's still the teaching because they're teaching you that there is nothing you can do (to gain fulfillment), that there is no one there ...

Andreas Müller: Yeah, but it is ...

Justin Allen: And nothing to learn here.

Andreas Müller: Of course, but it just isn't.

Justin Allen: Yeah.

Andreas Müller: Of course, I can say there is no method, and the "me" would turn it into, "Well, not doing a method in order to be enlightened is the right thing, is the right message."

Justin Allen: Is the message, yeah.

Andreas Müller: As if I used this kind of setup in order to get to the goal. No, it isn't; exactly that's not how it is. I'm not sitting there thinking that this is the best way to kill the "me."

Justin Allen: Right.

Andreas Müller: As if, "Forget meditation, forget this, forget that, come to me," were my point of view or my non-method; no, exactly not. But exactly that it's not like that, of course, turns this event into the kind of event that it is. Apparently there are effects and all that stuff, yeah. However, it's not about them, and they are not real, and I'm not doing it like that in order to bring something about.

Justin Allen: It's such a great non-message.

Andreas Müller: Yeah, I know. I know what you mean. It's gorgeous and meaningless like everything else.

Justin Allen: When you started giving these talks nine years ago, did you "feel" some kind of impulse; did you want to get out and communicate this to people?

Andreas Müller: No, not really.

Justin Allen: How would you say that it happened for you?

Andreas Müller: Well, this was actually kind of one of the most astonishing things: that there is no impulse from my side to pass on the message like in a mission sense.

Justin Allen: Right.

Andreas Müller: Maybe I could say in the story that I just liked those meetings, but I never had and still don't have anything to tell to anyone; there is no urge to spread this.

Justin Allen: Right. It's like ...

Andreas Müller: Even no real impulse to talk about it. It's not like, "That's how it is for me." It's not a general thing, and when I'm meeting a friend, it's not that the first thing I try to talk about is how there's no "me." It never was like that right away, and I don't know how these meetings started. It wasn't even planned for a long time or that at some point I thought, "Well, now I finally start doing it." I mean, of course, I have always been in surroundings where it is possible for something like that to happen, like with seeing gurus and then Tony, so the meeting setup where people stand in front of people and say something wasn't totally out of the world. But it was just a very general picture; it wasn't intended. All of a sudden it just felt like it's going to happen and it's right, kind of.

Justin Allen: It's also fun, I think at least that's a feeling that I get.

Andreas Müller: Yeah, absolutely, it's fun. I could almost say, "Fortunately it's fun." I don't do it because it is fun.

Justin Allen: Right, you could be doing it, and it could be terrible (laughing).

Andreas Müller: Exactly. Like so many other jobs that I've had. But no, it is fun, of course.

Justin Allen: This could become un-fun also.

Andreas Müller: Exactly, yeah totally.

Justin Allen: I can relate to it in the sense that generally I have fun talking with you. For sure I like the freedom that I can say what I want to say, also something that might be controversial, and it doesn't feel like you're ever pushing anything on me at all, like trying to convince me. I feel like it's totally open here.

Andreas Müller: Yeah.

Justin Allen: I really enjoy that. Before this, it was so rare for me in my circle, with the constellation of people in my life; to talk about the possibility that maybe you're not there would be something that nobody wants to talk about.

Andreas Müller: Mm-hmm (affirmative), yeah.

Justin Allen: Even in that sense it's enjoyable to just hang around with kind of like-minded people, also maybe people that are super desperate or people that are just really interested in those questions or people that are disappointed from past things.

Andreas Müller: Yeah.

Justin Allen: Then you're just kind of constantly in this setting or circle. Same if you like baseball; then you surround yourself with baseball people.

Andreas Müller: Yeah.

Justin Allen: I started to think it was weird talking about this in the sense how the message is in some way fixed and there's no evolution of it. We also talked about this in the very, very beginning.

Andreas Müller: Yes, totally.

Justin Allen: Generally you would think, "What's the point then?" because every other thing seems to have a progression, you know?

Andreas Müller: Mm-hmm (affirmative), yeah.

Justin Allen: Science is constantly figuring out a new chemical or a new virus or a new whatever, so it's constantly evolving and changing. The same with art and with technology and with building things. Then philosophy; historically there's been some progression. And in psychology there's always progression.

Andreas Müller: Exactly. I mean, the methods are quite old, but now they mix spirituality with therapy.

Justin Allen: Astrology (laughing).

Andreas Müller: Yeah (laughing).

Justin Allen: But this message is fixed. I imagine it could evolve, or if I were going to be involved in this, then my interest would always be the language that you'd use; maybe you'd refine the language more and more or something. But that's it.

Andreas Müller: Yeah.

Justin Allen: The fundamental idea will never or at least it seems like it will never change.

Andreas Müller: Yeah, because there is no message; there isn't really such a thing. I mean, it's both again. It's kind of fixed by not being fixed.

Justin Allen: Then you can just think, "Wouldn't that be boring?" Let's imagine your career should be forty years long or something, right (laughing)? So, for forty years it would just be kind of the same; if we listened to your first talk and then ten years later and then twenty years later; nothing would be really different (laughing).

Andreas Müller: Yes, it was actually quite amusing; someone once accused me of not developing at all.

Justin Allen: Yeah. The audience would come in, and they'd ask the same questions, and somebody would be like, "Well, we already asked that question ten years ago." (laughing)

Andreas Müller: Yeah. That's wonderful. Sun rises every day, sun sets every day, what to do (laughing)? Same, same but different.

Justin Allen: Yeah, so you picked a profession that has no promotion (laughing). Then again you can say that there is progression because even those talks are something that you can say has changed in a way.

Andreas Müller: That's what I mean; it's not really fixed. It's both. It's like what the whole message says; how it's being described:

There's no real change, but it's alive. There's nothing missing. There's no standstill, but it's not really moving or developing towards something else or something more.

Justin Allen: Yeah, I think that's just the same with life. Life also isn't actually evolving and changing.

Andreas Müller: Exactly, yeah.

Justin Allen: It's like basketball or tennis or any other sports game. There are fixed elements.

Andreas Müller: Yeah.

Justin Allen: Like the tennis court has a certain size, and the net has to be a certain height, and then the tennis rackets are built in a certain way, there are some rules, and maybe they change subtly or slightly, like the tennis balls and the tennis rackets. And then the game changes just because of the players that play on it, but the game of tennis never really changes. Still you hit a ball across a court.

Andreas Müller: Yeah, exactly. I mean, so many things don't really change.

Justin Allen: Right, it's the illusion of change.

Andreas Müller: It's still interesting, in a way.

Justin Allen: I think I've run out of things to talk about.

Andreas Müller: Yeah. What have we run out of?

Justin Allen: Things to talk about.

Andreas Müller: Yeah.

Justin Allen: At least for today. I was thinking about how we're going to have this talk and then you're going to give a Zoom talk.

Andreas Müller: Yeah. It starts in a few minutes actually.

Justin Allen: I was just curious and wondering if this is going to affect your Zoom talk.

Andreas Müller: Maybe, in an unknowable way.

Justin Allen: Some of this is going to percolate into your Zoom talk.

Andreas Müller: Yeah, definitely.

Justin Allen: Do you know how many people are going to be there?

Andreas Müller: No, actually not; it's the first time that I'm going to do it, and I have no idea.

Justin Allen: All right.

Andreas Müller: Not many, I guess, because you know, it's morning, I don't know.

Justin Allen: All right then.

Andreas Müller: All right.

Justin Allen: Maybe we talk next week.

Andreas Müller: Yeah, all right. Cool.

Justin Allen: Ciao.

Andreas Müller: Ciao, great to see you.

Justin Allen: Good to see you, too.

Andreas Müller: Yeah, bye.

Justin Allen: Bye-bye.

Andreas Müller was born and grew up in Southern Germany. After having become a spiritual seeker in his teens, he met Tony Parsons in 2009. Since 2011, Andreas has been holding talks and intensives throughout the world.

Justin Allen is an architect in Berlin, Germany. Justin has a background in philosophy and he is originally from upstate New York.